GUITAR STORIES
Volume Two

BY MICHAEL WRIGHT

Guitar Stories, Volume 2
By Michael Wright

Vintage Guitar® Books
An imprint of Vintage Guitar, Inc., P.O. Box 7301, Bismarck, ND 58507, (701)
255-1197, Fax (701) 255-0250, publishers of *Vintage Guitar*® magazine and of
Vintage Guitar® Online at www.vintageguitar.com.

ISBN 1-884883-08-7

Cover and Back photography: All photos except where noted by Mike Tamborrino
and Michael Wright. Alamo players courtesy of Michael Lee Allen. Chappie
D'Amato (sitting) and unknown model courtesy Maria Maccaferri. Kay and Veleno
headstocks from VG archives.

Cover Concept and Design: Vintage Guitar, Inc.

Printed in the United States of America

EXCLUSIVELY DISTRIBUTED BY

HAL•LEONARD®
CORPORATION
7777 W. BLUEMOUND RD. P.O. BOX 13819
MILWAUKEE, WISCONSIN 53213

VINTAGE
GUITAR
BOOKS

FOREWORD

Welcome to the second volume of *Guitar Stories*. The first thing you'll probably notice is that there are fewer chapters than in *Guitar Stories Volume 1*. Part of this is due to the fact that some of these histories — 80 years of Kay, for example — are far larger than anything we've undertaken before. Part is due to a combination of more detail and the addition of features such as instrument charts which should help you date instruments more conveniently.

You'll also notice that these subjects have previously appeared in the pages of *Vintage Guitar magazine*, however, it would be a big mistake to think of them as merely reprints. Since those were published, *much* new information has come to light, often with the help of generous readers, and the stories here been greatly revised, improved and expanded. In Kay alone, for example, new information about the transition from Stromberg-Voisinet to Kay has been found, and almost the entire chronology of instruments from 1948 to 1960 has been totally reconfigured based on additional catalogs provided by readers.

As always, be reminded that tracing guitar history is far from a precise science. These stories rely on a combination of notoriously inacurate anecdotal memories and the collation of press notices, advertising and catalogs, all with their own inherent unreliability, as well. We've tried as hard as possible to be complete and accurate, given the limitations at hand. Let us know if you find anything amiss, and we'll endeavor to correct it in subsequent editions.

Finally, these histories are born of my own lifelong love of guitars, and my desire to preserve for future generations as much as possible that is recoverable at this point in the instrument's history, however imperfect the effort may be. As time moves on, others may make improvements, and some improvements may become impossible. In the end, these stories are a tribute to a magnificent tradition in the culture of mankind. Please enjoy them in this spirit.

TABLE OF CONTENTS

ABOUT THE AUTHOR

Michael Wright is a professional writer, historian, musician and guitar collector who's been involved with the guitar since he began playing the ukulele in 1952. He began studying guitar two years later, and over the subsequent years performed and taught a variety of acoustic and electric music, including classical guitar. In addition, Wright has spent many years programming and hosting the all-guitar radio show, *Guitaromania*. He is ABD in Victorian English literature from the University of Wisconsin and spends his days in an advertising agency writing about biological and pharmaceutical products. His music criticism has appeared in pages of *Audio* and *Goldmine* magazines, and his guitar writings in *Vintage Guitar* magazine, *VG Classics*, *Acoustic Guitar*, and other magazines. He has also contributed to the 1994 books *Guitar Graphic Volumes 2 and 3* published in Japan by Rittor Music, and to *Classic Guitars of the '50s* (1996) and *Classic Guitars of the '60s* (1997) published in the U.K. by Balafon Books and in the U.S. by GPI Books/ Miller Freeman. His own *Guitar Stories Volume 1* was published by Vintage Guitar Books in 1995. He is the author of the histories contained in the authoritative annual *Vintage Guitar Magazine Price Guide*.

The author with his first guitar in 1956, with his sister Ginni.

ACKNOWLEDGEMENTS

For all their help and encouragement (and for giving me a voice), I'd like to especially thank Alan and Cleo Greenwood of *Vintage Guitar* magazine. For tolerance and understanding, I'd like to thank my wife Peggy and my son Benjamin. For an abiding interest in music I thank my mother and father, Mary and Frank Wright. A special note should be made of Mr. Charles Eilenberg, principal man behind the Alamo empire, who passed away shortly after I interviewed him. Another special acknowledgement goes to Mario Maccaferri whose great contributions to guitardom are often overlooked. Mr. Maccaferri unfortunately passed away before I began this research, but I'd like to thank his gracious wife Maria Maccaferri for her kind help in piecing together his story.

For helping me with information, tips, leads, hints, brochures, photos and guitars, I'd like to thank Michael Lee Allen, Frank Amiano, Akbar Anwari, Ron Wayne Atwood, Bill Baker, Bernunzio Vintage Instruments, Blue Suede Shoe, Dick Boak (Martin Guitars), Mary Bush (Photography By Mary), Ron Caimi, Frank Cammarata, Walter Carter (Gibson Guitars), Chelsea Guitars, Scott Chinery, Rich Chodak (Bluebond Guitars), John Ciarfella (Newark Musical Merchandise), Benny Cintioli (Cintioli's Music), Chip Coleman (Coleman Music), Paul Cowen, Dave's Music, Paul Day, Tod Dikemann, Chris and Sophie DiPinto (DiPinto Music), Jim Dulfer, Kelsey Edwards, Charles Eilenberg, Mark M. Fihen, Ryland Fitchett (Rockahaulix), Franklin Music, Steve Evans (Jacksonville Guitar Center), Scott Freilich (Top Shelf Music), Fret 'n Fiddle, Hirsh Gardner (Daddy's Junky Music), Steve Glazer, Gravity Strings, Kurt Grotyohann, Paul and Deb Grubich, Guitar & Music Center, O.J. Henley, Karl P. Huf, Jr. (Tinicum Guitar Barn), Stan Jay (Mandolin Brothers), Jim's Guitars, John Boy Vintage, Michael Katz (Serious Acoustics), Ron and Marsha Kayfield (Arpeggio Music), Marvin Kopermic, Mark Kremer, Doug Lesko, Hal Lewis (the Hal Lewis Group), Mike Longworth (Martin Guitars), Maria Maccaferri, Cameron MacLean, George Manno, Steve Margulis (Bluebond Guitars), Gilbert Matossian, Clark McAvoy (Clark's Music), Chris McGarry (McGarry's Pawn Shop), Larry "Mac" McKenzie, Elliot Mechanic (Mechanicland Vintage Guitars), Mike's Guitars, Etc., Johnny Milteer (Johnny's Guitars), Willie G. Moseley, Nui Luna Káne Guitars, Dr. Ben Nakashua, Richard Nesdale, Michael Newton, Joe O'Donnell, Fred Oster (Vintage Instruments), Joe Penissi, Jay Pilzer (New Hope Guitar Traders), Marvin Povernic, R&R Guitars, Jim Rhoads (Rhoads Music), Elizabeth Rimrott, Barney Roach, Rockville Music, Jay Scott (Nutty Jazz Guitars), Mike Sebren, Seductive Sound Guitars, Chris Smart (Krazy Kat Music), Mike Smith, Society Hill Loan, Maurice J. Summerfield, Sunrise Guitars, Michael Tamborrino, Ed Tauber, Ron Thorn, Chris Veleno, John Veleno, Robert Watkins, Way Cool Guitars, Gary Wood.

INTRODUCTION

Illuminating Guitar History

If you've ever pondered the fascinating textures of medieval book illumination, or perhaps a tapestry or stained glass, you've probably noticed that there is not only a main theme or story that dominates the page, there's also a series of subtexts. St. George slays the dragon while farmers till the soil down in the corner or, perhaps, colorful ladies go to market. These sideshows exist at the margins, but like everyday reality affect the interpretation of the main event often in quite significant ways. This same organizational infrastructure is true of observing Ozark forest environments in Arkansas, grassy beach dunes at the Jersey shore...and the subtleties of guitar history.

For most folks, the story line of guitar development is like the dominating events of St. George and his dragon. It goes something like this: there were some European acoustic guitars, which came to America with C.F. Martin, who invented the dreadnought, after which Orville Gibson invented archtop guitars, Leo Fender invented solidbody electric guitars, and then there were some others named D'Angelico, Epiphone and Gretsch. This is exaggerated thematic simplicity, of course, but it's the foundation upon which the edifice of writing about guitars — and the attendant phenomenon of guitar collecting — is built.

Of course, there's a kernel of truth contained in the commonly told tale. While guitars are part of the ancient cordophone family of instruments which probably hail from Egypt or Mesopotamia (and are found in cultures around the world), they are primarily a European development. The European tradition has had a significant direct and indirect — and little-studied — impact on American guitars and guitarmakers. And while there's no denying the significance of the contributions of Gibson and Fender, they are simply part of a larger nexus of innovators who have unrelentingly explored new ideas, some of which have ended up redirecting the mainstream. The guitar universe is filled to overflowing with the names of guitarmakers large and small, domestic and foreign, plus a host of importers and distributors, all of whom have shaped the history of the guitar.

This broader guitar universe is the province of these guitar stories. Chronicled here are histories that *should* be mainstream, such as the mighty Kay saga, but are, alas, not considered so by those who should know better. It was, for example, Kay, after all, which produced the first known commercially available electric guitars in 1928. The record is there, but rarely discussed. Also relayed here are tales of guitardom's Don Quixotes, of Florida's John Veleno and his carved aluminum guitars, and of Italy's Mario Maccaferri, whose remarkable plastic creations now overshadow his former challenge to the venerable Segovia hegemony. We even touch upon some of the lesser known products of mainstream brands, including the marvelous solidbody electric guitars built by Guild, one of the (unjustly) barely-sung legends of American lutherie, and the even more obscure electric guitars built by the acoustic giant Martin. And finally, we also take a look at one of the curious ill-illuminated corners of guitardom, the Alamo company out of — need you ask — San Antonio, Texas.

The "guitar stories" included here are only the proverbial tip of the iceberg. From massive factories to lonely artisans, the tapestry of guitar history is peopled by organizations, individuals and instruments whose main purpose has been to further the art of making music and the calming of that "rough beast slouching toward Bethlehem" lurking in the breasts of us all. Illumination of some of these stories may be found by taking up the lance, like St. George or Don Quixote, and turning the next page...

ALAMO
GUITARS AND AMPS

Remember the Alamo

Mention the Alamo and most of us conjure up a rich variety of images. Whether it's Davy Crockett (Fess Parker, *maybe* John Wayne) swinging his flintlock rifle as General Santa Ana's troops breached the walls, or Pee Wee Herman's futile quest for his stolen bicycle, or a symbol of modern Mexican-American political action, the Alamo means *something* to almost all Americans.

But to guitar fans, conjure up the name Alamo, and you've raised a spectre of a mystery, a puzzle made up of guitars and amplifiers that were built in San Antonio, Texas. And that's about it. What's the story about Alamo guitars and amps? How about we brighten up yet another dimly lit corner of American guitar history. Lights, camera, action...

The long search for the missing picture on Alamo guitars and amps was finally rewarded when San Antonio music dealer Chris Smart of Krazy Kat Music, who happened to own some of the remains of the Alamo guitar operation acquired when the Bruno warehouse was liquidated, provided

a lead to Mr. Charles Eilenberg. Mr. Eilenberg, it turns out, was the father of the Alamo empire, and he provided a foundation for reconstructing and remembering the Alamo story. Unfortunately, shortly after providing this information Mr. Eilenberg passed away. This story is dedicated to his memory.

As is often the case, a lot of this information is speculative reconstruction based on catalog sightings, observations and a generous helping of guesswork. Like many of the more obscure brands of instruments that have never been documented, there are gaps that still need to be filled, and the conclusions presented here may not necessarily be the last word, but it's about as close as we can get given the source materials available at this time.

1950s Alamo Model Amp 3, one of Alamo's first models (photo: Robert Watkins).

Jersey boy

Mr. Charles Eilenberg was born in Newark, New Jersey, and, upon graduating from

high school, traveled west to Wisconsin where he studied electronic engineering at the Milwaukee School of Electronics, affiliated with the University of Wisconsin. Interested in broadcasting, Eilenberg got his 1st Class license and got a job at a radio station in Jersey City, New Jersey. Jersey City was the stomping grounds, you'll recall, of Frank Sinatra, who had worked at Charles' first station and, according to Eilenberg, had been fired because he couldn't hold the key in which the band was playing.

Eilenberg worked in New Jersey for awhile and eventually joined the CBS network in New York, when World War II intervened. Charles went into the Navy as a communications engineer, coordinating communications for the big warships such as the Iowa and Missouri.

Southern Music

After the War, in late 1946, Eilenberg was contacted by Milton Fink, who had a large publishing company and music wholesaling business in San Antonio, Texas, called Southern Music. Mr. Fink wanted to recruit Eilenberg to help set up a manufacturing business. Eilenberg agreed and moved to San Antonio to establish Alamo Electronics (as you might guess, "Alamo" is a pretty common name in those parts).

Alamo Electronics got up and running in 1947 at a 2,000 square foot facility located at 105 W. Romana Street. The initial products included record players — luxury items unavailable during the War — and battery-operated radio sets. These were mainly dis-

Unknown early '60s R'n'B combo with Alamo guitars and basses (courtesy Michael Lee Allen).

(Left) 1950s Alamo lap steel, probably an early Futuramic Six (courtesy Clark McAvoy). (Right) Late '50s Alamo Embassy No. 2493 lap steel and Embassy No. 2463 amplifier (photo: Mike Newton).

tributed at post exchanges in Texas. At least one name used on these was Radioette. Very few retail outlets sold this early Alamo gear.

Among the activities of Southern Music at the time was distributing musical instruments. As part of that, the company had a great need for cases, and thus decided to get into the case manufacturing business. To that end, they bought the necessary equipment and began making cases, with the company divided into two areas, electronics and case manufacturing.

Into instruments

From instrument cases and radios it wasn't a big step to making instruments and amplifiers, a move which occurred in around 1949-50. Alamo began manufacturing amps and lap steel guitars. The earliest amps featured a wooden case of birch plywood with an "A" on the front, very similar to Epiphone amps of the time. The amp itself featured a top-mounted chassis, with tubes suspended downward.

Alamo's first amp and guitar combos were the AMP-3 Embassy amp and steel (the -3 signified the number of tubes), and the

AMP-4 Jet amp and steel, later to be augmented by the AMP-2 Challenger amp and Challenger steel. These can be seen in an undated catalog that features the Romana Street address and looks to be probably from around 1953.

By '53 the Alamo Embassy Electric Guitar ($54.50) had achieved its trademark shape. This was a cool six-string lap with a satin-finished light hardwood body in a symmetrical pear shape with two contrasting strips of walnut running along side the neck through the body. This had a clear lucite 'board with dots, a flat three-and-three head with Alamo logo, and one Alamo

Alnico pickup on a black plastic or lucite handrest assembly with volume and tone.

The '53 Alamo Embassy Amp-3 had a satin-finished birch A cabinet with drawer pull chrome handle. This had top-mounted controls with three inpus, a volume and tone control and, need we add, pilot light. It sported three tubes that put 6 watts through a 10" Jensen speaker. It cost $69.50 alone ($4.50 for water repellent cover). The Embassy combo was $136.

The '53 Alamo Jet guitar had a large triangular body, made of hardwood and finished in Alpine White. This had a white fingerboard with black "frets" and dots. There was a script Alamo Jet logo at the angular bottom of the fingerboard. This had the Alamo Alnico pickup on a black plastic or lucite handrest assembly, with volume and tone. The cord was permanently attached. This would set you back $39.50 back then.

The accompanying Alamo Jet Amplifier (sometimes called the Amp-4) came in a brown or white linen leatherette covering with a brown and gold plastic speaker grille and drawer pull handle. This had a top-mounted volume control and an on/off switch! This used three tubes pumping four watts through a 6" Jensen. Alone it cost $49.50. The Jet guitar and amp combo cost $99.

The Alamo Challenger guitar was around

Control panels of the '50s Alamo Models Amp 3 and Amp 5 (photo: Robert Watkins).

by '53. This had another typical Alamo shape with an asymmetrical pear-shaped body and a square three-and-three head. The Challenger had a small "German-carve" lip around the top. By '53 it had a natural hardwood finish and featured a black and silver lucite fingerboard with black dots and a light-colored plastic control and handrest assembly, with volume and tone controls for the Alamo Alnico pickup. It cost $45. Seen in another illustration, by the way, is another version of the Challenger with the same body but a black fingerboard with white dots. This also had a black handrest which seems to have been set slightly more forward than the large illustration. Strings attached at a slotted metal tailblock. Whether this was an earlier or later version is unknown, but you're now warned that this also existed in the early '50s.

The Challenger guitar could be had with the Alamo Amp-2, also known as the Challenger amp, for $116. The Amp-2 had a wooden A cabinet, drawer pull handle, and top-mounted control panel with two inputs and a volume control. Three tubes pushed power through an 8" Jensen speaker. Instead of birch, the Amp-2 came with a ³/8" veneer on the front and a solid top section. Alone it cost $59.50.

Three other lap steel guitars were available by around 1953 as well, the Futuramic model in three versions, the Futuramic 6 ($75), Futuramic 8 ($87.50) and Futuramic

1950s Alamo Model Amp 5 with the birch cabinet and "A" grille cutout (photo: Robert Watkins).

Dual 8 ($165). The single necked Futuramics had the same asymmetrical pear shape as the Challenger, with the player side slightly longer than the control side, both tapering down toward the head. These had

sort of square heads, but with a long small rectangular, round-edged extension or crown in the center. The Futuramic 6 and 8 both came with black and gold lucite fingerboards with a block letter Alamo logo running down the middle. The had Safe-Ti-String machines that were gold plated, fitted with gold tinsel buttons! These had what appear to be black lucite control panels and handrest covers. The single pickup was Alamo Alnico, with volume and tone controls. The Futuramic Dual 8 was similar except the wings were small and parallel to the fingerboards. Controls were mounted on a long center lucite strip and included voume, tone and a threeway neck select.

By '53 Alamo also offered the Amp-5 amplifier. This was a birch A amp with drawer pull handle. Mounted on the top were four inputs with a microphone channel, two volume controls, a master tone, on/off switch and pilot light, plus fuse. This had five tubes that punched 15 watts through a 12" Jensen speaker. It cost $110, with another $7.95 for a cover. This is probably what would later become the Montclair amplifier.

Finally, by '53 the Alamo Amp-6A amplifier had joined the line. This had the birch A cabinet and drawer pull handle. This now featured the electronic tremolo for which

1956 Alamo Paragon amplifier (photo: Mike Newton).

Back of the '56 Alamo Paragon amp (photo: Mike Newton).

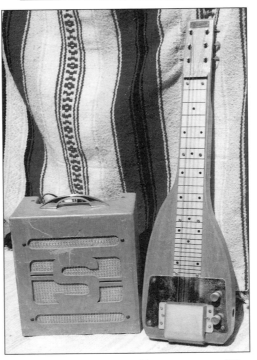

(Left) Late '50s Alamo Futuramic 6 lap steel and late '50s Alamo Challenger or Jet amplifier (photo: Chris Smart, Krazy Kat Music, San Antonio, TX). (Right) Ca. 1958 Somco Jet amp with 6" speaker and Futuramic 6 lap steel made for Southern Music by Alamo (photo: Chris Smart, Krazy Kat Music, San Antonio, TX).

single coil pickups on early Alamo laps were similar to what is generally encountered on their later Spanish electrics but slightly larger.

The details of the late '50s are pretty slim, due to lack of literature. By the late '50s the birch-cabinet amp line had expanded considerably to include model names which would continue often through the existence of the company.

Eventually the Alamo line would expand to include 14 or 15 models of amps, probably more than they should have, admitted Eilenberg.

Aloha

During the '50s Alamo also did a lot of OEM manufacturing. One of its primary clients was Aloha, the Hawaiian guitar and amp company. Many Aloha amps and guitars were made by Alamo. As Eilenberg recalls, Aloha only bought the AMP-3 Embassy amp and guitar. The Embassy was a tapered, roughly triangular hardwood lap with a "German carve" top. Later Alamo examples had black and red aluminum fingerboards, chrome handrest, extended range adjustable pickup, volume and tone, and Deluxe Safe-Ti string machine heads, in Alpine White; presumably Alohas were similar.

In around 1956, by the way, Aloha began making its own amps, an operation Eilenberg helped set up, but throughout they contin-

Alamo received a patent, with variable strength and speed, providing an "organ-like quality especially effective with electronic accordions," popular at the time. The Amp-6A had four inputs, with two volume controls, power switch, fuse, and pilot light. The coolest feature was five push-button tone controls, reminiscent of contemporary Premier amplifiers. The Amp-6A had seven tubes with 25 watts of power driving a 15" Jensen high fidelity concert series speaker. This cost a whopping $210, plus $9 for a cover. This is probably the amp which would later become the Alamo Paragon.

It's important to understand that Alamo amplifiers featured point-to-point wiring, adding a quality factor despite the fact that they were playing in a budget arena.

During this era, Alamo sold only to distributors. Probably the most famous was C. Bruno and Son, their major distributor through the glory years. They also did a brisk business down in Mexico and into Central and South America. Eilenberg recalls that one salesman own his own airplane and used to regularly fly south of the border to sell Alamo amps.

By sometime in 1953 Alamo had grown and relocated to a new 6,000 square foot facility in San Antonio.

Alamo built most — if not all — of its own lap steels over the years, although at least some have been reported that were made for Alamo by Valco. This is not confirmed. The

A collection of '50s Alamo wood-cabinet amps (photo: Chris Smart, Krazy Kat Music, San Antonio, TX).

ued to buy Alamo products, as well. Aloha, according to Eilenberg, acoustic guitars were sourced primarily from Harmony in Chicago.

Muddy waters

According to Mr. Eilenberg's recollection, Alamo production was limited to amps and lap steels until around 1960 when the company had to relocate again to a 25,500 square foot factory at 926 West Laurel Street. Alamo occupied the majority of this site, but leased out a part of it to tenants. And, according to Mr. Eilenberg, whose memory seemed to have been pretty good, it was in 1960 that Alamo increased the size of its woodshop and began the production of electric Spanish guitars.

However, the textual evidence raises chronology issues which are worth discussing, since they reflect on both the specific and broader problems of reconstructing guitar history (as well as other popular culture subjects). Personal recollections are notoriously imprecise. If you were called and asked if something happened 40 or 41 years ago, how accurate would you be? Mr. Eilenberg's memories were exceptionally good, but may not be as precise as historians (and guitar aficionados) might wish. The case in point is a catalog provided courtesy of collector Jim Dulfer, reproduced here. This has no date of publication. That is not unusual for guitar companies, who either didn't think dates were important, or expected to market the guitars for awhile and didn't want to "date" the literature so it would remain useful. When Dulfer got the catalog, it was supposedly dated, for an unknown reason, as being from ca. 1955. Mr. Eilenberg recalled that the company moved to West Laurel Street in 1960, when it made its first Spanish guitar. But the catalog has a Spanish guitar, and an address of 1415 N. Brazos Street on the warranty statement. The graphic style could easily be from 1955 to 1960. The Laurel street address does turn up on later catalogs. We have a more-or-less confirmed 1962 catalog, and the artwork is often the same, but the style is different. The Brazos Street address is still used. Did Alamo just not bother to change the address on the warranty statement? Or is this slightly earlier? Dulfer has seen catalogs of Alamo amps with

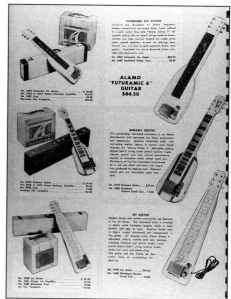
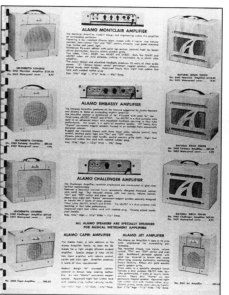

Ca. 1960 Alamo catalog showing the first electric Spanish guitar, the Texan (courtesy Jim Dulfer).

birch cabinets as late as '58. This catalog has birch amps plus vinyl-covered amps. The style of the *vinyl* amps could be from anytime during this whole period. The copy describing the guitar refers to its "new" neck design, but that could refer to an improvement, or imply the guitar is new.

So, what do we conclude? We will stick with Mr. Eilenberg's account here, that Spanish electrics debuted in '60, but understand that it could be a year or more earlier when Alamo Spanish guitars (and vinyl covered amps) appeared. In the cosmic scheme of things, it might matter if you had a '59 or '60 Gibson Les Paul, but not an Alamo gui-

tar! This is the "grain of salt" you must consider, and if you find evidence to correct this chronology, understand the difficulty of making these decisions based on the evidence at hand.

Transition

So, a good snapshot of the maturing Alamo line (and reflection of the old offerings) can be gleaned from the undated catalog, which can be assumed to date from 1960, but could actually date from a few years earlier.

Aside from an occasional exception, Alamo guitars and amps were all built in San

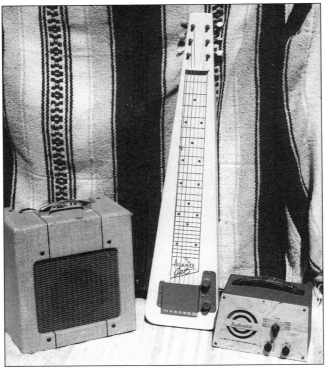

(Left) Ca. 1960 Alamo No. 2493 Embassy Lap Steel (courtesy Coleman Music, China Grove, NC). (Right) Ca. 1960 Alamo No. 2461 Jet amplifier and No. 2490 Jet lap steel, plus the Radioette (photo: Chris Smart, Krazy Kat Music, San Antonio, TX).

Antonio, Texas, as far as we know. Pickups were also made by Alamo. There were some early '60s guitars advertised in the music trade press made in Mexico which looked almost identical to Alamo guitars. The story behind these, or any possible connection with Alamo, may forever remain unknown. As far as can be determined with the evidence at hand, all Alamos were American-made.

By 1960 or so, the Alamo amplifier line had expanded to include at least seven basic models, all but one of which appear to have already existed prior to this catalog. These were now almost all offered in a choice of coverings, either in the old birch cabinet with the A cutout on the grill, or in a new, more modern "grey lite" leatherette offset with two vertical lines of dark grey beading on either side of the grille, and a dark grey plastic grillecloth. The handles for all were long rounded chrome-plated steel. Prices for either the birch A option or the leatherette were identical.

Still in the Alamo line were the Embassy, Challenger and Jet amplifiers of yore, although whether or not these had by this time undergone any upgrades is unknown. The Embassy featured three tubes, 6SL7GT, 6V6GT and 5Y3GT, a 10" Alamo speaker and 6 watts of output power. The No. 2563 came in leatherette, whereas the No. 2463 came in birch, both for $82.50.

The Challenger amp also had three tubes, 6SL7GT, 6V6GT and 5Y3GT, with two inputs, volume control, 8" Alamo speaker and 5 watts of output power. The No. 2562 in leatherette and No. 2462 in birch cost $62.50.

The No. 2561 Jet also had three tubes (including one 6SL7GT), two in-puts, volume control, 6" Alamo speaker, 4 watts output power, and only a leatherette option at this time, for $59.50.

Above these three was the Montclair. This had five tubes, 12AX7, 6SLGT, two 6V6GTs and 5Y3GT, with four inputs, tone control, 12" Jenson speaker and 15 watts of output power. The No. 2565 in leatherette and No. 2465 in birch cost $124.50.

Top of the line were two Paragon amplifiers. The Paragon guitar amplifier had seven tubes (unidentified), four inputs, two volume controls, a push-button tone control (bass boost), 15" Jenson Concert Series speaker and 25 watts output. The No. 2567 in leatherette and No. 2467 in birch cost $234.50.

The Paragon Special was a bass amp version with a 15" Jenson bass speaker. The No. 2569 in leatherette and No. 2469 in birch cost $259.50.

New in around 1960 was the Capri amp No. 2560. This had three tubes, two inputs, volume control, 6" Alamo speaker and 3 watts output. It was covered in brown leatherette with no beading and cost $46.50.

Five Alamo Hawaiian lap steels were available in circa '60, all having already been in-

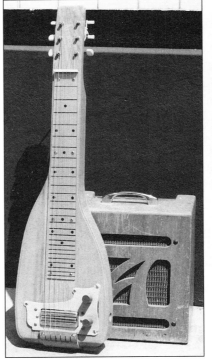

(Left) Ca. 1961 Alamo Futuramic 6 lap steel with possibly a ca. 1960 Alamo Jet amp (photo: Mike Newton). (Right) Ca. 1960 Alamo No. 2495 Futuramic Six lap steel.

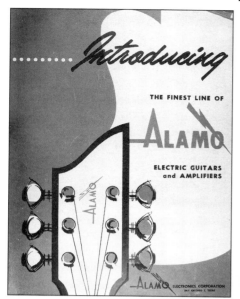

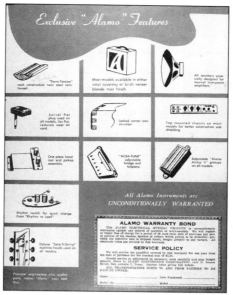

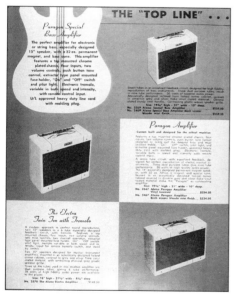

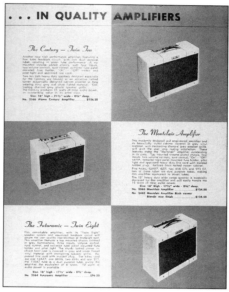

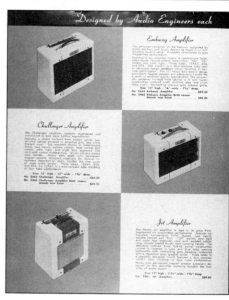

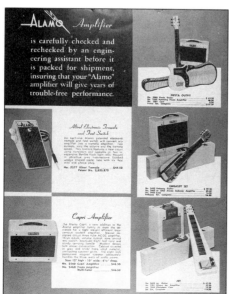

Ca. 1962 Alamo catalog, including the Futuramic and Tele-shaped Fiesta guitars (courtesy Jim Dulfer).

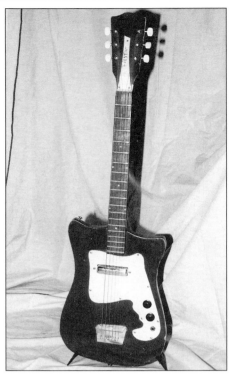

(Left) Ca. 1964 Alamo Titan Mark II. (Right) Ca. 1964 Alamo Fiesta Mark I with new double-cutaway shape and hollow body (courtesy Clark McAvoy).

troduced in the early '50s.

Top of the line was the No. 2499 Futuramic Dual Eight. This had two basically rectangular necks, the outside one now slightly elevated, the black and silver fingerboard with block ALAMO letters as position markers, *upward* facing four-and-four tuners, and a script Alamo logo on the front. Each neck had a single Alamo Alnico V pickup mounted under a chrome handrest. In between the necks was a rectangular chrome control plate with one volume and one tone control. Next to it was a two-way toggle select. Cost was $199.50 for the guitar, plus another $50 for hard case and $39 for legs.

The No. 2497 Futuramic Eight followed, with a single Alamo Alnico V pickup, chrome handrest/control assembly with volume and tone controls, black fingerboard with the block ALAMO markers, and a 25" scale. This had a flocked back. Gone was the gold tinsel trim, alas. Cost was a hefty $96.50 plus another $30 for a hard case.

The No. 2495 Futuramic Six was the same as the Futuramic Eight except for two fewer strings and an $84.50 price tag.

The old No. 2493 Embassy guitar was still around as before. The pickup was now descibed as being an Alamo Alnico V unit and the handrest assembly has changed from plastic to chrome. The lucite 'board had been

Ca. 1964
Alamo Tremolo Pedal
(photo: Chris Smart, Krazy
Kat Music, San Antonio, TX).

replaced by a red and black aluminum 'board with dots. Cost was now $59.50 with another $14 getting you a Gladstone flannel lined case.

Also still around was the No. 2490 Jet guitar, still with a large Alpine white triangular body. This too had the Alamo Alnico V pickup on a chrome handrest assembly,

with volume and tone. Cost was $47.50 plus $12.50 for a Gladstone case.

Both the Embassy and Jet lap steel guitars now had their respective names on the headstock, not Alamo.

The Embassy lap and amp and Jet lap and amp were still sold bundled together as guitar outfits. Gone by '60 was the little Challenger lap.

Enter Espana

Appearing for the first time in 1960 was Alamo's first Spanish electric duly dubbed the No. 2590 Texan Solid Body Spanish Electric. This was a solidbody guitar with two equal cutaways, sort of a cross between a Gibson Les Paul Junior and a Rickenbacker. The deep cutaways joined the neck right at the end of the fingerboard at the 20th fret, so it's probable that this was a glued-neck guitar. The neck was made of Northern maple and was called a FerroTorsion neck, with a "steel bar plate." This was probably a slab steel bar reinforcement similar to that on Danelectros of the period (soon this term would come to mean double steel bars, like on Danos, so it's probably safe to assume the design is a variation on that of their competitor). The headstock had a very dramatic French curve culminating in a high, pointed peak on the treble side. The logo was a headstock decal with the Alamo logo featuring a lightning bolt through the final "o." Tuners were Safe-Ti open-backed strips. The fingerboard on this (arguably) high point in Alamo Spanish guitars was ebony with four pearl block inlays which spanned the width of the fingerboard. The Texan's body was made of ash and finished in a natty Primavera Blonde. The pickguard was a conservative rounded black plastic shape, with a wide rounded part in the middle of the strings carrying a wide Alamo Alnico V pickup and extending down along the treble lower bout for volume and tone controls and jack. This had a third pushbutton rhythm tone control. It used a "new flat head phone plug," which would become an Alamo exclusive, basically a wide square

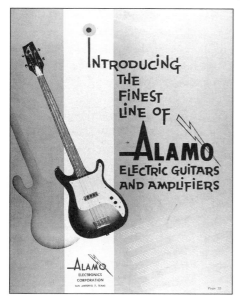

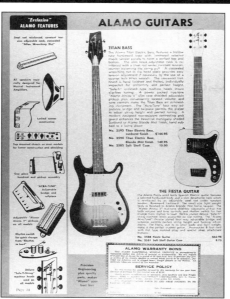

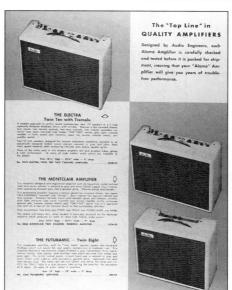

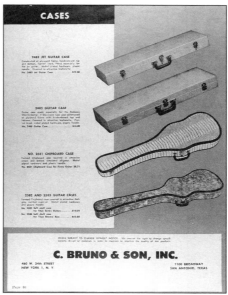

Ca. 1963 Alamo catalog, with the new Titan Bass and guitars (courtesy Jim Dulfer).

(Left) Ca. '64 white Alamo Fiesta; note unusual pickup spacing (courtesy Clark McAvoy). (Right) Ca. 1964 or early '65 Alamo Titan Bass with the Oriental A cutout in pickguard (courtesy Clark McAvoy).

plastic head with the plug coming out at a right angle. The bridge was a moveable adjustable type like those found on early Harmonies and Kays. The tail was a hinged trapeze.

This transitional lineup, including the new solidbody Texan guitar, probably lasted only a couple years until around 1962, when we can pick up the trail again with another Alamo catalog kindly provided by Jim Dulfer. This is also undated but probably from around 1962. While many of the line's mainstays remained in '62, a number of other changes and reshufflings were afoot. Again, this information could be plus or minus regarding date.

Also, it was sometime during this period that Alamo hooked up more exclusively with C. Bruno & Son, Inc., distributors, which were based in San Antonio, with a major office in New York City and later L.A. Bruno is not mentioned in the circa 1960 catalog, but is featured in some versions of the circa '62 catalog.

Into the '60s swing

In terms of '62 Alamo amps, the models were mostly still available in either the old birch cabinet or in a leatherette, now grey and silver flake vinyl, however, whereas before examples of both cabinets were illustrated in the catalog, now only the vinyl coverings were shown. Logos were on rectangular plates in the center of the top of the front of the cabinet. Still in the line and pretty much unchanged were the No. 2560 Capri, Nos. 2562 (vinyl) and 2462 (birch) Challenger, the Nos. 2563 and 2463 Embassy, Nos. 2565 and 2465 Montclair, Nos. 2567 and 2467 Paragon, and Nos. 2569 and 2469 Paragon Special, all still priced at '60 levels. Observation of many other brand catalogs shows similar stasis in prices during this period, contrary to the constant inflation seen in the '70s and '80s.

The old No. 2561 Jet also remained, but redesigned with grey and blue leatherette, with the center panel blue, grey beading and grey plastic grill. This still had three tubes (including 12AX7) and 4 watts output, for $59.50.

New by '62 were some Twins and the addition of a new patented electronic tremolo. (Note the correct designation of the tremolo, which is amplitude variation, not frequency variation, as on the Magnatone of the era. Guitars have "vibrato" systems, not tremolos.) The newer amps did not have the old birch option, and boasted interlocking cabinet corners for added strength.

The No. 2570 Electra Twin Ten with Tremolo had six tubes (unidentified), four inputs, two volumes and two tones, two channels, speed and intensity on the tremolo, two 10" Alamo speakers and 18 watts output. This came in grey and silver flake vinyl covering with a charcoal grey plastic grill, for $148.50.

Also new in '62 was the No. 2566 Century Twin Ten, with five tubes, two 10" speakers, four inputs, two volumes and one tone, 15 watts output, and the vinyl covering. At $136.50, this was almost the same as the Electra but without the tremolo.

In addition, the old Futuramic name formerly applied just to Hawaiian laps was transferred to the new No. 2564 Futuramic Twin Eight amp, with 12AX7, 6AV6, two 6v6 and 5Y3 tubes, two 8" speakers, 10 watts output and the grey and silver flake vinyl covering. This had a grey hammertone finish on the chassis, and cost $96.50.

Lastly, but not leastly, by '62 the No. 2460 Fiesta amp had debuted. This was basically identical to the old Capri, except it was offered in a speckled finish made up of multiple colors. It cost $46.50.

Three Hawaiian lap steels remained in 1962. The No. 2499 Alamo Dual Eight String Professional Model was the old Futuramic, still $199.50, with Alamo written down the middle of the fingerboard. This was a satin-finished hardwood, with chrome-plated control plate and handrests. Legs were optional. The No. 2493 Embassy guitar, with the walnut stripes, also remained, priced the same, with a red and black aluminum fingerboard and a chrome plated handrest. This still said Embassy on the headstock. The No. 2490 Jet, with the elongated triangular body and Alpine white finish, also remained the same, with a red and black aluminum fingerboard. Gone was the asymmetrical Futuramic Eight lap steel. The Embassy and Jet still had their names on the headstocks, not Alamo.

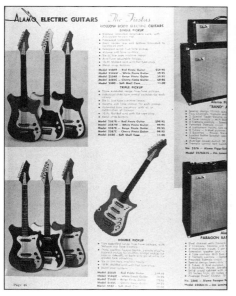

Ca. 1964 Alamo "stars" catalog (courtesy Chris Smart, Krazy Kat Music, San Antonio, TX).

(Left to Right) Ca. 1964 Alamo Fiesta Mark I, ca. 1965 Alamo Fiesta 2586W, and ca. 1964 Alamo Fiesta Mark II (photo: Chris Smart, Krazy Kat Music, San Antonio, TX). Red ca. 1967 Alamo No. 2598 Toronado and ca. '64 Alamo Titan Mark II (photo: Chris Smart, Krazy Kat Music, San Antonio, TX). Ca. 1965 Alamo Model 2591 Titan Mark II (courtesy Clark McAvoy).

New six-strings

Also gone in '62 was the Texan solidbody, replaced by the Futuramic Spanish electric solidbody, No. 2587. This was a similar equal double cutaway with a slightly thicker upper horn. It also appeared to have a glued-in neck, but this is unconfirmed. This was finished in a Blonde Mist. The three-and-three head still sported a French curve top, but this was much less dramatic, with a lower peak, than the Texan, still with Safe-Ti tuners. The logo was still the lightning bolt Alamo decal. The 20-fret fingerboard was now rosewood with dot inlays. The black pickguard was similar to the Texan, but was now squared off above the pickup, and still mounted in the middle of the body. Replacing the Texan's moveable adjustable bridge was a new Alamo Acra-Tune bridge/tailpiece assembly. This was remarkably similar to Danelectro's inimitable design. It was basically an angled piece of metal, hinged with adjustable height screws, with six holes for holding the strings in the back and an adjustable saddle at the front. This had volume, tone and a rhythm-lead toggle switch. The cost was $67.50.

New also was the No. 2588 Fiesta Spanish solidbody. This had a small, almost Tele-shaped single cutaway body, otherwise almost the same as the Futuramic. It was, like the Fiesta amp, available in a speckled, multicolor, "mar-resistant" paint, for $62.50. It's not clear whether this is a glued-in or bolt-on neck.

As before, Alamo offered various guitar and amp "outfits," including the Fiesta (matching guitar and amp for $117.50), plus the Embassy ($156) and Jet ($119) Hawaiian outfits. The Fiesta outfit shown in the catalog came with a guitar with speckled finish, matched on the amplifier.

Especially cool in '62 was the offering of the No. 2577 Altrol Electronic Tremolo and Foot Switch, essentially a foot pedal with the new patented electronic tremolo. In addition to an on/off switch, this had speed and volume knobs mounted on the side. All for a cool $44.50.

Expansion

In 1963 the Alamo line began to transmogrify again, taking a more familiar tack. A bunch of new Spanish electrics

bowed, as well as more new amps, seen again in an undated catalog provided by Jim Dulfer, probably from '63, very similar to our ca. '62 except for a change in the blue tint used on the cover.

Still in the amp line in '63 were the No. 2560 Capri (12AU6, 5OL6, 35Z5, 8" speaker); No. 2561 Jet; No. 2562 Challenger (12AX7, 6V6, 5Y3, 8" speaker, 5 watts); No. 2563 Embassy (same tubes, 10" speaker, 6 watts); No. 2564 Futuramic Twin Eight; No. 2565 Montclair (two 6V6, 5Y3GT, two 12AX7, ECC-83/12AX7, 6AN8, 12" speaker, 25 watts); and the No. 2570 Electra Twin Ten with Tremolo, all pretty much priced as before. Notice that gone now is the birch cabinet option; all are in the grey and silver flaked vinyl. Also, gone is the beading and a script Alamo logo is now on a little rectangular plate on the upper left corner of the grillecloth.

The Paragon and Paragon Special were still offered, though slightly redesigned. The No. 2567 Paragon Two Channel now had eight tubes (two 6L6GB, 5U4GB, two 12AX7, two ECC-83/12AX7, 6AN8), 15" speaker, two channels, four inputs, tremolo, treble

(Left to Right) Ca. 1965 Alamo Model 2587R Fiesta with three pickups. Ca. 1965 Alamo Model 2584W Fiesta (courtesy Clark McAvoy). Ca. 1965 Alamo Model 2586W Fiesta (courtesy Clark McAvoy).

and bass boost and 30 watts output (60 watts peak). The No. 2569 Paragon Two Channel Bass was similar (minus the tremolo), with six tubes (two 5881, 5U4GB, two ECC-83/12AX7, 6AN8), two channels, and 30 watts (60 watts peak).

New in '63 was the No. 2571 Galaxie Twin Twelve amp, with two 12" speakers, two channels (normal and tremolo), four inputs, patented electronic tremolo, seven tubes (two 6L6GB, 5U4GB, two 12AX7, ECC-83/12AX7, 6AN8), 25 watts output, for $199.50.

Still offered was the Altrol tremolo foot switch.

Reflecting the changing times, the Alamo Hawaiian line shrank still further. Gone in '63 was the old doubleneck. Still offered were the pear-shaped, walnut-striped No. 2493 Embassy and elongated triangular No. 2490 Jet laps.

Even more guitars

In terms of Spanish electrics, gone was the Futuramic solidbody, though the Tele-shaped Fiesta Spanish guitar remained, still a solidbody.

New in '63 was the Titan Series guitars and bass. These had even less dramatic French curves on the top of their heads, and featured hollow core bodies, a construction

Ca. 1965 Alamo No. 2570 Electra Twin Ten two-channel combo with vibrato (courtesy Clark McAvoy).

method usually associated with Alamo guitars. Headstocks still had the lightning bolt Alamo decals.

The Titan Series guitars consisted of two models, the Mark I and Mark II, slightly offset double cutaways (not unlike Magnatone Zephyrs) with one or two pickups, respectively. Pickups on the Titans, by the way, still have the Alamo humped metal covers but are significantly narrower, a design seen on most existing Alamo guitars. The pickguards had become almost Strat-like, covering most of the lower part of the guitar. The 20-fret rosewood fingerboards now had pearloid block inlays. The necks were definitely bolt-on. Bridge/tailpieces were the Alamo Acra-Tune. The Mark I had a single middle pickup, volume, tone and a rhythm-lead toggle switch. The No. 2589 Mark I was sunburst, at $89.95, while the No. 2590 Mark I was Blonde Mist, at $94.95. The Mark II was the same except for having neck and bridge pickup, and a threeway toggle replacing the rhythm switch. The No. 2591 Mark II was sunburst, at $109.95, while the No. 2592 Mark II was Blonde Mist, at $114.95.

The No. 2593 Titan Bass was Alamo's first bass, another hollow-body, with the slightly

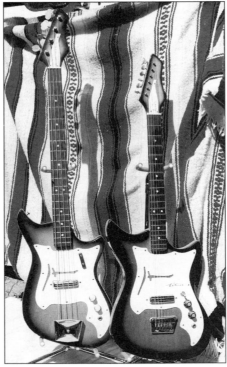

(Left)Ca. 1965 Alamo Model 2587R Fiesta and Alamo Model 2586R Fiesta (photo: Chris Smart, Krazy Kat Music, San Antonio, TX). (Right) Ca. 1967 Alamo Model 2593 Titan Bass and ca. 1965 Alamo Model 2589 Titan Mark I (photo: Chris Smart, Krazy Kat Music, San Antonio, TX).

offset double cutaway body, two-and-two head, volume, tone and Acra-Tune bridge/ tailpiece. This had a single, narrower pickup in the middle. A Blonde Mist Titan Bass set you back $144.50, while a Sunburst Titan Bass cost $149.50.

Mr. Eilenberg recalls the making of these hollowbodies. These were made of imported Swedish plywood because the specified thickness was 3 mm and European plywood came in metric sizes. The workers at Alamo would bend the sides on a form and then apply milk glue. Around forty guitars would then be stacked up with waxed paper between them and compressed with a hydraulic press while the glue dried. As Eilenberg states, the company never had a problem with bodies coming apart. Later on, milk glue was no longer available, and Alamo switched to a Tightbond type of glue.

Dazed and confusion

At this point we might as well admit to some little confusion. While these undated catalogs provide an excellent view of early Alamo instruments, there are a number of pieces which don't conveniently fit classification. One reason for this becomes clear when you trace this saga and note how often Alamo transferred one name to another instrument, causing obfuscation. Also, in terms of guitars, one suspects that the name Fiesta went on just about everything! Like they probably had a bin of Fiesta headstock plates and used them on anything. This perception may just persist because of the holes in our knowledge, however, remember that Alamo was not producing high end professional gear, but cheap beginner instruments where quality and consistency were not necessarily the most important ingredients. They certainly never thought someone would try to document them seriously…

Which is prefatory to discussing a few guitars which show up fairly frequently but which are not in the catalogs we have at hand. These bear both the Titan and Fiesta names. These carry a number of features which seem to mark a transition from the early '60s sightings and mid- and later-'60s models, so we can probably deduce that they date from a period from around 1963 and 1964. Most have a new flared three-and-three headstock which is more-or-less center-humped, "more-or-less" because some of the construction quality from this period is abysmal, and the hump kind of migrates around on some guitars! Some still have the old Alamo decal on the head, whereas others now begin to sport a large, downward-curved, anteater-shaped truss rod cover (almost like a Rickenbacker) with Alamo and the model name engraved on it. These covers are absent in '63 and standard by '65, so probably the presence or lack thereof indicates early or late in this period. Almost all of these have the Acra-Tune bridge assembly which was in place by '62 and the newer, more narrow pickup which debuted in '63. Most have a new pickguard design which featured what would become an Alamo trademark, a sort of squiggly tail on a squarish Strat-shaped 'guard, like an amoeba or polliwog or perhaps cartoon fetus. Well, you'll know it when you see it.

The Titans from this era seem to be pretty much a continuation as before, with the hollow core body but with the new broad center humped headstock, presumably still available in Mark I (one pickup) and Mark II (two pickup) versions. The example shown in the color photos is done up in a nifty plum purple color. This guitar, by the way, also has a remarkable treble edge to the neck: the maker must have figured out he was carving it too narrowly and at about the 9th fret or so it takes this curve outward to give it a bit more width, sort of like a flipped over 5-string banjo neck! It's quite startling to move up the neck and encounter this unique profile. Of course, I suspect they never expected an Alamo player to move up the neck…

The Fiesta also went through a further transition at this point. The old small solidbody Tele shape, which was fairly downplayed in the '63 catalog, appears to have briefly transformed into the double cutaway shape of the Texan, remaining a solidbody, with an Alamo decal on the head. However, soon enough this guitar changed into a small-bodied equal double cutaway hollow core body, with the slightly dipped cutaway horns almost perpendicular to the neck (which was almost parallel all the way down, much like a Harmony). These had the wide center-humped head, now with the Rickyesque truss cover, and the squiggly fetal pickguard. The Fiesta came with one (no fancy rhythm/lead switches) or two pickups, and at least in red and white finishes.

Beatlemania, more or less

On November 22, 1963, President John F. Kennedy was assassinated, one of the major media, cultural and psychological events of the decade. Several weeks later the Beatles' "I Want to Hold Your Hand" was released by Capitol records. By February of 1964 the song had reached #1 and the British Invasion of the U.S. pop music scene was underway. Later that month the Beatles made their historic appearance on the "Ed Sullivan Show." Electric guitars and amps took off in a stellar explosion. Magnatone, the important amp and guitar manufacturer in California, introduced its Starlite series of low-end amplifiers. An undated Alamo catalog with similar graphics introduced the "Stars of the Alamo Line…" that, based on a combination of deductive reasoning and the intuitive understanding that Magnatone

was a competitor of Alamo, is probably from 1964 as well. The style of the instruments supports this conclusion.

Black vinyl Professionals

The Alamo amps included in the '64 line mark the first appearance of black vinyl covering and gold sparkle grillecloths. Cabinets were mostly rectangular with front-mounted control panels slightly slanted back, although the piggy-back amps had back-mounted control panels. Larger amps had chrome drawer handles, while smaller ones had black vinyl strip handles. Larger amps had corner protectors. Early logos were still the rectangular Alamo plates, but some later versions had gold script logos outlined in black.

Top of the line was the Alamo Professional Series amplifiers, which included a couple Alamo piggy-back amps, Alamo's first head and cabinet units. The big unit was the Alamo No. 2578 Piggy-Back Super Band Amplifier with Loaded Baffle. The head came with two channels, tremolo and normal. Each channel had special taper volume control, plus Hi-Fi bass and treble con-

trols, and two inputs, coupled to power, standby and ground reverse switches. The patented tremolo channel also had speed and intensity controls. The Super Band was powered by eight tubes and offered 40 watts average power, 80 watts peak output. For $379.50 you got a cabinet with two 12" extended range speakers. For $679.50 you could get the Model 2578JL2-12 with a pair of 12" Jim Lansing speakers.

The Alamo No. 2576 Piggy-Back Band Amplifier was pretty much identical except it had a single 15" speaker and 30 watts average output, 60 watts peak, for $339.50. For $489.50 you could get the Model 2576JL15 with a 15" Jim Lansing speaker.

Next in the trio of piggies was the Alamo No. 2575 Piggy-Back Bass Amplifier. It was similar to the Band, except it substituted a bass channel for the tremolo channel. This offered six tubes, with 30 watts average output, 60 watts peak. For $319.50 the Bass came with a heavy duty 15" Special Bass speaker; for $469.50 you got the Model 2576JL15 15" Jim Lansing speaker.

Also included in the Professional Series were two redesigned Paragon amps, still combos. The Alamo No. 2568 Paragon Band had the same basic guts as the Piggy-Back Band with two channels, same controls, eight tubes, 30 watts (60 watts peak) and one 15" speaker for $289.50. The upgrade was the Model 2568JL15 with a 15" Jim Lansing speaker for $439.50.

The Alamo No. 2569 Paragon Bass Amplifier was basically the same as the previous year's model, with a $269.50 price tag for the single 15" speaker, $419.50 for the Model 2569JL15 Jim Lansing option.

Black vinyl Semi-Pros

Under the Professional Series in '64 were the Alamo Semi-Professional Amplifiers. Makes sense. Most of these were familiar names in the new packaging, although one shouldn't assume that no changes were implemented between these model years. Top of this series was the Alamo Model 2571 Galaxie Twin Twelve Piggy-Back Amplifier. This was introduced in '63 as a combo amp, but was now transmogrified into a head and cabinet. Electronics appear to be pretty much the same, with two channels, normal

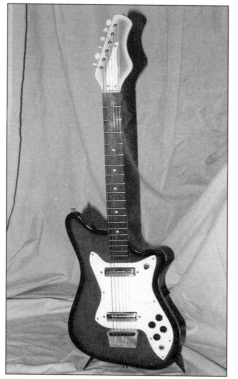

(Left) Mysterious ca. 1967 Alamo Fiesta, virtually identical to the Alamo Fury Standard solidbody (courtesy Clark McAvoy). (Right) Ca. 1967 Alamo Model 2583T-SB Fury Tremolo (courtesy Clark McAvoy).

and tremolo, four inputs, volume and tone controls on each channel, seven tubes, a pair of 12" speakers and 22 watts of output. This was stock for $249.50, or with 12" Jim Lansing speakers as the Model 2571JL12 at $384.50.

Under the Galaxie was the Alamo Model 2570 Electra Twin Ten Amplifier, at $159.50 another old model in new clothing. This again was similar in specs to the previous model. This had two channels, four inputs, seven tubes, two 10" speakers and 18 watts output. No Lansing option was offered.

Next came the evergreen Alamo Model 2565 Monclair Amplifier at $139.50. Again, two channels with four inputs, and seven tubes pushed 15 watts through a single 12" speaker.

New in '64 was the Alamo No. 2574 Reverb Unit. This was an outboard unit not unlike those sold by Kay, Premier and others. This used a Hammond Reverb system and offered a signal balance and intensity control, plus a remote control footswitch, all for $84.50.

Black vinyl Student amps

The tail end of the Alamo '64 amp line included the Alamo Student Amplifiers, again mainly a refurbishing of previous Alamo designs. Top of the series was a new Alamo Model 2572 Titan Amplifier at $119.50. This offered a single channel with four inputs, volume, tone, tremolo with speed and intensity controls, and a remote control jack. This had five tubes, a 12" speaker and 12 watts of power.

Our old friend the Alamo Model 2563 Embassy Tremolo Amplifier was back with three inputs, volume, tone, tremolo with speed and intensity, remote control jack, five tubes, 10" speaker, and 6 watts of power, for $89.50.

Also still around was the Alamo Model 2562 Challenger Amplifier, with three inputs, volume, tone, three tubes, 8" speaker and 5 watts of power, for $69.50.

The Alamo Model 2573 Fiesta Amplifier was perhaps most diffferent. Gone were the spackles for the new black vinyl. It had three inputs, volume, tone, tremolo with speed control, four tubes, 8" speaker and 3 watts of power, all for $69.50.

Finally, there was the familiar Alamo Model 2560 Capri Amplifier, with three inputs, volume, tone, three tubes, 8" speaker and 3 watts of power, at $47.50.

Stars Professional Guitars

As with the amplifier line, in '64 Alamo divvied up its guitars into three lines, the Professional, Semi-Pro and just plain Electric Guitars. By '64 the old French curve headstock was total history, with a new cen-

Ca. 1967 Alamo Model 2584T Fury Tremolo solidbody (courtesy DiPinto Guitars, Philadelphia, PA).

ter-humped design on most models, though by now the Fiestas had the angular 6-in-line design. By this time all pickguards except the Fiestas came with a highly stylized "A" cutout which we've dubbed the "Oriental A" for it's Eastern styling.

The top line was the Professional which consisted of the Eldorado Solid Body Electric Guitar, the Titan Hollow Body Electric Bass and a reworked combination of the old Embassy and Jet Hawaiians.

The Alamo Model 2598 Eldorado guitar was a solidbody made of Honduras mahogany. The body was sort of Stratish, with

offset double cutaways, a bit more widely flared than a Strat. The bolt-on neck had a three-and-three headstock with a large center-humped headstock. The truss rod cover was the new sort of Rickenbacker type with "Eldorado" engraved on it. It had two pickups, threeway toggle, two volumes and two tones, and a 20-fret rosewood fingerboard with block inlays. The pickguard was a large multi-laminate with a white Oriental A showing through the black, with a squiggly tail on the end. The Model 2598 ($149.95) was a stoptail in red cherry. The Model 2599 ($205.95) came outfitted with an original Bigsby vibrato.

The Alamo Titan Hollow Body Electric Bass was a hollowbody version almost identical in shape to the Eldorado, with widely flared double cutaways and a slightly thicker upper horn. The body was made of birch plywood. The bolt-on neck had the large-humped two-and-two headstock with the Ricky plate, Alamo and Titan engraved on the plate. The Oriental A pickguard was single-ply white or black, with the A exposing wood. One Alamo pickup sat in the middle with volume and tone controls. This had a chrome-covered stop Acra-Tune bridge. This was available in three versions, the Model 2593 in sunburst, the Model 2594 in blonde, and the Model 2597 in cherry.

By '64 Hawaiian music was pretty much passé, and many manufacturers dropped the lap steel from their inventories. Some, like Alamo retained a token vesitge. This was the Model 2493 Embassy Hawaiian Guitar, the old name of the Embassy applied to the long triangular Jet. This had a triangular body with a German carve relief around the edge, a black and red aluminum fingerboard, a squiggly black Alamo logo plate on the flat head, Safe-Ti tuners, chrome-covered pickup with volume and tone control, and an Alpine White finish. The Embassy cost $59.95 with another $15 getting you a hard case.

Stars Semi-Pro Guitars

The Alamo Semi-Pro Line included the old Titan Mark I and Mark II series. These were pretty similar to before, but now with the center humped or pointed headstock. If consistency is a problem, Alamo was not afraid to admit it because every model shown in the catalog had a somewhat different peak in the middle. Go figure. All had block inlays on 20-fret rosewood fingerboards. These had the Ricky-esque truss cover, single-ply 'guards with cutout Oriental As, and a covered Acra-Tune bridge. The Titan Mark I had a single Alamo pickup back near the bridge. Controls were a volume, tone and two-way rhythm/lead toggle near the pots. The Model 2589 came in sunburst ($89.95), the Model 2590 was blonde ($94.95), and the Model 2595 was cherry ($94.95). The Titan Mark II had two pickups and a three-way select on the lower horn end of the 'guard. The Model 2591 was sunburst ($109.95), the Model 2592 was blonde ($114.95), and the Model 2596 was cherry ($114.95).

Ca. 1967 Alamo flyer for psychedelic amps (courtesy Chris Smart, Krazy Kat Music, San Antonio, TX).

Stars Electric Guitars

Finally, the '64 Alamo Electric Guitars included a revamped Fiesta line. Little hint of the previous solidbody Tele, though if you squint at the new almost equal cutaways you can see the heritage. The new Fiestas were available in three configurations with one, two or three pickups, with four finish options, in a wide slightly offset double cutaway hollowbody, with squiggly pickguards, and a new elongated six-in-line headstock with the sorta Ricky truss cover. The head, by the way, had a slight French curve to the end or snout, which would become slightly more truncated shortly. All had an open Acra-Tune bridge, with volume and tone controls, and unbound 19-fret rosewood fingerboards. Pickguards did not have Oriental A cutouts. The Fiesta Hollow Body Electric Single Pickup guitar had a single bridge pickup, and, for $59.95, came as the Model 2584R in red, the Model 2584W in white, the Model 2584B in beige, and the Model 2584C in cherry. With two pickups, for $79.95, you got a three-way toggle on the

lower horn part of the 'guard, and a choice of the Model 2586R in red, the Model 2586W in white, the Model 2586B in beige, and the Model 2586C in cherry. With three pickups you got three sliding on/off switches plus three unidentified controls for volume and tone. The Model 2587R came in red, the Model 2587W in white, the Model 2587B in beige, and the Model 2587C in cherry, all for $99.95. Soft shell cases for all were $11.00 extra. The beige Fiestas lasted only a year, by the way.

Midway

1965 Alamo amps (and, for the most part, guitars) continued the look of '64. Amp cabinets were black-vinyl-covered and basically rectangular with metal corner protectors. Fabric grillecloth covered most of the front, with a little black rectangular logo plate in the upper left hand corner with a script Alamo logo with the lightning bolt. The better amps had loaded baffle speaker cabinets lined with acoustical fiberglass. Gone was the old chrome handle in favor of a "flexine plastic" carrying handle, ye old vinyl strap. While these look like solid state, they are still all tube units at this time.

Familiar names still in the combo amp line included the Model 2560 Capri (three tubes, three inputs, volume, tone, slanted front, 8" speaker, 3 watts, $47.50), Model 2573 Fiesta Tremolo (without color options!, four tubes, three inputs, volume, tone, tremolo speed, 8" speaker, 3 watts, $69.50), Model 2562 Challenger (three tubes, three inputs, volume, tone, 8" speaker, 5 watts, $69.50), Model 2563 Embassy Tremolo (four tubes, three inputs, volume, tone, tremolo speed and intensity, 10" speaker, 6 watts, $89.50), Model 2572 Titan, with five tubes, four inputs, volume, tone, tremolo speed and intensity, 12" speaker, 12 watts, $119.50), Alamo Reverb Unit No. 2574 (Hammond reverb system, balance and intensity controls, $84.50), Model 2565 Montclair (seven tubes, four inputs, two channels with volume, tone, tremolo with speed and intensity, 12" speaker, 15 watts, $139.50), Model 2570 Electra Twin Ten (seven tubes, four inputs, two channels with volume, tone, tremolo with speed and intensity, two 10" speakers, 18 watts, $159.50), the No. 2568 Paragon Band amplifier (eight tubes, two channels, tremolo and normal, four inputs, Hi-Fi bass and treble controls, tremolo speed and intensity, 15" speaker, 30 watts/60 watts peak, $289.50; the No. 2568JL15 with Lansings cost $439.50), and the Model 2569 Paragon Bass (six tubes, four inputs, two channels, volume, bass and treble controls, 15" speaker, 30 watts/60 watts peak, $269.50).

A new name in the '65 combo line was the No. 2567, note the same number as the old Paragon, now called the Futura with Reverb and Tremolo. This had eight tubes, four inputs, two channels, one with reverb and tremolo, volume, tone, 12" speaker, 15 watts, and a price of $199.50.

The piggy-back amps introduced in '64 continued on into '65 as well. These included the Model 2571 Galaxie Twin Twelve Piggy Back, the No. 2578 Piggy-Back Super Band, the No. 2576 Piggy-Back Band, and the No. 2575 Piggy-Back Bass amp. These were still offered with Jim Lansing speaker upgrades.

By '65 Alamo also offered two accordion amplifiers, by the way, though this was probably just marketing talk, since the amps appear to be the same as '64 models. Since the drawer pull handle was abandoned in '65, the only difference was probably in the use of leftover handles! Offered for accordions were the No. 2576 Piggy-Back Band Amp and the No. 2568 Paragon Band combo, both available in a Lansing option.

Also offered in '65 was our old friend the No. 2569 Paragon Special which was now being marketed to bass fiddle players. This also came with a Lansing speaker option. Again, I suspect this was simply a repositioning of older stock. Alamo, which was firmly in with the Bruno organization by this time, also sold the K720 Kay Heavy Duty Bass Amplifier.

Maximum guitars

The real news for '65 was a further redesign of Alamo's electric Spanish guitars into radical new "now" designs, as the hyperbole in the catalog copy enthused. Nowhere was this more evident than with the Fiesta. The sort of frumpy shape gave way to variation on a groovy hybrid between a Strat and a Jazzmaster, with the double cutaway horns sort of squashed outwards. The center-humped headstock gave way to four-in-line/six-in-line headstocks with a sort of squared-off Strat/Fender styling. Now standard fare was the more-or-less Strat-shaped pickguard,

with slightly more refined squiggles than on the previous fetal pickguard engraved with the "Oriental A" pickguard.

Alamo still divided its guitars and basses into three groups in '65, now called the Professional Line, the Artist Line and the Fiestas.

The '65 Professionals included the Titan bass, the Eldorado bass and the Eldorado guitar. The Titan bass ($159.50) continued

Ca. 1967-70 Alamo Model 2572 Titan amp with block letter logo (courtesy Arpeggio Music, Havertown, PA).

to have a hollow core construction. The body was the squashed Strat with a lower horn slightly thicker than the Eldorados. The 20-fret fingerboard was rosewood with dots. A white pickguard had the stylized Oriental A cutout, a single middle pickup and volume and tone controls. The bridge/tail-piece assembly was covered in chrome. The Titan bass now came in three finishes: Model 2593 in sunburst, Model 2594 in blonde, and Model 2597 in cherry.

The Eldorado guitar and bass were both still Honduras mahogany solidbodies. These were bascially the same as the '64 models. The 20-fret rosewood fingerboard was bound. The bass came in only one version, the Model 2600 in red cherry. The Model 2598 Eldorado guitar ($159.50) was a stoptail in red cherry. The Model 2598T

($219.50) came outfitted with an original Bigsby vibrato.

The '65 Artist Line included our old friends the Titan Mark I and Mark II. These were hollow core guitars with the squashed Strat shape of the Titan bass, with slightly thicker, squarish lower horn, and smaller, less squiggly Oriental A pickguard in white or black, depending on the guitar color. The Titan Mark I had a single pickup, finally moved back to the bridge position from the previous middle spot. The 20-fret rosewood fingerboards weren't bound, but they did have block inlays. The Mark I had volume and tone and the old rhythm/lead switch just in front of the volume knob. The Model 2589 was a stoptail in sunburst ($99.95), available as the Model 2589T with Bigsby ($159.95). The Model 2590 was blonde, the Model 2590T with Bigsby. The Model 2595 came in cherry, with the Model 2595T sporting a Bigsby. The Bigsby guitars all had metal adjustable compensated bridges, probably provided by Bigsby. The Titan Mark II added a neck pickup and a threeway select down by the lower horn (no rhythm/lead toggle). The Model 2591 ($119.95) came in sunburst, with the Model 2591T Bigsby option ($179.95). The Model 2592 came in blonde (Model 2592T with Bigsby). The Model 2596 came in cherry (Model 2592T with Bigsby).

Finally, the '65 line offered three Fiestas, with hollow core bodies and an even more radically squashed Strat/Jazzmaster body. Sort of Strat road kill. These each had slightly different pickguard shapes depending on how many pickups, each *without* the Oriental A, but with a cutout Fiesta just below the strings (although some examples are seen with nothing on the 'guard). The 19-fret rosewood fingerboards were dot-inlaid. The six-in-line heads had small Alamo truss rod covers. These had uncovered Acra-Tune bridge/tailpiece assemblies, with no Bigsby option. The one-pickup Fiesta had the pickup near the bridge, with volume and tone. The Model 2584R ($64.95) came in red, the Model 2584W in white, the Model 2584S in sunburst, and Model 2584C in cherry sunburst. The two-pickup Fiesta had volume and tone with a threeway toggle near the lower horn. The Model 2586R ($84.95) came in red, the Model 2586W in white, the Model 2586S in sunburst, and the Model 2586C in cherry sunburst. The three-pickup Fiesta had three pickups parallel to each other, with one volume and two tones, and three small plastic sliding on/off switches near the lower horn. The Model 2587R ($109.95) came in red, the Model 2587W in white, the Model 2587S in sunburst, and the Model 2587C in cherry sunburst.

Curiously enough, in the same Bruno catalog which featured the Alamo catalog, the old double-cutaway Alamo Titan Electric bass was also still offered. This was the older version with a hollow core body, Strat-style pickguard, and the old curved-top two-and-two headstock. This was still available as the No. 2593 in sunburst, No. 2594 in blonde, and No. 2597 in cherry, at $159.50. This, and the recycled Paragon amps for accordions and bass fiddles were probably left-over, slightly older designs.

The revamped Model 2493 Embassy lap steel remained.

Summer o' love

No picture is available of Alamos in 1966, but by 1967 the line had again undergone a fairly radical transformation, here with a catalog graciously provided by Scott Freilich of Top Shelf Music in Buffalo.

Alamo amplifiers in '67 had received yet another facelift, although not too drastically, when compared to the amps of two years earlier. The are still basically rectangular cabinets covered in black vinyl, but now with a darker black and silver grillecloth. Controls are now all face-mounted and the knobs sit on brushed aluminum plates. They are, however, despite the very "Standel" look, tube amps. Gone is the little logo plate in favor of a white plastic script Alamo lightning bolt perched at an angle on the upper left hand corner of the grill. Alamo now divides it amps into four lines, the PA Series, Professional Series, Artist Series and Studio Series. For an extra $20, all came with a set of optional castors.

The PA Series included four amps. Three of these were old friends, the piggy-backs. The Model 2578 was the Super Band Piggy-Back (eight tubes, two channels, tremolo, two 12" speakers, 35 watts/70 watts peak,

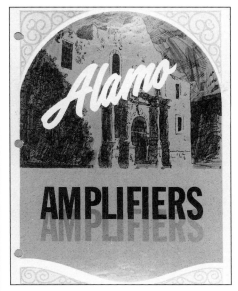

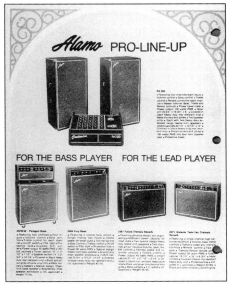

Late '60s or early '70s Alamo catalog illustrating the black vinyl-covered amplifier line.

$394.50), available, as before, in a Lansing option as the Model 2578JL12 ($694.50). The Model 2576 was the Band Piggy-Back (eight tubes, two channels, tremolo, 15" speaker, 35 watts/70 watts peak, $354.50), Lansing option Model 2576JL15 ($504.50). The Model 2571 was the Galaxie, mistakenly identified in the text as a Piggy-Back, but clearly still a combo (seven tubes, two channels, tremolo, two 12" speakers, 22 watts/44 watts peak, $249.50), Lansing option Model 2571JL12 ($384.50). New by '67 was the Alamo Pro Reverb Piggy-Back amplifier Model 2579. This had eight tubes, two channels, tremolo, reverb, two 12" speakers, 35 watts (70 watts peak), and cost $414.50 (no Lansing option).

The '67 Alamo Professional Series consisted of two three friends and one new face. Still around was the Model 2575 Piggy-Back Bass amp (six tube, two channels, 15" speaker, 35 watts/70 watts peak, $334.50), Lansing option Model 2575JL15 ($484.50). Also still pumping was the Model 2569 Paragon Bass combo amp (six tubes, two channels, 15" speaker, 35 watts/70 watts peak, $284.50), Lansing option Model 2569JL15 ($434.50). Also remaining was the Model 2567 Futura with Reverb and Tremolo (eight tubes, two channels, 12" speaker, 15 watts/30 watts peak, $199.50). New was the Model 2566 Fury Bass combo amp, with five tubes, three inputs, volume and two tones, 15" Jenson speaker, 20 watts output

(40 watts peak), and a $179.50 price tag.

The '67 Alamo Artist Series was basically familiar amps with the new look. Included were the Model 2570 Electra Twin Ten, Model 2564 Jet, Model 2565 Montclair, and Model 2572 Titan, all with the same specs and pretty much the same prices. Also included — with the new look — was the Model 2574 Alamo Reverb Unit.

Finally, the '67 Studio Series consisted mainly of a repackaging of other Alamo standbys, including the Model 2563 Embassy Tremolo, Model 2562 Challenger, and Model 2560 Capri, again the same except for the new cosmetics. One new amp joined the line, the Model 2573 Dart Tremolo, with four tubes, three inputs, tremolo with speed control, volume, tone, 10" speaker, 3 watts/6 watts peak power, and a cost of $47.50.

Fiesta siesta

Gone by '67 was the time-honored Fiesta amplifier (and, for the time being, anyway, Fiesta guitars).

Curiously enough, Alamo also offered the No. 2599 Q-T Practice Aid, a solid-state little box which served as a practice amp with a set of headphones ($46.50).

All amps had an optional cover. At least six different extension speaker cabinets were also available for various Alamo amp models.

Still hanging on in the '67 line was the Model 2493 Embassy Hawaiian guitar, with the tapered triangular body, finished in Alpine White, with the black and red aluminum fingerboard.

Guitar redux

Again in '67 the Alamo guitar line was redefined, although it still reflected the '65 look. Basically there were two groupings, the Professional Series and Fury guitars.

The '67 Professional Series consisted of one guitar and one bass. The guitar was the Model 2598 Toronado solidbody. This was a slightly more conservative interpretation of the offset double cutaway Strat, with more pointed horns. The pickguard was still the squiggly Strat-style with the engraved Ori-

ental A. The head was a slightly truncated Strat-style six-in-line, with more rounded features than its more angular predecessors. The elongated truss rod cover remained. This had a Honduras mahogany body finished in red cherry. The bolt-on neck had a 20-fret rosewood fingerboard with dots. It had two pickups, two volumes, two tones, and threeway toggle near the lower horn. The Model 2598 cost $145 with the covered Acra-Tune bridge assembly. The Model 2598T came equipped with a Bigsby and adjustable compensated bridge for $199.50.

The bass was our old friend the Model 2593 Titan. This remained a hollow core

Ca. 1976 Alamo No. 2564 Jet amp mixing transistors with 6V6 tube output (courtesy Daddy's Junky Music, Salem, NH).

beast, but now with a goofy, more angular offset double cutaway body profile, with the upper horn a large hump with an angle. It had one pickup and the Oriental A pickguard. The head was the more rounded version like the Toronado. It came in sunburst and cost $145.

The Fury series — not wanting to make things too easy for us — included both hollow core and solidbody guitars, all called Fury, which was engraved in script down under the strings! These all had the shorter, more rounded Strat-style heads, with the by now typical elongated truss rod cover. Fingerboards were all rosewood with dots.

The pickguards were identical to the previous, now defunct Fiesta guitars. These guitars were, for Alamo, fairly normal looking, aping fairly closely a Fender Jazzmaster shape.

The hollow core Furies were called "F" Hole Guitars because, as you might guess, they included, for the first time, a single f-hole on the lower bass bout. The Fury Standard was a stop-tail axe with the Acra-Tune bridge assembly. This came with either one bridge pickup (Model 2583, $59.50) or with two pickups (Model 2585, with four controls and threeway near the lower horn, $77.50). These could be had in sunburst or cherry sunburst.

The hollow Fury Tremolo was the same, except for the addition of a vibrato. This appeared to be a Japanese-made affair with a Bigsby-style spring, however, it doesn't look like most Japanese units, so it may, indeed, have been made for Alamo. The Model 2583T-SB (one pickup, sunburst) and Model 2583T-C (cherry sunburst) cost $74.50. The Model 2585T-SB (two pickups, sunburst) and Model 2585T-C (cherry sunburst) cost $92.50.

The solidbody Furies basically followed an identical pattern, except, of course, with no f-holes, but as Standards and Tremolos, with single or double pickups and sunburst or cherry sunburst finishes. The Model 2584 Fury Standard (one pickup) cost $59.50, while the Model 2586 Fury Standard (two pickups) cost $77.50. The Model 2584T Fury Tremolo (one pickup) cost $74.50, whereas the Model 2586T Fury Tremolo (two pickups) cost $92.50.

It should be noted that while the Fiesta guitar officially dropped from sight by the 1967 catalog, as can be seen in the example here, at least some Fiestas continued to be made in this later, more conservative style. Either the model was revived or, more likely, just continued to be made and not promoted. It is possible that the Fiesta came back to life

June 1973 Alamo catalog from David Wexler jobber book featuring amps with solid-state front end and tube output.

after the '67 catalog, or, for that matter, just before this same guitar became the Fury. Until more catalogs materialize, this will probably just have to remain a mystery.

Finally, in what seems to be the most Quixotic moment in the Alamo story, in 1967 Alamo offered a guitar kit so you could build your own! The was the Custom Electric Guitar Kit #0010 and Kit #0010-D, with either one or two pickups, respectively. These were basically the new hollow Fury Tremolo, with the main difference being that pickups were now slanted at an angle from bass to treble neck to bridge. These were available from Spanish Guitars Ltd. in San Antonio, and came with all the parts and instructions for building your very own Alamo!

In any case, that just about does it for Alamo guitars. No reference materials are available for after 1967, but everything we've described so far pretty much covers the Alamos encountered, so there are probably few new models introduced after this point in time. Don't be surprised to encounter other variations. It's not terribly likely that Alamo continued to put much energy into electric guitars much beyond this '67 line. In any case, by 1968 the market for beginner guitars pretty much went bust. Many Japanese companies went bankrupt, and the venerable Valco, which had just purchased the Kay company, bit the dust, too.

Valco/Kay

One final note, however. Eilenberg recalls travelling to Chicago for the Valco/Kay auction which occurred in August of 1969, a year after that company went bankrupt. He returned with several carloads of parts, including machine heads and fingerboards, which eventually went onto later Alamo guitars. Thus, if you find a late era Alamo with Kay or Valco parts on it, it just may be Kosher.

According to Mr. Eilenberg, Alamo guitars probably lasted until 1970 before going the way of all flesh. Or wood.

Happy Days

Alamo guitars were hardly ever contenders in the big-time guitar stakes, although obviously, as the picture of the rhythm and blues outfit illustrates, Alamo did have its advocates! Perhaps the crowning achievement, however, was the appearance of an Alamo guitar in the hands of Richie on the television sit-com "Happy Days."

Psychedelia

A curious sidebar occurred probably in 1967, as evidenced by yet another undated Alamo flyer. As with other amp manufacturers at the time, bigger was all of a sudden considered better, and Alamo produced a few monster amps. Basically these were four piggyback amps available with a five different

speaker cabinets and groovy psychedelic grillecloths and vinyl coverings. These were the Mod "M" Super Sound Amplifiers. As the copy enthused, "Over 120 watts of raw music power built to satisfy the demands of today's Rock and Folk groups. No gimmicks — no gadgets — but scientifically engineered to Alamo's quality standards to provide years of trouble-free service." These marked Alamo's first foray into integrating the new transistor technology into its time-tested tube gear.

There were basically two bass amps and two guitar amps. Top of the bass line was the Model 7 Plus 75 "MC" Bass Amplifier. This came in blue-green-black or red-orange-black floral patterned vinyl with a striped grille. The head had 120 watts, two channels, bass and normal, with two inputs per channel, a special taper volume, bass and treble controls for each channel, with power, standby and ground reverse switches. This came outfitted with three Dual-purpose tubes and a silicone rectifier. The cabinet provided had two Heavy Duty 15" CTS bass speakers with 54 oz. Magnet and a 2" voice coil. This monster listed at $469.95.

The second bass amp was the Model 7 Plus 75 "M" Bass Amplifier. This came in black vinyl with either red-and-grey striped grille or blue-yellow-black wavy lines. This had 120 watts and the same two-channel controls, tubes, and speaker cab as the "MC." This cost $454.95.

Top of the guitar line was the Model 7 Plus 79 "MC" Reverb Power Pack. This was supplied as a head only, with various cabinet choices. This had the same blue or red vinyl coverig options. It had 120 watts, two channels, one with tremolo and reverb, the other normal, with two inputs each. The reverb channel had volume, tone and reverb controls, plus speed and intensity for the tremolo. The normal channel had volume, treble and bass controls. The reverb unit was a Hammond. This had seven tubes (five dual purpose) plus two transisters and a silicon rectifier. Three switches included power, standby and ground reverse. A separate speaker jack and a tremolo and reverb remote jack for a dual purpose foot switch were also included. List price for the head was $300.

Five speaker cabinets were available for the "MC" amp, the Mod "MC" Columns, with the blue or red floral vinyl covering options. These all came with 42"x25"x10 °" cabinets. The Model 7 Plus 700 "MC" (don't ask me, I didn't name them) had two 12" Jenson Heavy Duty Speakers and cost $174.95. The Model 7 Plus 701 "MC" had one 12" Jenson and one 15" CTS Special Design speaker ($194.95). The Model 7 Plus 702 "MC" had two 15" Heavy Duty especially designed CTS speakers ($259.95). The Model 7 Plus 703 "MC" had two 12" Jim Lansing speakers ($497.95). The Model 7 Plus 704 "MC" had two 15" Jim Lansing speakers ($520.95).

The Model 7 Plus 79 "M" Reverb Power Pack was a second guitar head. This was essentially identical to the "MC" except for the black vinyl with the choice of red or blue (wavy) grille. Cost was $295.50.

Speaker cabinets were, again, the same as the "MC" but were the Mod "M" Column, with black vinyl and striped grilles, and cost $10 less.

Like most others in this class of mega-amp, they probably only lasted about a year before biting the dust.

Amps away

The Alamo story did not end with its guitars. Amps continued to be made in San Antonio into the 1980s! As we've seen, Alamo switched over to black vinyl coverings in the late '60s, one of the early companies to adopt what would become almost universal practice.

By the way, some Alamo amp models sighted in the ca. '67 line show up with rectangular logo plates on the grillecloth with Alamo in block letters. Presumably these are later models than those shown in the catalog.

Transition to transitors

Again, we are dealing with undated materials and not a little Sherlock Holmes here, but Alamo probably began the transition to integrating transistor technology with the tubes in around 1968. This makes sense given the existence of the psychedelic amps of '67-68, which openly tout hybrid technology. As far as we know, Kay had pioneered transistor amps as early as 1962. By '65 folks like Bud Ross of Kustom were experimenting with the new technology. By '67 transistor amps by Standel were all the rage. Truth to tell, this probably occurred gradually over time. Texas amp guru Gerald Weber recalls seeing handwired point-to-point amps which had a transistor wired into the reverb feedback circuit, which was powered by some of the output of the power tubes.

In any case, the further evolution in the black vinyl-covered Alamo amplifier line illustrated in an undated brochure which appears to by late '60s, possibly from 1968. These looked very similar to those seen in '67. However, no mentions of powerplants are made. Since some sightings of Alamo amps with transistor preamps and tube power outputs have been attributed as early as '68, and since we know of the psychedelic hybrids, it's pretty reasonable to assume that it was about 1968 that the combinations appeared and that this catalog is from about this time.

Alamo amps of ca. '68 consisted of three "line-ups:" the Pro-Line-Up, the Standard Line-Up, and the One-Niters. These were all basically rectangular cabinets with black mar-resistant vinyl covering and black and silver grillecloths, and white beading around the grill. Control panels were on the front, now in black. Logos were white script

Alamos on an angle in the upper left corner of the grill. Many of the names should be familiar by now, though the details have again changed.

The ca. '68 Alamo Pro-Line-Up consisted of two guitar amps "for the lead player," two bass amps and a PA system. Guitar amps were led by the 2567 Futura Tremolo Reverb. This had two 12" speakers, two channels, tremolo speed and intensity controls, reverb, and 45 watts RMS output. The 2571 Galaxie Twin-Ten Tremolo Reverb had one channel with volume, bass and treble controls, tremolo speed and intensity, reverb and 25 watts RMS output.

Bass-wise the 2575CW Paragon Bass was a piggy back. The head offered two channels, four inputs, volume, bass, treble and 40 watts RMS output. The cabinet carried a 15" speaker and an acoustically lined speaker enclosure. The 2566 Fury Bass amp was a one-channel combo unit with volume, bass, treble, 15" speaker and 30 watts RMS output.

The PA 200 system was driven by the PA200 Centurion, with four channels, eight inputs, with volume, bass, treble and reverb controls on each channel plus a master set. This pumped out 100 watts RMS, mixing the sound into two speaker cabinets with twin 12" speakers each.

The ca. '68 Alamo Standard Amplifier Line-Up featured six combo amps. Top of the line was the 2570 Twin-Ten with two channels, four inputs, volume and tone controls on each channel, tremolo with speed and intensity controls, two 10" speakers and 20 watts RMS output. The 2563 Embassy had a single channel, volume, tone, tremolo with speed and intensity, a 10" speaker and 10 watts RMS output. The 2562 Challenger had two inputs, volume, tone, no tremolo, 10" speaker and 10 watts RMS output. The 2573 Dart had two inputs, volume, tone, tremolo with speed and intensity, an 8" speaker and 5.5 watts RMS output. The 2560 Capri had two inputs, volume, tone, 8" speaker and 5.5 watts RMS output. The 2525 Special with two inputs, volume, tone, 6" speaker and 4 watts RMS output rounded out the line.

Finally, the ca. '68 Alamo One-Niters included three more combos. The 2565

Montclair Tremolo Reverb had one channel with two inputs, volume, bass, treble, reverb, tremolo, 12" speaker and 25 watts RMS output. The 2564 Jet-Tremolo Reverb had two inputs, volume, tone, reverb, tremolo, 10" speaker and 10 watts RMS output. The 2566 Fury Bass had two inputs, volume, bass, treble, 15" speaker and 30 watts RMS output.

Early '70s

The hybrid transistor/tube was certainly in place by 1973, at least, by which time Alamo was touting its solid-state front end and tube output. This change had occurred, in part, because RCA sold its tube manufacturing business to a Japanese company, leaving only Sylvania and GE as sources for tubes here.

According to a June 1973 Alamo catalog and price list from a David Wexler jobbers book, Alamo offered no fewer than 16 amplifier models that year, many, if not all, carrying familiar model names from the past. These were now divided into four "line-ups:" the Pro-Line-Up, Standard Amplifier Line-Up, Tremolo Line-Up and One-Niters series. These still had squarish plywood cabinets covered in black tolex with a black and silver grillecloth. These mostly had white script Alamo logos on a little black blob of plastic glued on the upper right corner of the grill. If you thought these were Japanese imports, given their appearance, you wouldn't be the first, but you'd be wrong.

The Alamo Pro-Line-Up included four variants for the lead player and three for the bass player. Lead amps included the Model 2567 Futura Tremolo Reverb ($409.95), a combo with two heavy duty 12" speakers, two channels, four inputs, volume, treble, bass, treble boost, reverb, tremolo, and 135 watts peak (45 watts RMS). The three remaining amps were known as the Paragon Super Reverb, each with a Model 7+79 Reverb/Tremolo Piggy Back Powerpak head. The Model 7+79 head had 210 watts peak (70 watts RMS) and basically the same controls as the Futura. The Model 7+700 Paragon Super Reverb ($585.95) added a cabinet with two heavy duty 12" speakers. The Model 7+701

Ca. 1976 Alamo catalog (courtesy Jim Dulfer).

Paragon Super Reverb ($609.95) had a cabinet with one 15" and one 12" speaker. The Model 7+702 Paragon Super Reverb ($654.95) had a cabinet with two 15" speakers.

Alamo Pro-Line-Up bass amps included the Model 2569 Paragon Bass ($339.95), a huge combo with 120 watts peak (40 watts RMS), two channels, four inputs, volume, bass and treble controls and a single 15" speaker. The Model 2565CW Paragon Bass Piggy Back ($399.95) — also called the Paragon Country Western Bass — consisted of a head version of the Paragon Bass and a single 15" speaker cabinet.

The Model 7+75 Paragon Bass Piggy Back ($559.95) — also called the Paragon Super Bass — had the Paragon head and a twin-15" speaker cabinet.

The '73 Alamo Standard Amplifier Line-Up included three combo amps. The Model 2562 Challenger ($91.95) had 36 watts peak (12 watts RMS), one 10" speaker, three inputs and volume and tone control. The Model 2560 Capri ($69.95) was similar with 12 watts peak (4 watts RMS). The Model 2525 Special ($54.95) offered 9 watts peak (3 watts RMS), a 5" speaker, two inputs and a volume control. The '73 Alamo Tremolo Line-Up included three combos. The Model 2570 Twin-Ten ($189.95) — also called the Electra Tremolo — offered 60 watts peak (20 watts RMS), two channels, four inputs, volume, tone, tremolo, and two 10" speakers. The Model 2563 Embassy ($115.95) had 36 watts peak (12 watts RMS), 10" speaker, three inputs, volume, tone and a tremolo with rate and depth controls. The Model 2573 Dart Tremolo ($79.95) had 12 watts peak (4 watts RMS) with 10" speaker, three inputs, volume, tone and tremolo.

Finally, there were three Alamo One-Niters combos in '73. The Model 2565 Montclair Tremolo Reverb ($249.95) had 75 watts peak (25 watts RMS), one 12" speaker, one channel, two inputs, volume, treble, bass, treble boost, vibrato and reverb. The Model 2564 Jet Tremolo Reverb ($179.95) offered 36 watts peak (12 watts RMS), one 12" speaker, volume, tone, reverb and tremolo. The Model 2566 Fury Bass ($225.95) was an all-tube unit with 105 watts peak (35 watts RMS), one 15" speaker, volume, bass and treble controls.

By '73 Alamo was also offering the Model 2574 Reverb Unit with a patented reverb system, three controls for mixer, contour and intensity.

Solid state (ca. 1980)

By around 1980, Alamo amps had finally become all solid-state. No information is available on these, but expect them to be similar to the previous line-ups.

Alamo amps continued to be made until around 1982 or so, when Alamo combined with a company called Southwest Technical Products and the Alamo legend again became the province of politics and warriors.

Exactly how many Alamo guitars and amps were made is hard to tell. At peak production, Alamo employed around 100 people, and produced between 36,000 and 40,000 amps a year, quite a hefty number. Guitar production was much smaller, running around 1,000 a year. Assuming approximately a ten-year run, that would be about 10,000 guitars, more or less.

Dating Alamos

Dating Alamo guitars and amps will be pretty hard, except by the broad-brush historical outlines presented here. Both guitars and amps had serial numbers which were recorded for warranty purposes, but the whereabouts of any records, if they even remain, is unknown. Where possible, pot codes should be helpful.

The End

And that concludes our remembrance of the Alamo, and fills in yet another piece in the wonderful mosaic that makes up American guitar history. Alamo amplifiers are probably among the most under-rated American instruments, and the older tube amps, while never powerhouses, are especially worth seeking out if you like that classic, warm sound. Alamo guitars, on the other hand, were at the very bottom of the American guitarmaking pecking order in terms of quality and performance. Still, they are fairly rare birds and reflect the heady days of the '60s and the Guitar Boom when you could sell anything with strings on it. It's unlikely you'd want to have to rely on one of these for a steady gig, but then, if you're reading this narrative, that's probably a pretty remote consideration anyway. Any good collection of American guitars from the '60s should have at least one example so you can properly "remember the Alamo."

Alamo Instruments

What follows is an *approximate* listing of Alamo amps, laps and guitars, based on the reference materials at hand. Please note that there are many holes and this should be taken as a rough guideline only. Also, since cosmetic changes occurred frequently and constitute one of the few guides for dating Alamo instruments, various models have been relisted when a design change is known. One pattern you should notice is that model numbers are coded to the finish, which becomes a clue to dating. It ain't perfect, but then, how much was known about Alamo amps and guitars before this? It's amazing we got this far! Alamo guitars all feature volume and tone controls, and threeway selects when two pickups are present. Electronics on guitars were never much beyond basic.

Amplifiers

Birch A cabinets

1949/50-61	AMP-3/No. 2463 Embassy Amplifier [3 tubes]
ca. 1950-59	AMP-4/No. 2461 Jet Amplifier [4 tubes]
ca. 1950-61	AMP-2/No. 2462 Challenger Amplifier [3 tubes]
ca. 1950-59	AMP-5 Amplifier [5 tubes]
1953-62	AMP-6A/No. 2467 Paragon Amplifier [7 tubes, 15" Jenson, 25w]
ca. 1954-61	No. 2469 Paragon Special Bass Amplifier [7 tubes, 15" Jenson, 25w]
ca. 1954-61	No. 2465 Montclair Amplifier [5 tubes, 12" Jenson, 15w]

Grey leatherette, beading stripes

by 1960-61	No. 2561 Jet Amplifier [3 tubes, 6", 4w]
by 1960-63	No. 2563 Embassy Amplifier [3 tubes, 10", 6w]
by 1960-63	No. 2562 Challenger Amplifier [3 tubes, 8", 5w]
by 1960-63	No. 2565 Montclair Amplifier [5 tubes, 12" Jenson, 15w]
by 1960-63	No. 2567 Paragon Amplifier [7 tubes, 15" Jenson, 25w]
by 1960-63	No. 2569 Paragon Special Bass Amplifier [7 tubes, 15" Jenson, 25w]
by 1960-63	No. 2560 Capri Amplifier [3 tubes, 6", 3w]
1962-63	No. 2570 Electra Twin Ten with Tremolo Amplifier [6 tubes, 2x10", 18w]
1962-63	No. 2566 Century Twin Ten Amplifier 5 tubes, 2x10", 15w]
1962-63	No. 2564 Futuramic Twin Eight Amplifier [5 tubes, 2x8", 10w]

Grey and blue leatherette

1962-63	No. 2561 Jet Amplifier [3 tubes, 6", 4w]

Colors

1962-63	No. 2460 Fiesta Amplifier [3 tubes, 6", 3w]
1962-64	No. 2577 Altrol Electronic Tremolo and Foot Switch

Grey & silver leatherette, no beading, rectangular logo plate

1963-64	No. 2560 Capri Amplifier [3 tubes, 8", 3w]
1963-64	No. 2561 Jet Amplifier [3 tubes, 6", 4w]
1963-64	No. 2562 Challenger Amplifier [3 tubes, 8", 5w]
1963-64	No. 2563 Embassy Amplifier [3 tubes, 10", 6w]
1963-64	No. 2564 Futuramic Twin Eight Amplifier [5 tubes, 2x8", 10w]
1963-64	No. 2565 Montclair Amplifier [7 tubes, 12", 25w]
1963-64	No. 2570 Electra Twin Ten with Tremolo Amplifier [6 tubes, 2x10", 18w]
1963-64	No. 2567 Paragon Two Channel Amplifier [8 tubes, 15", 30w]
1963-64	No. 2569 Paragon Two Channel Bass Amplifier [6 tubes, 15", 30w]
1963-64	No. 2571 Galaxie Twin Twelve Amplifier [7 tubes, 2x12", 25w]

Dark vinyl, tan and gold grillecloths, metal corner protectors (on better models), black rectangular logo plate in upper left corner of grill, drawer pull or vinyl strap handle

1964-66	Model 2560 Capri Amplifier [3 tubes, 8", 3w]
1064-66	Model 2573 Fiesta Tremolo Amplifier [4 tubes, 8", 3w]
1964-66	Model 2562 Challenger Amplifier [3 tubes, 8", 5w]
1964-66	Model 2563 Embassy Tremolo Amplifier [5 tubes, 10", 6w]
1964-66	Model 2565 Montclair Amplifier [7 tubes, 12", 15w]
1964-66	Model 2570 Electra Twin Ten Amplifier [7 tubes, 2x12", 18w]
1964-66	Model 2569 Paragon Bass Amplifier [6 tubes, 15", 30w]
1964-66	Model 2569JL15 Paragon Bass Amplifier [6 tubes, 15" Lansing, 30w]
1964-66	No. 2568 Paragon Band Amplifier [8 tubes, 15", 30w]
1964-66	No. 2568JL15 Paragon Band Amplifier [8 tubes, 15" Lansings 30w]
1964-66	Model 2572 Titan Amplifier [5 tubes, 12", 12w]
1964-66	No. 2574 Alamo Reverb Unit [Hammond]
1964-66	Model 2571 Galaxie Twin Twelve Piggy Back Amplifier [7 tubes, 2x12", 22w]
1964-66	Model 2571JL12 Galaxie Twin Twelve Piggy Back Amplifier [7tubes, 1x12" Lansings, 22w]
1964-66	No. 2578 Piggy-Back Super Band Amplifier [8 tubes, 2x12", 40w]
1964-66	No. 2578JL12 Piggy-Back Super Band Amplifier [8 tubes, 2x12" Lansings, 40w]

1964-66	No. 2576 Piggy-Back Band Amplifier [8 tubes, 15", 30w]
1964-66	No. 2576JL15 Piggy-Back Band Amplifier [8 tubes, 15" Lansings, 30w]
1964-66	No. 2575 Piggy-Back Bass Amplifier [6 tubes, 15", 30w]
1964-66	No. 2575JL15 Piggy-Back Bass Amplifier [6 tubes, 15" Lansings, 30w]
1965-66	No. 2567 Futura with Reverb and Tremolo Amplifier [8 tubes, 12", 15w]

Rectangular cabinets, black vinyl, black and silver grillecloth, white plastic script Alamo logo upper left corner

1967-68	Model 2578 Super Band Piggy-Back Amplifier [8 tubes, 2x12", 35w]
1967-68	Model 2578JL12 Super Band Piggy-Back Amplifier [8 tubes, 2x12" Lansings, 35w]
1967-68	Model 2576 Band Piggy-Back Amplifier [8 tubes, 15", 35w]
1967-68	Model 2576JL15 Band Piggy-Back Amplifier [8 tubes, 15" Lansing, 35w]
1967-68	Model 2571 Galaxie Amplifier [7 tubes, 2x12", 22w]
1967-68	Model 2571JL12 Galaxie Amplifier [7 tubes, 2x12" Lansings, 22w]
1967-68	Model 2579 Alamo Pro Reverb Piggy-Back Amplifier [8 tubes, 2x12", 35w]
1967-68	Model 2575 Piggy-Back Bass Amplifier [6 tubes, 15", 35w]
1967-68	Model 2575JL15 Piggy-Back Bass Amplifier [6 tubes, 15" Lansing, 35w]
1967-68	Model 2569 Paragon Bass Amplifier [6 tubes, 15", 35w]
1967-68	Model 2569JL15 Paragon Bass Amplifier [6 tubes, 15" Lansing, 35w]
1967-68	Model 2567 Futura with Reverb and Tremolo Amplifier [8 tubes, 12", 15w]
1967-68	Model 2566 Fury Bass Amplifier [5 tubes, 15" Jenson, 20w]
1967-68	Model 2570 Electra Twin Ten Amplifier [7 tubes, 2x12", 18w]
1967-68	Model 2564 Jet Amplifier [3 tubes, 6", 4w]
1967-68	Model 2565 Montclair Amplifier [7 tubes, 12", 15w]
1967-68	Model 2572 Titan Amplifier [5 tubes, 12", 12w]
1967-68	Model 2574 Alamo Reverb Unit
1967-68	Model 2563 Embassy Tremolo Amplifier [5 tubes, 10", 6w]
1967-68	Model 2562 Challenger Amplifier [3 tubes, 8", 5w]
1967-68	Model 2560 Capri Amplifier [3 tubes, 8", 3w]
1967-68	Model 2573 Dart Tremolo Amplifier [4 tubes, 10", 3w]
1967	No. 2599 Q-T Practice Aid

Psychedelic vinyl and grillecloths, hybrid transistor and tubes

1967-68	Model 7 Plus 75 "MC" Bass Amplifier [3 tubes, sili-

cone rect, 2x15", 120w]

1967-68	Model 7 Plus 75 "M" Bass Amplifier [3 tubes, silicone rect, 2x15", 120w]
1967-68	Model 7 Plus 79 "MC" Reverb Power Pack amplifier head [7 tubes, 2 trans, silicon rect, 120w]
1967-68	Model 7 Plus 79 "M" Reverb Power Pack amplifier head [7 tubes, 2 trans, silicon rect, 120w]
1967-68	Model 7 Plus 700 "MC" Mod "MC" Column speaker cabinet [2x12" Jensons]
1967-68	Model 7 Plus 700 "M" Mod "M" Column speaker cabinet [2x12" Jensons]
1967-68	Model 7 Plus 701 "MC" Mod "MC" Column speaker cabinet [12" Jenson, 15" CTS]
1967-68	Model 7 Plus 701 "M" Mod "M" Column speaker cabinet 12" Jenson, 15" CTS]
1967-68	Model 7 Plus 702 "MC" Mod "MC" Column speaker cabinet [2x15" CTS]
1967-68	Model 7 Plus 702 "M" Mod "M" Column speaker cabinet [2x15" CTS]
1967-68	Model 7 Plus 703 "MC" Mod "MC" Column speaker cabinet [2x12" Lansings]
1967-68	Model 7 Plus 703 "M" Mod "M" Column speaker cabinet [2x12" Lansings]
1967-68	Model 7 Plus 704 "MC" Mod "MC" Column speaker cabinet [2x15" Lansings]
1967-68	Model 7 Plus 704 "M" Mod "M" Column speaker cabinet [2x15" Lansings]

Square black vinyl cabinets, black grillecloths, white piping, black panels, transistors and tubes

1968-72	2567 Futura Tremolo Reverb Amplifier [2x12", 45w]
1968-72	2571 Galaxie Twin-Ten Tremolo Reverb Amplifier [2x10", 25w]
1968-72	2575CW Paragon Bass Amplifier [piggy back, 15", 40w]
1968-72	2566 Fury Bass Amplifier [15", 30w]
1968-72	PA 200 system/PA200 Centurion Amplifier [2-2x12", 100w]
1968-72	2570 Twin-Ten Amplifier [2x10", 20w]
1968-72	2563 Embassy Amplifier [10", 10w]
1968-72	2562 Challenger Amplifier [10", 10w]
1968-72	2573 Dart Amplifier [8", 5.5w]
1968-72	2560 Capri Amplifier [8", 5.5w]
1968-72	2525 Special Amplifier [6", 4w]
1968-72	2565 Montclair Tremolo Reverb Amplifier [12", 25w]
1968-72	2564 Jet-Tremolo Reverb Amplifier [10", 10w]

White script Alamo logo on black blob, solid-state preamps, tube output

| 1973-79? | Model 2567 Futura Tremolo Reverb Amplifier [2x12", 45w] |
| 1973-79? | Model 7+79 Paragon Super Reverb with Model 7+79 |

Reverb/Tremolo Piggy Back Powerpak Amplifier head [70w]

1973-79?	Model 7+700 Paragon Super Reverb Amplifier with 2x12 cabinet [70w]
1973-79?	Model 7+701 Paragon Super Reverb Amplifier with 15+12 cabinet [70w]
1973-79?	Model 7+702 Paragon Super Reverb Amplifier with 2x15 cabinet [70w]
1973-79?	Model 2569 Paragon Bass Amplifier [15", 40w]
1973-79?	Model 2565CW Paragon Bass Piggy Back Amplifier (Paragon Country Western Bass) [15", 40w]
1973-79?	Model 7+75 Paragon Bass Piggy Back Amplifier (Paragon Super Bass) [2x15", 40w]
1973-79?	Model 2562 Challenger Amplifier [10", 12w]
1973-79?	Model 2560 Capri Amplifier [10", 4w]
1973-79?	Model 2525 Special Amplifier [5", 3w]
1973-79?	Model 2570 Twin-Ten Amplifier [2x10", 20w]
1973-79?	Model 2563 Embassy Amplifier [10", 12w]
1973-79?	Model 2573 Dart Tremolo Amplifier [10", 4w]
1973-79?	Model 2565 Montclair Tremolo Reverb Amplifier [12", 25w]
1973-79?	Model 2564 Jet Tremolo Reverb Amplifier [12", 12w]
1973-79?	Model 2566 Fury Bass Amplifier [15", 35w]
1973-79?	Model 2574 Reverb Unit

All solid-state

| ca.1980-82 | [no information available] |

Hawaiian Lap Steels

1949/50-64	No. 2493 Embassy [pear-shape, map w/wal stripes]
1949/50-64	No. 2490 Jet [triangular]
ca. 1950-59	Challenger [asymm pear]
ca. 1953-61	No. 2499 Futuramic Dual Eight
by 1960-61	No. 2497 Futuramic Eight [asymm pear]
by 1960-61	No. 2495 Futuramic Six [assym pear]
1962-63	No. 2499 Alamo Dual Eight String Professional Model (Futuramic)
1964-67?	Model 2493 Embassy [triangular Jet]

Electric Spanish Guitars

1960-61	No. 2590 Texan [solid, 3/3 hs, 1 pu]
1962-63	No. 2587 Futuramic [solid, 3/3 hs, 1 pu]
1962-63	No. 2588 Fiesta Spanish [Tele solid, 3/3 hs, 1 pu]
1963	No. 2589 Titan Mark I [hollow, French curve 3/3 hs, 1 pu]
1963	No. 2590 Titan Mark I [hollow, French curve 3/3 hs, 1 pu]
1963	No. 2591 Mark II [hollow, French curve 3/3 hs, 2 pu]
1963	No. 2592 Mark II [hollow, French curve 3/3 hs, 2pu]
1964	Titan Mark I [hollow, center humped 3/3 hs, 1 pu]

1964	Titan Mark II [hollow, center humped 3/3 hs, 2 pu]
1963-64?	Fiesta [solid, 2-cut, center humped 3/3 hs]
1964	Fiesta [hollow, center humped 3/3 hs, 1 pu]
1964	Fiesta [hollow, center humped 3/3 hs, 2 pu]
1964-65	Model 2598 Eldorado guitar [red cherry solid, distorted Strat, Oriental A pg, 3/3 hs, 2 pu]
1965-66	Model 2598 Eldorado guitar [angular 6-hs in '65]
1964-65	Model 2599 Eldorado guitar [red cherry solid, distorted Strat, Oriental A pg, 3/3 hs, 2 pu, Bigsby]
1965-66	Model 2598T Eldorado guitar [renumbered the Model 2599, angular 6-hs]
1964-65	Model 2589 Titan Mark I [sb hollow, distorted Strat, Oriental A pg, 3/3 hs, 1 pu]
1965-66	Model 2589 Titan Mark I [angular 6-hs]
1964-65	Model 2590 Titan Mark I [blonde hollow, distorted Strat, Oriental A pg, 3/3 hs, 1 pu]
1965-66	Model 2590 Titan Mark I [angular 6-hs]
1964-65	Model 2595 Titan Mark I [cherry hollow, distorted Strat, Oriental A pg, 3/3 hs, 1 pu]
1965-66	Model 2595 Titan Mark I [angular 6-hs]
1964-65	Model 2591 Titan Mark II [sb hollow, distorted Strat, Oriental A pg, 3/3 hs, 1 pu]
1965-66	Model 2591 Titan Mark II [angular 6-hs]
1964-65	Model 2592 Titan Mark II [blonde hollow, distorted Strat, Oriental A pg, 3/3 hs, 2 pu]
1965-66	Model 2592 Titan Mark II [angular 6-hs]
1964-65	Model 2596 Titan Mark II [cherry hollow, distorted Strat, Oriental A pg, 3/3 hs, 2 pu]
1965-66	Model 2596 Titan Mark II [angular 6-hs]
1964-65	Model 2584R Fiesta [red hollow, 1 pu, offset 2-cut, 6-hs, 1 pu]
1965-66	Model 2584R Fiesta [squashed Strat/Jazzmaster, Fiesta 'guard cutout]
1964-65	Model 2584W Fiesta [wh hollow, 1 pu, offset 2-cut, 6-hs, 1 pu]
1965-66	Model 2584W Fiesta [squashed Strat/Jazzmaster, Fiesta 'guard cutout]
1964-65	Model 2584C Fiesta [cherry hollow, 1 pu, offset 2-cut, 6-hs, 1 pu]
1965-66	Model 2584C Fiesta [squashed Strat/Jazzmaster, Fiesta 'guard cutout]
1964-65	Model 2584B Fiesta [beige hollow, 1 pu, offset 2-cut, 6-hs, 1 pu]
1964-65	Model 2586R Fiesta [red hollow, 2 pu, offset 2-cut, 6-hs, 2 pu]
1965-66	Model 2586R Fiesta [squashed Strat/Jazzmaster, Fiesta 'guard cutout]
1964-65	Model 2586W Fiesta [wh hollow, 2 pu, offset 2-cut, 6-hs, 2 pu]
1965-66	Model 2586W Fiesta [squashed Strat/Jazzmaster, Fiesta 'guard cutout]
1964-65	Model 2586C Fiesta [cherry hollow, 2 pu, offset 2-cut, 6-hs, 2 pu]
1965-66	Model 2586C Fiesta [squashed Strat/Jazzmaster, Fiesta 'guard cutout]
1964-65	Model 2586B Fiesta [beige hollow, 2 pu, offset 2-cut, 6-hs, 2 pu]
1964-65	Model 2587R Fiesta [red hollow, 3 pu, offset 2-cut, 6-hs, 3 pu]
1965-66	Model 2587R Fiesta [squashed Strat/Jazzmaster, Fiesta 'guard cutout]
1964-65	Model 2587W Fiesta [wh hollow, 3 pu, offset 2-cut, 6-hs, 3 pu]
1965-66	Model 2587W Fiesta [squashed Strat/Jazzmaster, Fiesta 'guard cutout]
1964-65	Model 2587C Fiesta [cherry hollow, 3 pu, offset 2-cut, 6-hs, 3 pu]
1965-66	Model 2587C Fiesta [squashed Strat/Jazzmaster, Fiesta 'guard cutout]
1964-65	Model 2587B Fiesta [beige hollow, 3 pu, offset 2-cut, 6-hs, 3 pu]
1965-66	Model 2589T Titan Mark I [sb hollow, distorted Strat, Oriental A pg, angular 6-hs, 1 pu, vib]
1965-66	Model 2590T Titan Mark I [blonde hollow, distorted Strat, Oriental A pg, angular 6-hs, 1 pu, vib]
1965-66	Model 2595T Titan Mark I [cherry hollow, distorted Strat, Oriental A pg, angular 6-hs, 1 pu, vib]
1965-66	Model 2591T Titan Mark II [sb hollow, distorted Strat, Oriental A pg, angular 6-hs, 2 pu, vib]
1965-66	Model 2592T Titan Mark II [blonde hollow, distorted Strat, Oriental A pg, angular 6-hs, 2 pu, vib]
1965-66	Model 2596T Titan Mark II [cherry hollow, distorted Strat, Oriental A pg, angular 6-hs, 2 pu, vib]
1965-66	Model 2584S Fiesta [sb hollow, 1 pu, squashed Strat/Jazzmaster, Fiesta 'guard cutout, 6-hs]
1965-66	Model 2586S Fiesta [sb hollow, 2 pu, squashed Strat/Jazzmaster, Fiesta 'guard cutout, 6-hs]
1965-66	Model 2587S Fiesta [sb hollow, 3 pu, squashed Strat/Jazzmaster, Fiesta 'guard cutout, 6-hs]
1967-70	Model 2598 Toronado [red cherry solid, pointy Strat, stubby rounded 6-hs, 2 pu]
1967-70	Model 2598T Toronado [red cherry solid, pointy Strat, stubby rounded 6-hs, 2 pu, vib]
1967-70	Model 2583 Fury Standard [cherry sb or sb hollow, Jazzmaster, f-hole, Acra-Tune br, 1 pu]
1967-70	Model 2585 Fury Standard [cherry sb or sb hollow, Jazzmaster, f-hole, Acra-Tune br, 2 pu]
1967-70	Model 2583T-SB Fury Tremolo [sb hollow, Jazzmaster, f-hole, vib, 1 pu]
1967-70	Model 2583T-C Fury Tremolo [cherry sb hollow, Jazzmaster, f-hole, vib, 1 pu]
1967-70	Model 2585T-SB Fury Tremolo [sb hollow,

	Jazzmaster, f-hole, vib, 2 pu]		Oriental A pg in '64]
1967-70	Model 2585T-C Fury Tremolo [cherry sb hollow, Jazzmaster, f-hole, vib, 2 pu]	1965-66	Model 2593 Titan bass [sb hollow, distorted Strat, Oriental A pg, angular 6-hs]
1967-70	Model 2584 Fury Standard [cherry or sb solid, Jazzmaster, Acra-Tune br, 1 pu]	1963-65	No. 2594 Titan bass [blonde hollow, 2-cut, 2/2 hs, 1 pu; Oriental A pg in '64]
1967-70	Model 2584T Fury Tremolo [cherry or sb solid, Jazzmaster, vib, 1 pu]	1965-66	Model 2594 Titan bass [blonde hollow, distorted Strat, Oriental A pg, angular 6-hs]
1967-70	Model 2586 Fury Standard [cherry or sb solid, Jazzmaster, Acra-Tune br, 2 pu]	1963-65	No. 2597 Titan bass [cherry hollow, 2-cut, 2/2 hs, 1 pu; Oriental A pg in '64]
1967-70	Model 2586T Fury Tremolo [cherry or sb solid, Jazzmaster, vib, 2 pu]	1965-66	Model 2597 Titan bass [cherry hollow, distorted Strat, Oriental A pg, angular 6-hs]
c.1967	Fiesta [identical to Fury solid]	1964-66	Model 2600 Eldorado bass [cherry solid, distorted Strat, Oriental A pg, angular 6-hs, 1 pu]

Electric Basses

1963-65	No. 2593 Titan bass [sb hollow, 2-cut, 2/2 hs, 1 pu;	1967-70	Model 2593 Titan bass [sb hollow, angular offset 2-cut, humped upper horn, Oriental A pg, 1 pu]

GUILD
SOLIDBODY GUITARS

Underrated Americans

What always seems amazing is how myopic some guitar aficionados can be, scanning the classifieds and rooting through pawnshops in search of old Gibsons, Gretsches, Fenders and Martins, almost to the exclusion of anything else. Make no mistake, those estimable companies are responsible for many of the finest guitars built in America — indeed the world — over the years, but there are so many other names worth pursuing if one just broadens the gaze a bit.

One case in point is Guild guitars, perhaps the most underrated quality guitar line in American guitar history. Indeed, aside from Guild's highly esteemed electric archtops, which have managed to sustain interest among players and collectors alike, Guild's excellent acoustics have yet to be fully appreciated, and Guild's fine solidbody electrics are almost under the radar. Always the champion of the underdog, this is the story of the least-appreciated of Guild guitars, the solidbody electrics.

The chronologies of the guitars in this essay have been pieced together by triangulating between a combination of catalogs, contemporary press notices, partial company records and other published sources. Often guitars were produced before they appeared in catalogs or the press and sometimes after they ceased being promoted. This is made even more difficult by the fact that the Guild catalogs were not dated, but rather have codes which do not translate exactly into publication dates. For example, it would be tempting and convenient to attribute catalog No.7134 to 1971, but both the style and other evidence suggest that it is from somewhere between 1967 and 1970, probably 1969. An ad for the 1970 solidbodies lists the available catalog as 7367, and an ad from

'72 refers to catalog 7476-A. Two other guideposts can be seen in two price lists: the November 1, 1973, price list was No. 7851; the March

1959 Guild Aristocrat with replacement Gibson pickups (photo: Michael Lee Allen).

1, 1980, price list was No. 8826. And so it goes. The dates herein are close, but may be, in some cases, imperfect.

Born amidst a strike

Guild Guitars was founded in 1952 by Alfred Dronge, a New York City jazz guitarist (not a classical guitarist, as has been reported). The company was started coincidental to a labor strike at another New York guitar company, Epiphone. Epi Strathopoulis avoided unionization, but in the process lost a number of employees—stories have it primarily from New York's Little Italy—who subsequently ended up working for "Guild" (an old English term for a trade union). Some have suggested that Guild was actually begun by defecting Epiphone workers, but, rather, Guild was already in the works and merely profited from Epiphone's labor troubles and subsequent relocation from New York to Philadelphia's Manayunk neighborhood. For more information on the entire Guild story Hans Moust's *Guild Guitars* is most highly recommended.

As you might guess, with associations with both a jazz guitarist and Epiphone, Guild's early expertise was carved-top archtops (which still ruled the guitar world roost in 1952) and, secondarily, on its fine acoustic flattops. The company's reputation has almost always rested on its archtop electrics, indeed, the first Guild guitars were sold primarily to Alfred Dronge's friends in

(Left) Ca. 1958 Guild M-65 hollowbody, the antecedent of the semi-hollow and later solid M-75 (courtesy Bluebond Guitars, Philadelphia, PA). (Right) 1958 Guild Aristocrat, direct hollowbody ancestor of the later solid BluesBird (courtesy New Hope Guitar Traders, Fayetteville, TN).

(Left) Ca. 1963 Guild Polara S-100 solidbody with an unusual reverse six-in-line headstock (courtesy Way Cool Guitars, Charlottesville, VA). (Right) 1967 Guild BluesBird, early solidbody version, with replacement pickups (courtesy New Hope Guitar Traders, Fayetteville, TN).

the jazz community.

Guild guitars were born just as electric guitars had become the rage. Charlie Christian had thrust the electric into eyes of the public with his brief pre-War work with the Benny Goodman Quintet. Christian was followed after the War by such luminaries as Les Paul, who was voted most popular guitarist in 1952 music polls. Quickly Guild's archtops acquired pickups, usually DeArmonds, and the line expanded to include both full-body and thinline archtop electrics.

Guild endorsers in the early days included such influential luminaries as Johnny Smith ("Walk, Don't Run"), George Barnes, Charlie Byrd (of the Mark classicals), twangy Duane Eddy, George Benson, the Smothers Brothers and Richie Havens, to mention just a few.

Sixties guitar boom

Guild entered the solidbody arena slightly late in the game during the height of the guitar boom in the early '60s, just as the demand was making its transition from folksy flattops to rockier electrics.

From the very beginning, Guild established a penchant for distinctive styling for its solidbodies which were somewhat behind or ahead of their time (depending on your point of view), and which may account for why they didn't conquer the guitar world. Gibson had experimented with weirdness back in 1958 with the Explorer, Flying V and mysterious Moderne, but these quickly bit the dust, rejected by a market more in tune to the more conservative Spanish-shaped Les Paul or the way-modern contours of the Strat. As the '60s careened into the later years, exotic-shaped guitars became more attractive to Boomers entering their teens, but Guild never had a great impact on that electric scene.

Guild Gumbies

1964 Guild Jet-Star S-50 with a slightly more conservative shape than the upscale Thunderbird (courtesy Mike Smith).

Guild's first solids, introduced in 1963, were the strange-looking Thunderbird S-200, the Polara S-100 and the Jet-Star S-50, now among the more collectible of Guild's not-yet-discovered solidbodies. This first generation of Guild solids featured unique body shapes, glued-in necks, and originally a whimsical asymmetrical headstock design.

The top-of-the-line Thunderbird was the most curious, a lop-sided, Gumby-shaped offset double cutaway. In his *American Guitars* (Harper Collins), Tom Wheeler describes the shape as "melted Hershey bar," which is graphically right on! Its asymmetrical "Florentine" head sported an inlaid V-shaped Guild logo and a pearl thunderbird. The bound rosewood fingerboard had pearl block inlays. It was equipped with two metal-covered Guild Anti-Hum humbucking pickups (slightly smaller than later Guild humbuckers), activated by two on/off sliding switches. Somewhere during this run, by the way, the pickups were changed from 'buckers to single-coil DeArmonds. The controls were most interesting, with two separate tonal circuits, each with its own volume and tone control. The circuit sliding switch went from a fatter, rhythmic sound to a more trebly lead sound. In the down or lead position, another sliding switch activated in or out of phase when both pickups were engaged. Every time you pick up this guitar, you have to spend about a half hour remembering what the switches do, before you can begin to jam out on the Lovin' Spoonful's "Did You Ever Have To Make Up Your Mind." It would not be surprising to learn that a German had something to do with this guitar's design!

The Thunderbird also featured a vibrato which some published accounts attribute to Guild, however, which was actually a unit designed by the Swedish guitar company Hagstrom and found on their own name, Goya, Harmony and some other brands of guitars of the period. This was a fairly effective cross between a Bigsby and a Fender vibrato. It had a nickel or chrome base plate positioned over a small routed out opening to accommodate a single large Bigsby-like tension spring in the center. A second plate, with holes for string attachment, sat in a curved edge at the front, working with basically an early knife-edge mechanism. An adjustment screw passed through both plates and the spring, and could be tightened or loosened to adjust tension. A little sleeve with a thumb-screw was mounted on the lower side of the top plate into which a curved handle was inserted.

The coolest feature of the Thunderbird was a nifty built-in guitar stand, which was basically just a 12" chrome bar on a hinge mounted in the back of the guitar. Flip it out, and the guitar would perch on the two points of the lower bout and the stand. The Thunderbird came in Cherry Red "Starfire" and sunburst finishes. Evidence suggests these are pretty rare and were manufactured from 1963 through 1968.

The Polara S-100 had a considerably more symmetrical body than the Thunderbird, with more pronounced upper and lower horns and a bit more of an even scoop or cutout on the bottom bout. Curiously enough, the earliest of these Polara S-100s came with a reverse-tipped headstock, sort of like a Gibson Firebird, with six-in-line tuners. These probably did not last very long, and probably by '64 the Polara changed to the asymmetrical head of the early Thunderbird, with the so-

called "Chesterfield" inlay on the headstock. The Polara had an unbound fingerboard with dot inlays, Hagstrom vibrato and two Guild "Frequency-Tested" single coil pickups which were made by DeArmond. A simple threeway select toggle replaces the fancy sliding switches of the Thunderbird, but the built-in guitar stand remained. These were also made through 1968.

The Jet-Star S-50 was a single pickup version of the Polara, with the pickup curiously placed right in the center of the body, and without the stand. This had a curious bridge/tailpiece assembly with a square cover that was hinged at the bottom and flipped up for attaching the strings. A Jet-Star Bass was also manufactured at least from 1965 through 1967. This bass was not offered in the '64 catalog, so probably debuted in '65. No descriptions are available, but it no doubt had the Jet-Star shape and a single pickup. These appear to have been made only until 1967.

In addition to the guitars, there was also a Jet-Star Bass. This was basically identical to the S-200 Thunderbird in terms of shape. It had one pickup and a covered

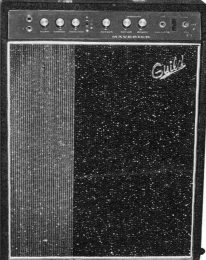

Ca. 1966 Guild Maverick amplifier, all tubes with tremolo, reverb and a pair of 10" speakers (courtesy Tinicum Guitar Barn, Ottsville, PA).

bridge/tailpiece assembly. There were two fingerrests on either side of the strings. Inlays were dots. These, too, were available in a cherry red "Starfire" finish and sunburst.

In the early '60s, the standard Guild headstock was reminiscent of the Gibson design, with an open-book dip in the center. As early as 1964 a redesigned headstock with a rounded crown began to appear on some acoustics. This became the new standard Guild headstock in 1965. As mentioned, the S-200 and S-50 had asymmetrical heads in around 1963. The earliest S-100s had the reverse six-in-line, but changed to the asymmetrical head, probably in '64. Somewhere between 1964 and 1966 (probably '65), the solidbodies lost their asymmetrical headstocks and adopted the new standard rounded crown style. However, you should note that Guild never bothered to change the illustrations in the catalog, and the asymmetrical headstocks were shown all the way through 1968 despite reality.

The advent of Avnet

In 1966, Guild was purchased by Avnet, Inc. At about this same time, the Thunderbird was changed to include two single-coil pickups instead of humbuckers, the rounded headstock, and a Thunderbird inlay. The electronics and guitar stand remained. It is possible that some of these guitars still featured humbuckers, but the only ones I've ever seen with the new standard Guild headstock had the single coils.

These early Guild guitars were not embraced by most mainstream professional musicians, however notable players included Muddy Waters (on the *Electric Mud* lp), as well as Zal Yanofsky, guitarist for the Lovin' Spoonful, who played a Thunderbird. Jorma Kaukonen of the Jefferson Airplane spun the psychedelic lines of *Surre-*

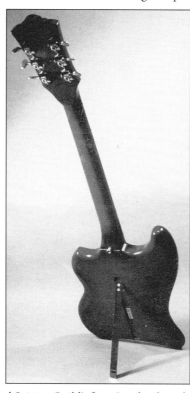

(Left) 966 Guild Thunderbird S-200, Guild's first Gumby-shaped solid, which Tom Wheeler described as melted Hershey bar. (Right) The built-in stand of the 1966 Guild Thunderbird S-200.

Ca. '69 Guild flyer No. 7134.

alistic Pillow on a Guild Thunderbird, too. It's possible that Banana of the Youngbloods also sported one of these, but, suffice it to say, the Thunderbird never really flew.

The first generation of Guild solidbodies technically lasted until around 1970, when the Polara was still being advertised in the newly founded *Guitar Player* magazine. However, based on production numbers of selected Guild guitars made between 1965 and 1969, production actually ended in 1968. This makes sense, because the electric guitar boom went bust at about that time, with companies like Valco/Kay going out of business.

Rare birds?

It is unknown exactly how many of these guitars were built in the six years between 1963 and 1968, but it is pretty certain that the number was relatively low. Guild was scurrying to keep up with demand for its acoustics in the mid-'60s, and it's doubtful that solidbody electrics occupied a great portion of production. That these are relatively rare is confirmed by how seldom these birds appear on the market.

Prior to 1965, Guild guitars all featured serial numbers in one large consecutive series. The

approximate last serial number from 1963 was #28943; from '64: #38636; from '65: #46606. If you have a Guild solidbody with a serial number within these parameters, you have a rough idea when it was made.

From 1965 to 1969, each model had its own prefix and was numbered consecutively within its own series. From 1965 through 1967, just 90 S-200 Thunderbirds (prefix SC) were made. From 1965 through 1968, 808 S-100s (prefix SB) were built. Between 1965 and 1967, some 1,174 S-50 Jet-Star guitars (prefix SA) and 677 Jet-Star Basses (prefix SD) were made. While total production would be a bit higher when 1963 and '64 quantities are

included, these are still not enormous numbers of units.

From New Jersey to Rhode Island

In 1967, Avnet began construction of a new factory in Westerly, Rhode Island, and began slowly moving production from Hoboken, New Jersey, where Guild had been located since 1956. Production continued at both facilities until 1971, when all guitars were made in Westerly. The Hoboken plant was closed down and headquarters were moved to 225 West Grand Street in Elizabeth, New Jersey.

Guild's relatively unsuccessful flirtation with Gumby guitars inspired a change to

1970 ad showing the new Guild S-100 Polara, JS Bass and M-85 solidbody, also mentioning the m-85 semi-hollows. (Right) 1971 ad for Guild's "great bass amps."

a more conservative approach in the next decade.

Guild's "SG"

In 1970, the Guild solid line was completely redesigned with a more conventional look inspired by Gibson's SG (the S series) and Les Paul (M series) guitars. Indeed, Guild's new solidbodies were quite reminiscent of the mid-'60s Hagstrom solidbodies, curious given the vibrato connection between the two companies. Ironically, Guild's '70s S guitars probably come as close as any to creating a strong identity for their solidbodies, yet even here the guitars are usually referred to as the "Guild SG," mixing company metaphors, as it were!

Initially, the S series included three guitars and two basses. Top of the line was the S-100, which bore virtually no resemblance to the older model that shared that number. Gumby was gone in favor of a more rounded-out look, more like a Gibson SG, with only slightly different sized cutaway horns.

The new S-100s featured two Guild humbuckers, a threeway select and two volume and two tone controls. Guild humbuckers had a stamped chrome cover with exposed pole pieces along one side and a rectangular elevation covering the other set of poles. The neck was glued in, with a bound 22-fret rosewood fingerboard and block ivoroid inlays. The headstock was the standard rounded crown with a Chesterfield inlay. The S-100 featured a little pickguard screwed onto the top just under the pickups. On the natural models, these were clear with Guild stenciled on them. In 1970, the S-100 came with a thin compensated bridge with a Hagstrom vibrato, however, soon, by '72 at least, bridges had become a finetune variety and tailpieces were a rectangular stop set at an angle toward the bass side. By '72, these were available in sunburst, cherry-red, black, walnut and natural finishes.

In 1970, when it was introduced, the S-100 was still called the Polara, after the '60s model. Sometime later, by '72 certainly, the S-100 would be referred to as the S-100 Standard.

Keeping up with the times, in 1973 the

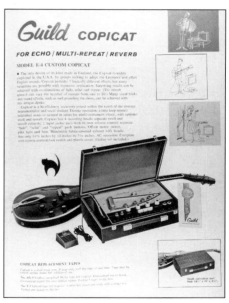

1968 Guild catalog; despite the illustrations, the guitars had acquired regular Guild headstocks by this time (courtesy Jim Dulfer).

S-100 was upgraded with a new set of improved, "hotter" humbucking pickups (using the same metal covers, so they look the same as the older versions) and the addition of a mini-toggle phase switch.

Joining the S-100 Standard in '73 was the S-100 DeLuxe. These were basically the same guitar except the S-100 DeLuxe added a Bigsby vibrato and Grover Roto-Matic tuners. Finishes were the same as before. By '73, at least, if not before, the natural finished models had clear plexiglass see-through pickguards with "Guild" stencilled on. Prices in '73 were $375 for the S-100 Standard and $420 for the S-100 DeLuxe.

Oak leaves

In 1974, the S-100 was improved again with the debut of the carved top model, the S-100C. This featured an oak leaf pattern carved into the body top, and was quickly imitated by many different brands, inspiring a whole spate of mostly imported guitars sporting various carved designs. This had the cool see-through plastic pickguard with "Guild" stencilled on. The only ones I've ever seen had a sort of walnut natural finish look. It's unknown if these were ever made in other finishes. These oak leaf Guilds hung around for about two years. These were very respectable guitars com-

Downscale

Nestling under the original S-100 in 1970 were two more guitars with the same basic shape, the S-90 and S-50. Both of these had plain headstocks (no Chesterfield) and unbound fingerboards with dot inlays. The S-90 had two Guild humbuckers set into a black/white/black pickguard assembly above and below the pickups, with one volume and one tone and threeway select. This had the same hinged, covered bridge/tailpiece assembly as the S-50 Jet-Star of the '60s.

The S-50 had a single humbucker in the middle (like the old S-50) set into a pickguard assembly that extended down to the volume/tone controls and jack. The catalog photo, by the way, looks more like a mini-humbucker or single-coil pickup, rather than the larger humbucker on the S-100 and S-90. This, too, had the hinged, covered bridge/tailpiece assembly.

Prices in 1973 were $300 for the S-90 and

$225 for the S-50. Finish options included sunburst, cherry red, black, walnut and natural.

By the middle of the decade, both the S-90 and S-50 had switched to the slanted rectangular stop tail combined with a finetune bridge. Later S-50s also clearly had a regular humbucker in the middle. These transitions had not yet happened by the November 1973 price list.

All these guitars could be had with a Bigsby vibrato, stereo wiring (on two-pickup guitars) and in left-handed versions. By '73 a phase switch option was also offered on twin-pickup models.

The bottom line

Two similarly shaped JS Bass 1 and 2 were also available in 1970, with one or two humbucking pickups, respectively. These

had Chesterfield inlays on the headstock and unbound rosewood fingerboards with dot inlays. These came equipped with a mini-toggle "tone" switch and could be had with both fretless and stereo options. In 1973 these were available in sunburst, cherry red, black, walnut and natural finishes. The JS Bass 1 cost $320 in 1973, the JS Bass 2 $400. For an added $25 you could have the two-pickup basses wired in stereo. Fretless was available free. Also, a 34 inch scale was optional. (These basses are also sometimes decribed with Roman numerals, by the way).

In 1974, the JS Bass 2 was offered with the carved oak leaf pattern on the body. By 1976, these could be had in sunburst, cherry, black, walnut and natural.

Ssseventies ssswan sssong

The S-100 Polara only lasted from 1970-1971 or maybe '72, after which it transmogrified into more familiar models. The S-100 Standard, S-90, S-50, JS Bass 1 and JS Bass 2 lasted in the catalog from 1970 through around 1976. The S-100 DeLuxe was in the catalog from '73 to around 1976. The S-100C and JS Bass 2C (with carved top) debuted in '74 and bowed

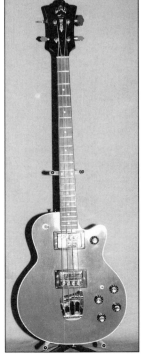

(Left to Right) 1972 ad for Guild's "different basses, the JS Bass II, JS Bass II Fretless, SF-Bass II (semi-hollow) and M-85-II Bass. 1971 Guild JS-11 Bass and a 1971 Guild M85-II Bass (Photo: Steve Glazer).

out in around 1976. No quantities are known because these were made during the period when production numbers were not encoded into serial numbers. The S-100 was revived again in 1994, but we'll get to that in due time.

Guild's Les Paul

In 1970 Guild introduced its *solidbody* M-75 BluesBird guitars and, by '72 at least, the M-85 basses, single cutaway Les Paul-shaped guitars which had previously been semi-hollow. The solid M-75 actually originated as the M-65 in the late '50s, a *hollowbody* with f-holes and a single neck pickup. This was followed by the two-pickup *semi-hollowbody* Aristocrat M-75 in 1959 or '60, which disappeared in around 1962. The semi-hollow Aristocrat then reappeared with the name changed to just the M-75 designation in 1967. These had Les Paul shapes which Guild dubbed "³/₄ size." These had a harp trapeze tailpiece with a finetune bridge, a pair of Guild humbuckers, elevated pickguard, two volumes and two tones, and a bound rosewood fingerboard with pearl block inlays. The headstock had a Chesterfield inlay. Both guitar and basses were available in black, sunburst or cherry red. In 1968 the M-75 guitar was also given the name "BluesBird."

In 1970 the BluesBird line bifurcated into two semi-hollowbody guitars and the new solidbody version. After '72, the semi-hollowbodies were offered with either gold or chrome hardware. These semi-hollows lasted until 1974, after which the M-75 was exclusively

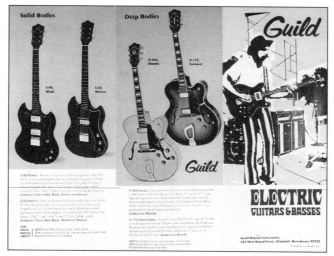

Ca. 1971 Guild flyer No. 7370-A.

a solidbody guitar.

The new M-75 solidbody introduced in '70 had a carved top, mahogany body, Chesterfield head inlay, a block-inlaid, bound ebony fingerboard, twin humbuckers, threeway select, finetune bridge, and the same harp-shaped trapeze tail as the semi-hollow, two volumes and two tone, stairstep elevated pickguard, and

1974 Guild S-100C, Guild's "SG" with oak leaf carving.

Grover Roto-Matics. By 1972 the tail changed to an angled rectangular stop-tail. Guild liked to describe these guitars as having ³/₄-size bodies, however, this was only in relationship to the thinlines; they were roughly equivalent to a Gibson Les Paul in

size. Initially, in 1970 the M-75 was divided into two models, the Deluxe ($495) and the Standard ($425), differentiated mainly by ebony fingerboard and gold hardware versus rosewood and chrome. By 1972 these had become the M-75GS for the ebony/gold Deluxe ($525 in '73) and the M75CS for the rosewood/chrome Standard ($475 in '73). These came in sunburst, cherry, black, walnut and natural.

By the mid-'70s, sometime after '73, the M series guitars had also acquired a phase switch. In around 1978 or so, they also began to be offered with a DiMarzio pickup option.

Two solid, Les Paul-shaped M-85-I and M-85-II basses were also introduced in 1972. These were also carved-top Les Paul shapes, otherwise basically identical in fea-

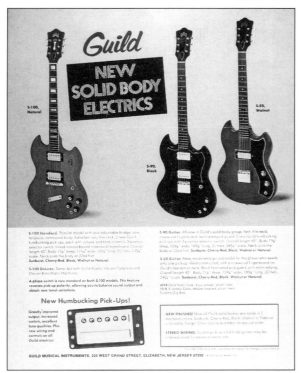

Ca. 1973 Guild flyer No. 7551.

tures and appointments to the JS Basses, with one or two humbucking pickups respectively. It's not clear how long the M-85-I was available, but it is *not* listed in the 1973 price list. In 1973, the M-85-II also came in sunburst, cherry, black, walnut and natural and cost $460.

In 1975, the M-85CS *guitar* joined the line, yet another upscale version of the solid Les Paul. These lasted until around 1980.

The M-75 and M-85 guitars and M-85 basses lasted throughout the '70s and until around 1980.

No information is available on quantities of these second generation Guild solidbodies, but they were probably more successful than their predecessors. Still, not many seem to appear on the market, which suggests either they're still hiding in closets, or that not that many were actually produced.

'70s dating

From 1970 through most of 1979, Guild had returned to a single series system of serial numbers, so it is impossible to determine totals with any exactitude. Again, the approximate final serial number for all gui-

tars of 1970 was #50978; of '71: #61463; of '72: #75602; of '73: #95496; of '74: #112803; of '75: #130304; of '76: #149625; of '77: #169867; '78: #195067; of '79: #211877. These can help you date your guitar, but yield no clues to totals, although remember that the majority of any year's production will be acoustic guitars. In 1979, Guild reverted to the prefix for individual models with their own series numbers, making quantities much easier to figure out.

In 1972, original founder Al Dronge was killed in the crash of his private airplane, and Leon Tell became the new president of Guild.

Japanese imports

In 1973 Guild introduced its Japanese-made Madeira guitars. These included solidbody electric copies of Gibson, Fender and Guild's own S-100 guitars, as well as acoustic copies (ironically) of Martin guitars. The Madeira electrics were essentially bolt-neck versions of their inspirations, most likely made by Kasuga, which was aggressively making its move into the American market at the time. Except for the bolt-on necks, these early Madeira's

were pretty close replicas except (for the most part) the headstock. Most heads featured a distinctive rounded crown, however, some were made with headstocks which were exact replicas of Gibson's open-book design. The copy of Guild's S-100 was the EG-100, while the copy of Guild's JS Bass 2 was the EB-100. These electrics were only promoted for about a year, with an ad appearing in *Guitar Player* as late as August of '74; whether they lasted much beyond 1974 or so is unknown. Probably not.

Madeira acoustics outlived their electric siblings. It's not known how long the Madeira acoustics lasted, but quite possibly through the '70s.

1979 Guild B-301 Bass (photo: Steve Glazer).

Bell-bottomed trousers

In 1977, the Guild line was completely redesigned again with the introduction of the S-60, a sort of bell-shaped offset double cutaway guitar with one Guild humbucking pickup in the lead position with one volume and one tone control. These had mahogany bodies and glued-in necks, the center-crown Guild headstock, unbound 24-fret, dot-inlaid rosewood fingerboards, a black/white/black pickguard, finetune roller bridge (similar to, if not actually, the one by Schaller), and a slanted rectangular stop-tailpiece. The headstock had only the Guild name inlaid into it. Finishes were sunburst, cherry, black, walnut, natural and white. In '80 the S-60 cost $339.

Introduced alongside the S-60 guitar was the B-301 long-scale bass. This was essentially the same thing with a Guild single-coil pickup, offered in the same finishes. This had a single bridge/tailpiece unit, and an added Chesterfield inlay on the head.

The bell-shaped S-60 and B-301 bass rapidly expanded to encompass a full line of solids which anchored the brand for the next few years. Reconstructing the precise chronology is hard, but we can get close.

By late 1977 or 1978, the line included the S-60, plus an S-60D, S-300, S-300A and S-300AD guitars, and a B-302 bass. The suffixes indicate a DiMarzio pickup option ("D") and the substitution of an ash body with maple neck ("A") for the standard all-mahogany construction.

The S-60D, rather than substituting a DiMarzio humbucker for the Guild version, actually offered two DiMarzio SDS-1 single-coils, with two volume and one tone control and a threeway select. Finish options included sunburst, cherry, black, walnut, natural mahogany and white, and it cost $439.

The S-300 was an upscale version of the S-60 with two Guild humbucking pickups, and unbound ebony fingerboard and the added Chesterfield inlay on the headstock. These had two volume and two tone controls, plus threeway select and a phase switch. Finish options included sunburst, cherry, black, walnut, natural mahogany and white, and the cost was $525. The S-300A ($565) was an ash/maple version of the S-300. The S-300AD was the ash/maple variant with a DiMarzio PAF pickup at

(Above) Summer of 1974 ad for Madeira guitars by Guild, including the EG-100 copy of Guild's S-100 and the MB-100 copy of Guild's own JS-100.

the neck and a DiMarzio Super Distortion at the bridge, available in blonde and sunburst and costing $625.

The B-302 was a two-pickup version of the B-301, with Guild single-coils, two volumes and one tone and a threeway select. Finish options included sunburst, cherry, black, walnut, natural mahogany and white. In 1980 the B-302 listed for $525, the B-301 for $450. At some point, certainly by 1980, since they're in the price list, ash-bodied versions of the B-302 and B-301 were added to the line, the B-302A ($565) and B-301A ($490), available in blonde or sunburst. The mahogany basses went out of production in 1980. By mid-'81 these basses were also offered in fretless and, for two-pickup basses, stereo wiring options. Production totals are not known, but at least 846 examples were built. The ash basses hung on until 1981, with at least 235 instruments constructed.

In either late 1978 or 1979, the line was further augmented with the S-70D and S-70AD guitars. These were the S-60D guitars with a third DiMarzio single-coil

1974 ad for the Guild M-75. (Right) June 1974 ad for the Guild PA-153A with a PA-300A Console and two CS-228H sound columns.

(Left) Mid-'75 ad for Guild's humbucker, offering "clean, distortion-free sound—with increased output and sustain," plus Guild strings and polish. (Right) Early 1974 ad for the Guild Starfire semi-hollowbody.

pickup, a fiveway select, one volume and one tone, a phase mini-toggle plus a bypass switch "to allow other pickup combinations." The bypass switch operated in the bridge position, activating both the bridge and neck pickups but bypassing the middle. Basically, the S-70D allowed eight different tonal variations, the five off the fiveway switch, plus a phase reverse between the neck and middle, the "bypassed" front and neck, and the position between the bridge and middle (because the neck pickup was added in to the mix). This seems somewhat complicated, but it was pretty effective and offered very flexible sounds. Finish options included sunburst, cherry, black, walnut, natural mahogany and white. In 1980 the S-70D listed for $550. The S-70AD was an ash bodied version with a maple neck which listed for $595. Ash bodied guitars were available in blonde or sunburst finishes.

At some point in 1979 or 1980 the S-65D joined the roster (it was listed in the March 1, 1980, price list), the older S-60 with a single DiMarzio Dual Sound humbuckers outfitted with a coil tap. Finish options included sunburst, cherry, black,

walnut, natural mahogany and white, and cost was $359.

By 1980, at least, the S-300D was also available ($585), basically the mahogany S-300 with the DiMarzio PAF at the neck and a DiMarzio Super Distortion (SDHP) at the bridge. At least one of these has been sighted in the mahogany finish with grey pickup bobbins and a very natty grey marbleized pickguard.

Also, in 1980 the line was capped by the introduction of the S-400, a neck-through-body variant of the ash/maple S-300AD with active electronic EQ and brass hardware.

All double-pickup guitars, by the way, were also available with a Bigsby option and optional stereo wiring. Basses could be ordered fretless, as well.

Finally, new in 1980 were the B-401 and B-402 basses. The B-401 ($625) was a long-scale with a maple neck, a laminated ash and walnut body and brass hardware. It had a single pickup run through an onboard preamp with EQ. The B-402 ($695) was the same except for having two pickups and an additional phase switch. These lasted for only about a year, and went out of production in 1981 after 335 were made.

Just like the other Guild solidbodies, the ungainly appearance of these guitars belies a surprising playability. The necks are comfortable and the glued-in (or neck-through) construction gives them nice sustain and a solid, reliable feel.

Like the Gumbies of the '60s, these bell-shaped guitars were somewhat off the beaten track of current taste and just did not win the hearts of the guitar playing universe. This series lasted for about four or five years, with most going out of production in 1981 and a few just stumbling into 1982 before disappearing from view. In all fairness, this may not have been entirely the fault of the guitars. It was right around

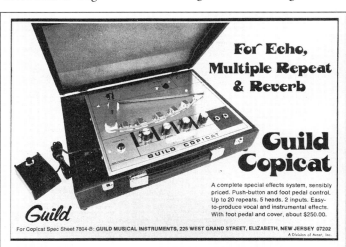

1974 ad for the Guild Copicat offering echo, multiple repeat and reverb.

Ca. 1960 Alamo No. 2493 Embassy Lap Steel.

Ca. 1962 No. 2566 Century Twin Ten amplifier.

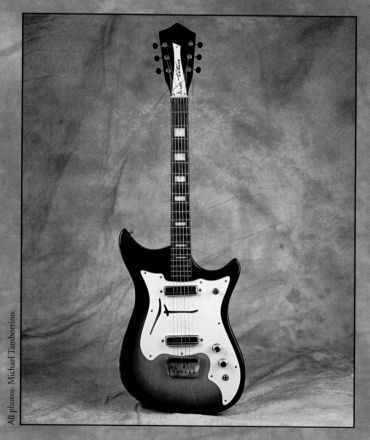

Ca. 1963 Alamo No. 2591 Titan Mark II.

Ca. 1963 Alamo No. 2589 Titan Mark I.

All photos: Michael Tamborrino.

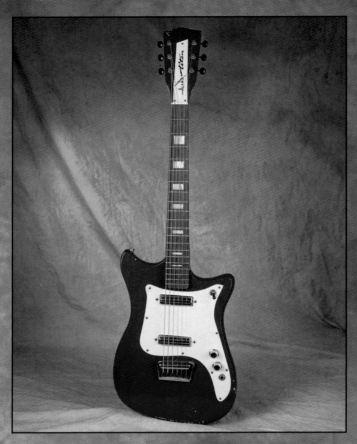

Ca. 1963-64 Alamo Titan II.

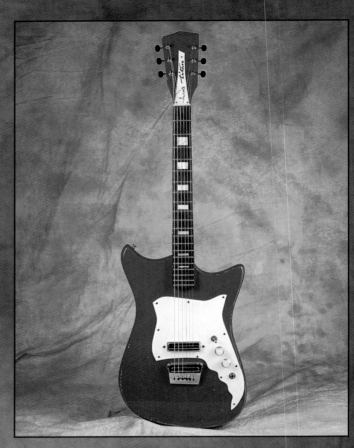

Ca. 1964 Alamo Fiesta I.

Ca. 1964 Alamo Fiesta II.

Ca. 1965 Alamo Model 2584R Fiesta.

All photos: Michael Tamborrino.

Ca. 1965 Alamo Model 2584W Fiesta.

Ca. 1965-66 Alamo Model 2586W Fiesta.

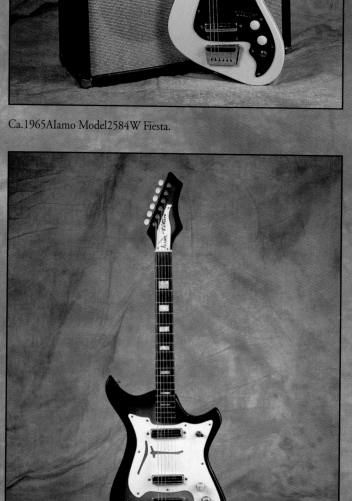

Ca. 1965-66 Alamo Model 2591 Titan Mark II.

Ca. 1966-67 Alamo Model 2586 Fiesta.

All photos: Michael Tamborrino.

Ca. 1967 Alamo Model 2583T-SB Fury Tremolo.

Mid--'70s Alamo Jet amplifier

Ca. 1965-66 Alamo Model
2589 Titan Mark I

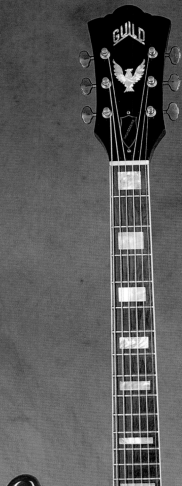

1966 Guild Thunderbird S-200

Photo: Michael Tamborino.

1974 Guild S-100NB

1977 Guild M-75
BCG BluesBird

1979 Guild
S-70D

All photos: Michael Tamborrino.

1983 Guild X-79

1984 Guild S-84 Aviator

All photos: Michael Tamborrino.

this time that the American economy sank into a fairly large recession which had a big impact on the guitar industry. However, the fact remains that Guild just never did manage to catch the wave of guitar taste and become a style leader.

Dating the bells

In 1979 Guild reverted to the practice of numbering each model with its own prefix and a consecutive number indicating the production quantities of that model, beginning with 1000001. Thus, for example, a later 1984 X-79 has the prefix AD, with the consecutive production number of 101505, making it the 1,505th one produced since the model began.

Again, since the bellbottoms antedate the implementation of this system, complete

(Left) Late '75 ad for the Guild M-80CS solidbody. (Right) 1976 ad for the Guild S-100.

production totals are not possible. Nevertheless, Guild records from 1979 on suggests that these Guilds, too, were not high production animals. No data on the neck-through S-400s is available, but these are undoubtedly quite rare. From 1979-82 about 470 S-300s had been made, while only 230 S-300As had been built. The S-60 made it to 500 pieces, while the S-60D consisted of a mere 207 guitars. The S-70 eked out 246 units. Even if you were to double the quantities recorded to cover those made from 1977 and '78, you'd still be in relatively rare territory.

Change for the '80s

In 1980 Guild began to rethink its solidbody line once again, beginning yet another phase which would last for the next few years. The first new design out of the gate was the M-80 guitar which was introduced in 1980.

The M-80 was a conventionally shaped, rounded double cutaway guitar, essentially a double-cut-

Mid-'75 ad for the Guild S-100 with hand-carved oak-leaf top and JS Bass 2.

away version of the M-75 BluesBird solidbody. The look was very reminiscent of the late '70s Epiphone Genesis. The short-lived M-80 had a glued-in three-piece maple neck, dot-inlaid two-octave ebony fingerboard, and rounded crown headstock with Chesterfield inlay. A bound carved maple cap topped a contoured mahogany body. In 1980 this model was introduced in two versions, the M-80CS ($695), with two pickups, phase switch and master volume control, and the M-80CSD ($755), with a DiMarzio PAF at the neck and a DiMarzio Dual Sound (DSHP) at the bridge. By the end of the line in '83 the M-80 came with an SP-6 quick-change stop tails (similar to a Gibson, no longer the slanted rectangle), two open-coil XR-7 humbucking pickups, and gold hardware. XR-7 pickups, by the way, were specially designed for Guild by DiMarzio. These M-80s had two volumes and two tones, with a threeway select. The buyer could specify a coil tap or phase switch. Later M-80s came in candy apple red, black, red sunburst and sunburst. M-80s were primarily produced in '81, although about 350 were actually produced between the end of 1980 and early 1983.

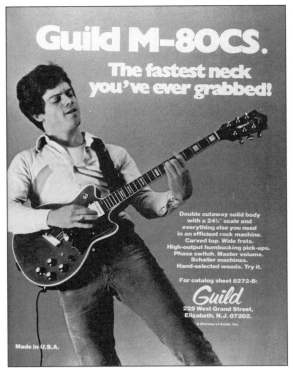

1976 ad for the Guild M-80CS.

Guild's first Strats

In 1981, the Guild line was expanded with some far more interesting pieces, including two conservative designs, the Strat-like S-250 and S-25, and two more radical visions, the X-82 and X-79 guitars. '81 also saw the debut of four new basses in the offset double cutaway mode, the SB-202, SB-201, MB-802 and MB-801.

The S-250s were essentially glued-neck Strats with mahogany bodies, bound tops, three-piece maple necks, Chesterfield crown heads, chrome hardware, two-octave rosewood fingerboards with dots, two XR-7 humbuckers, stop tails, finetune bridges, two volumes and one tone, and a choice of tap or phase. Color options included sunburst, black and candy apple red. According to later brochure copy from around 1982, jazz fusion keyboard ace and composer Jan Hammer used this guitar to write his guitar parts.

The S-25 was an unbound version of the S-250 with one volume and one tone, but otherwise identical.

Both the S-250 and S-25 were made until 1983, though again we're looking a pretty small quantities. Guild records reported in Gruhn list only 350 S-250s and 339 S-25s.

Holding up the "bottom" of the line in '81, were the new basses. The SB-200 series featured offset double cutaway bodies similar to Fender's classic style, with slightly more rounded lower bouts. These had glued-in necks, the crown two-and-two headstocks, Chesterfields, 21-fret fingerboards, dots, tailpiece/bridge assemblies and a rounded pickguard assembly reminiscent of the old Gibson Ripper. The SB-201 had one split-coil pickup with volume and tone. The SB-202 had one split-coil and one single-coil pickups, two volumes and one tone, plus a phase switch. These were offered with fretless and (for two pickup models) stereo wiring options.

Briefly appearing in 1981 were the MB-801 and MB-802. These were the companions to the M-80 guitar, with a rounded equal double cutaway body. Little information is available, but the MB-801 had a single pickup, and the MB-802 had two! Since these were similar to the guitar, they probably had two-octave ebony 'boards with dot inlays. Finish options at the time were sunburst, cherry, black and walnut. These probably lasted only about a year.

In 1983 two models appeared briefly, the S-260 and S-26. While no information is available on these, their date and numbers suggest that they were enhancements of the S-250/25. Only 30 S-260s and two S-26s were built in '83.

1978 Guild M-75.

1976 Guild catalog.

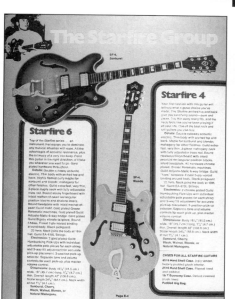

The Starfire Group

Starfire 6

Starfire 4

Starfire 2

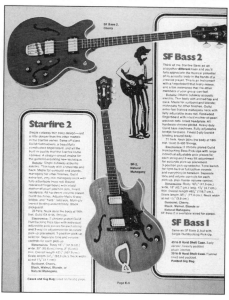

SF Bass 2

SF Bass 1

CASES FOR ALL STARFIRE GUITARS

Solid Bodies Solid Bodies Solid Bo

S-100 DeLuxe

Solid Body Guitars

S-100 Standard

Solid Body Guitars

S-90

S-50

Single Cutaway Solid Bodies

M-85-2 Bass

M-75CS Guitar

M-75GS

JS Solid Body Basses

JS Bass 2 LS

Long Scale

JS Bass 1 LS

JS Bass 2

JS Bass 1

Guild Electrics

Guild Catalog No. 7946

(Left to right, top to bottom) Mid-'77 ad for Guild's new S-300 "bell" guitar, "loaded with surprises." 1979 ad for the Guild S-300, their "most popular" guitar. Fall of '77 ad for the new Guild B-301 "bell" long-scale bass. 1978 ad for the Guild B-302 bass.

Guild's Dean

In contrast to the somewhat staid lines of the S-250/25s was 1981's X-82, basically a glued-neck copy of the Dean ML, a cross between an Explorer and a Flying V. This was initially nicknamed the Nova. This came with a unique new pointed three-and-three arrowhead headstock, a 24-fret ebony fingerboard, dots, a bound top, mahogany body and neck, chrome hardware, and a pair of the new XR-7 'buckers. These had the SP-6 stop tail and Adjusto-Matic finetune bridge. A threeway select was mounted on a little pickguard on the treble horn. Two volumes, one tone and either a phase or coil tap switch rounded out this baby. Fin-

ishes included sunburst, black, candy apple red, metallic blue, black sparkle and purple.

The X-82 was revamped somewhere between its advent in '81 and around 1983, when it appeared repackaged as the Starfighter. This was essentially the same except for the addition of an optional Kahler locking vibrato system and a change to a 24-fret rosewood or maple fingerboard, still with two open-coil DiMarzio-made humbuckers. By 1984 the X-82 had the new Guild pointy-droopy six-in-line headstock and a pair of EMG active pickups. The guitar shown in the circa 1984 catalog was finished in black with red binding around the top. A Floyd Rose vibrato system was offered as an option, as were unspecified custom color options. After '84 the Nova/ Starfighter X-82 got shot down, but it remains one of the cool guitars from this Guild era. About 460 of these various X-82s were built between '81 and 1984.

1979 Guild S-70D solidbody (courtesy New Hope Guitar Traders,

The X-factor

While the previous guitars were some-

what derivative, the '81 X-79 series was a dramatic departure, for once in a more attractive (versus Gumby) direction. The X-79 was a windswept double cutaway with a very extended upper horn and steeply sloped lower bout. These had glued necks with matching asymmetrical three-and-three headstocks, two-octave ebony fingerboards, dots, chrome hardware, two XR-7 humbuckers, stop tails, Adjusto-Matic bridges, two volumes and one tone, threeway, and optional coil tap or phase. A natty narrow pickguard ran along the lower edge.

By around 1982, at least, the X-79 had been joined by the X-79-3, which offered three single coil pickups instead of humbuckers, mounted on a larger pickguard. Finishes included white, sunburst, candy apple red, black, metallic blue, black sparkle, and purple. This was a well-balanced, lightweight guitar with a lot of punch combined with tonal flexibility. These guitars do not appear in later catalogs so probably were only around about a year.

In around 1983 the X-79 acquired the surname "Skylark." and was offered with

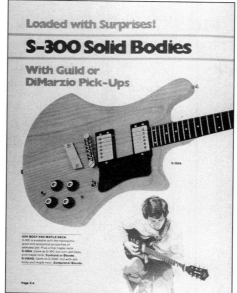

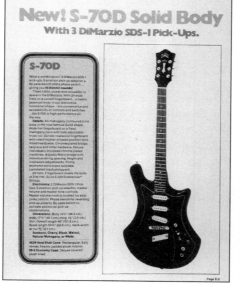

Ca. 1978 Guild brochure No. 8420-B.

either maple or mahogany neck options, rosewood or maple fingerboards and a top-mounted Kahler locking vibrato system.

The X-79 hung around until around 1985, although by the circa 1984 catalog it was no longer being actively promoted. Between 1981 and 1985 some 1,790 X-79s were made, making it one of the most popular of Guild's early '80s solidbodies.

Madeira redux

While the early '70s Madeira electrics quickly passed by the wayside, the brand was applied some more Japanese copy guitars in the early '80s, from late 1981

through around 1984 or so. A full accounting of these is not possible, but included were a number of near-copies (i.e., bolt-on necks) with the rounded crown headstock and some "original" designs, again with the rounded crown. One shown here is a bolt-neck version of a Gibson Les Paul Junior. It had electronics mounted on a circuit board, rather than the more typical hard wiring.

In January of '82 *Guitar Player* featured a news item on two Madeira guitars, the EG-250 and EG-330. These both had bolt-on three-piece necks, mahogany bodies with slightly offset double

cutaways, twin exposed-coil humbuckers, brass saddles, chrome hardware, 24-fret rosewood fingerboards, jumbo frets, and dot inlays. Both had two volume and two tone controls, threeway select, plus two coil-tap switches. The EG-250 had a plain mahogany top, whereas the EG-330 had a maple-laminate center, making it look like a neck-through. These have the same shape as a number of Electra, Westone, Westbury, and Vantage guitars of the era, all made by the legendary Matsumoku factory. Quite possibly, these were, too.

In around 1987 Guild switched to the

(Left to Right) Summer of '79 ad for Guild accessories, featuring a very nifty plexiglass S-300, presumably either a special promo guitar or one-off. Late '80 ad for the Guild S Series guitars.

502E bass, but it probably had a similar lifespan and limited production. References exist to an SB-501E bass from the same year, presumably a single pickup version, but no other information is available on that either.

Last but not least were the X-702 and X-701 basses with the windswept X-79 shape. The X-702 had a pair of single-coil pickups, two volumes and one tone, threeway on a large pickguard and a 22-fret dot neck. The X-701 had a single pickup. Colors were the same as the SB-200s. These held out a bit longer than the 200 series, making it until 1984, by which time some 235 units had been produced.

Burnside brand for its imports for a few years.

More Guild Fenders

By 1982 the Guild line had expanded a bit more on the base already established, as illustrated in a circa 1982 brochure. Still promoted were the M-80, X-82 Nova, X-79 series, S-250, S-25, SB-201 and SB-202. New was an upscale addition to the S-250/25 series, the S-275, and new basses including the semi-Fender-style SB-203 and active SB-502E, and the X-702 and X-701 in the dramatic X-79 styling.

Like the S-250/25, the S-275s were offset double cutaways with decided Strat inspiration, in terms of shape, with bound tops, plain or fancy maple caps, mahogany bodies, gold hardware, three-piece maple necks, two-octave ebony fingerboards with dots, Chesterfield crown heads, two XR-7 humbuckers, stop tails, finetune bridges, two volumes and one tone, and a choice of tap or phase. These were available in red sunburst and natural. While conservative designs, the S-275s were quite fetching. And quite rare. While the S-275 appeared in the 1982 catalog, only 110 were ever produced, and

those were in 1983.

Basswise, the SB-203 was an extension of the SB-200 line introduced a year earlier. The SB-203 — claimed to be an industry first — had the split-coil plus two single-coils, with one volume and one tone control, the pickups activated by three mini-toggles. The SB-502E was an active version with two volumes, bass EQ, treble EQ, phase switch, and a pre-amp on/off switch. Finish options included sunburst, white, black, candy apple red, metallic blue, black sparkle and purple.

The SB-203 bass lasted only a year until 1983. Only around 452 of the SB-201/202/203 basses were built. No information is available on quantities of the SB-

(Left to Right) Ca. 1982 Guild Madeira copy of a Gibson Les Paul Junior; note the rounded headstock shape (courtesy Sam D'Amico Music, Philadelphia, PA). Ca. 1982 Guild X-79 in candy apple red, with a stop tail and possible replacement neck pickup (courtesy Axe Factory/Guitars Wanted, Philadelphia, PA).

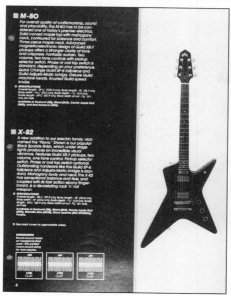

Ca. 1981 Guild brochure #8366.

(Left) July '82 ad for Guild solids, "when the thrill is gone…get it back" showing the X-79, S-275 guitars and SB-202 bass (Guild Guitars). *(Right)* Late '83 ad for Guild's new X-82.

A number of mystery guitars appear in a number of sources during this period. In 1983, Guild announced a new line of bolt-neck guitars — its first — about which nothing is known except they came with either a Guild or Kahler vibrato. These were the X-84V, X-97V and X-108V.

Fear of flying

Not quite as mysterious from 1983 were what would become two stalwarts of the Guild line, the S-280 Flyer guitar and the SB-600 series Pilot basses, plus some more wrinkles on the sweptwing shapes.

The Flyer was one of Guild's first documented bolt-neck guitars, entering production in 1983. This would basically prove to be Guild's answer to the increasingly popular guitars by Kramer and, later, Jackson/Charvel. Actually, there is some

confusion about both the numerical and name designations of this model. During the next few years it would not be uncommon for Guild to change the model name in subsequent years, although usually the numerical designation would remain con-

stant, with some minor discrepancies.

The initial Flyer S-280 was a bolt-neck offset double cutaway Strat-style guitar. It had a pair of humbucking pickups, possibly called "Pacific" humbuckers, in any case with open-coils. The headstock shape was the new blade-shaped modified Strat-style six-in-line headstock. These came, as did all '83 Guild electrics, with the option of a maple fingerboard with black dot inlays, or a rosewood fingerboard with pearl dot. Necks could be either maple or mahogany. The Flyer had a Kahler locking vibrato system. This had a contoured body, threeway select, one volume and one tone control. A hardtail may have been an option. Finishes were black, black sparkle, candy apple red, and pearl white, plus custom colors and graphic options.

In the circa 1984 catalog, the Flyer was shown as the S-270, sporting the blade head, 22 frets, a single EMG pickup and a Kahler locking vibrato system. Other

(Left) 1985 ad for Madeira by Guild electrics. *(Right)* Summer of '83 ad for the Guild M-80 solidbodies.

sources, however, identify the S-270 as a model called the Runaway, with a single EMG and a Kahler, a description that sounds like the '84 Flyer. In the ca. 1986 catalog, alas, the S-270 had become the Sprint, although, just to keep us thoroughly confused, elsewhere the Sprint is listed as being the S-271. Got that? The S-270 Sprint was available with either one or two EMG pickups and a Kahler.

By circa 1986, the Flyer was nominated the S-281. By now the Flyer had a bolt-on maple neck (hard or curly), either a poplar or flamed maple body, a 22-fret rosewood fingerboard with dots, a pointy droopy headstock and a pair of humbucking pickups, possibly called "California" pickups. The S-281 had a Kahler locking vibrato system and one volume and one tone with threeway select.

As we shall soon see, Guild entered on a bumpy business ride beginning in around 1986, when it was sold by Avnet, and this may account for some of this confusion regarding the Flyer. The Flyer was gone by 1987. It's not known exactly how many were made.

The Flyer body shape made it probably at least until 1987, by which time it had acquired the name Thunderbolt, with one

(Left) Summer of '84 ad for Guild "Flying Star" guitar and bass, endorsed by Mötley Crüe. (Right) 1984 Guild Brian May BHM-1, the first version of the Queen guitarist's classic axe ('94 version of the Signature or Pro behind it).

DiMarzio humbucker and two single-coils on a fiveway switch with coil tap, a Mueller vibrato, Sperzel Tremlock locking tuners and black hardware. From its debut in '83 through 1987 or so, at least 1,493 (and un-doubtedly a few more) of the S-280/281 were made, making it one of Guild's more popular solids.

Lighting the Pilot

Also debuting in 1983 was the popular Pilot bass. This was an offset double cutaway solid, like so many basses of the era, an extended exaggeration of the Fender bass inspiration. It had a bolt-on maple neck with the new blade-style four-in-line head and a 22-fret fingerboard with dot inlays. The SB-600 had a poplar body and a pair of DiMarzio pickups. The SB-601 had a single pickup, by '84 at least, an EMG. The SB-602 had a pair of EMG pickups in the P and J configuration, either a maple fingerboard with black dots or rosewood 'board with pearl dots. In '83, at least, the SB-602 came with a short 25 1/2" scale and 20 frets. By the ca. '84 catalog the Pilot SB-602 had a flamed maple body, black hardware plus a wonderful Kahler bass vibrato system. No descriptions of the SB-603 are available, but this probably had three pickups, like other basses ending in a "3." An SB-604 was briefly made for one year or slightly longer, with an offset pointy

(Left) Early '84 ad for the "hot" Guild X-82 solidbody. (Right) 1984 Guild X-79 Skylark, another original that proved relatively successful, as Guild solids go.

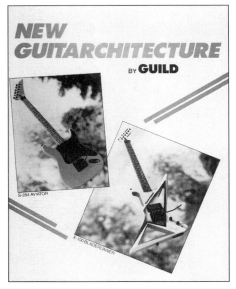
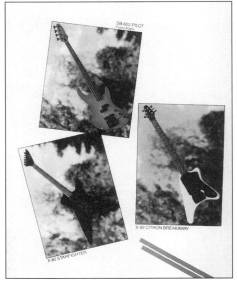

Ca. 1984 brochure for Guild's "new guitarchitecture."

droopy headstock design and EMG pick-ups; the model was still listed in the 1986 catalog. Most, if not all, of these were available in fretless options.

In 1986, the Pilot line was also joined by the SB-605, a five-string variation with a maple neck and body, EMG pickups, and rosewood fingerboard.

In 1987, just before the Fall, two more Pilots debuted, the SB-902 Advanced and SB-905 Advanced. These had flamed maple bodies, maple necks, 22-fret ebony fingerboards, fancy inlays and Bartolini P and J pickups connected to a Bartolini TCT preamp. The SB-905 was a five-string.

Complete quantities of all these Pilots is not known, but there were at least 1,726 of the SB-600/602/603s, about 616 of SB-604, and at least 177 of the SB-605, all through 1986.

By 1990 the Pilot bass was still being offered as the SB-602, SB-602M with maple body, SB-605 five-string (apparently with different timber), and the SB-605M with a maple body.

The Guild Pilot bass was the only solidbody bass to make it through the hard times, and it was still being offered in 1996, after the Fender acquisition.

Bass flying

Also in around 1983 an SB-280 Flyer bass was alluded to in Guild literature. Little is known of this beast but it probably had the Strat-style body with optional maple or mahogany neck, optional 22-fret maple or rosewood fingerboard and a $25^5/_8$" scale.

Reversing the trend

In 1983 another weird-shaped guitar made a brief appearance, a sort of "reverse" X-79 Skylark known as the X-80 Skyhawk. This had a short upper horn, extended lower horn and Explorer-style bottom angle. It had a pair of DiMarzio-made 'buckers, reverse X-79-style three-and-three head, two-octave maple fingerboard with black dots (rosewood optional), finetune bridge, stoptail, threeway, volume and tone. This, too, was available in black, black sparkle, candy apple red, pearl white, and in custom colors and with graphics. This guitar probably lasted only one year, because it was not in the catalog by '84.

Full flower

If you had to point to one most exciting year of Guild solids it would probably be the 1984 season. It was in '84 that a bunch of cool new guitars made their bows, how-

(Left) 1985 Guild Brian May BHM-1 #BHM00241 in blue with a flamed maple top and Kahler vibrato (photo: Ron Thorn). (Right) 1985 Guild X-88D Star guitar equipped with DiMarzios (courtesy Cintioli Music, Philadelphia, PA).

ever briefly. Included in the circa '84 catalog were the previous S-270 Flyer (the one-pickup version), the SB-602 Pilot bass, and X-82 Starfighter, already discussed. New were the S-284 Aviator, X-100 Bladerunner, X-88 Crue Flying Star, and X-92 Citron Breakaway. While this is a discourse on solidbody electrics, it should be noted that the F-44 Gruhn Model acoustic also appeared in 1984, along with the FS-48 Deceiver acoustic-electric (single cutaway, maple 'board, pointy droopy head, with piezo pickup and a *hidden humbucker* between the soundhole and bridge!). And these are only what was in the catalog...

Aviation

The S-284 Aviator was perhaps the least interesting of the new models to debut in '84. It was essentially a glued-neck Superstrat, with a Stratish-looking body but with equal double cutaways, pointy droopy headstock 22-fret rosewood fingerboard, dots, three EMG pickups in a humbucker/single/single arrangement, fiveway select, volume, tone and locking Kahler vibrato

system. The pickups and controls all mounted on a virtual copy of a Strat pickguard. The jack even sat on the top like a Strat.

Some sources also make reference to another early S-284 known as the Starling, with a humbucker and two single-coils. No other information is known about these birds, including exactly when, how long or how many were made.

Apparently, the EMG pickups did not prove to be universally popular. Guitar players have more generally preferred the loud, raucous — and somewhat noisy — hot output of passive pickups to the cleaner sound of active units. In any case, early on in the Aviator series the EMGs were changed out for some experimental DiMarzios which were designed for Leslie West, and shortly thereafter some were outfitted with Kent Armstrong (son of the legendary Dan Armstrong) pickups. The Aviator illustrated here was originally made for the EMGs but the battery cavity was never used and the DiMarzio "Leslie West" pickups were factory original. This means that if you find a guitar that was carved for an active system but is set up with passives, it may be original.

By 1986 the S-284 Aviator had changed slightly. Gone was the pickguard and the jack had moved to the side. Now the bodies could be of poplar or flamed maple, and necks of hard maple or flamed maple. The fingerboard had become ebony. Two pickup

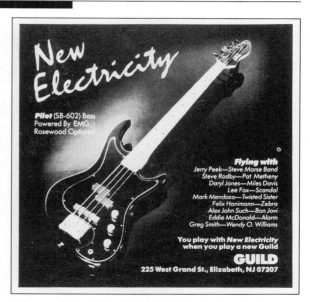

Winter of '84 ad for the new Guild Pilot SB-602 bass.

layouts were available, the usual humbucker/single/single with coil tap, or three single-coils with an optional "fat control."

For basically one year in '86, a deluxe Aviator S-285 was also now available, with a bound ebony fingerboard and headstock and fancy sunrise inlays. This had a Kahler vibrato system and EMG pickups in a humbucker/single/single arrangement. A second version with DiMarzios was also offered. Gruhn's *Guide* lists 19 of these as being built in 1986.

The Aviator made it into 1987 before biting the dust. In '87 the Aviator was offered only in poplar, still with an ebony fingerboard, Kahler fulcrum vibrato, humbucker/single/single DiMarzios (optional EMGs) with fiveway, volume and tone controls, and black hardware. At least 637, and undoubtedly a few more, of the S-284s were made. Gruhn lists only 19 S-285s from '86, definitely a guitar to keep on the lookout for.

Sci-Fi

Cooler by far, however, was the 1984 X-100 Bladerunner. This is a very curious guitar with a strange pedigree. It was originally invented by individual luthier David Andrews of David Andrews Guitar Research and ballyhooed in the guitar press. Andrews sold — or, based on subsequent developments, more probably licensed — his design to Guild, which then introduced

(Left) 1985 Guild S-284 Aviator, a glued-neck Superstrat. (Right) 1984-85 Guild X-100 Bladerunner, one of 95 made based on a design of luthier David Andrews (photo: Cameron MacLean).

(Left) all of '85 ad for the new Guild Aviator endorsed by Bobby Messano. (Right) "Would you play this guitar for 20 years?" asks a late 1985 ad for the first Guild Brian May Signature guitar, available in red, black, aqua and flamed maple.

the X-100 Bladerunner.

The X-100 Bladerunner was basically an X-shaped poplar guitar with the lower legs connected by a wooden span, with the whole body cut from a single piece of wood. The space between the lower legs was then cut out, as were holes in each of the upper horns. This had a glued-in poplar neck with a droopy pointy headstock, also with a cutout under the tuners. The fingerboard was 22-fret ebony inlaid with what were called "Mercedes stars." This had a single EMG 81 humbucker with a coil tap mini-toggle and what was called a "fat control." It was outfitted with a Kahler vibrato, and sported a very fancy multicolor paint job.

Basically, this was designed to be a nifty looking, very lightweight guitar capable of extended sustain. According to Guild literature, the first example of these was presented to Eddy Ojeda, then guitarist for Twisted Sister.

The distinctive X-100 Bladerunner actually stayed in the Guild line into the 1986 catalog, however, production records indicate that they were only made through 1985 and that only 95 (four prototypes and 91 production models) were ever made. This guitar eventually became the foundation of the Schecter Genesis line, being the first Genesis model in 1986, where it finally evolved to eliminate the cutout on the headstock and sport a bolt-on neck, but remained otherwise pretty much similar.

Some published sourses also list an SB-666 Bladerunner Bass which was offered from 1984-85, too. This apparently had a pair of EMG pickups and possibly a Kahler bass vibrato. Nothing else is known of this strange beast.

(Left) Early 1985 ad for the Guild Skyhawk X-79 and Pilot bass endorsed by Twisted Sister's Jay-Jay French and Mark 'The Animal' Mendoza. (Right) 1985 Guild Nightbird GG #BC100266 designed with George Gruhn (courtesy Ron Thorn; photo: Kelsey Edwards).

Ca. 1986 Guild brochure.

Catch a falling star

The 1984 X-88 Crue Flying Star was basically a more angularized version of the X-82 Starfighter. The "Crue" model shown in the catalog has a fancy paint job and may include a reference to the heavy metal band Motley Crue. In any case, this model is more generally known as the plain Flying Star, or, often just the Star guitar. The rounded points of the X-82 had become very pointed. The two-octave fingerboard had natty star-shaped inlays. Neck was bolt-on. The head was the new droopy pointy variety. The Flying Star had a single EMG pickup, one volume control, and a Kahler locking vibrato system.

Some design changes apparently took place subsequent to the '84 introduction of the X-88. By 1985 the model had bifurcated into two models, the X-88 and X-88D. Both now had an enlarged "spade" three-and-three headstock and DiMarzio pickups. The X-88 was basically the same as before except for the passive pickup, whereas the X-88D had two humbuckers and a Schaller bridge/tailpiece assembly. X-88s were built for only one year, in 1985, with some 457 being produced.

A companion SB-608 Flying Star Bass was also made, although it was not in the catalog. This came in two versions, a regular version SB-608 (probably two pickups) and the SB-608E with two EMG pickups. About 116 of these were made before the

model died in 1985.

Breakaway

The X-92 was an especially nifty little guitar. Designed by luthier Harvey Citron (of Veillette-Citron guitars), the X-92 was a full-scale guitar with a small quasi-V body from which the top wing detached by pressing a button so it would be easy to travel with. The body, actually not unlike a Randy Rhoads shape, had a little waist built in to the bottom to facilitate resting it on your knee. The maple neck was glued in. It had a V-shaped three-and-three headstock, 22-fret rosewood 'board, pearl dots, three EMG single coils on a black pickguard, fiveway select, one volume and active presence control with midrange boost, and optional Kahler vibrato. This is a very neat piece, a

member of the "travel guitar" category, which was becoming popular at this time. Compare it to Mark Erlewine's Chiquita, marketed at the time by Hondo. The X-92 was apparently relatively well received, since 637 were made before the model was retired in 1986.

Queen the First

Not in the '84 catalog was perhaps the best known of all Guild's solidbody endeavors, the Brian May BHM1. The Brian May was an official copy of the Queen guitarist's own guitar, the "Red Special," a double cutaway with three DiMarzio Brian May Signature humbuckers (modeled after the original Burns Tri-Sonics), a Kahler vibrato, and six mini-toggles which yielded up to seventeen different tonal variations. These

(Left) Early '86 ad for the Guild Liberator and Guild Detonator, endorsed by Earl Slick and Kevin Russell, both with David Bowie. (Right) Spring of '86 ad for the new Guild Nightbird, endorsed by Arlen Roth.

could have bound mahogany or flamed maple tops, solid mahogany bodies and necks, ebony 'boards, and dot inlays. These came with an outboard Power Booster, essentially a pre-amp, the size of a small pedal, with gain and intensity controls plus a footswitch.

The Guild was not the first May copy; it had been done several years earlier by the Fresher company in Japan, although it's unknown whether or not those had May's blessing or were sold anywhere other than in Japan.

The first edition of the Brian May guitar was not especially well received by players and eventually went the way of all flesh in 1986. Between 1984 and 1986, only some 316 of these guitars were made. Today, these have become highly sought by collectors. Guild would return to the May guitar later in the '90s.

One other guitar shows up in the Guild records, the S-282. No information is available on this,

except that it is probably related to the Aviators. Only 47 of these were made in 1984.

Exeunt Avnet

Most of the '84 line continued into '85, though development seemed to grind to a halt. It was probably a sign of impending separation. In 1986, Avnet sold Guild to a group of investors called the Guild Musical Instrument Corporation.

The 1986 solidbody line marked a consolidation and a retreat from the exotic shapes of the previous offerings. Still in the line was the trusty bolt-neck Flyer S-281, now in the fancier version as already discussed, and the new Pilot SB-605 bass. Also in the line was the S-270, the single pickup version, now called the Sprint (a.k.a. Flyer, a.k.a. Runaway), with one EMG pickup and a Kahler vibrato, basically competition for Kramer's Beretta. New in the '86 catalog were the T-200 Roy Buchanan, the solidbody Bluesbird and the semi-hollow Nightbird.

Roy Buchanan

The T-200 Roy Buchanan was basically a Telecaster copy designed in conjunction with that great Tele master. It was basically a Tele with two EMG single-coil pickups, a poplar body, maple bolt-on neck, the pointy droopy

(Left)Summer of '86 ad for the Guild Pilot bass and Guild/Hartke speakers endorsed by Jaco Pastorius. (right) Early '86 ad for Guild Pilot basses and Guild/Hartke speaker cabinets, endorsed by Gary Tallent (E Street Band), Will Lee (David Letterman Show), Daryl Jones (Sting).

headstock, 22-fret rosewood fingerboard, dots, and a solid, hand-machined brass bridge. No production numbers are available on these, but expect them to be especially rare. This was available for about a year.

Singing the blues

The Bluesbird was a resurrection of the old hollowbody of the late '50s, basically a single-cutaway Les Paul sort of guitar. This version was made of solid poplar or flamed maple and was designed in conjunction with Rockabilly ace Brian Setzer, entering production in 1985. The Bluesbird had a glued-in maple neck, the blade-style headstock, a 22-fret ebony fingerboard and three-piece pearl inlays, basically rectangular blocks with a center-notched abalone V. These had no pickguard, either three EMG single-coil pickups or a humbucker (with coil tap) and two singles, a fiveway select, volume and tone, and a Kahler vibrato system.

The Bluesbird was shown on the cover of the May 1986 *Guitar for the Practicing Musician* magazine touted by Aerosmith much as before but with two EMG humbuckers, a threeway and volume, tone, and top-mounted Kahler.

The Bluesbird was listed in the *Guitar*

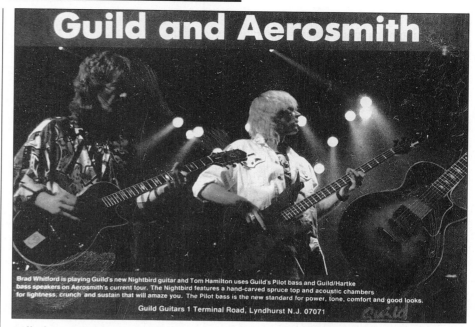

Fall of '86 ad for the Guild Nightbird, Guild Pilot bass and Guild/Hartke speakers, endorsed by Aerosmith's Brad Whitford and Tom Hamilton.

World 1987-88 Guitar Buyer's Guide, though by this time it had dropped the EMGs in favor of DiMarzio pickups.

The Bluesbird does not reappear in the *Guitar World 1988-89 Guitar Buyer's Guide*, so it probably went the way of all flesh in 1987, although some examples may have been produced into 1988 when things finally collapsed. How many Bluesbirds were actually produced is unknown, but by the end of 1986 only 215 or so had been made.

Into the night

While this is a discussion of Guild

December 1986 ad for Kahler vibratos showing on the right showing Steve "Plunk" Plunkett of Autograph playing a Guild Bladerunner (copyright American Precision Metal Works). May '86 cover of Guitar for the Practicing Musician magazine with Aerosmith sporting a Guild Bluesbird with two EMG humbuckers (© Cherry Lane Music). 1986 T-200 Roy Buchanan (photo: Akbar Anwari).

(Left) Early '87 ad for the Guild T-250 "Tele" endorsed by Joe Perry of Aerosmith. (Right) 1987 Guild Nightbird, a hollowbody descendent of the old M-75, one of the earliest made with Seymour Duncan pickups (courtesy Akbar Anwari; photo: Mary Bush, Photography By Mary, Branford, CT).

*solid*bodies, we can't help but mention the luxurious Nightbird, a single cutaway semi-hollowbody which also appeared in 1985. This guitar was designed in conjunction with vintage guitar guru George Gruhn, who earlier had worked with Guild to produce an acoustic model. The initial offering of the Les-Paul-shaped Nightbird had a mahogany body with a U-shaped acoustic chamber, blocks under the pickups to cut down on feedback, and a bound, carved Sitka spruce top. The glued-in mahogany neck culminated in a Guild three-and-three headstock, inlaid with the Guild chevron. The bound 22-fret ebony fingerboard had diamond inlays. These had stop tails, finetune bridges, a little elevated pickguard, threeway, one volume and one tone control, and either EMG or English-made Kent Armstrong pickups with coil taps. The initial offering came in a black finish with black hardware. Visually these are quite, quite stunning guitars.

By 1987 the Nightbird was being offered in two versions, the Nightbird I and II. The Nightbird II was basically the earlier Nightbird except that hardware had become

gold, and it came with slotted diamond inlays, and two EMG 60 humbuckers with coil tap and phase switch. The Nightbird I was a slightly less expensive version with a spruce top, rosewood fingerboard, two DiMarzio pickups, coil tap, phase switch and chrome hardware.

By the June of '88 Guild Price List the

Nightbird I was gone, replaced by the Nightbird Series. This included the Nightbird II with twin EMG humbuckers. Also new in '88 was the Nightingale, a semi-hollow body with carved spruce top, f-holes, mahogany body, pearl logo, and 2 EMG humbuckers. Joining these two were the Songbird I and Songbird Custom. The Songbird I was a hollow body with spruce top, round soundhole, x-bracing, multiple bindings, and a transducer pickup system with a preamp. The Songbird Custom was similar to the Songbird I but with gold hardware and custom color tops in either white, black, or black with red top.

The Nightbird returns in the *Guitar World 1989-90 Guitar Buyer's Guide*. Gone are the I and II denominations, and the Nightbird now came with EMG active pickups. The diamond inlays were now slotted. Still listed were the Nightingale and Songbird I.

The 1990 Guild catalog lists three Nightbirds, the Custom, the DeLuxe, and the Standard. The Custom is basically the same guitar listed in the *Buyer's Guide*. It was semi-hollow with a carved curly maple top and a mahogany body. The Nightbird DeLuxe was now a solidbody of carved poplar, rosewood 'board with dots, twin humbuckers (not EMG), standard stop-tail electronics, black hardware. The Nightbird Standard was another solidbody of solid poplar, but not carved, with twin 'buckers, rosewood 'board, dots, black hardware and

New Electric Guitars from Guild.

All featuring active pickup systems and Guild's exclusive Floyd-Rose licensed tremelo

Detonator II

Liberator II

Liberator Elite

1987 flyer with Guild Detonator II, Liberator II, and Liberator Elite.

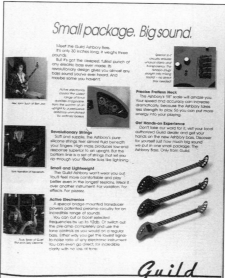

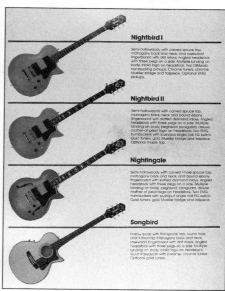
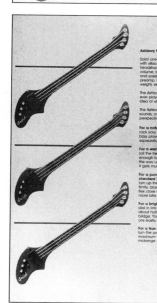

July 1987 2-page ad for the Guild Ashbory Bass endorsed by Alec John Such of Bon Jovi, Tom Hamilton of Aerosmith, and Rudy Szarzo of Quiet Riot (copyright Guild Guitars).

(Left to Right) Ca. 1987 Burnside by Guild Tele, with glued-in neck and "Superstrat" pickup layout (courtesy Society Hill Loan, Philadelphia, PA). Ca. 1987 Burnside by Guild Tele, with bolt-on neck-FOUR-PICKUP layout (courtesy Society Hill Loan, Philadelphia, PA). 1988 Guild Liberator Elite, with the mahogany body and flamed maple top (courtesy Cintioli's Music, Philadelphia, PA).

standard electronics. How long these were made is uncertain, but after this reference, the Nightbird flies off into the dark evening sky. Gruhn lists some 324 as having been made in '85 and '86; post-'86 production numbers are unknown.

Guild Teles

Guild continued to introduce some other interesting guitars not in the catalog in '86. One was the companion to the T-200 Roy Buchanan, the T-250 Telecaster copy, which debuted in 1986. This was very similar to the T-200, with a poplar body, maple bolt-on neck, rosewood fingerboard, dot inlays, a pair of EMG pickups, brass hardware and the droopy pointy headstock.

The Guild T-250 was offered again in 1987, this time with both the pointy droopy headstock and a "new Guild headstock." The pickups had been changed to DiMarzios, with optional EMG pickups and gold hardware. These were gone by 1988.

Minimalism

Another instrument that debuted in 1986 was the novel Ashbory bass. This was a fascinating minimalist short-scale bass looking not unlike the Fernandez Elephant. The poplar body was tiny, with a small reverse fan-shaped headstock with Schaller banjo-style tuners. The body and head were flipped-over images of each other. The total length was $29^1/2$ inch, with an 18 inch scale which was consciously designed to allow wider intervals than normal on a long-scale bass. What really made this nifty, however, was that the strings were made of silicon, very floppy, and rode over a bound fretless fingerboard. The bridge was a molded plastic affair with a piezo pickup built in. This had a volume, bass and treble active tone circuitry with an on/off switch allowing active or passive modes (LED indicates active mode). There was no truss rod on this guitar. These were apparently available from '86 through

to the end in '88. Only 23 were made in 1986. although in an '88 review in *Guitar Player* George Gruhn, speaking for Guild, says that more than 1,000 units had been shipped with back orders waiting for these strange birds. If you were looking for a Guild bass, this would be the one to check out!

Burnsides

In 1987 and 1988, by the way, Guild marketed imported solidbody electrics under the Burnside label, usually reading "Burnside by Guild." These were conservatively designed shapes, often with fanciful names such as "The Lance" (a Flying V). Many featured glued-in necks. The typical headstock was a very large triangular six-in-line shape, very angular, and not the most attractive. Most Burnsides were probably made in Japan, though it's impossible to rule out Korean origins; the feel is definitely Japanese. Often they had figured tops, ebonol fingerboards, locking vibratos and EMG Select pickups. Little information is available on these guitars, but they included, at least, the EG-53 (maple neck, Supermaxx humbucker and two single-coils, vibrato), the FE-1 (two EMG Select humbuckers, coil tap,

1988 Marshall amplifier ad featuring a Guild Bluesbird.

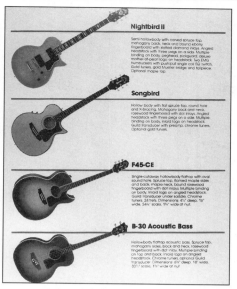

Guild electrics entering hiatus from the 1988 catalog [copyright Guild Guitars].

Accutune vibrato), the GE-27 (single cutaway, two EMG Select humbuckers), the HA-1 (offset headstock, one EMG Select humbucker, vibrato) and the SO-1 (EMG Select humbucker and two single-coils, Accutune vibrato). Two basses included the BB-111 (offset headstock, P/J pickup configuration) and the EB-151 (P/J pickup arrangement). Most are fairly handsome and well-built.

The two Telecaster variations shown here

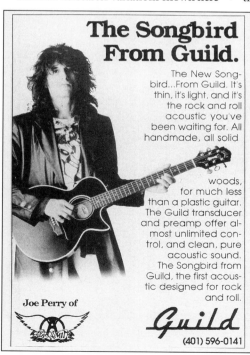

1988 ad for a Guild Songbird acoustic-electric, endorsed by Joe Perry of Aerosmith.

include a glued-neck guitar with h/s/s and a bolt-neck version with h/s/s/h pickup configuration. This later could possibly feature a later pickup alteration, but all signs suggest that it's original.

Detonation

After almost a quarter of a decade, an unbroken stream of solidbody electric guitars began to come to an end in 1987 with the introduction of the Detonator model.

The Detonator was a very conventional bolt-neck Strat-style with active EMG pickups (humbucker, single, single) and Floyd Rose vibrato. This had a poplar body, a new, straighter pointed six-in-line headstock, maple neck, a 22-fret rosewood fingerboard, dot inlays and black hardware. As usual, very well made, but quite undistinguished.

Going into 1988, the Detonator was offered in two versions. The plain Detonator now featured a Guild/Mueller vibrato system and DiMarzio pickups, whereas the Detonator II was the same as the original Detonator. By June of '88 the new Detonator was gone and only the Detonator II was in the price list. All were short-lived, as we shall see.

These Detonators were pretty good guitars, by the way. They really suffered most from appearing late in the

Superstrat craze and faced so much competition they were just too "me, too." They are, however, very nice American made guitars and represent an excellent value for the genre.

Liberation

Going out in a blaze of glory, in 1988 Guild introduced its gorgeous Liberator model. This was an offset double cutaway with a glued-in mahogany neck, the straight pointed six-in-line head, two octave fingerboard and the popular humbucker/single/single pickup configuration. Basically, the Liberator came in three models. At the bottom was the plain Liberator, with a poplar body, the Guild/Mueller non-locking vibrato system and DiMarzio pickups. By

MADEIRA®
Solid Body Electric Guitars and Basses
from Guild

(Left) Ca. 1990 flyer for Guild Madeira "copies." (Right) 1992 Guild Brian May prototype #BM20002 combining features of the '80s version and the '90s version (photo: Ron Thorn).

June of '88 these had disappeared from Guild price lists

Up a step was the Liberator II, another poplar guitar which featured a "seamless neck/body joint," EMG pickups controlled by three mini-toggles, a Floyd Rose licensed locking vibrato, and fancy rising sun inlays.

At the top was the Liberator Elite, a beautiful guitar with a flamed maple top over a mahogany body, a bound ebony fingerboard with the rising sun inlays, a rosewood faced headstock, gold hardware, Floyd Rose, active Bartolini pickups with an onboard boost, volume, tone, and three threeway minitoggles which let you coax an enormous variety of in- and out-of-phase tones from the beast. These came in Amberburst, Cherry Sunburst, and Transparent Charcoal.

Chapter 11

Guild had been owned by Avnet from the '60s until 1986, when it was sold to a group of investors led by Chattanooga investment banker Jere Haskew. Until 1988 vintage guitar dealer George Gruhn was part of the group, serving as vice president of product development and artist relations.

Alas, in 1988, the Guild Music Corpora-

tion defaulted on some bank notes and went into Chapter 11 bankruptcy. In 1989, Guild was purchased by the Faas Corporation of New Berlin, Wisconsin, later called U.S. Mu-

sical Corporation, owners of Randall amplifiers. Clearly, as quantities suggest, Guild had never scored big with its solidbody electrics, and, given the financial difficulties, solidbodies went into hiatus, while the company refocused on its real strengths. The production of fine flattop acoustics and archtop electrics at the Westerly facility continued, but not of solidbodies.

Madeira revisited (again)

While the new owners did not immediately continue U.S. production of solidbodies, it did revive the Madeira name in around 1990 or so with a series of imported electric and acoustic guitars. There were four basic electric models based on popular guitar designs.

The ME-500 "Traditional Style" was a two-pickup Les Paul Custom copy with bound rosewood fingerboards, block inlays, finetune bridge and stoptail. Pickups were two EMG Select humbuckers. These had a clever three-and-three headstock that was shaped like the multiple-humped Guild head, but the humps were painted white, while the face was black, with a Gibson top shape without the center dip. These had the

(Left to Right) 1993 Guild Brian May Signature #ME00019 intended for export (courtesy Ron Thorn; photo: Kelsey Edwards). 1994 Guild Brian May Special #BHM30082 in dark green (courtesy Ron Thorn; photo: Kelsey Edwards). 1994 Guild Brian May Standard #BHP00030 in turquoise (courtesy Ron Thorn; photo: Kelsey Edwards).

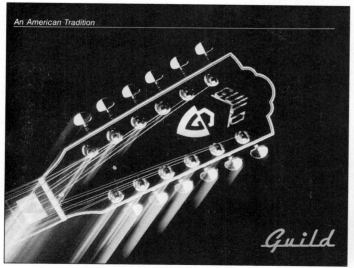

GX Series

A new direction by Guild designers . . . the GX Series with the solid body electric guitar player in mind. Feels and plays like a solid body, but sounds like an acoustic electric guitar. Perfect for the guitar player that doesn't want to change the feel from one guitar to the next. It is light weight and perfectly balanced.

Guild Active Acoustic Pick-Ups

All Guild acoustic electric guitars use a Fishman transducer and active pre-amp specifically designed for Guild. With sustained quality and deep booming bass response.

the pick-ups used, have a hi-fi E.Q. Bass and Treble and have fully separated active controls at 1 K.C. The treble control is plus or minus 12Db. The bass control is plus or minus 7.5 Db.

GX Specifications
Hollow body, spruce top, round hole. X-bracing. Bolt-on maple electric neck. Guild Deluxe Transducer with active pre-amp. A routed one piece mahogany side and back. Scale 25-5/8", nut width 1-5/8". Available in Black, White, Candy Apple Red and Electric Blue. Deluxe hard case available #42P.

The Guild 5 String Bass
Preferred by professional bass players like, Kevin O'Neal (Tracy Chapman), Glen Browne (Ziggy Marley Band).

Pilot Bass 605M
Solid maple body. Same features as 605. Available in: Amberburst, Cherryburst, Blueburst and Transparent Charcoal

Pilot Bass-605
5-string Pilot, for high C or low B string. Features a wider neck and bridge and two EMG pick-ups, one tone and two volume controls. Black hardware, Mueller bridge, scale 34", nut width 1-1/2". Options: Fretless fingerboard, maple body. Black, White, Candy Apple and Electric Blue. Pilot deluxe case available #4529B.

Kevin O'Neal (Tracy Chapman)
"Comfortable neck, smooth action, hot sound. Great contour, streamlined design, feels comfortable. With the low B string, I am able to get to the bottom of the music—places where only keyboard players dare to tread.
If finding a direction in music and expressing it to others is your goal, the Guild Pilot five string is my compass and steering wheel."

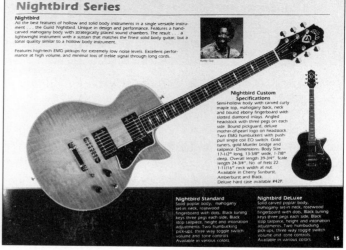

Nightbird Series

Nightbird
All the best features of hollow and solid body instruments in a single versatile instrument . . . the Guild Nightbird. Unique in design and performance. Features a hand-carved mahogany body with strategically placed sound chambers. The result . . . a lightweight instrument with a sustain that matches the finest solid body guitar, but a tonal quality similar to a hollow body instrument.

Features high-tech EMG pickups for extremely low noise levels. Excellent performance at high volume, and minimal loss of treble signal through long cords.

Nightbird Custom Specifications
Semi-hollow body with carved curly maple top, mahogany back, neck and bound ebony fingerboard with slotted diamond inlays. Angled headstock with three pegs on each side. Bound pickguard, deluxe mother-of-pearl logo on headstock. Two EMG humbuckers with push-pull single coil EQ switch. Gold tuners, gold Mueller bridge and tailpiece. Dimensions: Body Size 17-1/2" long, 13-3/8" wide, 1-7/8" deep. Overall length 39-3/4". Scale length 24-3/4". No. of frets 22. 1-11/16" neck width at nut. Available in Cherry Sunburst, Amberburst and Black. Deluxe hard case available #42P.

Nightbird Standard
Solid poplar body, mahogany set-in neck, rosewood fingerboard with dots. Black tuning keys three pegs each side, Black stop tailpiece, height and intonation adjustments. One humbucking pick-up, three way toggle switch volume and tone controls. Available in various colors.

Nightbird DeLuxe
Solid carved poplar body, mahogany set-in neck, rosewood fingerboard with dots, Black tuning keys three pegs each side, Black stop tailpiece, height and intonation adjustments. Two humbucking pick-ups, three way toggle switch volume and tone controls. Available in various colors.

1990 Guild catalog, "an American tradition."

Pilot Bass Series

The perfect electric bass . . . sleek with lines and a shape that accents your individuality. Comfortable enough to play all night long, and the kind of sound and punch that means mountains.

Perfectly balanced and lighter than most electric basses, the Pilot's smooth, clean lines make it seem like an extension of your body. Features the best neck in the business . . . a satiny smooth, specially-shaped neck that lets you reach 22 frets and burn through tough licks like lightning. No matter what your playing style, the Pilot delivers the fullest sound you can imagine.

The Pilot is also available as a fretless model. Like all Guild instruments, the Pilot is handcrafted by skilled artisans using only the finest materials available. The Pilot has become one of the best selling new basses in years. Find out why . . . buy one for yourself! The Pilot bass—only from Guild.

Greg Rzab

Pilot Bass 602M
Solid maple body. Same features as 602. Available in: Amberburst, Cherryburst, Blueburst and Transparent Charcoal

Pilot Bass-602
Solid poplar body, bolt-on maple neck, rosewood fingerboard with dot inlays. Two EMG pick-ups, one tone and two volume controls. Black hardware, Mueller bridge. Scale 34", nut width 1-1/2". Options: Fretless fingerboard, maple body. Black, White, Candy Apple and Electric Blue. Pilot deluxe case available #4529B.

old Chesterfield inlay. Finish options were black, white, antique sunburst and wine red.

The ME-300 "Rock/Metal Style" was a Superstrat with a Strat-style body, no pickguard, unbound rosewood 'board, dots, the old Burnside droopy pointy six-in-line headstock, humbucker/single/single EMG Select pickup arrangement, fiveway select, traditional vibrato, and side-mounted jack. Colors were black, red and white.

The ME-200 "Traditional Style" was a Strat copy, with three single-coil pickups on a pickguard, maple fingerboard, black dots, traditional vibrato, and top-mounted jack. The ME-200 had the droopy pointy head. Available in black, white and candy apple red.

The MBE-100 "Traditional Style" was essentially a Fender-style bass with one split coil and one single-coil EMG Select pickup, and the droopy pointy head, available in black, white and red.

These were still listed in the January 1991 price list, but disappear soon thereafter.

Revival

The early '90s saw a resurgence of interest in Guild solidbodies primarily due, ironically, to the success of the so-called grunge rock movement centered in Seattle. Grunge rockers were notorious for eschewing mainstream rock guitars like Strats, Teles and Les Pauls in favor of unloved — though not necessarily inferior — models they could pick up relatively cheaply. Young guitar players — and the collector markets — quickly followed suit, as demand for Melody Makers, Mustangs, Jazzmasters and Jaguars skyrocketed once they'd been seen on MTV.

1996 Guild Guitars catalog, the first after Fender ownership, showing the Guild S-100 (copyright Fender Musical Instrument Corporation).

Among the beneficiaries was the honorable Guild S-100 from the '70s. Suddenly, people wanted them.

In response to the new-found demand, in 1994, Guild tentatively reentered the solidbody market with two "reissue" guitar models, one of its '70s S-100 and the other an improved version of the Brian May, which had by this time caught the eye of collectors.

The S-100 Reissue was basically an exact replica of the original. Precise measurements were taken of an older example provided by Guild expert Jay Pilzer and reproduced in the new version. The new S-100 had a mahogany body, a little black pickguard, a glued-in mahogany neck, the old crown headstock with a Chesterfield inlay, 22-fret bound rosewood fingerboard, block inlays, chrome hardware, finetune bridge, slanted rectangular stop tail, small black pickguard, two Guild HB-1 humbuckers, two volumes and two tones, threeway select and a coil tap. An S-100G option was available with gold hardware. Both came with black, green stain, natural, red stain, vintage white and white finish options. These listed for $1,000 and $1,200. These latter day S-100s have proved to be fairly successful, and production continues on a limited basis to this day. Some guitarists found the

original HB-1 humbuckers to be a bit to microphonic — they were not, after all, designed to be run through rows of Marshall stacks to fill large stadiums — so Guild has built some with a Seymour Duncan JB at the neck and a Seymour Duncan 59er at the bridge. These may have the coils exposed, or may be covered.

Queen the 2nd

The relatively unsuccessful Brian May was also brought back in 1994. The new version attempted to correct some of the inaccuracies that had gotten into the previous guitar, and reportedly was built after meticulously measuring and scoping out May's own Red Special.

Actually, prototypes of the new Brian May began to be produced as early as 1992. These earliest prototypes actually combined features of the previous mid-'80s models and what would become the new guitar. By 1993 the new version was finalized and actually some production was begun, even though the official introduction

didn't take place until '94.

Initially, only a limited number of the Brian Mays was planned, with 500 being made for the U.S. market and another 500 for export. These are often referred to as the Brian May Signature, and feature a reproduction of May's signature on the back of the headstock. American models were shipped with either a BHP or BHM prefix to the serial number, while the European models featured an ME prefix, reported to stand for "May Europe," or perhaps "May Export." It is also reported that some 50 of these exports were inadvertantly shipped in the U.S. There were no differences in domestic or export models.

The Brian May Signature was a slightly offset double cutaway with a mahogany body, bound mahogany top, glued-in mahogany

Kim Thayil of Soundgarden with his Guild S-100 on the cover of Guitar Player (Guitar Player).

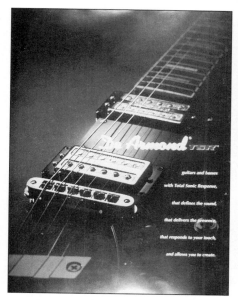

These American-made pickups give DeArmond guitars

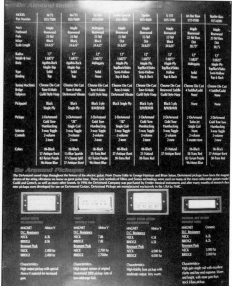

The 1998 Fender/Guild DeArmond catalog of imported "reissues" of Guild classics.

neck, three-and-three headstock, bound 24-fret ebony fingerboard, pearl dot inlays, finetune bridge, a Schaller replica of May's knife-edge vibrato, chrome hardware, three Seymour Duncan replicas of the old Burns Tri-Sonic pickups, and six sliding switches which serve as on/off and allow all sorts of in- and out-of-phase tonal variations (not unlike the previous Liberator, to be honest). Aside from the complexity of figuring out all the little sliding switches, these are quite remarkable guitars and well worth seeking out.

The limited edition Brian Mays were fairly well received, and have continued in the Guild line, with some significant differences. After the initial limited run of 1,000 instruments, the May signature was removed from the back of the headstock, the serial numbers were changed, and the guitar continued in production as the Brian May Pro, with a list price of around $1,800.

In addition, Guild followed up on the Pro with a slightly less expensive version called the Brian May Special, which was basically the same as the Pro except for having a rosewood fingerboard and a tunomatic bridge with stop tail.

Finally, in response to players wanting the tone but not the fuss of figuring out the sliding switches, Guild introduced the Brian May Standard, which was similar to the Special except for the use of a fiveway pickup selector switch.

These later Brian Mays all feature the Seymour Duncan single coil pickups and come in black, transparent red, transparent green and white, and listed at around $1,800, $1,500 and $1,000 respectively. Brian Mays were made into 1995, but were gone by the time of the Fender acquisition. While the Signatures are the most desirable, production numbers of the later models may even be smaller, and, certainly, like most Guild solidbodies, none were produced in massive numbers.

Looking backward, looking forward

In November of 1995, Guild Guitars was purchased by Fender Musical Instruments, primarily because of its top-notch line of acoustics. Fender had long wanted to be a player in the acoustic arena, going back to the early '60s when Leo Fender hired Roger Rossmeisl to design the company's first acoustic boxes. Despite some interesting examples over the years, Fender never seemed to make a mark in the acoustic field. The purchase of Guild gave Fender the credibility of extremely good acoustics, while adding some much needed marketing clout to the Guild brand.

Obviously Guild's solidbodies represented somewhat of a competitive factor for Fender, but Fender chose to keep the venerable S-100 solid in the line. The Guild S-100 "SG" continued to be offered into 1999, at least.

The cool Guild solidbody heritage has received a nod from the new Fender/Guild alliance in the revival of yet another honored name in guitardom, DeArmond. DeArmond is the namesake of Toledo guitarist Harry DeArmond, one of the pioneers of finger-tapping technique, who is best known as a manufacturer of so many pickups on early guitars, including the early Guilds. Fender purchased the rights to the DeArmond name in 1997. In January of 1999 Guild introduced a line of -hollowbody and solidbody guitars imported from Korea bearing the DeArmond brand name (the first guitars to do so), based on vintage Guild designs, called the DeArmond TSR ("Total Sonic Response) guitars and basses. These consisted of two series, a set-neck series and a bolt-neck series. All featured American made De-Armond-brand pickups.

The '99 DeArmond set-neck guitars included two single-cut, solid M-style inspirations (available in sparkle finishes!), the M75 and M75T (Bigsby); two Thunderbird gumby copies (asymmetrical head), the Jet Star (blocks) and Jet Star Bass; three thinlines, the Starfire (double-cut), Starfire Special (single-cut, Bigsby), and StarfireBass;andafull-bodiedsingle-cutjazzbox,theXl55. Bolt-neckmodels included three single-cut M-styles, the M55, M65, M65C (blocks, pickguard); and two Thunderbird-style gumbies, the Jet Star Special and Jet Star Special Bass. These appear to be of excellent quality and were offered at reasonable prices.

Guild solidbodies have always been extremely well made, but for various reasons just have never quite been able to win the hearts of legions of players, and thus have languished in undeserved obscurity. Often produced in small quantities, many of these qualify as extremely rare birds, indeed. Clearly, great possibilities exist for the savvy collector to find very interesting instruments which are pedigreed American guitars built by one of our great companies. Perhaps now with increased awareness Guild solidbodies will take their rightful place as bona fide American treasures.

Guild Solidbodies 1963('59)-1999

Here's a listing of Guild's solidbody electric guitars and basses (plus a few of the semis mentioned in the text). Unless otherwise indicated, you can assume that necks are bolted on, although it should be remembered that Guild produced far more glued-neck solidbody electric guitars than most other U.S manufacturers, except for Gibson.

Approx. Years in Production	Models
Guitars	
1959/60-62	Aristocrat M-75 (semi-hollow 1-cut, glued, f-holes, 1 pu)
1963-68	Thunderbird S-200 (gumby offset 2-cut, glued, 3/3 Florentine hs, bound rw fb, blocks, 2 Guild Anti-Hum hb, on/off slid sw, 3v/1t, Hagstrom vib, stand; reg hs, 2 De Armond sc pu by '65)
1963-68	Polar S-100 (gumby offset 2-cut, glued, rev Firebird 6-hs, rw fb, dots, 2 Guild/DeArmond "Frequency-Tested" sc pu, 3-way, v/t, Hagstrom vib, stand; Florentine hs by '64)
1963-67	Jet-Star S-50 (gumby offset 2-cut, glued, 3/3

	Models
	Florentine hs, rw fb, dots, 1 DeArmond sc pu, v/t, stop)
1967-74	Deluxe M-75 (semi-hollow ∫-size 1-cut, glued, 3/3 Chesterfield hs, bound rw fb, blocks, 2 Guild hb, 3-way, 2v/2t, elev pg, finetune, trapeze; called Bluesbird in '68)
1970-76; 1994	Polara S-100 ("SG" eq 2-cut, glued, 3/3 Chesterfield hs, bound 22-fret rw fb, blocks, pg, 2 Guild hb, 3-way, 2v/2t, Hagstrom vib; named Standard w/stop by '72; improved hb and phase in '73)
1970-76	S-90 ("SG" eq 2-cut, glued, 3/3 hs, 22-fret rw fb, dots, pg, 2 Guild hb, 3-way, v/t, br/tp; stop, opt Bigsby ca. '74)
1970-76	S-50 ("SG" eq 2-cut, glued, 3/3 hs, 22-fret rw fb, dots, pg, 1 mini-hb, v/t, br/tp; Guild hb, stop ca. '74)
1970-80	M-75 (solid 1-cut, carved top, glued, 3/3 Chesterfield, bound rw fb, blocks, 2 hb, 3-way, 2v/2t, elev stairstep pg, finetune, trapeze; stop by '72; phase after '73; DiMarzio pu opt in '78)
1970-80	Deluxe M-75 (solid 1-cut, carved top, glued, 3/3 Chesterfield, gold, bound eb fb, blocks, 2 hb, 3-way, 2v/2t, elev stairstep pg, finetune, trapeze; stop by '72, phase after '73; DiMarzio pu opt in '78)
1973-76	S-100 DeLuxe ("SG" eq 2-cut, glued, 3/3 Chesterfield hs, bound 22-fret rw fb, blocks, pg, 2 Guild hb, 3-way, 2v/2t, phase, Bigsby, opt stereo)
1974-76	S-100C ("SG" eq 2-cut, glued, 3/3 Chesterfield hs, bound 22-fret rw fb, blocks, carved oak leaf pattern in top, clear pg, 2 Guild hb, 3-way, 2v/2t, phase, stop, opt Bigsby, opt stereo)
1975-80	M-85CS (solid 1-cut, carved top, glued, 3/3 Chesterfield, bound eb fb, blocks, 2 hb, 3-way, 2v/2t, phase, elev stairstep pg, finetune, stop)
1973-74	Madeira EG-100 (bolt copy of Guild S-100)
1973-74	Madeira copies (bolt copies of Gibson and Fender guitars, with round crown or open book hs)
1977-82	S-60 (offset 2-cut bell, glued, 3/3 hs, 24-fret rw fb, dots, pg, 1 Guild hb, v/t, finetune, stop)
1977/78-82	S-60D (offset 2-cut mah bell, glued, 3/3 hs, 24-fret rw fb, dots, pg, 2 DiMarzio SDS-1 sc, 3-way, v/t, finetune, stop)
1977/78-82	S-300 (offset 2-cut mah bell, glued, 3/3 Chesterfield hs, 24-fret rw fb, dots, pg, 2 Guild hb, 3-way, 2v/2t, phase, finetune, stop, opt Bigsby, opt stereo)
1977/78-82	S-300A (offset 2-cut ash bell, glued, 3/3 Ches-

	Models
	terfield hs, 24-fret rw fb, dots, pg, 2 Guild hb, 3-way, 2v/2t, phase, finetune, stop, opt Bigsby, opt stereo)
1977/78-82	S-300AD (offset 2-cut ash bell, glued, 3/3 Chesterfield hs, 24-fret rw fb, dots, pg, 2 DiMarzio hb, 3-way, 2v/2t, phase, finetune, stop, opt Bigsby, opt stereo)
1978/79-82	S-70D (offset 2-cut mah bell, glued, 3/3 hs, 24-fret rw fb, dots, pg, 3 DiMarzio SDS-1 sc, 5-way, v/t, phase, bypass sw, finetune, stop)
1978/79-82	S-70AD (offset 2-cut ash bell, glued, 3/3 hs, 24-fret rw fb, dots, pg, 3 DiMarzio SDS-1 sc, 5-way, v/t, phase, bypass sw, finetune, stop)
1979/80-82	S-65D (offset 2-cut mah bell, glued, 3/3 hs, 24-fret rw fb, dots, pg, 2 DiMarzio Dual Sound hb, 3-way, v/t, coil tap, finetune, stop, opt Bigsby, opt stereo)
1980-82	S-400 (offset 2-cut ash bell, glued, 3/3 Chesterfield hs, 24-fret rw fb, dots, pg, 2 DiMarzio hb, 3-way, 2v/2t, phase, active EQ, brass hdw, finetune, stop, opt Bigsby, opt stereo)
1980-82	S-300D (offset 2-cut mah bell, glued, 3/3 Chesterfield hs, 24-fret rw fb, dots, pg, 2 DiMarzio PAF and Super Distortion hb, 3-way, 2v/2t, phase, finetune, stop, opt Bigsby, opt stereo)
1980-83	M-80 (eq 2-cut, carved map top, mah body, glued, 3/3 Chesterfield hs, 24-fret eb fb, dots, 2 hb, 3-way, v, finetune, stop; 2 XR-7 hb, 2v/2t, gold, opt phase or coil tap by '83)
1980-83	M-80CSD (eq 2-cut, carved map top, mah body, glued, 3/3 Chesterfield hs, 24-fret eb fb, dots, 2 DiMarzio PAF+Dual Sound hb, 3-way, v, finetune, stop)
1981-84	Madeira EG-250 (offset mah 2-cut, 24-fret rw fb, dots, 2 hb, 3-way, 2v/2t, 2 coil taps, stop)
1981-84	Madeira EG-330 (offset mah/map 2-cut, 24-fret rw fb, dots, 2 hb, 3-way, 2v/2t, 2 coil taps, stop)
1981-84	Madeira copies
1981-83	S-250 (offset mah 2-cut, bound top, 3/3 Chesterfield hs, chrome, 24-fret rw fb, dots, 2 XR-7 hb, 3-way, 2v/1t, phase or tap, finetune, stop)
1981-83	S-25 (offset mah 2-cut, 3/3 Chesterfield hs, chrome, 24-fret rw fb, dots, 2 XR-7 hb, 3-way, v/t, phase or tap, finetune, stop)
1981-84	X-82 Nova (mah V/Expl, bound top, 3/3 arrowhead hs, chr, 24-fret eb fb, dots, 2 XR-7 hb, 3-way, 2v/1t, phase or coil tap, finetune, stop; called Starfighter by '83; pointy droopy

Approx. Years in Production	Models
	hs, opt Floyd Rose by '84)
1981-85	X-79 (assym offset 2-cut, glued, asymm 3/3 hs, 24-fret eb fb, dots, chr, 2 XR-7 hb, 3-way, 2v/1t, phase or coil tap, pg, finetune, stop; called Skylark, opt rw/map fb, Kahler in '83)
1982-83?	X-79-3 (assym offset 2-cut, glued, asymm 3/3 hs, 24-fret eb fb, dots, chr, pg, 3 sc, finetune, stop)
1983	S-260 (probably similar to S-250)
1983	S-26 (probably similar to S-25)
1983	S-275 (offset 2-cut, map/mah, 3/3 Chesterfield hs, gold, 24-fret eb fb, dots, 2 XR-7 humbuckers, 3-way, 2v/2t, phase or coil tap, finetune, stop)
1983	X-84V (no information available)
1983	X-97V (no information available)
1983	X-108V (no information available)
1983-84	X-80 Skyhawk (rev. x-79, glued, asymm 3/3 hs, 24-fret map/rsw fb, dots, 2 DiMarzio hb, 3-way, v/t, finetune, stop)
1983-86	S-280 Flyer (offset 2-cut, blade 6-hs, mah or map neck, opt rw/map fb, dots, 2 hb, 3-way, v/t, Kahler, opt stop)
1984-85?	S-270 Flyer/Runaway/Sprint (offset 2-cut, blade 6-hs, 22-fret fb, 1 or 2 EMG pu, Kahler)
1986?	S-271 Sprint? (offset 2-cut, blade 6-hs, 22-fret fb, 1 EMG, Kahler)
1986	S-281 Flyer (offset 2-cut, pop or fl map body, pointy-droopy 6-hs, 2 hb, 3-way, v/t, Kahler)
1987	Thunderbolt (former Flyer, offset 2-cut, pointy-droopy 6-hs, black, Sperzel Tremlock tuners, 1 DiMarzio hb+2 sc, 5-way, Mueller vib)
1984-87?	S-284 Aviator (eq 2-cut, glued, pointy-droopy 6-hs, 22-fret rw fb, dots, pg, 1 EMG hb+2 sc, 5-way, v/t, Kahler; some DiMarzio Leslie West hb and Kent Armstrong hb; no pg, eb fb, opt hb/sc/sc with coil tap or 3 sc with "fat control" by '86; DiMarzio or EMG hb/sc/sc, 5-way, v/t, Kahler fulcrum vib in '87)
1984?	S-284 Starling (hb+2 sc)
1984	S-282 Starling (no information available)
1984-85	X-100 Bladerunner (X-shaped pop cutout 2-cut, glued, cutout pointy droopy 6-hs, 22-fret eb fb, Mercedes star inlays, 1 EMG 81 hb, coil tap, fat control, Kahler)
1984-85	X-88 Crue Flying Star (star eq 2-cut, bolt, pointy-droopy 6-hs, 24-fret rw fb, star inlays, 1 EMG hb, v, Kahler; spade 3/3 hs, DiMarzio hb in '85)

Approx. Years in Production	Models
1984-86	X-92 Citron Breakaway (quasi-Rhoads V eq 2-cut, detachable wing travel guitar, glued, V 3/3 hs, 22-fret rw fb, dots, pg, 3 EMG sc, 5-way, v/active presence, opt Kahler)
1984-86	Brian May BHM1 (slightly offset 2-cut, glued, 3/3 hs, eb fb, dots, pg, 3 DiMarzio Brian May Signature hb, 6 mini-toggles, Kahler, outboard Power Booster preamp)
1985	X-88D (star eq 2-cut, bolt, spade 3/3 hs, 24-fret rw fb, star inlays, 2 DiMarzio hb, 3-way, v/t, Schaller br/tp)
1985-87/88	Bluesbird (pop 1-cut, glued, blade 6-hs, 22-fret eb fb, 3-pce pearl/ab blocks, 3 EMG sc or opt hb+2 sc w/coil tap, 5-way, v/t, Kahler; 2 EMG hb, 3-way by '86; DiMarzio hb by '87)
1985-87	Nightbird (semi-hollow mah 1-cut, bound spr top, glued mah, 3/3 hs, blk hdw, bound 22-fret eb fb, diamonds, 2 EMG or Kent Armstrong hb, 3-way, v/t, coil tap, elev pg, finetune, stop)
1986-87	S-285 Aviator (bound 6-hs, bound eb fb, sunrise inlays, 1 EMG hb+2 sc, Kahler; opt DiMarzio pu)
1986-87	T-200 Roy Buchanan (pop Tele 1-cut, pointy-droopy 6-hs, 22-fret rw fb, dots, 2 EMG sc, brass br)
1986-88	T-250 (pop Tele 1-cut, pointy-droopy 6-hs, 22-fret rw fb, dots, 2 EMG sc, brass br; gold, DiMarzio pu, opt EMG in '87)
1987-88	Nightbird I (semi-hollow mah 1-cut, bound spr top, glued mah, 3/3 hs, chr hdw, bound 22-fret rw fb, slotted diamonds, 2 DiMarzio hb, 3-way, v/t, coil tap, phase, elev pg, finetune, stop)
1987-90	Nightbird II (semi-hollow mah 1-cut, bound spr top, glued mah, 3/3 hs, gold hdw, bound 22-fret eb fb, slotted diamonds, 2 EMG 60 hb, 3-way, v/t, coil tap, phase, elev pg, finetune, stop; called just Nightbird in '89)
1987-88	Burnside FE-1
1987-88	Burnside EG-53
1987-88	Burnside GE-27
1987-88	Burnside HA-1
1987-88	Burnside SO-1
1987-88	Burnside BB-111
1987-88	Burnside EB-151
1987-88	Detonator (pop offset 2-cut, bolt, pointed 6-hs, black hdw, 22-fret rw fb, dots, EMG hb+2 sc, 5-way, Floyd Rose; Guild/Mueller vib, DiMarzio hb in '88)

Approx. Years in Production	Models
1988	Detonator II (pop offset 2-cut, bolt, pointed 6-hs, black hdw, 22-fret rw fb, dots, EMG hb+2 sc, 5-way, Floyd Rose)
1987-88	Liberator (offset pop 2-cut, straight 6-hs, 24-rw fb, dots, hb+sc+sc, 5-way, Mueller vib)
1987-88	Liberator II (offset pop 2-cut, straight 6-hs, 24-rw fb, rising suns, EMG hb+2 sc, 3 mini-toggles, Floyd Rose)
1987-88	Liberator Elite (offset mah/map 2-cut, glued, straight rw 6-hs, gold, bound 24-fret eb fb, rising suns, 1 active Bartolini hb+2 sc, 3 mini-toggles, v/t, boost, Floyd Rose)
1988-90	Songbird I (1-cut hollow, round sh, binding, transducer pu, preamp, stop)
1988-89	Songbird Custom (1-cut hollow, colored top, round sh, binding, gold, transducer pu, preamp, stop)
1988-90	Nightingale (mah 1-cut semi-hollow, carved spr top, f-holes, glued, 3/3 hs, 2 EMG hb, finetune, stop)
1990-91	Nightbird Custom (mah 1-cut semi-hollow, carved curly map top, glued, 3/3 hs, black, rw fb, dots, 2 hb, 3-way, finetune, stop)
1990-91	Nightbird Standard (pop 1-cut solid, glued, 3/3 hs, black, rw fb, dots, 2 hb, 3-way, finetune, stop)
1990-91	Nightbird DeLuxe (carved pop 1-cut solid, glued, 3/3 hs, black, rw fb, dots, 2 hb, 3-way, finetune, stop)
1990-91	Madeira ME-500 "Traditional Style" (1-cut LP, 3/3 hs, bound rw fb, blocks, 2 EMG Select hb, 3-way, finetune, stop)
1990-91	Madeira ME-300 "Rock/Metal Style" (offset 2-cut Strat, pointy-droopy 6-hs, rw fb, dots, EMG Select hb+2 sc, 5-way, vib)
1990-91	Madeira ME-200 "Traditional Style" (offset 2-cut Strat, pointy-droopy 6-hs, map fb, dots, pg, 3 sc, 5-way, vib)
1993-94	Brian May Signature (slightly offset mah 2-cut, bound top, glued, 3/3 hs, bound 24-fret eb fb, dots, pg, 3 Seymour Duncan Burns Trisonic replica hb, 6 sliding sw, finetune, Schaller/May knife-edge vib)
1994-95	Brian May Pro (slightly offset mah 2-cut, bound top, glued, 3/3 hs, bound 24-fret eb fb, dots, pg, 3 Seymour Duncan Burns Trisonic replica hb, 6 sliding sw, finetune, Schaller/May knife-edge vib)
1994-95	Brian May Special (slightly offset mah 2-cut, bound top, glued, 3/3 hs, bound 24-fret rw fb, dots, pg, 3 Seymour Duncan Burns Trisonic replica hb, 6 sliding sw, finetune, stop)
1994-95	Brian May Standard (slightly offset mah 2-cut, bound top, glued, 3/3 hs, bound 24-fret rw fb, dots, pg, 3 Seymour Duncan Burns Trisonic replica hb, 5-way, finetune, stop)
1994--	S-100 Reissue (2 Guild HB-1 hb, tap, opt: Seymour Duncan JB/59er)
1994--	S-100G (gold hdw)
1998--	DeArmond M75 (1-cut solid, glued, 3/3 hs, Chesterfield, bnd 22-fret rw fb, blocks, 2 DeA Gold Tone hb, pg, 2v/2t, 3-way, finetune, harp)
1998--	DeArmond M75T (1-cut solid, glued, 3/3 hs, Chesterfield, bnd 22fret rw fb, blocks, 2 DeA 2K sc, pg, 2v/2t, 3-way, finetune, Bigsby)
1998--	DeArmond Jet Star (gumby offset 2-cut solid, glued, asym 3/3 hs, eagle, bnd 22-fret rw fb, blocks, 2 DeA Gold Tone hb, pg, 2v/2t, 3way, finetune, stop)
1998--	DeArmond Jet Star Special (gumby offset 2-cut solid, bolt, 3/3 hs, eagle, 22-fret rw fb, dots, 2 hb, v/t, 3-way, finetune, stop)
1998--	DeArmond Starfire (eq 2-cut thinline, f-holes, glued, 3/3 hs, Chesterfield, bnd 22-fret rw fb, dots, 2 DeA Gold Tone hb, pg, 2v/2t, 3-way, finetune, harp)
1998--	DeArmond Starfire Special (1-cut thinline, f-holes, glued, 3/3 hs, Chesterfield, bnd 22-fret rw fb, dots, 2 DeA 2K sc, pg, 2v/2t, 3-way, finetune, Bigsby)
1998--	DeArmond Xl 55 (1-cut full hollowbody, f-holes, glued, 3/3 hs, Chesterfield, bnd 22-fret rw fb, blocks, 2 DeA Gold Tone hb, pg, 2v/2t, 3-way, adj br, harp)

Basses

Approx. Years in Production	Models
1965-67	Jet-Star (gumby offset 2-cut, glued, 2/2 hs, rw fb, dots, 1 DeArmond sc pu, v/t, stop)
1970-76	JS Bass 1 ("SG" eq 2-cut, glued, 2/2 Chesterfield hs, rw fb, dots, 1 hb, tone sw, v/t, stop, opt stereo, opt fretless)
1970-76	JS Bass 2 ("SG" eq 2-cut, glued, 2/2 Chesterfield hs, rw fb, dots, 3 hb, 3-way, tone sw, 2v/2t, stop, opt stereo, opt fretless)
1972-73	M-85-I (solid ∫-size 1-cut, glued, carved top, 2/2 Chesterfield hs, bound rw fb, dots, 1 hb, v/t, elev pg, stop)
1972-80	M-85-II (solid ∫-size 1-cut, glued, carved top, 2/2 Chesterfield hs, bound rw fb, dots, 2 hb,

Approx. Years in Production	Models
	3-way, 2v/2t, elev pg, stop)
1973-74	Madeira EB-100 (copy of Guild JS Bass 2)
1974-76	JS Bass 2C ("SG" eq 2-cut, glued, 2/2 Chesterfield hs, rw fb, dots, carved oak leaf top, 3 hb, 3-way, tone sw, 2v/2t, stop, opt stereo, opt fretless)
1977-80	B-301 (offset 2-cut mah bell, glued, 2/2 Chesterfield hs, 24-fret rw fb, dots, pg, 1 Guild hb, v/t, br/tp)
1977/78-80	B-302 (offset 2-cut mah bell, glued, 2/2 Chesterfield hs, 24-fret rw fb, dots, pg, 2 Guild sc, 3-way, 2v/2t, br/tp)
1979?-81	B-301A (offset 2-cut mah bell, glued, 2/2 Chesterfield hs, 24-fret rw fb, dots, pg, 1 Guild hb, v/t, br/tp)
1979?-81	B-302A (offset 2-cut ash bell, glued, 2/2 Chesterfield hs, 24-fret rw fb, dots, pg, 2 Guild sc, 3-way, 2v/2t, br/tp)
1980-81	B-401 (offset 2-cut ash/wal bell, glued, 2/2 Chesterfield hs, 24-fret rw fb, dots, pg, 1 pu, v/t, active EQ, brass hdw, br/tp)
1980-81	B-402 (offset 2-cut ash/wal bell, glued, 2/2 Chesterfield hs, 24-fret rw fb, dots, pg, 2 pu, 3-way, 2v/2t, EQ, brass hdw, active br/tp)
1981-83	SB-201 (offset 2-cut, glued, 2/2 Chesterfield hs, 21-fret rw fb, dots, pg, 1 split coil pu, v/t, br/tp, opt fretless)
1981-83	SB-202 (offset 2-cut, glued, 2/2 Chesterfield hs, 21-fret rw fb, dots, pg, 1 split coil+1 sc pu, 3-way, 2v/1t, phase, br/tp, opt fretless, opt stereo)
1981-82	MB-801 (eq 2-cut, 1 pu)
1981-82	MB-802 (eq 2-cut, 2 pu)
1982-83	SB-203 (offset 2-cut, glued, 2/2 Chesterfield hs, 21-fret rw fb, dots, pg, 1 split coil+2 sc pu, 3 on/off toggles, v/t, phase, br/tp)
1982-83	SB-502E (offset 2-cut, glued, 2/2 Chesterfield hs, 21-fret rw fb, dots, pg, 1 split coil+2 sc pu, 3 on/off toggles, 2v/bass+treble EQ, phase, preamp on/off toggle, br/tp)
1982-84	X-702 (assym offset 2-cut, glued, asymm 2/2 hs, 22-fret fb, dots, pg, 2 sc, 3-way, 2v/1t, br/tp)
1982-84	X-701 (assym offset 2-cut, glued, asymm 2/2 hs, 22-fret fb, dots, pg, 1 sc, v/t, br/tp)
1983-88	SB-600 Pilot (offset pop 2-cut, bolt, blade 4-hs, 22-fret fb, dots, 2 DiMarzio pu, 3-way, br/tp)
1983-88	SB-601 Pilot (offset 2-cut, bolt, blade 4-hs, 1 pu, br/tp; EMG pu by '84)
1983-88; 1990	SB-602 Pilot (offset 2-cut, bolt, blade 4-hs, blk hdw, rw/map fb, dots, 2 EMG P+J pu, Kahler; flamed map by '84)
1983-88	SB-603 Pilot (offset 2-cut, blade 4-hs, 3 pu)
1983-86	SB-604 Pilot (offset 2-cut, pointy-droopy 4-hs)
1983	SB-280 Flyer (offset 2-cut, 22-fret map/rw fb, br/tp)
1984-85	SB-666 Bladerunner (X-shaped pop cutout 2-cut, glued, cutout pointy droopy 4-hs, EMG pu, Kahler)
1984-85	SB-608 Flying Star Bass (star eq 2-cut, bolt, rw fb, star inlays, 2 pu, br/tp)
1984-85	SB-608E Flying Star Bass (star eq 2-cut, bolt, rw fb, star inlays, 2 EMG pu, br/tp)
1986-88; 1990	SB-605 Pilot (offset map 2-cut 5-string, rw fb, 2 EMG pu, br/tp)
1987-88	SB-902 Advanced Pilot (offset 2-cut, flamed map body, map nck, 22-fret eb fb, fancy inlay, 2 Bartolini P+J pu, Bartolini TCT preamp, br/tp)
1987-88	SB-905 Advanced Pilot (offset 2-cut 5-string, flamed map body, map nck, 22-fret eb fb, fancy inlay, 2 Bartolini P+J pu, Bartolini TCT preamp, br/tp)
1986-88	Ashbory (pop mini-fan body, fan 4-hs, banjo tuners, silicon str, fretless, molded plastic br/tp, piezo pu, active v/bass/treb, active/passive on/off, LED)
1990-91	Madeira MBE-100 "Traditional Style" (offset 2-cut, pointy-droopy 4-hs, dots, 1 EMG split-coil+1 sc, br/tp)
1990-91	SB-605M Pilot (offset 2-cut, map body, br/tp)
1990-91	SB-602M Pilot (offset 2-cut, map body, 2 pu, br/tp)
1998--	DeArmond Jet Star Bass (gumby offset 2-cut solid, glued, asym 2/2 hs, eagle, bnd 22-fret rw fb, dots, 2 DeA Turbo Jet sc, pg, 2v/lt, 3way, br/tp)
1998--	DeArmond Jet Star Special Bass (gumby offset 2-cut solid, bolt, 2/2 hs, 22-fret rw fb, dots, 1 split coil pu, v/t, br/tp)
1998--	DeArmond Starfire Bass (eq 2-cut thinline, f-holes, glued, 2/2 hs, Chesterfield, bnd 22-fret rw fb, dots, 2 DeA Gold Tone hb, 2v/2t, 3way, br/tp)

KAY
MUSICAL INSTRUMENT COMPANY

Stromberg-Voisinet, Kay Kraft and Kay Guitars 1890-1969

Ironies abound when it comes to the history of instruments, and nowhere is this more true than when it comes to the subject of Kay guitars. After the Harmony Company, no one in America made as many guitars as the Kay Musical Instrument Company. Indeed, it was companies like Kay and Harmony, catering to the mass market, selling through America's great mass manufacturers, which can be said to have built the vast American guitar market, feeding the country's rich musical heritage. As wonderful and as significant as guitars by Gibson and Martin may have been, they have always been relatively expensive, and were not the main instruments shipped to young America through the mail or played in suburban garages, fuelling teenage fantasies of wealth and fame across the nation. More often than not, those guitars came from manufacturers like Kay.

Yet, despite such an important role, precious little is known about the history of Kay guitars. Some general outlines have been available, but no detailed account of this great guitar giant has been collected. Until now.

Following yet another labyrinthine trail — and with *lots* of help from my friends — it's now possible to illuminate something about this curious major corner in American guitar history. Welcome to the story of Kay guitars.

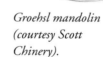

Groehsl mandolin (courtesy Scott Chinery).

Chicago and guitars

To trace the history of the Kay guitars, we have to wade a bit into the thick, juicy stew of early 20th Century Chicagoland lutherie.

Chicago had already begun to become the powerhouse of instrument making. The city was experiencing a massive influx of European immigrants and the new Americans brought with them guitarmaking and woodworking skills, and set about making musical instruments for the rapidly expanding nation.

Chicago's central geography was perfectly situated to foster this growth and, with its huge network of railroad conduits, was quite literally the crossroads of the na-

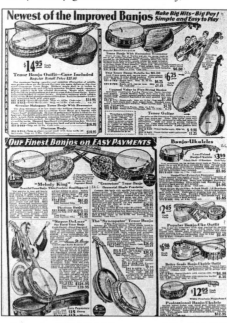

(Left to Right) Stromberg guitars and mandolins from the 1925-26 Montgomery Ward Fall/Winter catalog . Stromberg banjos and Venetian tenor guitar from the 1929 Montgomery Ward Spring/Summer catalog. Stromberg guitars from the 1929 Montgomery Ward Spring/Summer catalog (courtesy Mike Newton).

Ca. 1927 Oahu flattop made by Stromberg-Voisinet, except for finish and bridge identical to the Stromberg C-737 in the 1925-25 Ward's catalog (photo: Mike Newton).

tion during this critical era of Manifest Destiny. The access to transportation for distribution in turn encouraged the explosion of mass marketing, becoming the cornerstone of the success of perhaps the greatest evangelist of American consumer culture, the mail-order catalog. Among the many consumer items reaching the far corners of the country via that remarkable American institution — through catalogs produced by Montgomery Ward, Spiegel and the mighty Sears, Roebuck and Company — were guitars, made in Chicago.

The Roaring '20s

The big player in Chicago in the late 19th Century and early 20th was Lyon & Healy, the big music retailer. In addition to providing guitars for both Wards and Sears, Lyon & Healy made the well-known brand Washburn. Lyon & Healy remained a force until the '20s, when it lost interest in manufacturing instruments. By that time, the Harmony Company, then actually owned by Sears, had become the largest Chicago guitar manufacturer. Lyon & Healy eventually sold the Washburn name and its factory to the J.R. Stewart Company in the spring of 1928. Stewart, with ties to the big distributor Tonk Brothers, went bankrupt in 1930, when the young Regal company purchased the old Lyon & Healy holdings, but that's another story. It's from this often inbred world of Chicagoland guitars that the Kay tale spins.

Groehsl

What was eventually to become the Kay Musical Instrument Company actually began in Chicago in 1890 as the Groehsl Company (sometimes also spelled Groehsel). (Later Kay catalogs would promote the company with the claim of "since 1890.")

Basically little is known of Kay's original forebear, the Groehsl Company, except that they began making bowl-backed mandolins, adding banjos and then guitars to the stable in 1918. From the instrument example shown on page 154 in George Gruhn and Walter Carter's *Acoustic Guitars* (GPI/Miller Freeman Books), Groehsl clearly had a predilection for strange shapes. This ca. 1920 Hawaiian guitar had a standard Spanish lower bout but then swooped up to the headstock in a taper not unlike those found on some harp-guitars of the era. This has a spruce top and rosewood body, with snowflake inlays and a bunch of cool pearl trim around the top and soundhole. Perhaps there was a tradition of weirdness from which the later exotic Kay Kraft Venetian shapes would spring, wrapped up in the emergence of the Kay name.

Stromberg-Voisinet

In 1921, Groehsl changed its name to the Stromberg-Voisinet Company, with a factory at 316 Union Park Court. The stolid midwestern pronunciation of "Voisinet" is Germanicized to "Voy-zin-et," not the expected French ending, by the way. At least one of its divisions under vice-president C.G. Stromberg manufactured the Mayflower brand of mandolins and guitars. While Stromberg-Voisinet was the actual name and its instruments carried the "Stromberg" label, Chicago luthiers always *referred* to the company as *Voisinet*, to distinguish it from Boston's *Stromberg* company, which a different Charles Stromberg had founded around the turn of the century and later produced the classic archtops built by Charles' son Elmer.

Hank Kuhrmeyer

It was during the early Stromberg-Voisinet era that the major personality — and namesake — in the Kay saga enters the picture. Based on the account provided in an obituary notice, which appeared in *Instrumental-*

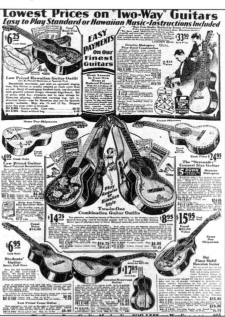

(Left) Stromberg banjos and mandolins from the 1929-30 Montgomery Ward Fall/Winter catalog. (Right) Stromberg guitars, including a Venetian Hawaiian, from the 1929-30 Montgomery Ward Fall/Winter catalog (all courtesy Mike Newton).

(Left to Right) Ca. 1929 Stromberg flattop with rosewood body and Venetian bridge; identical to the '29 Ward's E-748. Back of the ca. '29 Stromberg guitar; note the fancy marquetry. The carved leaf pattern on the back of '29 Stromberg guitar's Venetian headstock (photos: Mike Newton).

ist magazine in May of 1956, Henry Kay Kuhrmeyer joined Stromberg-Voisinet in 1923 and was secretary of the company (perhaps even running it), by 1925. In any case, it would be Kuhrmeyer who would forge Stromberg-Voisinet into a major force in American guitar history.

Plywood pioneers?

Stromberg-Voisinet guitars became one of the principal players in the volatile Chicago instrument-making scene in the '20s, climbing to success on the backs of mass merchandising. Among the Chicago manufacturers of the time, Stromberg guitars were some of the best made within their mass-market niche.

Kay itself claimed in '50s literature that it — or actually Stromberg-Voisinet — pioneered the process of laminating guitar tops and backs, i.e., introducing plywood instruments, in 1924. It's possible that this was the case, though many surviving instruments from the '20s have solid timber. Lamination in guitarmaking goes back to the 19th Century, at least, so Kay's claims probably related to processes rather than the concept. In any case, the plywood in question is not the dust-filled stuff of today, but a three-ply

laminate of quality wood. Three plies of rosewood might be employed (better grade on the outside), though there are reports of rosewood/maple/rosewood combinations. Examples of these possibly from the late '20s are seen. By '33 Kay's resonator instruments appear to be laminates. In 1937, Kay developed laminated basses and cellos. Some of the higher end archtops of the later '30s had laminated backs.

Expansion

According to some reports, Stromberg-Voisinet was looking to set up an expanded factory in Chicago in around 1925. Such expansion would fit with what we know about the aggressive moves Stromberg-Voisinet was making at the time. By 1925, in addition to its own instruments, Stromberg-Voisinet was making many of the instruments for Sears' major competitor, Montgomery Ward, and supplying guitars to other companies as well, including possibly even Lyon & Healy.

Early Stromberg guitars (Chicago)

Complete information about the early

Mid-'20s Stromberg non-Venetian mandolin with Venetian headstock and built-in tuners (photo: Mike Newton).

(Left) Late '20s Avalon mandolin made by Stromberg-Voisinet with newer symmetrical headstock, not the old Venetian shape (photo: Mike Newton). (Right) 1944 Kay ad claiming to have pioneered ply molding "as far back as 1924." (courtesy Michael Lee Allen).

Stromberg guitars of the 1920s remains sketchy, but some things are known.

In the 1925-26 Montgomery Ward Fall/Winter catalog #104, most of the lower grade instruments were made by Oscar Schmidt in New Jersey, whereas the better guitars and most of the banjos were supplied by Stromberg-Voisinet.

The top of the Stromberg guitar line was the C748 ($14.95), a small-bodied Spanish "Professional Concert Guitar," with spruce top, rosewood body and mahogany neck with a rosewood-faced slothead. This snazzy little guitar had and ebony fingerboard with dot inlays and an ebony pyramid bridge. Top and soundhole were inlaid with colored marquetry. Postage, by the way, was $.24 extra!

Next down was the C737 ($12.25), another small flattop with a spruce top, mahogany back and sides, round soundhole and slotted headstock. The top had a large, elaborate vine decal in blue, gold and maroon extending from the belly to the upper bouts. The top was bound in celluloid and featured an additional band of colored marquetry around the top and soundhole. The ebony fingerboard was bound in white celluloid. The pyramid bridge was ebony. This beautiful guitar was identical to models offered as late as 1931, so it's

1920s Regal "fancy scroll model" mandolin which probably influenced the Venetian shape (photo: Mike Newton).

probably safe to assume it had been around before 1925 as well.

Other pretty cool Strombergs included the C738 ($10.95) "Koa Wood Finish Hawaiian Guitar." The operative word, of course, is "finish." This was a Spanish guitar made of birch with a koa finish. Neck was basswood with slotted head. This had an ebonized fingerboard and pyramid bridge, a belly decal and "Hawaiian designs" inlaid around the top. This was set up with a tall nut and came with a method, fingerpicks and metal slide.

The C743 ($9.85) was another Spanish with spruce top and rosewood-finished birch. This had marquetry and a little celluloid pickguard glued on the top. The C740 ($7.95) was a birch-bodied guitar finished in mahogany (with a small belly decal). The mahogany-finished birch C742 ($6.45) held up the bottom of the Stromberg line. All had slotheads.

Early Stromberg banjos

The '25-26 Ward's catalog also offered a number of Stromberg-Voisinet banjos. Top of the line was the C770 Orchestra Tenor ($35). This had a three-piece walnut neck, bound ebony fingerboard with snowflake inlays and a nickel-plated hoop. The C753 Melody King ($19.95) had a small resonator on a shell, and no cast flange as seen on later models. The rim was laminated curly mahogany; the bowl resonator finished in mahogany. The ebony fingerboard was pearl dot inlaid. The C765 Tenor Banjo ($14.45) had a birdseye maple rim, as did the Popular Tenor Banjo ($9.95). A C786 Tenor Banjo Ukulele ($12.25) with "tone amplifier" resonator (curly mahogany rim) and C780 Banjo Ukulele ($9.45) with birdseye maple rim were also offered.

Early Stromberg mandolins

Stromberg mandolins included typical pear-shaped flattops with several unique features. These had glued-in necks and an S-curve Venetian headstock which would typify Stromberg instruments of the later

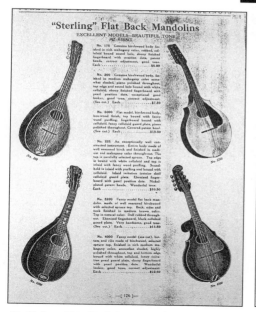

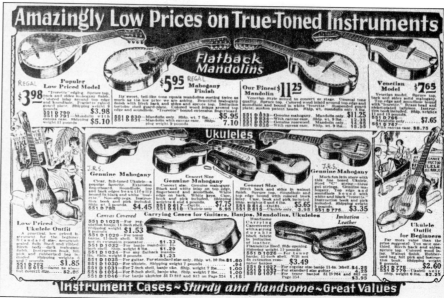

(Left) Late '20s Tonk Bros. Sterling version of the Regal fancy mandolin (courtesy Mike Newton). (Right) Flatback and Venetian Stromberg mandolins from the 1929 Montgomery Ward & Co. catalog (courtesy Mike Newton).

'20s and early '30s. This headstock had built-in tuners enclosed within the head itself. These had large black washers or grommets on the front and the black-plastic buttons came out of the side. The company referred to this design as "imbedded tuning pegs." The back was solid wood with a stamped-in design, another feature typical of many better Strombergs. This arrangement was somewhat reminiscent of the patented design used by Joseph Bohmann, another Chicago guitarmaker.

The '25-26 Ward's catalog featured a mandolin which marked the first documented appearance of the distinctive Stromberg Venetian shape which would later be associated with Kay Krafts. This was the C753 flatback mandolin ($9.95), a mahogany-body flattop with the two-point Venetian body and the S-curve Venetian headstock with enclosed "imbedded" tuners, as on other Stromberg mandolins. The spruce top was celluloid-bound with a band of colored marquetry inlays. It had a large, elevated pickguard, a simple moveable bridge and small tailpiece. We'll return to this instrument in a moment, because it's at the heart of a puzzle that's as yet not completely solved.

Information on mid-'20s Stromberg guitars becomes scarce at this point; however, there was probably little change until 1927

when three key Chicago luthiers joined Stromberg-Voisinet.

Discount prices

By the way, just to give you an idea of relative value, Montgomery Ward & Company usually discounted its Stromberg-Voisinet and later Kay guitars by about 40 percent off the usual list price, so other retail outlets might sell them for considerably more.

Joseph Zorzi and friends

By the 1920s Chicago's guitarmaking firms employed a sizeable number of luthiers who designed instruments and supervised production. Among these were three Lyon & Healy luthiers who figure greatly in the Kay Kraft story: Joseph Zorzi, Philip Gabriel and John Abbott.

Joseph Zorzi was yet another Italian luthier who's had a big impact on American guitars. A Sicilian, Giuseppe Zorzi was born in Messina in 1878 into a musical family related to the Panormo clan, the famous guitarmakers. Joseph's parents were guitarists. Through these connections, Zorzi was apprenticed to the Milanese luthier Leandro Bisiach, with whom he studied violin- and cello-making from age 16 to 19. From another luthier in Milan, Gaetano Antoniazzi, Zorzi learned how to make gui-

Ca. 1930 Stromberg Venetian guitar with Venetian bridge and pearloid fingerboard (courtesy Mike Newton).

Closeup of the belly scene on the ca. '32 Stromberg guitar. Ca. 1932 Stromberg guitar with decal scene. (photos courtesy Mike Newton).

tars.

In 1898, Zorzi was recruited from Bisiach's shop by Lyon & Healy and moved to Chicago to build Washburn guitars. Diligent effort got him promoted to production chief in 1899, which gave him the opportunity to design his own instruments. Fancy inlays were characteristic of his work. Zorzi worked in the guitar department at Lyon & Healy for almost a decade, after which he moved on to violins. By the 1920s, Zorzi was building fancy "presentation" guitars for Lyon & Healy.

Reportedly, in 1923, a general disgruntlement about inadequate pay ran through Chicago's instrument-making companies. A Lyon & Healy luthier named Angelico Boselli, whom Zorzi had helped recruit from his old employer in Italy, Bisiach, left Lyon & Healy to work for their competitor, William Lewis & Son, which offered him substantially more money. Zorzi tried to get Lyon & Healy to match the salary being paid to Boselli, but was turned down. This disagreement over wages ultimately led to the first meeting, in July 1924, of the American Guild of Luthiers, of which Zorzi

was one of the original founders. Other names you might recognize who were at that initial meeting included Gibson's Lloyd Loar, Joseph Virzi and C.F. Martin III.

From Lyon & Healy to Stromberg-Voisinet

Needless to say, management did not approve of the Guild activities (even though there was more casual camaraderie than political action) and it was pretty much suppressed until the '30s.

However, Zorzi apparently did attempt to carry the torch and in 1926 he put up a notice of a Guild meeting at Lyon & Healy, and was promptly fired. Two of Zorzi's good friends, the luthiers Philip Gabriel and John Abbott, also walked out in protest.

In need of new talent for its expanding business, Stromberg-Voisinet hired luthier Joseph Zorzi and his pals Gabriel and Abbott in either 1926 or '27. Zorzi and his friends got the job of developing a new line of instruments, with Zorzi as foreman, responsible for designing archtop guitars.

Essentially, Stromberg-Voisinet was looting of some of Lyon & Healy's best talent.

Whether this loss had anything to do with Lyon & Healy's decision to divest itself of guitar manufacturing is unknown, but since that company had closed down virtually *all* instrument manufacturing by mid-1928, the luthiers' defection is unlikely to have caused the collapse of an empire.

Besides extensive experience, Zorzi and friends brought important technical knowledge and creative ideas to Stromberg-Voisinet. Among the technical things Stromberg-Voisinet got was an intimate understanding of Lyon & Healy's new "rolling pin" technique, which involved cutting wood larger than necessary and then trimming it back to reduce cracking problems.

The Venetian body shape

It appears, as nearly as we can reconstruct it, that the earliest signs of this new luthier presence at Stromberg-Voisinet was the elevation of the emphasis on the *Venetian* shape as part of the Stromberg identity, a form that would be a crucial part of the emerging Kay identity, as well.

Of course the exotically shaped mandolin was pioneered by Gibson beginning in 1902 with its F, F-2, F-3 and F-4 archtop

1932 Stromberg #58 tenor banjo in walnut (photo: Mike Newton).

mandolins with arched backs (but *not* bowls), multi-pointed bodies and the scroll on the upper bass bout. These proved to be popular and set the standard for years to come. It's probable that most exercises in adding points and sometimes scrolls to the more common pear-shaped "flattop" mandolins were attempts to compete directly or indirectly with Gibson.

However, the more immediate progenitor of the Stromberg Venetian shape appears to be a mandolin made by Regal beginning in the 'Teens. This was the Regal No. 4000, a "fancy model" flattop mandolin with the addition of two equal sharp points on the shoulders of the upper bout, and an S-curve on the upper treble bout which ended in a sharply cutaway plain scroll on the upper bass bout. The headstock had an asymmetrical oval dropping off to the treble side, much like the heads on '60s Fender 12-strings. Further suggestive evidence that Stromberg-Voisinet may have been inspired by this design comes from the fact that not only is there a relationship between the

Stromberg instruments from the 1928 C.M.I. catalog; basically the transitional line. The first production electrics!: Stromberg Electro Instruments from the '28 C.M.I. catalog (photos courtesy Michael Lee Allen).

Ca. 1929 Key Kord baritone ukulele made by Stromberg-Voisinet, fitted with a button chording device. Closeup of the '29 Key Kord button device without its cover (photos: Mike Newton).

shapes; the construction methods are almost identical. In both the earlier Regal and the later Stromberg, the entire area under the upper bout above the soundhole is a large solid block of wood into which the neck is set, and the sides below the points are made of a single bent piece of wood. The Regal No. 4000 was offered from the teens until at least 1929, so it's pretty impossible that Stromberg-Voisinet guitar designers would be *un-aware* of it.

It was this Regal which also influenced — one might even say "dictated" — some of the mandolins the Larson brothers designed for Stahl in Milwaukee, which were almost identical in appearance to the old Regal shape. The

cheaper versions of these Stahl mandolins were built by Regal, the better ones by the Larsons.

Published accounts have attributed the invention of the Kay Kraft Venetian shape to Joseph Zorzi. However, now, with the evidence of the Stromberg Venetian mandolin in the 1925-26 Ward's catalog, a good two years prior to the defection of Lyon & Healy's luthiers to Stromberg-Voisinet, the truth seems to be a little more complex, although there's no denying Zorzi played a major role in its implementation.

The development of the Stromberg Venetian shape may *perhaps*, in fact, be credited to Zorzi's friend Philip Gabriel, though this is by no means assured. It is reported that Gabriel designed a two-point Venetian mandolin while employed at Lyon & Healy. His employer did not like the design, and never produced it. Indeed, some Chicago old-timers have said that Gabriel had been planning to jump the Lyon & Healy ship for Stromberg-Voisinet for a considerable time prior to Zorzi's firing. Thus, it is easy to believe that perhaps Gabriel, using the older Regal shape for inspiration, developed the Venetian shape and sold it independently to Stromberg-Voisinet in around

1930-31 Continental Venetian tenor guitars. 1930-31 Continental No. 2096 glued-neck Venetian flattop guitar with a Venetian headstock, Venetian bridge and pearlette-covered body and fingerboard (courtesy Michael Lee Allen).

1925, after Lyon & Healy rejected the idea. Stromberg-Voisinet luthiers then produced the Venetian mandolin. Such things *could* have happened in those days in the close world of Chicago guitarmaking.

Whether or not the Stromberg Venetian shape was inspired by the Regal No. 4000 or was actually invented by Philip Gabriel, we know that Joseph Zorzi was playing around with it at least by 1926. At that time, Joseph Zorzi built his first version of what would eventually become the Kay Kraft Venetian guitar shape, a Venetian mandolin.

There's probably no way to clear all this up, but a plausible resolution is possible. It seems fairly probable that Gabriel came up with the Venetian shape on a mandolin. The "Gabriel" design, like the Regal before it, was a very small mandolin with narrower points and with a solid block of wood from just above the soundhole to the heel-block. While that worked fine for a small mandolin, it would be totally impractical to build a guitar with solid wood in the upper bout. It is quite likely that it was Zorzi who adapted this design to guitar production, and, specifically, came up with the shimmed adjustable neck design which would come

to typify Kay Kraft, versus Stromberg, instruments.

Whether or not this redesign was Zorzi's contribution, this *was* indeed what took place between the old "Gabriel" mandolin and the expanded Stromberg line.

What is not in doubt is that by mid-1927, not long after Zorzi, Gabriel and Abbott joined the company, the Venetian shape emerged as the hallmark of Stromberg-Voisinet's progressive guitar designs, and would soon be part of what appear to be *the first American production electric guitars!*

Stromberg Venetian Guitars

Probably Stromberg-Voisinet began to offer its newly redesigned and expanded instrument line featuring the new two-point Venetian body on a series

Luthier Joseph Zorzi in a 1924 photograph (courtesy George Manno).

of glued-neck, flattop guitars, tenor guitars and mandolins as early as 1927. Evidence is contained in a variety of distributor catalogs dated from approximately 1929 to 1932, although examples (not Stromberg-branded) appear as late as 1935. While these descriptions come from different dates, probably the instruments described were available throughout the entire period.

Most of these S-V Venetians featured the old Stromberg half-slotted S-curve Venetian headstock design which had slots going almost all the way through, like a classical, but with a solid piece of wood on the back. This piece of wood had the trademark stamped design in it. Except for the mandolins (why change a good thing you've already tooled-up for?), these all had the new hollow construction.

In the Montgomery Ward Spring/Summer catalog #110 of 1929, Stromberg Venetian guitars included the D730 and D731, "Our Finest Hawaiian Guitar." These were glued-neck flattops with the two-point body, the Stromberg Venetian headstock and a new Venetian fixed bridge design, unveiled in 1928, with rounded edges curving to a neat downward point in the center, like an upside-down mustache. Older Stromberg bridges had been of the standard rectangular pyramid type. Except for the point, this is almost identical to the design used on earlier Lyon & Healy guitars, and illustrates the growing infusion of ideas that came with Zorzi, Gabriel and Abbott. This bridge would become known in later Kay literature as the "Venetian bridge."

The '29 D730 ($13.95) had a mahogany body, neck and top. The spruce-topped D731 ($19.95) was covered in nifty gunmetal gray pearloid (however, not on the headstock or fingerboard, as on later guitars)! Both had tops and soundholes bound in multiple white and black "ivorette." According to the illustration, these appeared to have bound ebony or ebonized fingerboards; however, the description mentions a "white pearlette fingerboard with dark pearlette position guides," which was, in fact, how these guitars came. They came with picks, a steel bar and two nuts for either Hawaiian or Spanish playing.

Also in this '29 catalog was one Venetian "Concertone" Tenor guitar, the D845 ($9.98, $11.25 with case). This was a mahogany-bodied guitar with a spruce top (colored marquetry inlay), bound fingerboard, floating bridge, tenor banjo tailpiece and tenor banjo-style headstock with banjo tuners. It offered "Sweet, clear guitar tones

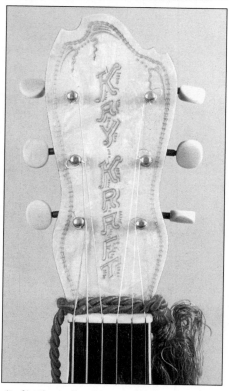 

(Left) Plastic-faced asymmetrical headstock of the ca. '32 Kay Kraft Style B (courtesy Society Hill Loan, Philadelphia, PA). (Right) Ca. 1933 Kay Kraft Style B designed by Joseph Zorzi, with maple body (courtesy Society Hill Loan, Philadelphia, PA).

with tenor banjo neck scale—acclaimed by radio and vaudeville entertainers."

In the subsequent Ward's catalog #111 Fall/Winter 1929-30, the Venetian Hawaiian guitars were replaced by the E560 ($15.95), basically the previous D730 with the addition of a small Hawaiian decal on the top, and the E731 ($19.95), the same pearloid-covered guitars as the D731. The E560 had mahogany body, neck and top (bound in black and white celluloid bands). No pickguard is shown in the illustration. The fingerboard was white pearlette with dark pearlette position markers. The E731 had a fingerboard of the gunmetal pearlette. Headstocks were the half-slotted Venetian shape. Bridges were fixed Venetians. More early Stromberg Venetian instruments are listed in the C.M.I. (Chicago Musical Instrument Company) catalog from 1929-30, including the No. 67

Tenor Guitar, a flattop with a glued-in neck, spruce top and mahogany body.

The tenor is described as sporting "the new and popular Venetian shape" and has the Stromberg Venetian headstock shape, unslotted, with four banjo-style tuners. The model shown in the C.M.I. catalog had a bound fingerboard, colored marquetry inlays, no pickguard, a plain moveable bridge, and a banjo-style small tailpiece. This was probably a slightly older version, because other examples in both the catalog and in *The Music Trades* had the new fixed Venetian pin bridge, indicating that the model had evolved thusly by late '29.

Stromberg Venetian guitars continued to be made pretty much as long as the Stromberg line itself existed, although archtop examples of these guitars would be sighted until 1936 or so. A good glimpse of the latter Stromberg Venetians is seen in the 1930-31 Continental catalog. The No. 2096 guitar ($33) was our old friend the Venetian flattop with a glued-in neck, spruce top, half-slotted Venetian headstock (no design pressed into the back, if the il-

1930-31 Continental Venetian flatback mandolins with the old Venetian headstock with built-in tuners (courtesy Michael Lee Allen).

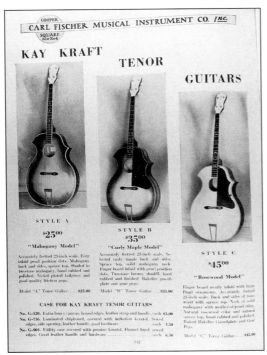

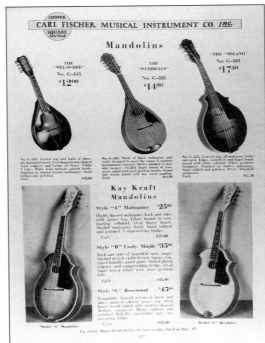

(Left) Kay Kraft Tenor Guitars from the 1935 Carl Fischer catalog (courtesy Clark McAvoy). (Right) Kay Kraft Mandolins from the 1935 Carl Fischer catalog; note the Kay-made Venetian mandolin still available (courtesy Clark McAvoy).

seems to mark the death of the Stromberg Venetian flattop.

Stromberg Venetian mandolins

Three Stromberg Venetian mandolins were offered by Montgomery Ward in 1928, the D766, D833 and D835. All had the new two-point body, but conventional pegheads, not the enclosed Venetian style of earlier models. These had spruce tops, moveable bridges, elevated pickguards and little tenor banjo-style tails. The D766 ($7.65) was plainest with a mahogany body. The D833 ($11.25) was also mahogany, but with white celluloid binding and color marquetry inlays around the top. The D835 ($14.95) was similar with a rosewood body.

In the subsequent Ward's catalog #111 Fall/Winter 1929-30, the E766 Venetian mandolin ($8.95) was also offered, identi-

lustration can be believed) and new Venetian bridge. This guitar's body was covered in pearlette like the older E731/D731 Strombergs. On the top was a matching pearlette pickguard. In the illustration this appears to have a plastic fingerboard, too, although no mention is made in the copy.

Two Venetian Tenor Guitars were offered by Continental in '30-31, the No. 2470 ($15) was a glued-neck flattop with a cherry finish, pearlette fingerboard and pickguard, Venetian bridge, old Venetian headstock with banjo tuners, marquetry around the top and soundhole and a decal on the belly (Stromberg No. 48). The No. 2472 ($30) was the same only far fancier, with the body, fingerboard, headstock and pickguard covered in mottled pearlette.

Stromberg-brand Venetian instruments are still seen in the 1932 C.M.I. catalog. The 6-string available was the Stromberg No. 76 Guitar, a Venetian with a glued neck, birch body, spruce top, checkerboard binding and rosette, centerpoint Stromberg bridge, half-slotted Venetian head, and Bakelite pickguard.

The Stromberg No. 76 Guitar continued to be offered in the 1932-33 Conti-

nental catalog as the No. 2111 Venetian Style Guitar. This marked the swan song of this beauty.

Two Stromberg Venetian tenors appeared in the '32 C.M.I. catalog, the No. 76T and No. 48. The No. 76T was spruce topped with a birch body, checkerboard binding, Venetian head with banjo tuners, centerpointed bridge and Bakelite 'guard. The No. 48 had a spruce top, birch body, marquetry, centerpoint bridge, Venetian head with banjo tuners, white pearlette fingerboard, and white pickguard.

Essentially the Stromberg brand disappeared after 1932, perhaps into 1933; however, the instruments can still be sighted at least into 1935 in the Carl Fischer catalog. Still around was the Fischer No. G-670 Venetian-shaped guitar, basically the old Stromberg No. 48. Also still around was the No. G-850 Venetian Tenor Guitar, the old Stromberg No. 76T. The Venetian shape continues in guitars slightly beyond '35, and way beyond then in mandolins, but '35

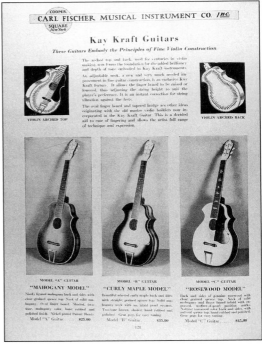

The Kay Kraft Guitar line from the 1935 Carl Fischer catalog; these are the same illustrations used throughout the run beginning in '32 at the earliest (courtesy Clark McAvoy).

cal to the previous D766.

Prior to the Ward mandos, in October of 1928, Stromberg-Voisinet officially announced a new line of instruments which included a Venetian mandolin sporting a newly redesigned *symmetrical* headstock with twin center humps similar to the '60s Epiphone design. These were not reflected in the Ward's catalog, indicating that several headstock designs were available at the same time.

Yet another Stromberg mandolin appeared in the 1929-30 C.M.I. catalog, the No. 600 Mandolin. This had a glued-in neck, mahogany body, spruce top and appears to be a flattop. The strings passed over a very thin moveable bridge and fastened to a typical small tailpiece on the lower bout. These had a screwed-on pickguard. The mandolin *shown* in the C.M.I. catalog had the same Stromberg Venetian-shaped headstock as the earlier Venetian mandolin from 1925, but it's *described* as "new style," celluloid-

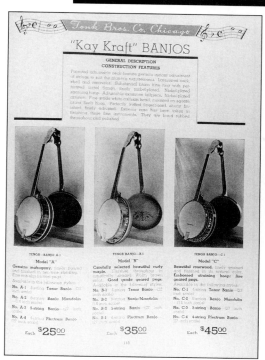

(Left) Kay Kraft Banjos from the 1935 Tonk Brothers catalog (courtesy Robert Watkins). (Right) Venetian flattop guitar from the 1935 Carl Fischer catalog; these were available as early as 1930 (courtesy Michael Lee Allen).

Kay Kraft Jumbo Guitars from the 1935 Carl Fischer catalog (courtesy Clark McAvoy).

faced and unslotted, indicating that the catalog has an older illustration. The description suggests the new asymmetrical head found on contemporary Kay Krafts.

Two Venetian mandolins were offered in the 1930-31 Continental catalog, both flatbacks with the old Venetian headstock with built-in tuners. The No. 2230 ($13.50) had a birch body (Stromberg No. 450), while the No. 2232 ($16.50) had a mahogany body (Stromberg No. 600). These continued through the '31 catalog.

Five Stromberg-brand Venetian mandolins were offered in the 1932 C.M.I. catalog. The No. 75 ($12) had an atypical squared-off headstock, spruce top, mahogany body, basswood neck, ebonized fingerboard with four dots, checkerboard binding, and Bakelite pickguard. The No. 76 ($15) was similar except the body was birch, the body and ebonized fingerboard had a wider "line" design, and the head was the symmetrical "Epi" style. The No. 450 ($13.50) was another spruce/birch mando with symmetrical "Epi" head, plain white

body binding. The No. 600 ($18) had the symmetrical head, spruce top, mahogany body, and colored wood inlays. The No. 750 ($22.50) was the same as the No. 600 except for a rosewood body and marquetry strip down the center of the back. It's interesting to note that while some Stromberg guitars and tenors still had the older S-curve Venetian head, these all had the symmetrical "Epi" style.

While the Venetian shape would continue for many years hence, these C.M.I. Strombergs would mark the end of the Stromberg mandolin line.

Later Stromberg Spanish guitars

Later Stromberg-Voisinet Spanish guitars are seen in both the Ward's and C.M.I. catalogs reflecting the later days of the Stromberg line.

Spanish flattop guitars in the Spring/ Summer 1929 Ward's catalog included a wide range of models. Top of the line was the D817 "Serenader" Concert Size Guitar ($24.95), "acclaimed by Broadway artists." This had a mahogany body and glued-in neck, a standard slotted headstock, spruce top bound in white ivorette, with mother-of-pearl top and soundhole purfling, and a

(Left) Venetian flattop mandolin with new symmetrical headstock from the '35 Carl Fischer catalog; this also was available as early as 1930 (courtesy Michael Lee Allen). (Right) 1933-34 Arch Kraft tenor guitars (identical to Kay Kraft Deluxe Tenor guitars) and Venetian mandolins sold by Targ & Dinner (courtesy Mike Newton).

bound ebonized fingerboard inlaid with a pearl vine. The bridge was a relatively plain rectangular pin variety.

Next in line was the D769 "Troubadour" Concert Guitar ($19.75), in which "memories of old romance dwell in the lilting tone." "Praised by professionals for its brilliant performance," this had a rosewood body, spruce top, mahogany neck, and ebonized fingerboard with white pearlized binding and pearl diamond inlays. The headstock was the half-slotted Venetian type; the bridge was Venetian. The top had black/white ivorette binding.

Under these beauties were the D748 ($15.95) with rosewood body, spruce top and mahogany neck. Head was slotted, bridge pyramid, top and soundhole bound with colored marquetry. The D736 ($10.75) was a similar guitar with a mahogany body, pyramid bridge, marquetry, half-slotted Venetian headstock and a Hawaiian island scene decoration. Curiously enough, the D741 ($11.95) was an auditorium-sized *12-string version!*

The D800 ($8.75) was a mahogany-finished birch "Two-in-One Guitar Outfit," a glued-neck guitar with the half-slotted Ve-

netian headstock, rectangular pin bridge, a pair of nuts for Spanish or Hawaiian playing, marquetry and the fancy top decoration of the old C737. The D723 ($6.45) was a rosewood-finished birch Students' Guitar, with slothead and colored marquetry. A D727 el cheapo ($3.85) guitar with a slothead, moveable bridge, cheap trapeze tailpiece and a couple hand-painted flowers on the top was probably a Stromberg, as well.

Two Spanish-shaped Hawaiians rounded out the guitar offerings, the D737 ($9.98) had a birch body, spruce top, Venetian half-slotted head, marquetry and elaborate top decorations. The D905 ($5.95) was all-birch with the Venetian headstock and more fancy scroll top decorations.

The Stromberg Spanish guitar line as represented in the Fall/Winter 1929-30 Montgomery Ward catalog was pretty much the apex of the brand.

The slothead E817 "Serenader" was still offered at $24.95, still the same. The E748 ($17.85) was the same as the previous D748 with the exception of the Venetian half-slotted headstock. Two Two-in-One Combination Guitar Outfits were offered, the

E805 ($14.75) and E800 ($8.95). The E805 had top marquetry, a small celluloid pickguard, a rectangular pin bridge, the Venetian half-slotted headstock and an elaborate Hawaiian scene covering the entire belly. The E800 was basically a repeat of the D800/C737 with the Venetian headstock. Both came with two nuts for Spanish or Hawaiian playing. The slothead E723 ($6.95) was the old D723 birch student guitar. The budget E727 was the old D727 with a price of $4.05. The E905 ($6.25) was the old D905.

The '29 C.M.I. catalog featured one Stromberg, the No. 167 Guitar. This was a standard, small-bodied Spanish with a glued-in neck, mahogany body, spruce top, and a fixed rectangular pyramid pin bridge. The

Mid-'30s Kay flattop Venetian mandolin with the old Kay Kraft headstock shape (photo: Mike Newton).

ebonized fingerboard had pearl inlays. This had the typical Stromberg rosewood-faced, half-slotted Venetian headstock.

A variety of Stromberg-made Spanish guitars appeared in the 1931 Continental catalog. The No. 2122 Guitar was a concert size, basically a Stromberg No. 34P, with half-slotted Venetian head, marquetry, small pickguard, made of birch with a spruce top, very similar to the E805. The No. 2108 Guitar was a Stromberg No. 65M with an all-mahogany guitar with white celluloid binding and fancy inlays on the fingerboard, and black and white "line" purfling around the top and soundhole. The No. 2104 Hawaiian Guitar was a little guitar with a spruce top, mahogany body, white celluloid binding and a stenciled vine inlay extending from the belly up around the top edges.

The '31 Continental catalog also featured three Regal-brand guitars made by Stromberg-Voisinet. The No. 2106 ($21.50) was slothead guitar with a spruce top, figured mahogany body, colored wood purfling around the top, soundhole and back center strip. A veneered head had a pearl star inlay. The fingerboard was ovalled — a Kay trademark — with pearl dots and nickel silver frets. The slothead No. 2110 Guitar ($26) had a spruce top, rosewood body, mahogany neck, inlaid soundhole, top and center back strip. The No. 2112 ($34.50) was similar with top-grade lumber, and thin black and white strip purfling.

The Stromberg flattop Spanish guitars also continued to be offered, more or less, at least through 1932. The ca. 1932 Karl Fischer catalog included several Spanish flattop guitars which were also probably Strombergs, including one with the pointy fixed Venetian bridge and pearlette-faced slotted headstock, the all-mahogany, Grand Concert sized No. G-680 Guitar. The No. G-860 Handcraft Tenor Guitar was a Grand Concert with all-mahogany construction and the new asymmetrical head soon to be associated with Kay Kraft.

Headstock of the ca. '34 Recording King Style B (photo: Gilbert Matossian).

The last gasp can be seen in the '32 C.M.I. catalog. The No. 34P ($15) was a Spanish guitar with a half-slotted Venetian head, spruce top, birch body, celluloid binding, basswood neck, pearlette fingerboard, pyramid bridge, small pickguard and Hawaiian scene on the front. The No. 49 ($15) was similar with a squared off slothead, spruce top, birch body, marquetry purfling,

white celluloid binding, basswood neck with pearlette fingerboard, Stromberg centerpointed bridge, small gunmetal pickguard and matching headplate, and the same Hawaiian scene. The No. 65M guitar ($15) was the same as the figured mahogany '31 Continental No. 2108. The No. 65M Tenor Guitar ($15) was the same with four strings. The No. 60 Guitar ($19.50) was a more conventional slothead guitar with spruce top, mahogany body and neck, ebonized fingerboard, black and white celluloid binding, bound veneered head, back centerstrip and nickel plated patent heads.

And that's all she wrote on *Stromberg* Spanish guitars.

Later Stromberg banjos

Later-day Stromberg-Voisinet banjos were featured by Wards in '29, worth noting is the "Super Deluxe" D757, which had a shell, resonator, fingerboard and peghead covered in white pearloid with fancy colored engraving. The metal hardware was engraved and gold-plated! This may have been the most highly decorated Stromberg-Voisinet instrument ever produced. It cost a whopping $124.95.

Also offered were the old D696 "Melody King" ($67.85) with pearlette covering and hand engraving, the D762 "Syncopator" Tenor ($36.45) with a walnut shell and pearloid fingerboard, the regular D842 Tenor Banjo Outfit ($14.95) with birdseye maple rim, and several Banjo-Ukuleles.

By 1931, as seen in the Continental catalog, there were six Stromberg banjos, illustrated as Tenors but also available as Plectrums. The No. 2016 Tenor Banjo (Stromberg No. 17, $24) had a 7-ply laminated shell of birdseye maple, nickel-plated tone flange with 20 brackets, one-piece maple neck, white pearlette fingerboard, and flower decal on back. The head was an elaborate symmetrical design. The No. 2018 Tenor Banjo ($42) had solid walnut

Ca. 1934 Kay Kraft Style B bearing the Recording King brand from Montgomery Ward (photo: Gilbert Matossian). 1933-34 S.S. Maxwell No.728, one of Kay's earliest f-hole guitars, built for Targ & Dinner (courtesy Mike Newton).

1933-34 S.S. Maxwell Credenza and Florenza Model resonators made by Kay. 1934-35 Kay Kraft Deluxe archtop guitars from the Sorkin catalog (Photos courtesy Mike Newton).

walnut resonator.

These 1932 banjos mark the end of the Stromberg brand for banjos, though the tradition continued with Kay Kraft and Kay.

Pearloid

But before we move on to more exciting things, let's wrap up our discussion of Stromberg-Voisinet by mentioning the company's skill at working pearloid. Pearloid was a type of plasticine, which antedates our more modern polymers. It was generally opaque, or translucent at best. Stromberg-Voisinet was certainly not the only company to favor this material, but they certainly used their share. Not all of it was the usual white. As mentioned, the company was selling guitars with bodies covered in a gray plastic. Apparently they also made some Serenader

resonator, neck and rim. The ebonized fingerboard had pearl dots. The flange was metal. The No. 2022 Tenor Banjo (Stromberg No. 130, $36) had a laminated shell with side covered in white pearlette, nickel plated flange, 20 brackets, 5-ply neck, white pearlette fingerboard, engraved, gold-filled position markers, gunmetal pearlette on back, engraved with two circles, and armrest. The No. 2010 Tenor Banjo (Stromberg No. 51, $30) had a 7-ply laminated mahogany shell with a nickel plated tone flange, 20 brackets, 5-ply mahogany neck, mahogany resonator, pearl inlay on head, bound ebonized fingerboard with diamonds, and a flower decal on the back. The No. 2012 Tenor Banjo (Stromberg No. 14, $20) had a 7-ply birdseye maple shell with a nickel plated flange, 20 brackets, a bound laminated resonator with ring decal, and an ebonized fingerboard with pearl dots. Finally, the No. 2014 Tenor Banjo ($40) had a 7-ply laminated walnut shell with colored wood inlay on the sides, a 20 bracket flange, 5-piece walnut neck, bound white pearlette fingerboard, carved heel, laminated walnut resonator with inlaid marquetry flower basket.

Stromberg banjos lasted into 1932 and

were shown in the C.M.I. catalog. These were Stromberg-branded banjos basically the same as those seen the year before sold as Continentals. It is curious to note that these all had "the adjustable neck feature," a reference to Joseph Zorzi's probable contribution. Also, all models were available in tenor, plectrum, banjo mandolin, and 5-string versions. Still offered were the Stromberg No. 14 (Continental No. 2012), No. 17 (Continental No. 2016), No. 51 (Continental No. 2010), and the No. 130 (Continental No. 2022). Three other Stromberg banjos were listed in the '32 C.M.I. catalog. The open-back No. 1 ($10.50) had an 11" laminated maple shell, 16 brackets, maple neck, ebonized fingerboard, and four pearl dots. The No. 9 ($15) was similar to the No. 1 except for having a 13" laminated birdseye maple resonator and two-tone shaded amber finish with a rose decoration. Lastly, but not leastly, was the No. 58 ($45) with a laminated walnut shell, 28 bracket flange with "extra heavy brass tone band," celluloid-inlaid sides, laminated walnut neck, ebonized fingerboard with fancy mother-of-pearl inlays, and burl

1933 Oahu Deluxe Jumbo Guitar Style No. 60 built by Kay (courtesy Jim Dulfer).

banjos for Bugeleisen & Jacobson in New York which had a rose pink color, covered in clear lacquer, which nowadays usually appears a salmon color. Another banjo made for Leedy has been seen which had a non-pearloid beige covering with little dark brown and white swirls. This instrument also had checker binding and gold sparkle dot inlays!

This predilection for pearloid would come to the fore soon in the Kay Kraft guitars, and make a curious historical background against which one can view those bizarre Kelvinator headstocks of the late '50s.

America's first production electrics?

However interesting Venetian shapes and pearloid covered guitars and banjos may be, they pale in comparison to the fact that in 1928, Stromberg-Voisinet became America's first company to produce electric guitars.

The usual canon is that George Beauchamp and Karl Barth, failing to convince National to produce their electric Hawaiian "Frying pan" in 1931, left to join with Adolf Rickenbacker in the formation of Electro, producing the first electric gui-

tars in 1932. These would later become called Rickenbackers. While these *were* the first commercially produced electric guitars with modern electro-magnetic pickups, the credit for producing the first-ever electric guitars goes to Stromberg-Voisinet, some four years earlier.

These first electrics were basically the Stromberg line announced in October of 1928, including the Venetian tenor guitar, but offered as Stromberg Electro Instruments, "Electrically Amplified Guitars, Tenor Guitars, Banjos and Mandolins." These were very early acoustic-electric instruments with electronics which seem to have been designed, or "perfected," at least, by Stromberg-Voisinet's rising star, Henry Kuhrmeyer.

Because these are such curiosities, let us

quote *The Music Trades* (October 20, 1928), at length:

"*New Sales Avenue Opened with Tone Amplifier for Stringed Instruments*/H.C. [sic] Kuhrmeyer Perfects Electrically Operated Device That Produces an Increased Volume of Tone for Any Stringed Instrument When Used with Phonographs or Radio Receivers.

"A tone amplifier for string instruments which, observers declare, is destined to bring the guitar, in particular, into its own as a 'professional' instrument has been perfected by H.C. Kuhrmeyer, secretary of the Stromberg-Voisinet Co., 316 Union Park Court, Chicago. Patents have been applied for on the device and the first production unit is now under way at the Stromberg-Voisinet factory. Experimental units have already proved highly successfully in use here by radio broadcasting organizations and professional orchestras.

"This tone amplifier is electrically operated, either by alternating or direct current. It consists of two major units — an electro-magnetic pick-up and an amplifying unit. The electro-magnetic pick-up is built within the instrument and is attached to its sounding board. This unit is connected with the amplifier, which produces the tone volume required of the instrument.

"**How It Works.** The electro-magnetic pick-up operates to convert the me-

Stromberg Venetian Flattop Body Sizes				
The following guide to body sizes Stromberg Venetian flattop instruments was compiled by guitar aficionado Mike Newton.				
	Lower bout	Upper bout	Depth	Scale
Guitar	$13^{1}/_{4}$"	10"	$3^{1}/_{2}$"	$24^{1}/_{4}$"
Tenor	11"	8"	3"	23"
Mandolin	$9^{3}/_{8}$"	$5^{1}/_{4}$"	$2^{3}/_{4}$"	14"
Bout (across points)				

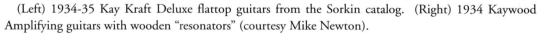

(Left) 1934-35 Kay Kraft Deluxe flattop guitars from the Sorkin catalog. (Right) 1934 Kaywood Amplifying guitars with wooden "resonators" (courtesy Mike Newton).

Oahu Jumbo Guitar

.... same size, same tone quality as The De Luxe Jumbo

This instrument is a part of the famous .. *Oahu* .. family, for the person who appreciates a plain instrument without pearl work, and the only consideration is tone quality and workmanship, we recommend this instrument as the best that money can buy. .... *Guaranteed to last a lifetime.*

Has the best gear pegs. .... Each instrument has a special guard plate, reinforced gridge and *Oahu* polished strings. Hand rubbed. De luxe Oahu finish.

IN buying a musical instrument consider the reputation, and trade name of the manufacturer. More *Oahu* Hawaiian Guitars are sold than any other kind. Considering the tone quality, the construction and the guarantee *Oahu* instruments have never had a competitor — be your own judge — tune to any program of the *Oahu Serenaders*, NBC artists. The value of any musical instrument lies in its tone quality. "When better guitars are made, *Oahu* will be the first to make them." Play safe — buy from the world's largest guitar dealers. The biggest mistake any person can make is to buy a guitar from some one who can not even play same.

Style 68B. OAHU JUMBO

PRICE

$98.00

Terms if desired, or your present instrument taken in trade.

HAWAIIAN GUITARS AND ACCESSORIES

Style No. 65m

Genuine Hawaiian Mahogany, natural finish, standard size, piano polish, manufactured under the most exacting conditions. For a standard size instrument, tone quality and workmanship is incomparable. This is the same instrument used by hundreds of radio and recording artists. Carries the regular lifetime "OAHU" guarantee. Present owners of this instrument refuse to part with them.

PRICE

Style No. 65m Each $65.00

Style No. 51

Built for long hard service. Has an exclusive "OAHU" design. Finished in black, imitation pearlette finger board. For those who desire an excellent inexpensive instrument. We recommend this model. Carries the regular "OAHU" guarantee.

PRICE

Style No. 51 Each $27.50

The Guitarist Who Is "Wise," Buys Nothing But "OAHU" Supplies.

(Left) 1933 Oahu Jumbo Guitar Style No. 68B made by Kay. (Right) 1933 Oahu Style No. 65m made by Kay (photos courtesy Jim Dulfer).

chanical vibrations of a bridge or sound board to electrical impulses. These impulses, in turn, are amplified, thereby increasing the tone of the instrument as many times as desired.

"The device is particularly adapted for use with the guitar, tenor guitar, banjo and violin, but can be applied, as well to any stringed instrument, and the amplifying unit alone produces an increased volume and pleasant tone when used with phonographs and radio receiving sets. In all cases it is operated from either AC or DC with converter.

"**Valuable To Orchestras.** Its utility has been found to be particularly valuable and significant when used by orchestras as it enables the banjoist to play either tenor guitar or guitar, and have that instrument stand out above others in the orchestra. The want of volume in these string

instruments has restricted their importance as units of an orchestra; but this device, amplifying the instrument's tone without distortion of any kind, now removes that

restriction, it is claimed, and enables these instruments to take their proper place as orchestral units and as solo instruments for the stage and large auditorium.

"**Now In Production.** The device was perfected by Mr. Kuhrmeyer during the past six months, working largely in the acoustic laboratories of the United Reproducers Corp., St. Charles, Ill. Now in production at the Stromberg-Voisinet factory here, they are being manufactured complete, that is, the string instrument equipped with the electro-magnetic pickup and the separate amplifier. The entire set will be sold ready to be attached to a power unit and played. A single amplifier can be used for other orchestral instruments equipped with the electro-magnetic pick-up. The amplifiers are made in a carrying case design, measur-

The Oahu De Luxe Jumbo Guitar

... the aristocrat of them all

is GUARANTEED to be the finest and best Guitar ever manufactured by anyone. You can secure it for Hawaiian or Spanish playing. It is made of the finest African Rosewood.

The beauty of this instrument is such that you will be proud to have it grace any orchestra trio or musical group.

As to Tone Quality, be your own judge. Just tune to any program of the Oahu Serenaders and you will be convinced of the incomparable tone quality of this instrument.

Rich or Poor—Young or Old—Amateur or Professional players all acknowledge that Oahu Guitars have no equal.

"Johnny was a guitar player, very hard to please. Whenever he played in public, he tons nervous and ill at ease. One day he bought a Jumbo, and now I'll have you know. He's the happiest, cheeriest fellow —wherever he happens to go."

The head of this instrument, the entire length of the neck, edges of the face and sound hole are richly inlaid with the very best Waikiki polished genuine pearl. All pearl work is skillfully done by hand and elaborately finished Hand rubbed. De Luxe finish. This instrument is guaranteed a lifetime. Equipped with the new SafeTiString posts (See page 19).

Style 68K — Square Neck — Hawaiian Style

Style 69K — Round Neck — Spanish Style

PRICE

$158.00

Terms if desired, or your present instrument taken in trade

The Oahu Jumbo Guitar

is the same size and has the same tone quality as The De Luxe Jumbo. This instrument is one of the members of the famous Oahu family. For one who appreciates a neat looking instrument without elaborate handiwork and whose primary interest is tone quality and workmanship, we recommend this instrument as the best that money can buy. It is Guaranteed to last a lifetime.

Each instrument is equipped with the new SafeTiString posts (See page 19), a special reinforced bridge, Oahu polished strings and an Oahu De Luxe hand-rubbed finish.

Style 71K—Square Neck Hawaiian Style

Style 72K—Round Neck Spanish Style

PRICE

$98.00

Terms if desired, or your present instrument taken in trade

"You May Have Seen All the Rest—Make Up Your Mind Now to Buy the Best"

When buying a musical instrument one should pause to consider the reputation and trade name of the manufacturer. Day by day the popularity of Oahu Guitars increases. Consider the tone quality, the construction and the guarantee Oahu instruments have and let your judgment guide you.

The value of any musical instrument lies in its tone quality. "When better guitars are made, Oahu will be the first to make them." Play safe and buy from the world's largest guitar dealers.

For distinctive instruments with unequaled tone quality, follow the crowd to Oahu Dealers.

(Left) 1937 Oahu De Luxe Jumbo Guitar Style 68K made by Kay. (Right) 1937 Oahu Jumbo Guitar Style 71K made by Kay (photos courtesy Jim Dulfer).

ing about 18 in. x 15 in. x 19 in.

"One of the first complete units in a Stromberg-Voisinet guitar to be manufactured is now being shown and demonstrated in the banjo shop of Milton G. Wolf, 816 Kimball Building, Chicago, where it is attracting widespread interest and praise. The amplifier is also being used there with a portable phonograph with really amazing results.

"String instruments equipped with the device have been used with singular success here by 'The Vagabonds' in broadcasting programs. 'The Vagabonds' — Dean and Paul Upson and Curt Poulton, are Brunswick recording artists and are numbered among the leading radio entertainers of this section. It was used in a broadcast-

Early guitar amplification

The technology for making portable amplifiers had been developed in 1926 and '27, making the Stromberg Electros possible. Since it applies directly to these first production electric guitars, let's look briefly at the evolution of early amplifiers.

Experiments in amplification were already underway by the early '20s, if not before. As mentioned, both Lyon & Healy and Lloyd Loar were playing around with the idea of amplification as early as 1923. Recall that sound on film only first appeared in 1923, but took a few years to catch on because there was no amplification in theaters. [It's amusing to note that while I was researching this article, I encountered editorials in *The Music Trades* in the late '20s optimistically proclaiming that there was no way "talkies" would put *theater organists* out of work!]

We have no idea what these early electric instruments were played through. Wall-outlet AC power had yet to become universal, and ways to use AC current in electrical appliances remained to be developed. There were no efficient power output tubes yet, and no cone speakers. A good speculation would be that Lloyd Loar's amplifier was probably much like the audio output section of contemporary radios. Radios had one '01A pre-amp tube, either a '12A or '71A output tube, and a horn speaker. These ran off wet-cell batteries and may have had between 1 and 2 watts of power output. A little hard to imagine dragging this rig to a gig. Hardly a Marshall stack!

The breakthrough to modern amplifiers began in 1926. At that time Western Electric and RCA came up with large PA systems which used large 211 tubes which had originally been developed for telephone and radio broadcasting. These systems ran off AC current, not batteries. These were the first theater amplifiers for the talkies, still entirely too large to provide portable amplification for guitars.

In 1926, Western Electric also came up with the first magnetic phono cartridge. Indeed, this may have been a direct ancestor of the pickup used in the Stromberg Electros. In 1927, RCA introduced its Radiola 18, the first home radio to employ a rectifier tube and power transformer, which allowed it to run off AC wall current.

By 1928, there were two rectifier tube options, the 80, a single diode tube, and the 81, which was about half the power of the 80 and used in pairs in the big theater amplifiers. Two preamp tubes were also available, the 26 and 27. The 26 was used in some radios, but the 27 was the preamp tube used in virtually all amplification circuits.

In 1928, RCA also announced the 45 and 50 power triode output tubes. These were the first fairly compact, powerful power

tubes, but were not generally available until 1929, well after the Stromberg amplifier. The next small power tube was the 42, which wasn't developed until 1932-33. All these tubes were triode tubes, by the way; pentodes had yet to be invented.

Lastly, but not leastly, at the beginning of 1928, Jenson came out with the first modern cone speaker powered by a field coil. Prior to these developments, it would have been pretty difficult to build a portable guitar amp.

It was some combination of these elements, which made up Stromberg's amplifiers. By the way, this evolutionary history explains why the contemporary hype suggested that the new amp could also enhance your phonograph player, since that was likely to have an old horn speaker and no comparable amplification.

These were a long way away from being hi fi components, featuring specs like 100 to 5,000 cps with 5 percent distortion (by comparison, typical modern hi fi equipment has distortion levels at around .002 percent!), but they made noise and you could carry them around.

Just exactly what configuration the Stromberg amps used is unknown, but with some research and deductive reasoning Mike Newton has been able to speculate with a high degree of probability. Given availability and general usage, it's probable that they were two-stage amps using an 80 rectifier, a 27 pre-amp tube, and a pair of '71A output tubes and may have put out around 3 watts of power, but keep in mind that this is just guesswork. The cabinets measured 18" x 19" x 15" and carried a 12" Jenson speaker. One reason these early amps were so expensive is that the 12" speaker would have run somewhere between $25 and $50 wholesale. No mention is made of controls. We know there were no volume controls on the instruments, and there probably were none on the amp either: like some other early amps, these first Strombergs probably ran wide open. When Kay returned to electrics in the mid-'30s, the first generation had no volume or tone controls.

While we don't know what these sounded like, it's possible to speculate that they may have been about as loud as a Fender Tweed Champ, only cleaner. We won't know for sure till one shows up.

In any case, Henry Kay Kuhrmeyer was one of the first people out of the gate with this, then, state-of-the-art technology!

As with most other things, the Depression intervened to halt development in amplification until the mid-'30s when technology took another great leap forward. By the beginning of 1939, most of the large tubes used in guitar amps had been invented, including the classic 6V6GT glass power output tube. It would not be until March of 1948 that the first miniature preamp tube, the 12AX7, would appear.

(Left) 1937 Oahu Style No. 112K Tenor with a Stromberg bridge made by Kay. (Right) 1937 Oahu Styles No. 66K and 65K made by Kay (photos courtesy Jim Dulfer).

ing program staged on Columbus Day, at the seventh Annual Chicago Radio Show where it was widely acclaimed, and by Guy Lombardo's Orchestra at the Grenada Cafe, noted in Chicago for its singularly fine dance music. Arrangements are also being made to introduce these Stromberg-Voisinet instruments at other prominent Chicago dance places, notably the Aragon Ballroom."

[Note that Henry Kuhrmeyer is incorrectly identified as "H.C.," whereas it should be "H.K."]

This sounds like a very early transducer pickup! As the catalog describes it, "The tone in these instruments is amplified many times, through a magnetic pickup built into the instrument which takes the vibrations direct from the sounding board, and passes it through a two-stage amplifier. Every tone is brought out distinctly and evenly, with a volume that will fill even a large hall..." In the illustrations, the instruments show no evidence of pickups except for having *two* cords coming from the area of the end-pin. These were positive and negative leads with $1/8$" phone tips like those used at the time to connect aerial leads on radios. Basically

the amplified Stromberg Electros corresponded to the No. 167 Spanish guitar, No. 67 Tenor Guitar, No. 51 Tenor Banjo, No. 600 Mandolin, plus a banjo mandolin.

The amplifier had one cone speaker on the side and positive/negative inputs for three separate instruments (cost, a whopping $165). The Electro Guitar, Spanish or Hawaiian style, Tenor Guitar and Mandolin all cost $40; the Tenor Banjo, which in an acoustic version was more expensive than Stromberg guitars, cost $50.

While Stromberg-Voisinet's Electro instruments didn't use the same version of electro-magnetic technology, which would eventually establish the electric guitar, they were indubitably electric guitars.

Rare birds

Stromberg Electros are rare. Sometime in 1937 Rickenbacker challenged Kay's right to make electric guitars, and in his response, Kuhrmeyer alludes to his previous electric escapades. He says, "In fact,

we put out several hundred electrical instruments as far back as 1927. At that time our patent attorney informed us that it would be impossible to control any method of electrical amplification for musical instruments, as it was already covered by patents held by A.T. & T." (unpublished company letter). Since the announcement of the Stromberg Electros didn't hit the press until October of '28, Kuhrmeyer's recollection of 1927 was probably slightly off, probably recalling early developments, not actual production, which was most likely in 1928.

Indeed, it's quite probable that the '28 Stromberg Electros were carrying on from earlier electronic experiments. According to some second-hand accounts, as early as 1923 Lyon & Healy had an electric bass, although this had an unfortunate de-

1937 Oahu Volu-Tone with flattop guitars made by Kay (courtesy Jim Dulfer).

sign flaw which made the player the ground, thereby killing anyone who happened to sweat while he played... There are also reports seeing another Stromberg-Voisinet guitar which looked to be closer to 1924, although, based on the timeframe of technological developments, this was most likely an earlier guitar with an electric retrofit, but maybe not. In '24 Lloyd Loar was also working on a primitive capacitance pickup and installed it in a string bass and viola and even performed several recitals with this device, although no one knows what sort of amplification he used.

In any case, it's clear from what Kuhrmeyer's patent attorney advised

(Left) 1935 Carl Fischer catalog with the Handcraft Tenor Guitar by Kay (courtesy Clark McAvoy). (Right) 1935 Tonk Brothers catalog with the "old standby" Venetian mandolin created by Regal in the 1920s, still around (courtesy Robert Watkins).

that the race for electric guitars was well on by the time the Stromberg Electros appeared. And, since Stromberg-Voisinet actually produced these guitars, that makes them (until another candidate is found), and not Electro/Rickenbacker, the first American electric guitar company! Most certainly, as one pundit has put it wryly, these marked "the *last* time Kay was on the cutting edge of technology!!"

Unplugged

Just why Stromberg Electros didn't take the world by storm is unknown. Part of it could have been poor timing — the Depression struck in 1929 — but since they had about a year to get a toehold, there's probably another reason. As mentioned in *The Music Trades*, they *were* featured on the radio. However, the real possibility exists that they just may not have sounded too good, providing a tone comparable to strapping a phonograph cartridge under the soundboard of a small flattop. Still, no electrics had existed before, so how would anyone know if the sound sucked? What-

ever the reason, after 1929 Stromberg Electros slip into oblivion. By that time, perhaps inspired by the Stromberg Electros, both Gibson and Vega were experimenting with amplification, but the Depression definitely put that on hold, until Electro charged into the fray in 1932.

The Transition from Stromberg-Voisinet to Kay

While the Stromberg brand name continued on into the early '30s, there's little doubt that the Stromberg Electros marked its high point of achievement. However, this was a period of rapid change, for both American society — with the Great Depression — and the company, which was undergoing a transition from Stromberg-Voisinet to Kay. Unfortunately, we have lots of murky "facts" about this era, but few conclusive answers. Published dates for the change from Stromberg-Voisinet to Kay have ranged from 1928 to 1931. Let's try to sort some of this out.

What appears to be the situation is that, as Hank Kuhrmeyer increasingly dominated the company, Stromberg-Voisinet

1935 Carl Fischer catalog with the Venetian Tenor Guitar (courtesy Clark McAvoy).

Oahu Custom Built ELECTRICS WITH *Mellow Tones*

OAHU electric guitars and amplifiers pictured on these pages are CUSTOM BUILT. In them has been incorporated the beauty and dignity of fine wood and the vibrant richness of mellow tones.

Every source has been probed to its depths to give the artist an instrument with technical completeness. Oahu does not tolerate flexibility in the various parts used in the building of its sets. They must meet the most rigid specifications.

It is the usual desire of the musician that his instrument respond in an easy, efficient manner to his perfected ability to perform. Oahu Electrics have been designed to serve the artist in this respect.

At your finger tips has been placed control of the richest tones ever to have been produced by this type of instrument. Full, deep, mellow bass tones or clear, vibrant trebles are governed by no more exertion than the curving of your little finger.

One would naturally say a guitar of this type is now complete, but we have gone a step farther. A "TOUCH CONTROL" on the back of the instrument—a miniature slide switch—gives the player with a soft touch an added range of volume with which to work and a great amount of sustained tone. It compensates for the loss of volume encountered when a foot pedal is used and steps up the volume for satisfactory operation on a battery amplifier.

Tonemaster

Solid mahogany body; White ivoride binding; Patented Safe-T-String Posts; 16" scale; Equipped with "High Bass" scientifically gauged monel wound strings; Volume and Tone controls; "Oahu" patented metal string bridge; "Touch control."

No. 229K—Tonemaster $37.50

No. 263K

No. 229K

Diana DeLuxe

Oahu's "DIANA DELUXE" is built in like manner to the Tonemaster except that underneath its final coat of lacquer has been placed a gold leaf design, combining the dignity of beautiful wood with the richness of old gold.

No. 263K—DIANA DELUXE $63.50

Standard Amplifier

8" clear-tone dynamic speaker; 12 watts peak power output; Dual controlled, high and low gain inputs accommodate two instruments, or one microphone and one instrument; Easily accessible fuse protection on instrument panel; Pilot light; Four leaded hum-free, non-microphonic tubes; Has been power output tubes; Sturdy veneer case covered with airplane luggage material; Attractive "Oahu" grill backed with gold cloth protects speaker cone; A special cover protects Voice Coil of the speaker against detrimental dirt or metal particles.

● Cautious designing has resulted in an absolute minimum A.C. hum, and sorting of tubes as well as floating them in rubber has rendered this amplifier free from mechanical rattles, vibrations, and annoying feed-back, so commonly experienced.

No. 230K—Standard Amplifier for 110-volt, 50-60 cycle A.C. operation $77.50

For different A.C. voltages and frequencies, additional $5.00

See "Electrical Briefs" page 13, paragraph 4.

No. 230K

NOTE THE RADIO DIALS UNDER THE KNOBS

Ca. 1938 Oahu catalog showing the No. 263K Diana, No. 229K Tonemaster and No. 230K Standard amplifier by Kay (coutesy Michael Lee Allen).

began shifting its identity, and this happened over a period of time, not cleanly. This shift seems to be associated with the Venetian creations of Zorzi, Gabriel and Abbott. Most accounts suggest that the Kay name derived from the middle name of S-V's dynamic secretary, Henry Kay Kuhrmeyer. We have no reason to doubt that, though, as we shall see, there are confusing facts even here. A plausible reconstruction is that S-V introduced a new line of Venetian guitars called the "Kay Kraft" line in late 1927. Kay Kraft would become the most recognized brand name until 1937, at least, occasionally showing up in catalog copy beyond that time. From evidence

we'll discuss, the Stromberg-Voisinet Company officially became the Kay Musical Instrument Company sometime between 1931 and 1934. The Kay brand name itself first appeared on guitars in 1936 or 1937.

The German connection

Muddying the waters somewhat is the fact that the Kay brand was actually first used in 1925 by Stromberg-Voisinet for a business that imported and exported violins and cellos built by both the Loewendahl and Kreuzinger factories in Germany. Apparently some inexpensive flattop guitars were also imported from these German plants in the early '30s, too. It is entirely possible that this "Kay" name may in fact have been taken from the initial letter of Kreuzinger and that the connection with Kuhrmeyer on this business may have been purely coincidental, but there's no way to know for sure, and it really doesn't matter in the cosmic scheme of things. Stromberg-Voisinet's as-

sociation with the German string industry probably in part accounts for Kay's later reputation as a maker of stand-up basses, by the way. The German Kay affiliation lasted until 1936, when Hitler ascended to power. American companies ceased buying German instruments, and shifted import activities to suppliers from France and England. Curiously enough, about a year after the German suppliers were cut off Kay began using the Kay brand for guitars and a year later began making its own stand-up acoustic basses.

Evidence

Among the first documented evidence for the shift from S-V to Kay is a story in *The Music Trades* of August 1928. The company is still clearly identified as S-V, but the release announces the *addition* of a mandolin, tenor guitar, tenor banjo and Jumbo guitar to the *Kay Kraft* line. To quote, "The additions to the line were inspired by the success of the Kay Kraft guitars, introduced last year." Illustrated in the story is a Kay Kraft Model A Mandolin. While no technical details are visible or discussed, this appears to be the Gabriel/Zorzi Kay Kraft. This is strong evidence

(Left to Right) 1935 Oahu. 1937 Oahu No. 229K Tonemaster made by Kay, with early "horseshoe" pickup. Ca. 1939-40 Oahu Tonemaster made by Kay, without the G-clef.

1985 Guild X-88D

Ca. 1982 Madeira by Guild

1988 Guild Liberator Elite

Ca. 1987 Burnside by Guild

All photos: Michael Tamborrino.

1995 Guild Brian May Signature

1985 Guild Brian May, 1994 Guild Brian May Special, 1994 Guild Brian May Pro, 1994 Guild Brian May Standard

1932 Stromberg #49

1932 Stromberg #76 Venetian

Photo: Michael Tamborrino.

1940 Oahu Tonemaster Lap Steel and 1939 Oahu Tone
Master Amplifier

Ca. 1933 Kay Kraft Model B

Photos: Michael Tamborrino.

1938 Kay Violin Archtop

1941 Silvertone Crest

Photos: Michael Tamborrino.

1954 Kay K161 Thin Twin

that these instruments first appeared in 1927, to which we'll return in due time.

Company literature published in the '50s in a way corroborates this observation, for there it states that Kay began in 1928. However, as late as January 19, 1929, Henry Kuhrmeyer was still identified as the *secretary* of Stromberg-Voisinet. At that time, Kuhrmeyer was appointed to the prestigious position of President of the Chicago Zone of the Association of Musical Merchandise Manufacturers (A.M.M.M.). By that time, Stromberg-Voisinet had increased in volume so as to be almost as large as its neighbor, the Sears-owned Harmony.

Kuhrmeyer's tenure as an officer of the A.M.M.M. lasted for a year until 1930, when Harmony's President Jay Kraus replaced him. The first mention of Kuhrmeyer as *president* of Stromberg-Voisinet appeared in *The Music Trades* in March of 1931. As late as August of 1931, the company was still identified as Stromberg-Voisinet. The next reference I've encountered in the trade press is not until 1934, by which time the company had most assuredly become Kay.

However, in minutes of early National board meetings reproduced in Bob Brozman's *The History and Artistry of National Resonator Instruments* (Centerstream), conversations about the new El Trovador model in February of 1932 indicate that they will be made by "Kaykraft," not Stromberg-Voisinet. By March of '32 the references are simply to "Kay." All this would confirm that Stromberg-Voisinet went the way of all flesh in late 1931 and became Kay. The Stromberg brand name was gone by 1932, replaced by Kay Kraft. As previously mentioned, the Stromberg brand was used into 1932, after which it disappears.

Thus, to recap, what seems to have happened was that, under Henry Kay Kuhrmeyer's leadership, Stromberg-Voisinet introduced the Kay Kraft brand name in late 1927. S-V continued to be

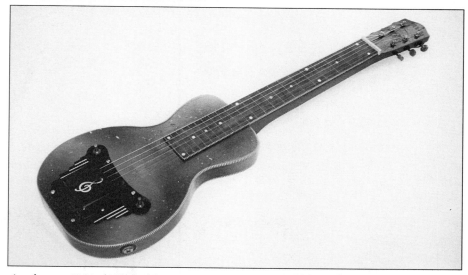

Another ca. 1939-40 Oahu Tonemaster made by Kay with G-clef and different dots (photo: Mike Sebren).

the company name at least into 1931, but the company increasingly became known as Kay Kraft. Sometime in late 1931, most certainly by 1934, Stromberg-Voisinet became the Kay Musical Instrument Company.

Enter George Nicholas Einsele

Hank Kuhmeyer's ascent to power was clearly due to his energy

The front and back of a ca. 1937 Oahu No. 230K amplifier.

and vision, but it's possible that Henry had a backer. Reportedly Kuhrmeyer's accession to the presidency of Stromberg-Voisinet was related to another Chicagoland music magnate George Nicholas Einsele. Einsele reportedly became a multi-millionaire in the real estate business just before

the stock market crash in '29. One of Einsele's ventures was the Perfection Musical String Company, one of the largest string manufacturers at the time. Einsele reportedly also owned pieces of Regal, J.R. Stewart, the Steger Piano Co., Kimball, E.H. Roth and C.M.I. When the Depression hit, Stromberg-Voisinet, like many other companies, got mired in hard times between 1929 and 1931. Einsele apparently loaned Stromberg-Voisinet considerable amounts of money to help them through the hard years. Hank Kuhrmeyer is said to have been Einsele's man for protecting his investment, becoming president of Stromberg-Voisinet sometime in early 1931.

Kay Kraft

Which, like a revolving record, brings us back to the Kay Kraft brand, which is an inextricable part of the emerging Kay identity. Generally speaking, the Kay Kraft brand name is associated with the unique Venetian-shaped instruments probably designed by Philip Gabriel and probably refined by Joseph Zorzi, as we've previously discussed. Again, we are faced with some facts and inconclusive answers.

Ca. 1936 Kay flattop with a fake flame maple finish (photo: Mike Newton).

As mentioned previously, one of the first sighted mentions of the "Kay Kraft" brand name was in the August 1928 *The Music Trades* article. In this notice, new instruments were being added to the line of "Kay Kraft guitars," which had been successfully introduced a year earlier...in late 1927. No evidence exists, to my knowledge, of anything other than the classic Kay Kraft Venetian instruments associated with that brand prior to their introduction. Gabriel and Zorzi were already working for S-V, and are reported to have been working on the Venetians in the mid-'20s. A range of dates for the debut of the Kay Krafts has been proposed, from 1929 to 1931 (confused by the fact that they were indubitably introduced in the trade press in '31). We know from one documented example that 14-fret Kay Krafts existed by 1929, since it is signed by Zorzi inside and dated 12/29.

The copy goes on to say, "All are of the violin type of construction, with the exception of the banjo. They have the arched top and back type of construction, used for centuries in violin making and which forms the foundation for the added bril-

liancy and depth of tone embodied in Kay Kraft. The oval fingerboard and tapered bridge are other ideas originating with the old master violin builders. This is a decided aid to ease of fingering and allows the artist full range of technique and expression...

"Our Kay Kraft guitars met with success from their first launching," the spokesman told *The Music Trades.* "The demand has surpassed our expectations and musicians have given the instruments strongest endorsement. We feel that the Kay Kraft guitar which embodies many of the secrets that the great craftsmen of old and modern times considered essential in the perfect instrument, was a distinct achievement in the fretted instrument line. The new mandolin, tenor guitar, tenor banjo, and the Jumbo guitar — the largest size made — have all the merit of the Kay Kraft guitar in the matter of tone quality, beauty of design and construction."

This description is clearly not the flattop Venetian guitars sold under the Stromberg brand name and as Stromberg Electros. Such language also perhaps brings to mind Joseph Zorzi's recent experience with violins at Lyon & Healey. This copy would be repeated almost verbatim later in the 1931 description of Kay Kraft instruments.

Reconstruction

We know that the Venetian *shape*, in glued-neck Stromberg guitars were around by 1927. The evidence presented in *The Music Trades* suggests that the first Kay Kraft Venetian guitars were introduced in '27 as well, followed in '28 by the Kay Kraft mandolin, tenor guitar, tenor banjo and Jumbo guitar. The photograph in the '28 story shows

a Model A Kay Kraft Mandolin with the classic Venetian shape and the new asymmetrical headstock, faced in plastic. The new instruments are described as being put out in three finishes, mahogany, maple, and rosewood, similar to the guitars, suggesting the Models A, B, and C which would appear later.

What are we to make of this? We know for sure that the Kay Kraft Venetians exist in late 1929, based on the signed Zorzi example. Tom Wheeler cites their first appearance in a December 1930 price list. These do not appear in any jobber's books before 1930. We also know that in March of 1931 the Kay Kraft line was fully (re-?) introduced in *The Music Trades.* In May of that year, *The Music Trades* ran a notice that the "Kay Kraft Guitar Makes Debut." By August, 1931, the full Kay Kraft line had been described, "built by skilled artisans under the direction of H. Kay Kuhrmeyer, head of the company."

One final factoid might provide a clue. There are, indeed, some 12-fret Kay Kraft Venetians extant, however, by late 1929 the Zorzi signature had 14 frets, and the gui-

(Left) Ca. 1936 Kay Arch Kraft archtop, typical of late '30s Kays (photo: Mike Newton). (Right) 1938 Kay Violin guitar with "lips" on top and back, one of the earliest guitars bearing a Kay name.

(Left) Typical Kay archtops from the 1937 Tonk Bros. catalog. (Right) Decorative flattops from the 1937 Tonk Bros. catalog: note the tripart top (probably Philip Gabriel's "wax paper" technique) and the lyre-soundhole (photos courtesy Mike Newton).

tars introduced in 1931 and sold thereafter also had 14 frets.

Thus, the probable sequence of events goes like this. Upon joining Stromberg-Voisinet, Zorzi, Gabriel and friends set to

Another 1938 Kay Violin guitar (in search of some parts) with the "cello" headstock.

work establishing the Venetian style. In '27 the Stromberg brand Venetian flattops hit the street, evolving into the Stromberg Electros. In late 1927, the more radical Kay Kraft Venetian archtop guitars bowed, probably in a 12-fret version. The rest of the Kay Kraft line followed in 1928. Then came 1929 and the crash. By this time Kay Kraft guitars had become 14-fret instruments. Business went into a tailspin. Hank "Kay" Kuhrmeyer took the reigns as president of S-V in early 1931 and the company regrouped under the Kay Kraft banner, relaunching the line in the spring of 1931.

If this reconstruction is correct, it may go a long way toward clearing up some of the confusion over the emergence of the Kay company name, since reports range from '28 to '31, the very period that the Kay Kraft name was emerging.

Zorzi's Kay Kraft archtops

So, how about the guitars? We'll pick up the descriptions as of May, 1931. As we've seen, the Kay Kraft archtop guitars came out of Stromberg-Voisinet's interest in the Venetian shape and reflected the input of the company's new luthiers Joseph Zorzi, Philip Gabriel and John Abbott. As we already discussed, the Venetian shape was

probably invented by Gabriel and refined and developed by Zorzi. Zorzi's "improvements" probably included the hollow body, perhaps the new asymmetrical headstock shape, possibly the new Venetian bridge and probably the adjustable neck and pressed (versus carved) top features (note that the famous instruments made by the contemporary Larson Brothers of Chicago favored "stressed" arch tops which were also not carved). These new guitars were known as the Kay Kraft Styles A, B and C (or sometimes also referred to as *Models* A, B and C).

Adjustable neck

Kay Kraft guitars had a very curious bolt-on neck design. This clever feature actually dates back to the 1840s and the cello maker Nicholas Vuillaume, at least. Indeed, even C.F. Martin employed a similar technique briefly, using a key and clockwork mechanism in the heel to adjust angle.

The design involved making a convex curve on the part of the heel that snuggled up against the body. A concave shim was inserted between the heel and body. The neck attached to the body by means of a big bolt coming through the shim and body and fastening with a large wing nut inside. To adjust the neck, you simply

Late '30s Kay cello (courtesy Society Hill Loan, Philadelphia, PA).

reach inside, loosen the nut, slide the neck up or down in its shimmed cradle, and tighten the nut again. The fingerboard extended over the body to the soundhole, of course. This whole arrangement works quite well, by the way, although the resulting neck joint is not as stable as a glued one, so probably had limitations for any proto-Eddie-

Van-Halens of the era, if such existed.

These guitars also featured a new asymmetrical headstock. Besides the elaborate shape, these were faced in fancy pearloid imprinted with designs and a gold vertical Kay Kraft logo.

Styles A, B and C

Basically, the Kay Kraft creations were available as guitars, tenor guitars and mandolins, offered in three basic styles, Styles (or sometimes Models) A, B, and C.

Style A, at $25 in 1931, had a mahogany body and neck, a "shaded" spruce top and a bound, dot-inlaid fingerboard. The headstock sported the new asymmetrical design. Gone were the slots and Stromberg Venetian S-curve in favor of more of a banjo shape, with indented sides and a rounded peak with a little hump on the left side. This was faced in "Pearlette" plastic. The bridge was a tapered moveable affair with rounded ends. Strings attached to a fairly plain, utilitarian trapeze tailpiece. Early catalogs show the Style A without a pickguard, although by 1934, at least, it had certainly acquired one, and probably most were produced with one.

The Style B, at $35, was similar to the A except it featured a curly maple body and "a rich violin brown shaded" finish. This had a large pickguard in black.

The Style C, at $45, had a natural top,

rosewood body, and pickguard. The Style C, typical of Zorzi's taste for ornamentation, also had fancy snowflake inlays.

"An adjustable neck, a new and very much needed improvement in fine guitar construction," enthused the copy, "is an exclusive Kay Kraft feature. It allows the fingerboard to be raised or lowered, thus adjusting the string height to suit the player's preference. It is an instant correction for string vibration against the frets."

The sound of these Venetian guitars is not loud, but is very crisp and well-balanced, excellent for fingerstyle, although with a fair zip for plectrum playing as well. The neck had a very comfortable V shape. It's not reinforced, but thickened gently as it moves up.

The Kay Kraft Tenor Guitars and Mandolins essentially followed patterns identical to the regular guitars, with similar materials in the Styles A, B and C, arched tops and backs, and the adjustable neck feature on the tenor, although the mandolins had glued-in necks.

In addition to the Zorzi Venetian instruments, the Kay Kraft line also featured banjos. These, too, came in Styles A, B and C, with mahogany, curly maple and rosewood resonators, respectively. Kay Kraft banjos also featured the "patented adjustable neck," presumably Zorzi's design. These were available as tenors, or, by special order, as

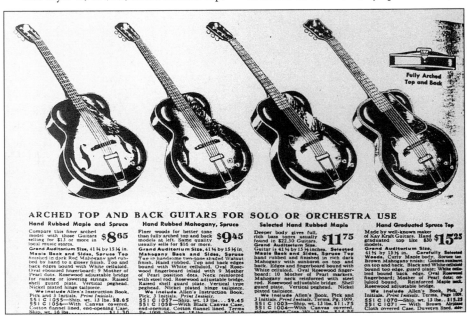

(Left) 1939 Kay Television archtops. (Right) Kay archtops from the 1939 Ward's catalog (photos courtesy Mike Newton).

plectrum, banjo-mandolin or 5-string banjos.

Kay Kraft Jumbo Guitars

Finally, there were three Kay Kraft Jumbo Guitars, Spanish flattops in similar Styles A (mahogany, $30), B (curly maple, $40) and C (rosewood, $50). Descriptions do not mention the innovative Zorzi adjustable neck, so presumably these are regular glued-neck guitars. The headstocks, however, are in the new, asymmetrical Pearlette Kay Kraft style. Each had a Bakelite pickguard. The bridge was a fixed pin bridge design, which also appeared on later Stromberg-Voisinet Venetian flattop guitars. As on other instruments, inlays on the rosewood Style C were large, elaborate snowflakes.

Kay Kraft guitars were marketed by most of the major distributors of the day, including Continental, Targ and Dinner, Chicago Musical Instruments, Karl Fischer and Bugeleisen and Jacobson (which had sold Strombergs bearing its Serenader label earlier), to name but a few. Some of these were also sold by Montgomery Ward bearing their Recording King label, and possibly some of the later ones were marketed by Spiegel under their Old Kraftsman brand name. In 1932, some of the guitars were being sold by Vega.

The Kay Kraft Venetian and Jumbo guitars, tenor guitars, and mandolins lasted basically until 1935, the Kay Kraft banjos sticking around at least two more years until 1937.

Depression

The '30s were hard times. Amusingly

1939 Kay guitars from the Grossman catalog (courtesy Robert Watkins).

(or not), *The Music Trades*, in the wake of the 1929 stock market crash, predicted a good year in 1930. When the truth of the Great Depression finally dawned on everyone, the trade press became more political than ever, ignoring new introductions of instruments (there probably weren't many) in favor of covering attempts at recovering. During this period, it should be noted, Hank Kuhrmeyer assisted in drafting a set of operating principles for the music industry which included, among other things, 40-hour limits on the work-week for employees, a standard many still take for granted today.

(Left) 1939 Gretsch acoustics: the natural-finished one is a Kay; note the lefty guitarist in the picture (courtesy Mike Newton)! (Right)Kay guitars in the 1939 Grossman catalog, including more "wax paper" models (courtesy Robert Watkins).

graved block inlays. The example shown in Tom Wheeler's *American Guitars*, by the way, has been substantially modified, and is not representative of what these guitars looked like except in terms of shape. While the catalog shows the Style A with no pickguard, most of these which turn up either have a 'guard or evidence that they once did. As previously mentioned, some earlier examples had necks which joined the body at the 12th fret. Photos exist of Josh White, Curley Weaver and Buddy Moss playing 14-fret Style As, taken in 1933.

Arch Kraft

While the Venetian instruments were top of the line, Kay did not ignore more conventional Spanish designs. In the 1933-34 Targ & Dinner catalog the Arch Kraft Tenor Guitars and Mandolins are introduced. Unlike their predecessors, the tenors had

Kay Kraft variations

A number of variations occurred within the Zorzi/Kay Kraft line during its reign, although it's pretty much impossible to trace these with anything but guesswork. Typical of the times, Kay seems to have taken one set of catalog photos when the guitars were introduced and those were picked up in all subsequent distributor catalogs.

Some Kay Kraft Venetian guitars, notably the Style B guitar, had a gold leaf design stenciled on the belly. This was a feature which shows up on a lot of other guitars in around 1933, so may be a dating clue. Whether or not Chicago's 1933 Century of Progress exhibition influenced any of these Kay Kraft variations remains to be discovered, but it wouldn't come as a surprise

to find out it did.

Others, such as the guitar pictured in George Gruhn and Walter Carter's book *Acoustic Guitars* (Miller Freeman) had en-

(Left) Kay mandolins (upper right, lower center and right) from the '39 Grossman catalog. (Right) Kay Venetian mandolins from the '39 Grossman catalog (photos courtesy Robert Watkins).

Spanish bodies, arched tops and backs, round soundholes, elevated Kay pickguards, moveable bridges, and simple trapeze tails. These had 14-fret mahogany necks with the adjustable feature. They have the old Kay Kraft asymmetrical headstock, plain-faced with an Arch Kraft logo that looks somewhat like Dick Tracy's police badge, and banjo-style tuners. The No. 921 ($22.50) was otherwise constructed like the Venetian Style A, with mahogany body and neck, and spruce top, most likely pressed, not carved, and the fancier Venetian moveable bridge. The No. 920 ($15) was similar except for a birch body and a small, plain bridge.

The two '33-34 Arch Kraft Mandolins were Venetian-shaped with glued-in necks, the asymmetrical Kay Kraft headstock. The No. 1515 (also $22.50) had the mahogany body, the No. 1514 ($15) had the birch.

By the 1934 Targ & Dinner catalog, the Kay-made Arch Kraft line had expanded greatly to include three Grand Auditoriums and four Auditoriums, all roundhole archtops.

The Grand Auditoriums all had the adjustable neck feature, with symmetrical three-and-three heads with Arch Kraft shield logos, round soundholes, trapeze tails, bound ovalled fingerboards, dot inlays, the tapered moveable bridge, and elevated pickguards. The No. 820 ($20) was made of birch, with purfling binding, mahogany neck, ebonized fingerboard, and two-tone brown finish. The No. 825 ($25) was similar but with a spruce top and mahogany body. The No. 830 ($30) was also similar, but with two-piece matched curly maple body, nine pearl dots, and Grover De Luxe machines, in two-tone "rich golden brown." Note the correlation between the model numbers and price.

The Auditoriums all had squared-off slothead and plainer thin rectangular bridges, with simple trapeze tails and dot inlay. The Arch Kraft shield logo was on the head. The No. 800 ($13.50) was all birch with white celluloid binding, bass-

wood neck, ebonized fingerboard, probably flat, and possibly a glued-in neck. The No. 802 ($15) was similar with the addition of an ovalled fingerboard and adjustable neck arrangement. The No. 804 ($18) was all-mahogany, with white celluloid binding, ovalled fingerboard, and adjustable neck. The No. 805 ($18) was identical to the No. 804 except for a spruce top.

F-holes

It would be another year or two before Kay would change over to making modern f-hole archtop guitars as we generally know them, but in around 1933 Kay's first experiments with f-hole guitars began to appear. Among these were guitars carrying the S.S. Maxwell brand name marketed by Targ & Dinner. Most Maxwells at this time were standard flattops made by either Regal or Harmony (some with fancy belly stencils, as on some Kay Krafts), however, one made by Kay stood out. Ballyhooed as "The Latest In Guitar Design" in the 1933-34 Targ & Dinner catalog, this Kay-made No. 728 guitar was a Spanish flattop with f-holes at the waist (rather than on the lower bout), as was common at the time. This was a glued-

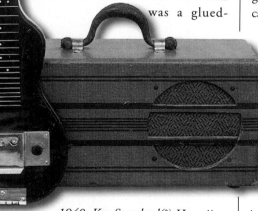

1940s Kay Standard(?) Hawaiian (photo: Jim Dulfer).

neck guitar with a moveable bridge and the old simple trapeze tail. The bridge was clearly inspired by the Venetian shape, but with more rounded ends, sans point. Also reminiscent of the Kay Krafts (and

Kay Venetian Mandola (and Mando-cello) from '39 Grossman catalog (courtesy Robert Watkins).

Stromberg's predilection for pearloid), the highly tapered snakehead headstock was faced in pearloid with a gold "S.S. Maxwell" logo running vertically down the center. This was basically a cheap flattop, at $9.50, with painted "binding," a birch body and "dark brown shaded mahogany" finish, but it was probably Kay's first f-hole guitar. It was still offered in the '34 T&D catalog.

It is possible that Kay also made its first *archtop* f-hole at this time. In the same 1933-34 Targ & Dinner catalog as the S.S. Maxwell flattop f-hole is advertised the No. 778 Auditorium Size archtop ($12.40). The illustration for this instrument is a Harmony archtop, however, the catalog description describes the guitar as having "arched top and back, new Arch Kraft model. Built similar to a violin with F holes, giving it more volume of tone. Rich reddish brown piano gloss finish with strongly contrasted shading, white striped edges, oval fingerboard with 14 frets clear of the body." Details such as the arched top and back and the oval 14-fret fingerboard definitely suggest that this was a Kay and that they had begun to tinker with the modern archtop

1941 Kay-made, carved solid spruce-top Silvertone Crest, one of the first guitars to carry Sears' famous brand name.

as early as 1933. This guitar was probably also sold carrying the Arch Kraft brand, and was also seen in the Targ & Dinner catalog carrying the Marveltone brand name, all identified as the No. 778.

Resonator guitars

Toward the end of the Kay Kraft tenure, Kay began building resonator guitars. By 1933 Kay was making mahogany-bodied El Trovador guitars for National. Apparently, Kay was also making S.S. Maxwell Amplifying Guitars for Targ & Dinner and some Hollywood-brand guitars for the Shireson Bros. These were basically Kay guitars with resonator parts provided by the Shireson Bros. For some unknown reason, National abruptly yanked its contract from Kay and awarded the business to Harmony, which subsequently built some El Trovadors (very similar to Harmony's own Trojan model). It's quite possible that Kay's affiliation with

Shireson Bros., National competitors, may have been the reason for National's change.

In any case, at least two S.S. Maxwell models were built by Kay in around 1933-34, the Credenza Model and the Florenza Model. Both had mahogany bodies and glued-in necks, arched backs, the "new design" symmetrical headstocks, fancy snowflake fingerboard inlays, twin "violin" f-holes on the upper bout, and Shireson/Maxwell resonator cones and coverplates. The Credenza ($27) had a shaded mahogany top, while the Florenza ($35) was fancier with a bound fingerboard and a natural spruce top.

Apparently, Kay was left holding some El Trovador bodies after National cancelled its contract, and some of those were built containing Shireson/Maxwell resonators. In other words, there are some Maxwells out there, which are half National El Trovadors, half Shiresons.

While, as we shall see, it would be another several years before the Kay company would adopt the Kay brand name, a number of these have been seen labeled as Kay Krafts and at least one which was branded

as a "Kay Deluxe." This may have been the first time the Kay name was used alone, without the "Kraft" appended.

Kaywood Amplifying guitars

In 1934 Kay also introduced the Kaywood Amplifying guitars. These were a bizarre alternative to the resonator guitars pioneered by the Dopyera Bothers in California and built by Kay in '33. Kaywoods included four models, which took the "resonator" idea into a logical dead-end. Basically, instead of metal resonators, these guitars isolated a round wooden plate in the belly of the guitar. Let's let the purple prose of the catalog describe what this was supposed to do:

"These guitars embody a system of amplifying which has been used in other ways and is accepted as correct in theory and practice which has never before been used in musical instruments of the string type. The amplification does not give the tinny tone but maintains the soft mellowness so much desired in guitars at the same time giving a carrying and penetrating quality, which gives ample capacity for an orches-

(Left to right) Ca. 1941 Kay Professional archtop which was notched above the earlier Television series (photo: Mike Newton) 1945 Kay Imperial bought from Ward's for $33.75 (photo: Mike Newton). Ca. 1947 Kay K36 all-mahogany archtop (photo: Gilbert Matossian).

tral instrument. These instruments are made in the super-grand size with the body 15$\frac{1}{2}$ inches wide and 20$\frac{1}{2}$ inches long. The scale is 25$\frac{3}{4}$ inches with the new slim tapered fingerboard permitting easy fingering of all positions. All models have the neck clear of the body at the 14th fret, and have the adjustable neck feature."

All had the new symmetrical headstocks, moveable bridges, boring tailpieces and some sliced soundholes cut in the upper bouts. The No. 1 Kaywood Guitar ($25) had a 3-ply maple top and back. The No. 2 ($35) had a 3-ply mahogany top and back. The No. 3 ($50) had a laminated curly maple top and back. The top-of-the-line No. 4 ($75) had laminated rosewood top and back, plus "a very beautiful gold leaf floral decalcomania," an engraved, mother-of-pearl inlaid headstock, and Grover Deluxe tuners.

The Kaywood idea did not set the guitar world on fire and died about a year later, although its last gasp actually appeared in the 1937-38 Continental catalog, which featured the No. 1121 ($9.50) with a "specially ribbed resonating wood diaphragm

(Left) Ca. 1955 Kay K34 archtop, with carved spruce top and laminated maple body (courtesy Ron Wayne Atwood). (Right) Ca. 1948 Lark Junior electric archtop made by Kay.

with neat round soundhole perforations." This had a birch body, a glued neck, slothead and a pair of Regal-style f-holes on the upper bout.

It is possible, by the way, that Joseph Zorzi had something to do with the Kaywood guitars, since they featured his adjustable neck idea, which would depart along with Zorzi (and actually, the Kaywood) in 1934, although this is only speculation.

Exit Zorzi

In any case, Joseph Zorzi left Kay in 1934 to start his own private shop. Upon Zorzi's departure, Philip Gabriel was made shop foreman. It was Gabriel who would come up with the unique technique of painting a flamed-maple pattern on waxed paper, which was then overlaid on birch backs to make them look like genuine flamed maple!

Kay Kraft DeLuxe guitars

In 1934, Kay officially re-

placed the Venetian guitars with three new archtop guitars with Spanish-shaped bodies called the Kay Kraft Deluxe Guitars series. These were Grand Auditorium sized guitars (15$\frac{1}{2}$" wide) with round soundholes, shaded finishes, 14-fret necks, **moveable bridges, boring utilitarian trapeze tails,** and the adjustable heel joint. Gone **was** the asymmetrical headstock in favor of a "new design" dramatically scalloped symmetrical design. The K20 ($20) had a birch body and spruce top. The K25 ($25) had a mahogany body. The K30 ($30) had a curly maple body, multiple bindings, a tortoise pickguard, and Grover Deluxe individual tuners.

Kay Kraft DeLuxes also included a budget line, the K4 ($12), the K8 ($13.50), and the K2 ($15.90). These were slightly smaller "Auditorium" sized guitars, still with the adjustable neck. The K4 had a flat spruce top, glued-in basswood neck, ebonized fingerboard, the later pointy Stromberg Venetian fixed bridge, four dots, slotted head, and no pickguard. The K8 had a flat figured (striped) mahogany top and body, with other features like the K4. The K2 was an archtop with a spruce top, birch body, basswood neck, slothead, moveable

1948 Kay-made No. F451 Electric Spanish guitar and No. F461 Hawaiian from the Targ & Dinner catalog (courtesy Mike Newton).

(Left to Right) Ca. 1948 Kay K46 Artist archtop, with replacement tuners, and non-original tail made by John D'Angelico (photo: Frank Cammerata). Late '40s Kay K136 lap steel (coutesy Tinicum Guitar Barn, Ottsville, PA). Ca. 1948 Paramount archtop, built by Kay, similar to the K42. 1948 Kay-made Rex Aragon archtop with fancy engraved headstock and checkerboard binding on head, neck and body (courtesy John Boy Vintage, TX).

bridge, boring tailpiece, and elevated pick-guard.

Continuing in the line at this time were two archtop Kay Kraft Tenor Guitars, the K1 and K2 [sic], which were identical to the Arch Kraft tenors introduced the year before. The K1 at $15.90 was an all-mahogany guitar, while the K2 at $20.00 had a white spruce top and mahogany body.

The last Venetian guitars

An archtop Venetian guitar appeared in the Montgomery Ward catalog at least until the Spring/Summer 1936 edition. Unlike previous guitars, however, these were glued-neck, 14-fret models with no binding on the back, smaller pickguards and conventional slotted headstocks. They did, however, have the stenciled gold designs on the belly. Cost was $9.75 in '35, $9.45 in '36!

While echoes of the Venetian guitar might still be heard in later years, this distinctive guitar finally disappeared by 1937, the year in which Philip Gabriel and John Abbott left Kay.

New digs

Kay continued to thrive as the '30s and the Depression chugged on into the decade. In April of 1935 the company moved into a new, larger factory at 1640 West Walnut Street, by now named the Kay Musical Instrument Company. Indeed, in an amusing aside, in 1936 Oahu printed a catalog with a photo factory tour and a picture of their new factory; the pictures were of the new Kay plant, with a hand-drawn Oahu sign pasted down over the Kay name! Photos of Venetian bodies can just barely be discerned in the tour photos, indicating they were still being made in the new factory, though for which models it is impossible to ascertain.

Several Kay-made guitars appeared in the 1935 Carl Fischer catalog. Fischer sold the No. G-860 Handcraft Tenor Guitar with the old asymmetrical head and center-pointed Stromberg bridge. The No.

G-850 Venetian Tenor Guitar was the old Venetian-shaped flattop tenor with the Stromberg bridge.

1948 Kay Artist archtops with the "ribbon" bridges from the Targ & Dinner catalog (courtesy Mike Newton).

Kay glued-neck guitars

In 1935 Kay was still providing Montgomery Ward with mail-order guitars. It was at this time that the old adjustable-necked guitars gave way to more traditional glued-necked f-hole archtops (with *adjustable bridges* rather than adjustable necks) and flattops, most in a conventional Spanish shape. Except for the last vestiges of the Venetian guitar (still available until '36), shown in the Fall/Winter 1935-'36 Wards catalog were an auditorium (15" wide) sized flattop and an archtop. Both were fairly plain dot-neck models with painted trim.

The adjustable bridge that replaced Zorzi's adjustable neck is worth noting. This was a svelte affair with a wooden base and a black Bakelite top resting on thumbwheels. In catalogs, this is referred to as the "Kay adjustable bridge," and it lasted until at least 1938 or so. It was actually sold by some distributors as an accessory. While other variations could occur,

(Left to Right) Ca. 1948 Kay-made Rex Royal (?) with fake flamed finish and label that says "Rex Professional" (courtesy Tinicum Guitar Barn, Ottsville, PA). Probably late '40s or '50s Sherwood Deluxe version of the K23 jumbo-sized flattop marketed by Montgomery Wards (courtesy Bernunzio Vintage Instruments, Penfield, NY). Ca. 1948 Sherwood Deluxe version of the Kay No. F451 sold by Montgomery Ward (photo: Gilbert Matossian).

Closeup of the late '40s K23 showing natty white/tortoise binding and curly maple rims (courtesy Bernunzio Vintage Instruments, Penfield, NY).

if you find an old Kay with a Bakelite bridge, you know that the bridge, at least, dates from the late '30s. By late '38 and after, the bridge changed to a wooden design, and catalog descriptions change, too.

Also appearing in the 1935 Carl Fischer catalog, in addition to the Kay Kraft Venetian line, was the Handcraft Tenor Guitar No. G-860, a glued-neck Spanish Grand Concert four-string in all-mahogany, with a bound fingerboard, bound top and soundhole, screwed-on pickguard, and the asymmetrical Kay Kraft-style head with banjo tuners.

The Spring/Summer 1936 Wards catalog provides a better snapshot of Kay guitars from this transitional period. Kay was still supplying a lot of the Wards line, although by this time Regal and even Gibson were also represented in the Wards catalog. At this time, the Kay Kraft name was still in use, however, it was now being applied in somewhat more generic fashion to Kay-made guitars, with no specific identification with the Venetian shape remaining.

This catalog contained two "hand carved," super-auditorium-sized, Kay-made archtops, a fancy model made of "genuine rosewood," with a carved spruce top, f-holes, bound Brazilian rosewood fingerboard, tortoise pickguard, a "Kay adjustable bridge" and plain trapeze tailpiece. This had a large engraved pearl block inlays (recalling the Venetian guitar shown in Gruhn's book). The cost of this beaut was $35.95 ($75 value, cash or $4 down); the mahogany Gibson cost $39.95. The plainer guitar had a "rosewood grained" maple body, a black pickguard and an unbound "ebonized" fingerboard with dot inlays. Cost was $14.94, "lowest price we know of for a hand-carved guitar!" enthused the copy. Darned right, too!

In addition to the glued-neck Venetian guitar (it's last bow), the '36 line included the "Biggest Guitar Made!," the "famous Kay-Kraft guitar in the new, tremendous *Super-Jumbo* size. This was basically the old Kay Kraft Jumbo archtop, here with spruce top and Honduras mahogany body. Interestingly, the neck was advertised as being steel reinforced. This had a bound fingerboard and a dot-neck joining the body at the 14th fret. The headstock was a fancy version of the Kay Kraft symmetrical type.

In '36 there was also a "Regular $20 Kay Kraft! Big super Auditorium size" archtop, with carved spruce top and mahogany-finished maple body. Cost was $11.25. An auditorium sized Kay Kraft archtop made of birch was also available for $7.45. These had the symmetrical Kay Kraft headstock and 14-fret necks.

One Kay-made roundhole flattop was also included, promoted as "The Most Beautiful Guitar We've Ever Seen!," a Spanish guitar with the latter-day Stromberg Venetian bridge and a five-color floral design on the belly *and* fingerboard.

This catalog also contained two Venetian-shaped mandolins made by Kay, one with f-holes and another with an oval soundhole. Both of these had the old Kay Kraft asymmetrical headstocks, by the way.

Kay Electric Amplifying Guitar

Topping off the Kay-supplied Wards line in '36 was the appearance of a new "World's Finest Electric Amplifying Guitar." "For Orchestra! For Radio!," this was a super-auditorium-sized flattop with a spruce top and curly maple body. It had a moveable adjustable bridge and standard trapeze tail-

Ca. 1952 Kay K21 archtop (photo: Gilbert Matossian).

piece. The neck was steel reinforced. The dot-inlaid fingerboard was rosewood. The headstock was slotted. The neck joined the body at the 14th fret. Instead of a soundhole, this had a rectangular pickup with a large celluloid surround. *No controls* were on the guitar. It offered: "Superb tone! Every string is individually amplified — a tiny mike element under each string is wound to amplify that string only — will not pick up pick-

noise, wood vibration, etc. Other electric guitars amplify two or three strings at a time — and the result is that chords run into each other, sound 'fuzzy.' With Wards guitar you can 'break' a chord as cleanly as you can on an unamplified guitar." These came with an adapter to allow either Spanish or Hawaiian playing and a two-input amplifier. The cost for the entire outfit was $85, $93.50 on time payments.

Bigger and better

Several new and curious guitars appear in the subsequent Fall/Winter 1936 Ward's catalog, including lots of Gibsons. Two super auditorium-sized archtops and one auditorium size are still in the line. The top guitar ($16.45) was a carved top advertised as being "made by the maker of the famous Kay Kraft." The middle guitar ($9.95) had a pressed top and was still identified as being made by the maker of Kay Kraft. Both of these still had the symmetrical Kay Kraft headstocks. The bottom archtop ($7.50) had a slothead and doesn't mention Kay Kraft.

New in late '36 was a "Full Grand Concert" guitar, 15" wide with an arched top but a round soundhole. This had a 14-fret dot-neck, moveable bridge and trapeze tail. The headstock was the narrow humped variety. Cost was $5.35.

The Electric Amplifying guitar was still present, although it had changed slightly

(This page and next page) 1950 Kay catalog (courtesy Jim Dulfer).

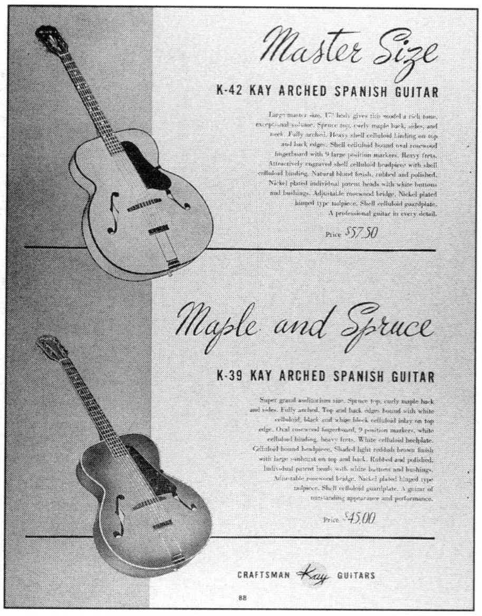

Master Size

K-42 KAY ARCHED SPANISH GUITAR

Large master size, 17" body gives this model a rich tone, exceptional volume. Spruce top, curly maple back, sides, and neck. Fully arched. Heavy shell celluloid binding on top and back edges. Shell celluloid bound oval rosewood fingerboard with 9 large position markers. Heavy frets. Attractively engraved shell celluloid headpiece with shell celluloid binding. Natural blond finish, rubbed and polished. Nickel plated individual patent heads with white buttons and bushings. Adjustable rosewood bridge. Nickel plated hinged type tailpiece. Shell celluloid guardplate. A professional guitar in every detail.

Price $57.50

Maple and Spruce

K-39 KAY ARCHED SPANISH GUITAR

Super grand auditorium size. Spruce top, curly maple back and sides. Fully arched. Top and back edges bound with white celluloid, black and white block celluloid inlay on top edge. Oval rosewood fingerboard, 9 position markers, white celluloid binding, heavy frets. White celluloid heelplate. Celluloid bound headpiece. Shaded light reddish brown finish with large sunburst on top and back. Rubbed and polished. Individual patent heads with white buttons and bushings. Adjustable rosewood bridge. Nickel plated hinged type tailpiece. Shell celluloid guardplate. A guitar of outstanding appearance and performance.

Price $45.00

CRAFTSMAN Kay GUITARS

88

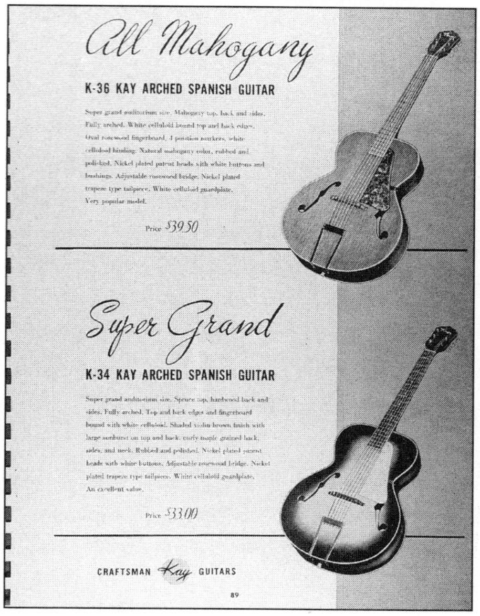

All Mahogany

K-36 KAY ARCHED SPANISH GUITAR

Super grand auditorium size. Mahogany top, back and sides. Fully arched. White celluloid bound top and back edges. Oval rosewood fingerboard, 4 position markers, white celluloid binding. Natural mahogany color, rubbed and polished. Nickel plated patent heads with white buttons and bushings. Adjustable rosewood bridge. Nickel plated trapeze type tailpiece. White celluloid guardplate. Very popular model.

Price $39.50

Super Grand

K-34 KAY ARCHED SPANISH GUITAR

Super grand auditorium size. Spruce top, hardwood back and sides. Fully arched. Top and back edges and fingerboard bound with white celluloid. Shaded violin brown finish with large sunburst on top and back, curly maple grained back, sides, and neck. Rubbed and polished. Nickel plated patent heads with white buttons. Adjustable rosewood bridge. Nickel plated trapeze type tailpiece. White celluloid guardplate. An excellent value.

Price $33.00

CRAFTSMAN Kay GUITARS

89

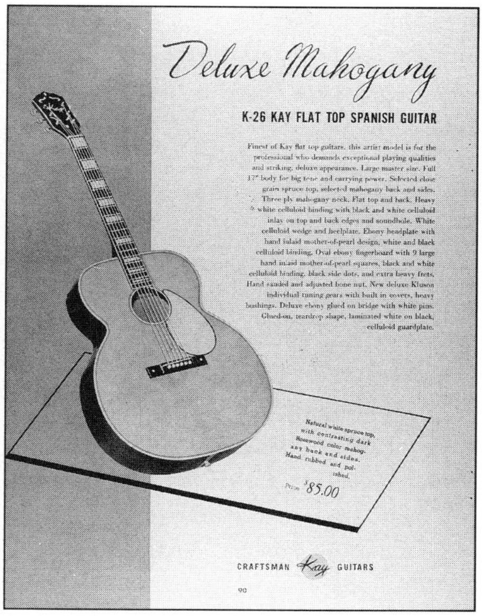

Deluxe Mahogany

K-26 KAY FLAT TOP SPANISH GUITAR

Finest of Kay flat top guitars, this artist model is for the professional who demands exceptional playing qualities and striking, deluxe appearance. Large master size. Full 17" body for big tone and carrying power. Selected close grain spruce top, selected mahogany back and sides. Three ply mahogany neck. Flat top and back. Heavy white celluloid binding with black and white celluloid inlay on top and back edges and soundhole. White celluloid wedge and heelplate. Ebony headplate with hand inlaid mother-of-pearl design, white and black celluloid binding. Oval ebony fingerboard with 9 large hand inlaid mother-of-pearl squares, black and white celluloid binding, black side dots, and extra heavy frets. Hand sanded and adjusted bone nut. New deluxe Kluson individual tuning gears with built in covers, heavy bushings. Deluxe ebony glued on bridge with white pins. Glued-on, teardrop shape, laminated white on black, celluloid guardplate.

Natural white spruce top, with contrasting dark Rosewood color mahogany back and sides. Hand rubbed and polished.

Price $85.00

CRAFTSMAN Kay GUITARS

90

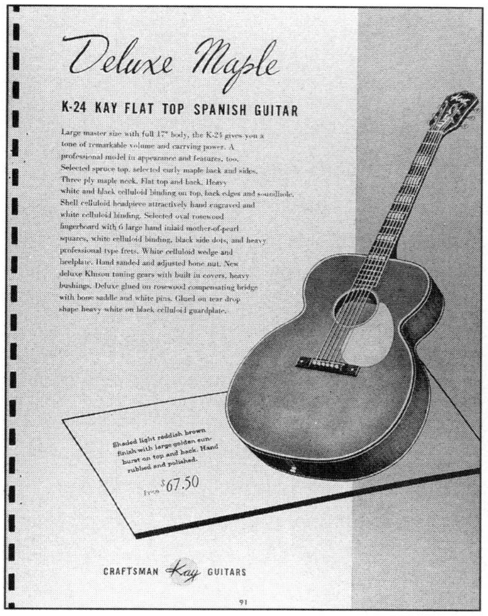

Deluxe Maple

K-24 KAY FLAT TOP SPANISH GUITAR

Large master size with full 17" body, the K-24 gives you a tone of remarkable volume and carrying power. A professional model in appearance and features, too. Selected spruce top, selected curly maple back and sides. Three ply maple neck. Flat top and back. Heavy white and black celluloid binding on top, back edges and soundhole. Shell celluloid headpiece attractively hand engraved and white celluloid binding. Selected oval rosewood fingerboard with 6 large hand inlaid mother-of-pearl squares, white celluloid binding, black side dots, and heavy professional type frets. White celluloid wedge and heelplate. Hand sanded and adjusted bone nut. New deluxe Kluson tuning gears with built in covers, heavy bushings. Deluxe glued on rosewood compensating bridge with bone saddle and white pins. Glued on tear drop shape heavy white on black celluloid guardplate.

Shaded light reddish brown finish with large golden sunburst on top and back. Hand rubbed and polished.

Price $67.50

CRAFTSMAN Kay GUITARS

91

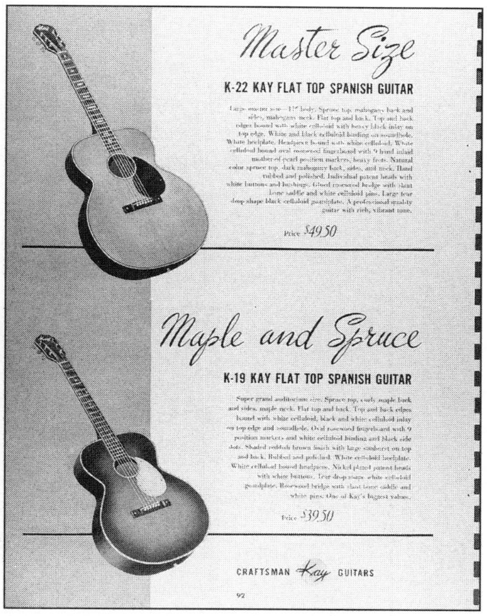

Master Size

K-22 KAY FLAT TOP SPANISH GUITAR

Large master size—17" body. Spruce top, mahogany back and sides, mahogany neck. Flat top and back. Top and back edges bound with white celluloid with heavy black inlay on top edge. White and black celluloid binding on soundhole. White heelplate. Headpiece bound with white celluloid. White celluloid bound oval rosewood fingerboard with 9 hand inlaid mother-of-pearl position markers, heavy frets. Natural color spruce top, dark mahogany back, sides, and neck. Hand rubbed and polished. Individual patent heads with white buttons and bushings. Glued rosewood bridge with slant bone saddle and white celluloid pins. Large tear drop shape black celluloid guardplate. A professional quality guitar with rich, vibrant tone.

Price $49.50

Maple and Spruce

K-19 KAY FLAT TOP SPANISH GUITAR

Super grand auditorium size. Spruce top, curly maple back and sides, maple neck. Flat top and back. Top and back edges bound with white celluloid, black and white celluloid inlay on top edge and soundhole. Oval rosewood fingerboard with 9 position markers and white celluloid binding and black side dots. Shaded reddish brown finish with large sunburst on top and back. Rubbed and polished. White celluloid heelplate. White celluloid bound headpiece. Nickel plated patent heads with white buttons. Tear drop shape white celluloid guardplate. Rosewood bridge with slant bone saddle and white pins. One of Kay's biggest values.

Price $39.50

CRAFTSMAN Kay GUITARS

92

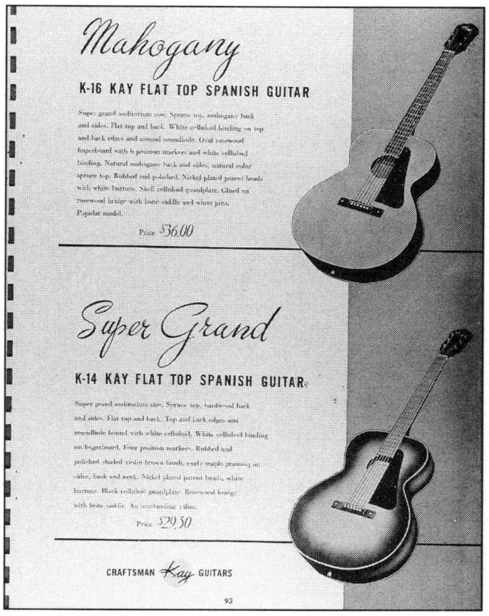

Mahogany

K-16 KAY FLAT TOP SPANISH GUITAR

Super grand auditorium size. Spruce top, mahogany back and sides. Flat top and back. White celluloid binding on top and back edges and around soundhole. Oval rosewood fingerboard with 6 position markers and white celluloid binding. Natural mahogany back and sides, natural color spruce top. Rubbed and polished. Nickel plated patent heads with white buttons. Shell celluloid guardplate. Glued on rosewood bridge with bone saddle and white pins. Popular model.

Price $36.00

Super Grand

K-14 KAY FLAT TOP SPANISH GUITAR

Super grand auditorium size. Spruce top, hardwood back and sides. Flat top and back. Top and back edges and soundhole bound with white celluloid. White celluloid binding on fingerboard. Four position markers. Rubbed and polished shaded violin brown finish, curly maple graining on sides, back and neck. Nickel plated patent heads, white buttons. Black celluloid guardplate. Rosewood bridge with bone saddle. An outstanding value.

Price $29.50

CRAFTSMAN Kay GUITARS

93

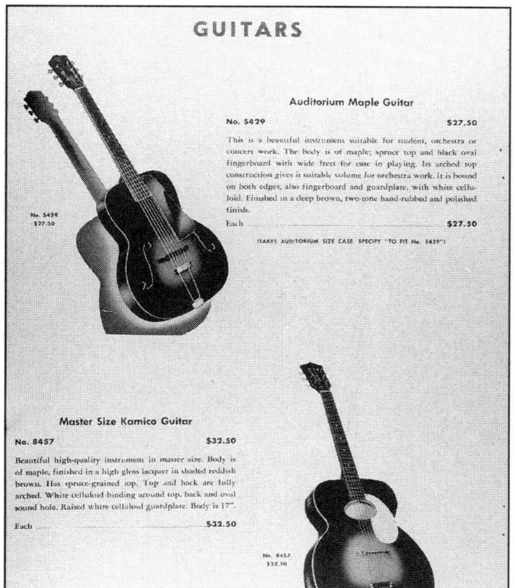

GUITARS

No. 5429
$27.50

Auditorium Maple Guitar

No. 5429 **$27.50**

This is a beautiful instrument suitable for student, orchestra or concert work. The body is of maple; spruce top and black oval fingerboard with wide frets for ease in playing. Its arched top construction gives it suitable volume for orchestra work. It is bound on both edges, also fingerboard and guardplate, with white celluloid. Finished in a deep brown, two-tone hand-rubbed and polished finish.

Each **$27.50**

(TAKES AUDITORIUM SIZE CASE. SPECIFY "TO FIT No. 5429")

Master Size Kamico Guitar

No. 8457 **$32.50**

Beautiful high-quality instrument in master size. Body is of maple, finished in a high gloss lacquer in shaded reddish brown. Has spruce-grained top. Top and back are fully arched. White celluloid binding around top, back and oval sound hole. Raised white celluloid guardplate. Body is 17".

Each **$32.50**

No. 8457
$32.50

94

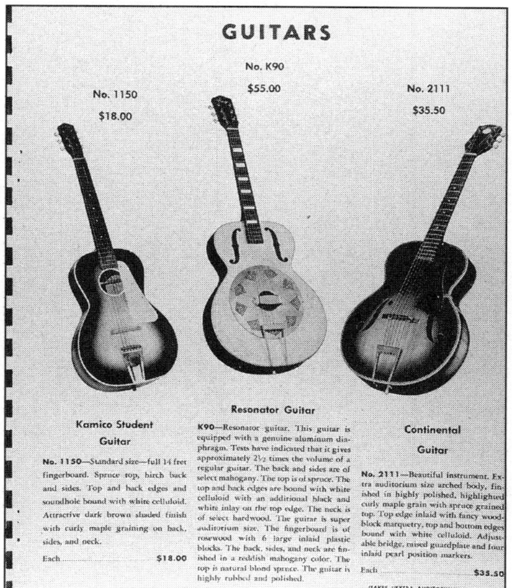

GUITARS

No. K90
$55.00

No. 1150
$18.00

No. 2111
$35.50

Kamico Student Guitar

No. 1150—Standard size—full 14 fret fingerboard. Spruce top, birch back and sides. Top and back edges and soundhole bound with white celluloid. Attractive dark brown shaded finish with curly maple graining on back, sides, and neck.

Each **$18.00**

Resonator Guitar

K90—Resonator guitar. This guitar is equipped with a genuine aluminum diaphragm. Tests have indicated that it gives approximately 2½ times the volume of a regular guitar. The back and sides are of select mahogany. The top is of spruce. The top and back edges are bound with white celluloid with an additional black and white inlay on the top edge. The neck is of select hardwood. The guitar is super auditorium size. The fingerboard is of rosewood with 6 large inlaid plastic blocks. The back, sides, and neck are finished in a reddish mahogany color. The top is natural blond spruce. The guitar is highly rubbed and polished.

Price **$55.00**

K91—Resonator guitar. Same as above but with mahogany top to match.

Price **$55.00**

Continental Guitar

No. 2111—Beautiful instrument. Extra auditorium size arched body, finished in highly polished, highlighted curly maple grain with spruce grained top. Top edge inlaid with fancy woodblock marquetry, top and bottom edges bound with white celluloid. Adjustable bridge, raised guardplate and four inlaid pearl position markers.

Each **$35.50**

(TAKES "EXTRA AUDITORIUM" SIZE CASE)

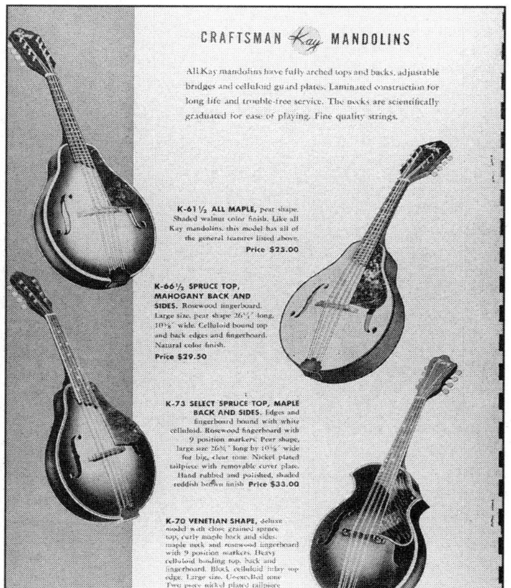

CRAFTSMAN Kay MANDOLINS

All Kay mandolins have fully arched tops and backs, adjustable bridges and celluloid guard plates. Laminated construction for long life and trouble-free service. The necks are scientifically graduated for ease of playing. Fine quality strings.

K-61½ ALL MAPLE, pear shape. Shaded walnut color finish. Like all Kay mandolins, this model has all of the general features listed above. **Price $25.00**

K-66½ SPRUCE TOP, MAHOGANY BACK AND SIDES. Rosewood fingerboard. Large size, pear shape 26¾" long, 10⅝" wide. Celluloid bound top and back edges and fingerboard. Natural color finish. **Price $29.50**

K-73 SELECT SPRUCE TOP, MAPLE BACK AND SIDES. Edges and fingerboard bound with white celluloid. Rosewood fingerboard with 9 position markers. Pear shape, large size 26¾" long by 10⅝" wide for big, clear tone. Nickel plated tailpiece with removable cover plate. Hand rubbed and polished, shaded reddish brown finish. **Price $33.00**

K-70 VENETIAN SHAPE, deluxe model with close grained spruce top, curly maple back and sides, maple neck and rosewood fingerboard with 9 position markers. Heavy celluloid binding top, back and fingerboard. Block celluloid inlay top edge. Large size. Unexcelled tone. Two piece nickel plated tailpiece with removable cover. Hand rubbed and polished, shaded reddish brown finish. **Price $39.00**

96

to include an oval pickup surround and a single control knob on the front. It still came with a 5-tube amp, but the price had dropped to $79.95.

Aluminum Hawaiian steel

Also offered new in '36 was an "All-Metal Hawaiian Model," made by Kay. This curious piece had a small Spanish shaped body like Gibsons of the era. Here's how the catalog described it: "The new electric metal guitar. For Hawaiian playing only. One piece cast aluminum model. Electric pickup mounted beneath the strings. Metal body maintains greatest sustaining vibration — more than any wooden guitar. Scientifically designed to give rich, clear tone." This had one chicken-head control knob on the top, and came with the same amp for $65. The pickup appears to have been a magnetic contact unit attached to the bridge saddle, probably a descendant of the Stromberg design.

Oahu Publishing Company

Since its beginning in 1927, Stromberg-Voisinet and then Kay supplied instruments to Harry Stanley's Oahu Publishing Company in Cleveland, which was big in the Hawaiian genre. Some of the early guitars were small flattops with the Venetian headstock as found on Strombergs, and some of the later guitars were quite fancy and listed for high prices. These Oahus were basically the old Kay Kraft Jumbo Model B Spanish guitars all gussied up. The 1933 Oahu Style No. 60 De Luxe Jumbo had a body made "of the finest Hawaiian curly maple" (whatever that is), with the symmetrical headstock and a bound, vine-inlaid fingerboard encrusted with "the very best Waikiki polished genuine pearl." This beauty cost $158, $2 less than a 1933 Martin 00-45 ($160). Its companion, at $98, the 1933 Style No. 68B Oahu Jumbo was a bit plainer, with dots on the fingerboard and Bakelite 'guard, but with a gold stenciled design on the belly. These were endorsed by those famous NBC artists, the Oahu Serenaders.

One other Kay guitar was also offered in '33. The Oahu Style No. 65m was an all-

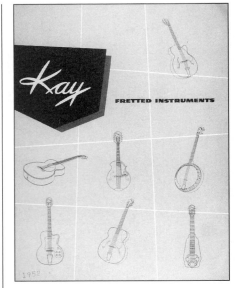

(This page and next page) 1952 Kay catalog, with the debut of the first cutaways and the Kay Thin Twin.

mahogany Kay with the triple-humped head, standard size, checkerboard binding, pin bridge, and $65 price tag.

The Oahu De Luxe Jumbo was offered at least until 1938. No longer "Hawaiian curly maple," by 1936 the De Luxe was now made of "the finest African rosewood" with a spruce top. The fingerboard still has an elaborate vine inlay, with smaller pearl inlays on the "new design" symmetrical head. Top trim and rosette are also pearl inlaid. The neck joined the body at the 12th fret. This was available as the Style 68K Square Neck for Hawaiian style and the Style 69K Round Neck for Spanish style. The advertising included a poem worth preserving for posterity:

"Johnny was a guitar player,
very hard to please,
Whenever he played in public,
he was nervous and ill at ease.
One day he bought a Jumbo,
and now I'll have you know
He's the happiest, cheeriest fellow
— wherever he happens to go."

(Left to Right) 1954 Kay Thin Twin K161, the beginning of the modern Kay electric era (courtesy Mike Newton). Another ca. 1954 Kay Thin Twin K161 with a white headstock and lightning 'guard. Another mid-'50s Kay Thin Twin K161 (photo: Steve Evans, Jacksonville Guitar Center, Jacksonville, AK).

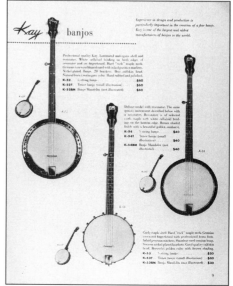

(Left) '53 Spiegel Old Kraftsman alongside a comparable '56 Sears Silvertone (photo: Mike Newton). (Right) Ca. 1955 Kay K161 Old Kraftsman made for Spiegel with stenciled headstock (photo: Gilbert Matossian)

By 1938 the Oahu De Luxe Jumbo had acquired a 14-fret neck, slightly fancier headstock inlays, and a very cool double row of triangular position markers along either edge of the fingerboard, in addition to the fancy vine inlay. The price was still $158!

The Oahu Jumbo continued to be offered at least through 1938, if not longer. This appears to have remained pretty much the same as when it was introduced, with the gold stencil on the belly. By the 1937 catalog it had been renumbered to become Styles 71 and 72, with slightly abbreviated belly design and no pickguard, but otherwise pretty much the same. The Style 71K Square Neck and Style 72K Round Neck could be had for $98, terms available if desired, trades welcomed. "For distinctive instruments with unequalled tone, follow the crowd to Oahu Dealers." Its poem went:

"You may have seen all the rest —
Make up your mind now to buy the best."

A number of other Kay guitars graced the Oahu line in '36, including the Styles No. 66K (Hawaiian; 67K Spanish) and No. 65K (Hawaiian; 64K Spanish), both built of mahogany, both with symmetrical headstocks, dot necks and no pickguards. The 66K was a wider "concert size," while the 65K had a narrower body with a larger soundhole, "built for long, hard service." The Style No. 112K was a wide-bodied Tenor Guitar with several throwback features including the older Kay Kraft asymmetrical headstock and the pointy Venetian bridge. The 112K had a mahogany body and a

spruce top and a pickguard. All three guitars carried $65 price tags. The old Style No. 50 from '33 was now the Style No. 50K Hawaiian and the Style No. 23K Spanish. New were the Style No. 53K Round Neck Spanish and Style No. 54K Square Neck Hawaiian, with all-mahogany construction, dots, and symmetrical slotted head. These were available at least through 1938.

In 1937 Oahu began to market the Volu-Tone, an electric guitar system produced independently but shown mounted on Kay 66K guitars. The Volu-Tone had a very large roughly 6"x3" pickup mounted on flattops with no soundholes, plus a cord coming out of the bottom of the unit going to a large Volu-Tone amplifier. This had five tubes and a microphone attached. Volu-Tone appears to have been an L.A.-based provider of early electronics components, either associated with or at least distributed by Shireson Brothers.

Goodbye Kay Kraft

1937 pretty much marks the end of the Kay Kraft brand name. In the '37 Tonk Brothers catalog, the Kay Kraft line of banjos, Models A, B and C, as before, was of-

Sunburst ca. 1952 Kay K21 Cut-Away Professional archtop, ca. 1954 Kay K27 Jumbo flattop (with DeArmond pickup), and ca. 1956 Kay K112 Rhythm Special archtop in blonde (photo: Gilbert Matossian).

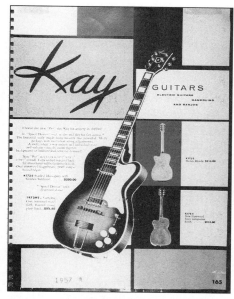

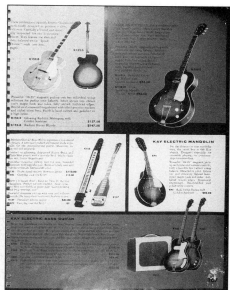

1956 Kay catalog, just before the advent of the Kessels and Kelvinators (courtesy Jim Dulfer).

(Left) Ca. 1955 Kay Electronic Bass Guitar K160 (courtesy Tinicum Guitar Barn, Ottsville, PA). (Right) Ca. 1954 Kay K172 Professional Spanish Electric Archtop, predecessor of the Barney Kessel Pro (photo: Jay Scott).

fered for the last time under that name. Gone for good are the Venetian guitars, with their hallmark Stromberg/Kay Kraft shape. Except for the Tonk banjos and an occasional reference to the "maker of the famous Kay Kraft" left over in certain Montgomery Ward catalogs, the Kay Kraft name entered the annals of guitar history.

Also, by 1937, the cool Kay amplifying electrics were gone, too, not to reappear until after the War.

Hello, Kay (at last)

As nearly as can be determined from catalogs and other sources, the first guitars using the *Kay* brand name probably appeared in late 1936, most certainly by 1937. You'll recall the mention of a ca. 1934 "Kay Deluxe," but this seems to be more an aberration than a beginning. You'll also recall that imported German-made Kay basses were discontinued in 1936.

By 1937 distributor catalogs clearly feature Kay-brand instruments. Although it is still probable that some distributors received Kay-made guitars with their own logos attached, Kay was in a strong enough position to be able to leverage its own name on its instruments, and after '37 distributors marketed "Kay" guitars.

Gabriel's wax-paper flame?

In 1937-38, both Continental and Tonk Brothers were offering a few curious other Kay-made flattops, the No. 2092 with a flat headstock and what looks like a three-piece top, the center being a "stipled maple color panel running the length of the guitar," which could mean paint, but actually may be the wax-paper technique invented by Philip Gabriel. The No. 2091 was a flattop with a diamond design on the top and a groovy lyre-shaped soundhole. The headstock on this was straight and slotted with the plain center hump typical of a zillion later cheap Kay guitars, pale reflections of the company's early days. Some of these had small square shield logos with the "Kay" name.

There were also three Kay-made archtops. The Tonk No. 4315 Super-Grand-size body ($22.50) was the old curly maple, carved spruce top Kay which had been holding the top of the line for years, complete with a fancily inlaid "vase-and-tendril" design and the name "Kay Superb" logo on a variant of the old Kay Kraft style symmetrical headstock. The No. 4313 ($18) was the standard birch pressed-top archtop with the humped headstock. This was a direct descendant of the Arch Kraft guitars. Continental had a similar No. F-3, with "koa wood graining" on the neck, at $15. The Tonk No. 4311 (Continental No. 5400) was a curious hybrid of the birch-body archtop and the flattop with the lyre soundhole. Gone was the diamond design, but the lyre soundhole made this quite a nifty deal at $15. A number of these guitars featured the small square Kay shield logos.

Two Kay-made Venetian mandolins — a flattop and an arched top — were still being advertised in the 1937-38 Continental catalog, sporting the old Kay Kraft asymmetrical headstock.

This transitional Kay line stumbled on into 1938, though its vitality seemed to be fading. Seen in catalogs from both Continental and Tonk Brothers, Kay was still making the three-part flattop design, now curiously sporting the old Stromberg Venetian bridge, and the flattop with the lyre-shaped soundhole. The birch-bodied

Bluesmeister Jimmy Reed with his Kay Thin Twin, hence the nickname "Jimmy Reed" model applied to the K161.

archtops were also still available, in humped or slotted headstocks.

Violin guitars

A fascinating aberration appeared in '37 and '38, sold both by Tonk and Continental. This was a Violin Style Guitar. This "distinctively new and different style guitar" was the old birch-body archtop with a cool scrolled headstock, similar to the shape found much later on the Baldwin Burns guitars, and a long violin-style tailpiece. The top

and back on this guitar were extended over the sides to form a pseudo-violin "lip." The top was pressed plywood; basically it looked cooler than it sounded. The finish was a thin "antique violin" brown. It'll be hard to find one of these without damaged "lips" because the moment you pick one up the edges start getting in the way. This guitar came in a number of variations, including with a humped headstock typical of contemporary Kays and a version with a very narrow "cello" scrolled headstock shape.

Doghouse basses

Perhaps not coincidentally, it was in 1938 that Kay's first upright acoustic basses, known affectionately as "doghouses," appeared. Undoubtedly the new violin guitars reflected some of the company's enthusiasm for the basses, which would become major sellers for Kay over the years.

Ca. 1955 Kay K11B blondie (photo: Gilbert Matossian).

The Normandie

Another Kay from the era was a spectacular Normandie sold by Continental from around 1936 to '38. This was the old curly maple/carved spruce archtop with a huge 18" "dreadnought size body!" It had a steel-reinforced mahogany neck (one of Kay's earliest reinforcements), "Kay adjustable bridge," and the old awful trapeze tail. Most interesting were a new headstock design with a center point, faced with "ivory" and a fingerboard covered in "ivory celluloid" with "seven hand engraved and colored position markers." Yowza! The pickguard was also engraved and colored

Ca. 1955-56 Kay K192B (courtesy Sunrise Guitars, Baldwin, NY).

ivory celluloid. To top this off, the "instrument is finished in a contrasting shaded metallic finish. Two bright finish spots highlight the f-holes. Cost was $49.50. Given the spelling of the name and the extra large size, it is quite possible that this guitar was named after the huge French Art Deco ocean-liner, the Normandie. This was a very swell guitar, which met an undeserving death quickly (foreshadowing the liner, which was sunk by saboteurs in the N.Y. harbor in 1942).

Continental mandolins

Two of our old friends the Venetian mandolin were being offered by Continental in 1937-38, the No 2224 and No. 2225. Both had the two point Venetian shape and the asymmetrical headstock, oval soundhole, and black Formica pickguards. Necks were glued-in. The No. 2224 ($7.80) had a birch body and basswood neck, with two-tone shaded burl fruitwood finish. The No. 2225 ($10) was similar, birch and basswood, with a shaded amber finish.

Oahu's next electrics

Beginning in 1937, Kay also supplied

 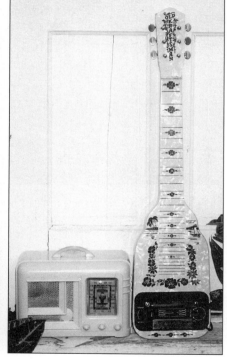

(Left) Kay lap steel. (Right) Fada radio and an Old Kraftsman lap steel.

(Left to Right) Ca. 1956 Kay Gold K Line K8990 Upbeat in natty black (photo: Gilbert Matossian). Ca. 1956 blonde Kay Gold K Line J1700 Barney Kessel Pro and ca. 1959 Kay K1700 Pro in blonde (photo: Gilbert Matossian). 1956 Kay K142 mini-Les Paul in copper finish.

Oahu with its next electrics to follow the Volu-Tones of early '37. Offered by Oahu were the Spanish-shaped No. 229K Tonemaster mahogany Hawaiian lap steel outfitted with an "Oahu patented metal string bridge," a fancily lacquered, gold-leaf encrusted No. 363K Diana DeLuxe, and a No. 230K Standard Amplifier (8" speaker), all Kay-made. Both had headstocks reminiscent of the old Kay Kraft symmetrical style, with oval Oahu logos. The earliest versions of the Diana, at least had horseshoe pickups that look very much like Rickenbacker pickups. Knobs were the radio-dial style, volume and tone on either side of the pickup assembly. How long these early Oahus were offered isn't known for sure, but at some point after 1938 the pickup was changed to a more conventional design. At some point probably in around '39, the Oahu headstock changed to the center-peaked variety with script stenciled Oahu logos and the model name stenciled diagonally down the center of the face. The Diana had lost the gold leaf and acquired "Oahu" letters down the center of the fingerboard. The pickup was contained in a plastic assem-

bly with two Bakelite knobs on either side. The Tonemaster was still considerably plainer, with a large black plastic pickup assembly, usually with an Oahu G-clef on the front, though some examples do not have this feature. Position markers also vary on these later Oahus, which probably provides some clue to vintage, but that's a mystery for another day. By around 1941 Oahu had switched to selling Hawaiian lap steels made by Dickerson, the precursor of the Magnatone line.

The early Kay "horseshoe" pickups, by the way, may have been what inspired Rickenbacker's lawyer to complain to Kuhrmeyer, as previously mentioned. In the Kuhrmeyer letter responding to Rickenbacker, Hank states that Kay had licensed the electronics from Meissner Inventions, Inc., 18 Main Street, Milburn, New Jersey. Meissner claimed to control the patents that governed the Kay pickup, and Kuhrmeyer suggested that Rickenbacker take up any dispute with Meissner. Meissner was also actively involved with Vega and Epiphone at this time, and Meissner held patents that show up on the early Electar guitars from this

period. In late '37, shortly after the Rickenbacker/Kuhrmeyer exchange Herb Sunshine of Epiphone applied for his patent on a non-horse-shoe pickup. By 1938 Kay, too, was putting more conventional pickups on its Oahu steels. As far as is known, the horseshoe pickups never appeared on Kay-branded instruments, though if you find one, that would change this observation. Just what Meissner's connection was with the horseshoe pickups and licensing is still unknown.

As seen in the 1941 catalog, Oahu also offered the Valencia Spanish Electric Guitar No. 303K ($57.50). This was a Super Grand size f-hole archtop with maple body, spruce top and the old humped headstock, essen-

Ca. 1956 Kay K21 Rhythm Special with rare Kelvinator headstock (courtesy Scott Chinery; photo: Jay Scott)

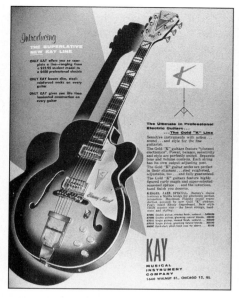

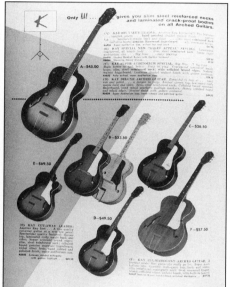

1957 Kay catalog from the '58 David Wexler jobber book (courtesy Robert Watkins).

(Top) Ca. 1957 Kay K6700B Barney Kessel Artist (courtesy Chelsea Guitars, NY; photo: Jay Scott). (Bottom) Ca. 1957 Kay K8921S Masterpiece and a 1958 Kay K8921S Masterpiece (coutesy Nutty Jazz Guitars, New York, NY; photo: Jay Scott).

bingers of some of the good things to come. The Televisions were still archtops, the genre which Kay had hired Joseph Zorzi to design back in 1927 and in which it had excelled, in its price category, ever since.

The Televisions came in two versions, the K60 and K62. Basically these were the same guitars, with the K60 in "artistically shaded walnut brown" sunburst finish, and the K62 in "white natural finish," i.e., blonde. Both were Super Grand size, with highly flamed maple bodies and three-piece neck, bound carved spruce tops, bound f-holes, 14th fret neck/body joint, and fancy swirled celluloid pickguards. Fingerboards were rosewood with distinctive line and quadrant or "sharkfin" mother-of-pearl inlays. The headstock was a new design, with concave top tapers culmi-

nating in a flat top about an inch wide. These were faced with rosewood and inlaid with a big block-lettered Kay logo. The back of the head was painted black. Also new was a swell adjustable bridge that looked like a scrolled ribbon, with the bass end pointing down and the treble end up. Gone — praise be! — was the boring functional tailpiece in favor of a fancy wire trapeze. These were very nice guitars, indeed, and a steal at $60.

Why exactly Kay chose the Television name is unknown, but it was definitely a *modern* idea. TV, of course, was first demonstrated back in 1926 and had been the hit of the 1932 Chicago World's Fair. The first public broadcasts had begun in London in 1936. Kay was ahead of the game, for Americans had to wait until 1941 for the first television broadcasting. Fender's Broadcaster wouldn't appear yet for more than a decade.

The '38-39 line...

At least two other archtops and two flattops were introduced bearing the Kay brand by 1938 and seen in the C.M.I. catalog.

'38 archtops included the K20 ($22), an all-Honduras mahogany Super Auditorium size with a center pointed head, bound ovalled rosewood fingerboard, nine pearl dots and tortoise pickguard. The K5 ($15) was a downscale Auditorium size version in Honduras mahogany.

'38 flattops in-

cluded the Model K6 Auditorium size Spanish Guitar ($16.50) with a spruce top and Honduras mahogany body, rectangular bridge, ovalled rosewood fingerboard, and pickguard. The K2 ($11) was standard size in all-Honduras mahogany, with rectangular pin bridge, square-top headstock and no pickguard.

These were joined in '39 (though these were *probably* also available in '38) by additional models. The K25 ($27.50) Super Auditorium was a slightly downscale model of the Television, still with curly maple body, spruce top, and rosewood fingerboard. The head was the newer pointed version intro-

tially the same as the '39 Kay Spanish Electric Guitar. This had a large single-coil pickup at the neck and a volume and tone control, one on each shoulder of the upper bout. This came with an Oahu De Luxe Amplifier, with a 12" High Fidelity speaker, made by Kay.

Professional-grade Televisions

The fancy appointments of the Normandie were a sign of changes in the wind. In 1938 Kay introduced its first truly "professional" archtops, the Kay Television Model, with the company logo written in the natty "modern" cursive script that would last through the War.

As seen in the 1938 C.M.I. and 1939 Tonk Brothers catalogs, topping the new Kay Television Model guitars were definitely an evolutionary step forward for Kay and har-

Ca. 1957 Kay K6700S Barney Kessel Artist (courtesy Chelsea Guitars; photo: Jay Scott).

duced a year before. The K18 ($20) was maple-bodied, with the older humped headstock. The K10 ($16.50) was an even plainer maple version. Both still had spruce tops. The K20 and K5 were still around.

Flattops offered in '39 (again, probably available in '38) were the K8 ($16.50) Auditorium Mahogany Hawaiian Guitar, with a Honduras mahogany body, heavy square neck and spruce top. This had a pin bridge, tortoise celluloid pickguard and a pointed headstock. The K4 ($13.50) was an all-Honduras-mahogany auditorium-size guitar with a rectangular pin bridge, square-top headstock and no pickguard. The K6 and the K2 were still available, too.

Five Venetian Kay mandolins were offered in '39, if not earlier, reflections of our friend Zorzi. These all had the old Kay Kraft asymmetrical headstocks. The Model K70 ($27.50) was an f-hole model with curly maple body and spruce top. The K68 ($22) was all Honduras mahogany. The K66 ($16.50) was mahogany body and spruce top. The K61 ($15) was all mahogany. The K30 ($11)

(Left to Right) Ca. 1957 Kay K6437 (courtesy Paul Cowen, photo: Elizabeth Rimrott). Ca. 1957 Kay K6118B Cut-Away (courtesy Rockville Music, Dallas, TX). Ca. 1957 Kay K6700S Artist (courtesy Scott Chinery).

was all mahogany with an oval soundhole. Also in the line were three "new pear shaped models." These were the K71 flattop ($9), with mahogany-finished birch body and oval soundhole. The K72 ($15) archtop/back had hardwood body and spruce top and f-holes. The K73 ($25) had arched top and back with spruce top and curly maple body.

The 1939 Grossman catalog carried the same instruments plus the No. 4009 "Winton" Venetian Model mandolin ($7.50), similar to the previous Continental mandos, with birch body and two-tone "rich, brown color" in "skillful graining.

Despite the introduction of the Kay brand, Kay continued to sell to Montgomery Ward, Oahu and some surprising other outlets.

In the Fall/Winter 1939 Wards catalog five Kay-made Grand Auditorium archtops were still offered, four pressed-tops with the old humped headstocks ranging

Ca. 1957 Old Kraftsman K157 Student Hawaiian with a probably Dano amp (photo: Jim Dulfer).

from the all-birch model ($7.15) to maple/spruce ($8.65), mahogany/spruce ($9.45), maple/spruce ($11.75), and carved spruce/curly maple, checkerboard-bound model ($15.25). The last two had the new ribbon bridge. The carved-top had the newer pointed headstock, and had the usual Wards "Kay Kraft" attribution.

Curiously enough, while this Wards catalog still sold instruments under its own label and relegates identifying the maker to a casual mention in the copy, it now promoted its guitars as the "Same Quality sold by Music Stores...Three of the best known makers of fretted instruments in the country made the models on these pages. They're made of the same costly materials as those guitars which bear the makers' own names..." Read, "same as the Kay guitars now sold in music stores."

Other Pre-War electrics

Three Kay electric guitars and two amplifiers were offered in both the 1939 Grossman and Tonk catalogs. These included the Spanish Electric Guitar and the Hawaiian De Luxe and Hawaiian Standard Models.

(Left) Ca. 1958 Kay K8901B Combo (courtesy Scott Chinery).
(Right) 1957 Kay K136 in Spring Green and White Mist finish
(photo: Mike Newton).

The Kay Spanish Electric Guitar was a Super Grand archtop in maple, with an unbound fingerboard, dots, and a center-humped head. A single thin covered pickup sitting on a large surround was in the neck position, with one "radio dial" volume and one tone control, one on each upper shoulder! This was shown with a small amplifier in a squarish sort of cabinet with a round speaker cutout with a Kay "K" shield insert. The covering was a light brown tolex (called "aeroplane cloth") with two thick and a bunch of thinner vertical stripes. This had 8-10 watts output and had two channels with separate volume controls.

The Kay Hawaiian De Luxe Model was what would become the classic multi-level stairstepped all-mahogany body. This had a large hump in the head, more dramatic than usual. A handrest covered one pickup, with "radio dial" volume and tone knobs on either side. A slotted rectangular tailpiece completed the piece. This was also shown with the "aeroplane" amp.

The Kay Hawaiian Standard Model had a shape that crossed a Spanish guitar with a Bosch pear. Also of mahogany, this had a more standard center-humped head, handrest covered pickup, radio volume and tone on either side, and slotted tail. The accompanying amp was a smaller version with a round grille, plain covering, 6-8 watts, and two inputs.

Kay and Gretsch

In 1939 Kay (and Harmony) briefly also supplied none other than Gretsch. Among the Kays was the new Grand Concert Size Spanish Guitar No. 20 ($20). This was a "sweet-toned, real mahogany" flattop in a jumbo size with a spruce top, rectangular pin bridge, 14-fret neck, tortoise pickguard, dot inlays and tapered notched headstock.

More curious was the Gretsch "Electromatic" Hawaiian, an example of which you can see on page 37 of George Gruhn and Walter Carter's *Electric Guitars* (GPI/Miller Freeman Books). This looked much like the old Kay aluminum body, but this was made of mahogany. This had one pickup, an elevated pickup cover/handrest, and volume and tone controls with radio-style silver foil inserts under the knobs. Binding was the checker style popular with Kay at the time; dots were multi-colored. Most curious was a unique six-in-line headstock with Harlin tuners made by Kluson (G-400V). These were six tuners set on a curved plate with gears at a diagonal angle, requiring worm gear stems to get longer as they went from treble to bass. Around the edges was a bevel easily described as a German carve.

Accompanying the Hawaiian was a Gretsch "Electromatic" Spanish guitar, an archtop with volume and tone controls. Both were supplied, at $110, with a matching Kay-built Gretsch "Electromatic" electric amplifier with a 7-inch speaker, the "entire unit enclosed in aeroplane cloth case with water-proof zipper-closing cover." These were related to the '39 Kay Spanish Electric Guitar and amplifier.

The Kluson "Special Harlin" six-in-line tuners appeared later on Valco-made Gretsch lap steels and Oahu Iolanas, by the way.

The Kay line continued on pretty much as usual as the '40s dawned. By 1939, of course, World War II had begun in Europe, and the expectation of the entry of the United States into the conflagration continued to grow.

(Left) Ca. 1958 Kay K8990 Upbeat in sunburst (courtesy Jim's Guitars, Baltimore, MD). (Right) Ca. 1957 Kay K673 Swingmaster in sunburst (courtesy Blue Suede Shoe, Dallas, TX).

Sears, Silvertone and Kay

In 1940, Kay received its first order from mighty Sears, Roebuck and Company, two models of lap steel guitars. This was a significant event for guitardom not so much because Sears got its first guitars from Kay, but because it signaled the imminent arrival of one of the most famous brand names in guitar history, Silvertone.

Sears had for years relied on its subsidiary Harmony (and occassionally other companies such as National) for its supply of guitars and other fretted instruments. Harmony had begun in Chicago back in 1892 and had ridden to great success making ukuleles after their introduction in 1915. In order to better meet its customer demand for ukes, Sears purchased Harmony in 1916. Harmony remained a Sears company until 1940, providing Sears with guitars, banjos and mandolins bearing the *Supertone* label.

In early 1940, Sears decided to divest itself of the Harmony company. Long-time Harmony president Jay Kraus resigned in February of 1940, whether because of or causing the imminent divestiture is unknown. In any case, in December of 1940 Sears sold Harmony to a group of employee investors with Jay Kraus being the majority shareholder. In January of 1941, Harmony relocated to new, larger facilities. This transition away from the parent Sears company was probably quite amicable, because after 1941 Sears went back to relying on Harmony.

In any case, it was during this period of reorganization at Harmony that Sears turned to other suppliers, including Kay and Regal, for its instrument needs. The earliest non-Harmony Sears' instruments were still called Supertone, however, one Supertone archtop was called the Supertone Silvertone model. Someone at Sears clearly liked that name, and shortly thereafter these Kay- and Regal-made guitars became the first to bear the new moniker, *Silvertone*. When Sears returned to buying Harmony instruments, the name Silvertone was retained.

Kay Silvertones

The first two Kay guitars for Sears appeared in the 1940-41 catalog, which still contained almost all Harmony-made guitars. These were a pair of electric Hawaiian lap steels, the #2307 ($18.95) and the #2331, a fancy deluxe model ($39.95). The deluxe version is illustrated on page 38 of George Gruhn and Walter Carter's *Electric Guitars*, showing a swell guitar with a flamed maple top, a plastic-faced 3-and-3 headstock and a plastic fingerboard with multi-colored rectangular position markers. This had the same electronics as the Gretsch Electromatic, with a single pickup, handrest and two knobs with the radio-style foil inserts. These lasted only about a year and were replaced by National-made steels the following year.

In 1941 the Sears line was fully revamped reflecting its "alternative" suppliers, and the brand was renamed Silvertone. Kay/Silvertones that appear in the 1941-42 Sears catalog included six Kay archtops.

Ca. 1958 Spiegel Old Kraftsman version of a Kay K6100 Country dreadnought, this with spruce top and maple body (photo: Gilbert Matossian).

Top of the line was "Our Finest Silvertone," the Super-Artist, at $49.95. This was identical to the Kay Television model which had appeared in 1939, and was available in either a natural blond or violin brown finish. This had the fancier trapeze tails, the new ribbon bridge, quadrant inlays and a curly maple neck, again with steel reinforcement.

The Blonde Silvertone ($19.95) and the Silvertone Crest ($29.95) were mid-level high-end models (the ones recommended for "orchestra or studio"). These were both Grand Auditorium carved-spruce tops with curly maple bodies, f-holes, 14-fret necks and the pointed headstock. Both were fancy guitars, the former in natural, the latter sunburst with checker binding (including on the pickguard) and nine inlays, including some horizontal designs which look to be rectangular in the catalog. On some examples the non-dots are diamonds. Bodies were maple-faced plywood, necks were curly maple. The sunburst Crest had been offered as Kay's top-of-the-line in the '39 Ward's catalog, differing only in that it fea-

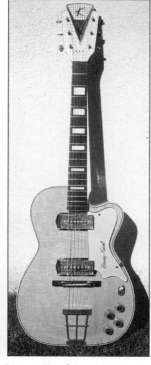

(Left) Ca. 1958 Kay K1700 Barney Kessel Pro in sunburst. (Right) Ca. 1958 Kay K1700 Barney Kessel Pro in blonde (photos: Ed Tauber).

(Left) 1959 Kay K8980 Upbeat in sunburst (photo: Mike Newton). (Right) Imagine being a Mummer on this Kay U.S. tenor banjo of unknown vintage, probably '50s but could be earlier or later.

tured the new "ribbon" bridge.

The Kay-made Silvertone Crest had a nice crisp tone, offering sharp cut-through in a rhythm section. This guitar is often referred to as the "Big Boy Crudup" guitar since he was shown in RCA publicity photos paying one capo'd up to the seventh fret. One would never confuse this with a truly professional guitar like a Gibson L-5, but it's not bad for a guitar delivered to your door by the postman in 1941.

The remaining three Kay Silvertones were auditorium size. The DeLuxe Playtime ($13.95) had a sunburst finish, spruce top and maple body. The Blond Playtime ($9.95) was the same guitar in natural. The Prep All Maple ($7.95) was a sunburst maple guitar. All had the humped headstocks.

Curiously enough, this Sears catalog had one Kay mandolin, the Professional, a maple/spruce archtop *Venetian* ($11.95).

By around 1941 the Television line had acquired a notch above it, the Kay Professional, a fancy archtop guitar with a multi-bound spruce top, maple body, huge pick-guard, a fancy Kluson trapeze tailpiece, the ribbon bridge, bound f-holes, a bound ebony fingerboard with mini-rectangle inlays, and a tapered, inlaid headstock. The rosewood front-and back-faced headstock had a series of sort of Moderne rectangular inlays, and very fancy individual Kluson tuners. This model, in slightly more restrained form, would survive the War as the Kay Artist model.

Songbirds

At least one other brand was produced by Kay in the late '30s and possibly '40s called the Lark brand. These usually had little bird decals located on the body. The Lark Junior was one curious example with two normal f-holes and a mini-f-hole just under the fingerboard!

Wartime

By 1942 World War II was in full gear, and guitar production slowed to a crawl for everyone as almost all industrial manufacturing was refocused toward the War effort. Kay continued to produce guitars during the war years, but in very limited numbers. It was during this period that Kay's first 17" flattop guitars appeared.

Evidence of the reduced wartime production can be seen in the Spring/Summer 1945 Wards catalog. Kay was still providing instruments for that great mail-order house, but the selection was drastically curtailed. For the first time, these guitars are specifically identified as being Kays. Of four guitars and one bandello (a banjo-mandolin), two archtops and the bandello were Kays. One flattop, a Regal, and another unknown archtop (and the bandello) were stamped "NOT AVAILABLE." Thus, the only guitars available from Wards in 1945 were the Kay Professional and the Kay Imperial guitars.

The Kay Professional ($49.50) was our old friend the carved-spruce-top curly maple f-hole archtop done up in a natural blond finish. This had a laminated curly maple neck. The Kay Imperial ($33.75) was similar, with a carved spruce top, flamed maple body, and a poplar neck(!), finished in a dark mahogany sunburst. These had tortoise 'guards and dot-necks. Both had the humped headstock, but the Professional had the pre-war block-lettered KAY logo set in a celluloid face, whereas the Imperial had the metal cursive script Kay logo which first appeared in 1939 and is usually associated with Kay in the '40s.

Kay was still marketing electric steels by the mid-'40s, including the Kay Hawaiian DeLuxe Model. This was the Art Deco-stairstep-shaped "modernistic design," with a single pickup, three-and-three tuners (no six-in-lines), and the radio dial knobs. It came with a small 8-10 watt Kay amplifier similar to those pre-War ones also seen earlier sold by Oahu and Gretsch.

Spiegel Fall/Winter 1959 catalog with Kay guitars (courtesy Paul and Deb Grubich).

Kay Body Sizes

The following guide to Kay body sizes was compiled by Mike Newton. Kay — and other manufacturers — typically used these terms to describe the body sizes of their guitars. Most, in fact, were quite inconsistent in their use of these descriptions, so you should use this as a *rough* guide only.

Size	Lower bout	Typical model	Dates
Standard	12³/₄"	Early Stromberg-Voisinet	ca.1925-30
Standard	13¹/₄"	Later Stromberg-Voisinet/Kay	ca.1928-40s
Grand Auditorium	14¹/₄"	Kay Kraft Jumbo	1931-ca.1937
Auditorium	15"	Small archtops and flattops	ca.1935-50s

Size	Lower bout	Typical model	Dates
Super Grand	15¹/₂"	Standard archtops	1936-38
Super Auditorium	15¹/₂"	Standard archtops	1939-50s
Super Grand	17"	Large archtops	1939-46
Master	17"	Large archtops and flattops	1947-50s
Super Jumbo/ Dreadnought	18"	Normandie	1936-38

Occasionally the term Concert or Grand Concert is employed, and this usually translates to either a Grand Auditorium or Auditorium size. Some Grand Auditorium guitars, such as the Kay Kraft Deluxes, were actually 15¹/₂" wide. Don't expect consistency!

Even though this is a guitar book, here's the 1957 Kay acoustic (and electric) bass catalog…where else will it be preserved? (courtesy Robert Watkins).

1958 Kay Upbeat K8995 with three pickups and gold hardware (photo: Gilbert Matossian).

Post-War: Archtops

In 1947, Kay was back in stride and introduced its new post-War line. It's interesting to note that Kay's Sales Manager was Bob Keyworth, who would play a big role in the mid-'50s.

The new Kay line was illustrated in the '47-'48 Targ & Dinner catalog and included seven acoustic archtops, six flattops and four electric guitars.

Top of the archtop line included three guitars dubbed Kay Artist guitars. The *sine qua non* remained the K48 curly maple, carved spruce top beast, now in a Master size with a 17" body. This had bound f-holes, bound top and back, bound fingerboard and bound humped headstock. As with all these guitars, the logo is now a consistent cursive script Kay with additional triangular mother-of-pearl inlays. The laminated curly maple neck now had a center ebony strip. The fingerboard was now ebony, with split pearl block inlays, the splits alternating in diagonal and vertical positions. The fingerboard ended with an angled extension toward the treble side. The fancy deluxe "ribbon" or s-shaped bridge now graced the belly. The finish was

a dark reddish brown sunburst or a natural blonde. The familiar utilitarian Kay trapeze tailpiece was replaced by a large fancy, cast plated affair. The old utilitarian price was replaced by a respectable $200 tag, too!

The master size Kay Artist K46, at $97.50, was a bit closer to usual Kay fare. This, too, had a carved spruce top and curly maple body in brown sunburst. The f-holes weren't bound, but it had the ribbon bridge and bound (square ended) fingerboard. Inlays were the sharkfin quadrants with mother-of-pearl "eighth notes" on the rosewood-faced headstock. The boring trapeze was back. The Kay Artist K44 ($76.50) was pretty much the same, with bound f-holes, and block inlays. The headstock was celluloid-faced with a different decoration.

These Artists were reportedly very well received by dealers at NAMM that year. Sales Manager Keyworth was quoted: "We're mighty proud of this instrument. At $200 retail, the Artist Model is our answer to the many requests we have had for an exceptionally fine guitar to sell to those who want the best money can buy." Subtract the sales hype and you still have some pretty decent guitarflesh.

The K42 was another curly maple axe for $52.50. This had pearl dot inlays, a plain rosewood bridge, a smaller pickguard, and a celluloid-faced head with a fleur-de-lis decoration.

The other three archtops were Kay Arched Guitars. The super grand auditorium K39 ($42.50) had an "arched" spruce top, curly maple body, light reddish brown sunburst finish, and bound rosewood fingerboard with dot inlays. This had a plain humped headstock with the script Kay logo. The K36 ($32.50) was an all-mahogany guitar, and the K34 ($26.50) was made of spruce and a "hardwood" body.

With the exception of the K34, which lasted until 1956, these archtops appear to have lasted until around 1951.

'47 Flattops

Kay's '47 flattops included three Master size (17") and three super grand auditoriums. All had a nicely rotund jumbo shape and were quite handsome. Top of the line was the Artist K26 ($85) made of ma-

hogany with a spruce top, round soundhole, a rectangular pin bridge and a glued-on white/black laminated pickguard with sort of a Martin shape. The bound ebony fingerboard had large pearl block inlays. The multi-humped symmetrical headstock had the cursive script Kay logo with little flourishes around it. The K24 ($67.50) was similar except for a curly maple body and a rosewood fingerboard. The K22 ($48.50) had a mahogany body, smaller rectangular inlays and a plain black pickguard.

The super auditoriums were similar, just plainer. The K19 ($36.50) had a curly maple body, spruce top, sunburst finish, bound rosewood fingerboard and dot inlays. The white guardplate was screwed on. The K16 ($30) had a mahogany body, tortoise guard and was finished in clear natural. The K14 ($23.50) had a hardwood body, a violin brown finish and a black guard.

Except for the K22, these flattops also lasted until around 1951.

Kamico

It was also in 1947 that Kay introduced its truly budget line called Kamico, for, pre-

Ca. 1960 Kay Thinline Pro Series Model No. 1993 in blonde (courtesy MIke's Guitars, Etc., Erial, NJ).

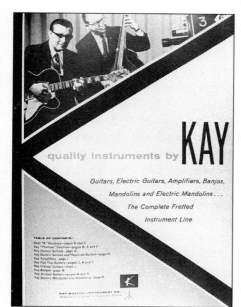

1960 Kay catalog seen in the '61 Targ & Dinner jobber book; thinline electrics and acoustic guitars, banjos and mandos were the same as those shown in the 1961 catalog following (courtesy Jim Dulfer).

sumably, *Kay Musical Instrument Company*. The Kamico No. 1150 Student Guitar was a flattop with spruce top, birch body, with white celluloid binding, dark brown shaded finish, and curly maple graining on the back, sides and neck. Narrow center-humped head and dots. The Kamico No. 8457 Master Size Guitar was an archtop with spruce top, maple body, and oval soundhole. The Kamico No. 5429 Auditorium Maple Guitar was another archtop with spruce top, maple body, and f-holes. The No. 5429 was basically the same as Kay's pre-War archtops like the F-3. The Kamicos drop from sight by 1951.

Back to resonators

New in the '47 line were the K90 and K91 Resonator Guitars, a genre Kay dabbled in briefly fifteen years earlier. Both had mahogany bodies, hardwood necks, f-holes on the upper shoulders, rosewood fingerboards, humped headstocks with the script Kay logo and plastic block inlays. The resonator cones and plates were genuine National Dobro parts. The K90 had a spruce top and the K91 a mahogany top. In '49 these were also sold through Gretsch for $55. In 1950 Kay Resonators went for $49.50. These were gone by 1952, at the latest.

Electric Spanish and Hawaiian guitars

1947 Kay Electric Guitars, as shown in the '47-'48 Targ & Dinner catalog, consisted of two Spanish and two Hawaiian models. All were available with or without an amplifier. The Spanish models were much as seen before the War. The master size (17") F451 was a standard Kay f-hole archtop with curly maple back, mahogany sides and spruce top in sunburst. The bound rosewood fingerboard had small rectangular pearl inlays. The pickup had individual pole pieces, an oval surround and was placed in the center perpendicular to the strings. A volume and tone control were

placed on the top shoulder of the upper bout. Guitar alone was $107.25, with amp $217.25. The F453 was basically the same with deluxe covered tuners, the ribbon bridge and a shaded light brown mahogany finish. Cost was $132, $242 with amp. The headstocks shown in the catalog look remarkably like the old symmetrical Kay Krafts, though with the new script logo. Descriptions are vague, but there may have been a difference in pickups between the two models.

Shortly after these models appeared the

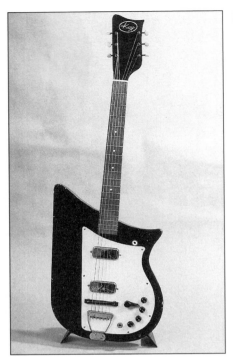

1960 Kay K4102 Solo King, the ugliest guitar in the world: care to argue about it?

K160 Kay Deluxe Spanish Electric Guitar appeared in the Wexler catalog, with the controls moved down to the lower treble bout. The pickup was similar but now angled toward the bridge on the treble side. The bridge was the new ribbon variety. This had the '50s-style symmetrical headstock with the Kay script logo. The guitar alone was $120, with a 5-tube High Fidelity Amplifier $210.

The '47 Hawaiians lap steels in the '47-'48 Targ & Dinner catalog were no longer mini-Spanish shaped nor stair-stepped, but a sort of tapered arrowhead shape. The F461 had a mahogany body with a curly maple top and brown sunburst finish. It had a flocked non-slip back and a single pickup with volume and tone controls. It, too, had the old-style symmetrical headstock with three-and-three tuners. Alone $71.50, with amp $181.50. The F463 was the same except for contrasting curly maple on the top, a shell on white celluloid fingerboard with hand engraved position

markers, and a special shell-on-white celluloid plate for the pickup. Again, the F461 is described as having a "magnetic pickup" while the F463 had a "deluxe magnetic pickup," but whether this is merely sales jargon or a real difference is unknown. Cost: $99, $209 with amp.

The 5-tube amp with 12" speaker cost $110. This had a large wooden cabinet of mahogany with a curly maple front, bone-shaped grill cutouts, two large eyebrow cutouts above, and a drawer-pull handle. The cabinet was 18$\frac{1}{2}$" high, 14$\frac{1}{2}$" wide, and 8$\frac{1}{4}$" deep. There were two instrument inputs with their own volume controls, and a microphone input with volume, tone and "high fidelity" controls.

Here's what Bob Keyworth said about the new Kay electrics in the June 1947 *The Music Trades.* Recall this is sales hype, but there's also probably a great deal of insight into the workings of Kay at the time under Kuhrmeyer's leadership.

"Just any amplifier or pick-up won't do. The amplifier and the pick-up must be engineered to the job of getting the most out of the specific instrument, both as to its range and its tone characteristics. Various tests prove that the new Kay

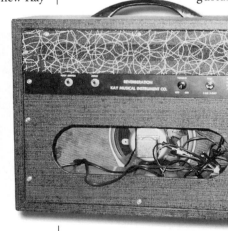

(Left) 1960 Kay K540 Reverberation Unit, last of Kay's tube amplification gear. (Right) Rear view of the Kay K540 Reverberation unit which connects with "alligator" clips (courtesy DiPinto Guitars, Philadelphia, PA)!

'electrics' accomplish these objectives to an appreciable degree." Such a claim fits with what we know of Hank Kuhrmeyer's dedication to audio excellence.

Shortly thereafter, the K159 Kay Hawaiian Electric Guitar was introduced, essentially the same as the F463, with a handrest inscribed with the Kay script logo. Alone this was $90, with the amp, $180.

The Rex line

Other interesting guitars of note included the Rex line of archtops and flattops that were sold through the Gretsch catalog and others. These were basically the same as the '48 Kay line and carried names like the Rex Lancer, Rex Aragon and Rex Royal archtops and the Rex Playboy flattops. The Rex Lancer was an auditorium in all mahogany. The Rex Aragon was a super auditorium spruce top and curly maple body. The Rex Royal was another super auditorium in all mahogany but with curly maple graining. The Playboys came as a 15" auditorium Spanish, a $\frac{3}{4}$ size model "For Ladies and Juveniles," and a Tenor. These appear to have been gone by '48, however, it's possible that the Rex line extended out on either side of this catalog sighting.

Cutaways

In 1952 Kay announced its "first new guitar in five years" in *The Music Trades.* Quoting Kuhrmeyer, Kay described itself as a company not inclined to introduce "face-lifts" just for the sake of looking new year after year. "It's the dealer we're thinking about," said Hank, "because frequent changes mean all-too-frequent mark-downs at the dealer's expense." The new guitars were Kay's first cutaway archtops, marking Kay's joining of the modern guitar world. Kay cutaways were basically the same as their previous line enhanced by the popular new cutaway feature and included the K21 Cut-Away Professional, the K11 and the K1. These were shown in the '52 Kay catalog.

The K21 Cut-Away Professional was a spectacular guitar. The K21 had a master-size 17" wide body with a carved one-piece spruce top and fiddleback maple sides and back, all bound in wide white celluloid. The 7-ply maple neck had a wide, bound triple-humped headstock with "Seal Fast" enclosed tuners, script Kay logo, and a decoration with two triangles facing two parallel strips. The bound ebony fingerboard had mother-of-pearl inlays, alternating diagonally split blocks and vertically split ovals. The end of the fingerboard was diagonal and scalloped, matching the lines of the large white, winged pickguard (engraved with a Kay shield). This had an ebony "ribbon" bridge, stock flatwound strings attached fancy, heavy-duty cast tailpiece. At $200 this came in sunburst or natural blonde. Necks were reinforced by a u-shaped bar.

New also was a second cutaway archtop, the K11. This was also 17" master sized, with bound spruce top and curly maple body. The head was triple-humped, with

script Kay logo and mirror-image "eighth note" design. The bound rosewood fingerboard had line and quadrant inlays. The bridge was ribbon, the tailpiece with a large, grooved rectangular piece for string attachment. The pickguard was a large white affair, but not the wing. At $110 it could be had in sunburst or blonde. This guitar would become known as the Rhythm Special later in the '50s.

The Kay K1 was the third in the trio, another 17" master size. This had a spruce top, curly maple body, binding, plain triple-humped head with script Kay logo, bound rosewood fingerboard, alternating single/double large dot inlays, plain rosewood bridge (not ribbon), and old-style plain trapeze tail. The large white pickguard had a natty hook on the end. At $65 this came in sunburst. The K21, K11 and K1 cutaways hung around till '56.

'52 non-cut archtops

Five non-cutaway archtops were offered in '52, most basically versions of earlier guitars.

New was the K45, a handsome 17" master size with spruce top, curly maple body, triple-humped head faced in torch-engraved tortoise, bound rosewood 'board,

Ca. 1960 Kay Style Leader No. 1983 (photo: Ed Tauber).

block inlays, ribbon bridge and the grooved trapeze. This was $85 in blonde. The K45 lasted until 1954.

The K43 ($49.50) was another 17" master, with spruce, curly maple, hardwood neck, triple-humped head, bound rosewood 'board, single/double dots, plain bridge, simple trapeze and sunburst finish.

The K37 ($29.50) was a 15½" super grand auditorium in all-mahogany with unbound rosewood 'board and single dots.

The K34 ($33.50) was another super grand auditorium with spruce top, maple plywood body, rosewood fingerboard, dots, plain bridge and trapeze, in shaded brown sunburst.

The K30 ($27.50) was a 15" Auditorium in all-maple plywood, spruce graining on top, walnut fingerboard, dots, plain bridge and trapeze, and sunburst finish.

The K43, K37, K37T, K34, and K30 lasted until 1956.

'52 Flattops

In '52 the Kay flattop line got some new numbers, though these were similar to previous guitars. The necks had the new u-bar reinforcement.

Top of the line was the K27 ($95), a 17"

(Left) Ca. 1960 Kay Upbeat K8995. (Right) Ca. 1960 Kay K6533.

(Left) Ca. 1960 Kay K8995S (courtesy Scott Chinery). (Right) Ca. 1960 Kay Pro Series Thinline No. 1993 (photo: Paul & Deb Grubich).

master size with spruce top, walnut-finished curly maple body, white and black celluloid binding, 5-ply maple neck, bound triple-humped head, bound ebony fingerboard, pearl block inlays, belly-bridge, and a small teardrop-shaped pickguard which was glued on. The K23 ($69.50) was almost the same except for having a rectangular bridge, rosewood fingerboard, tortoise 'guard, and blond finish.

The K22 ($53.50) was a continuation of the previous 17" master size version. Under it was the Super Grand Auditorium K20 ($40), 15½" wide, with spruce top, curly maple body, hardwood reinforced neck, white and black binding, rosewood fingerboard, alternating single/double dots, rectangular pin bridge, and screwed-on pickguard. The K15 ($32.50) was also a Super Grand Auditorium, with spruce top, maple body, white binding, rosewood 'board, dots, rectangular pin bridge, screwed-on 'guard, and sunburst finish. The K15T was a tenor version. The K10 ($27.50) was an auditorium at 15", in all mahogany.

These were all offered until 1956 except for the K10 and K20 that ended in around 1954.

Early '50s Mandolins and Banjos

A curious snapshot of Kay mandolins comes from the '52 catalog. Our old friend with the Venetian shape topped the line with the K72. This had a bound triple-humped head with a script Kay logo and elaborate fleur-de-lis design. The fingerboard had block inlays. Top was spruce with a curly maple body. The celluloid pickguard repeated the fleur-de-lis design. Finishes were sunburst or maple ($65). The K70 ($44) was a less fancy version without the designs and with dots. Two pear-shaped mandos finished the line. The K68 was spruce and mahogany, with dots ($32.50). The K64 ($23.50) was all maple.

Three basic banjo models were offered in '52, each available in five-string, tenor and banjo mandolin versions. The K52 had

Ca. 1961 Kay Vibrato Leader No. 504 amplifier.

a mahogany resonator, nickel-plated flange, 20 brackets, maple neck, old asymmetrical head and rosewood fingerboard with dots ($60). The K54 ($40) had a curly maple

resonator and 16 brackets. The K53 ($30) had a curly maple shell and no flange or resonator. Except for the banjo mandolin option, which disappeared after '56, these would anchor the line till the end. By '61 the K52 was called the Professional Model, the K54 the Deluxe Model, and the K53 the Leader. In '66 the K52 would add a plectrum option. But otherwise, these would last until 1968.

Thin Twins

In 1952 (it's possible some examples may have been produced as early as '51) Kay began its participation in the modern electric age with the introduction of the K161 Thin Twin Spanish Electric, the so-called "Jimmy Reed" model, nicknamed for its most famous player, the legendary bluesman. The Kay Thin Twins appeared in the '52 catalog and were first *advertised* in the Fall of 1953.

The Kay Thin Twin appeared in the middle of the industry rush toward providing cutaway guitars with pickups. The Gibson ES-175 had appeared with one pickup in '49, with two in '53. The Gibson Les Paul appeared in mid-'52. Both size-wise and conceptually the Kay Thin Twin was somewhere between these two guitars.

The Kay Thin Twin was actually a semi-hollowbody guitar and, despite the name, was only "thin" in relationship to big super-auditorium-sized archtops. The Thin Twin had a wood block that ran down the center under the pickups to decrease feedback. This was years before Gibson introduced its semi-hollow ES-335, by the way. At 15", the lower bout was narrower than the big jazzers, though wider then a Les Paul, and at 2¾" the body was only slightly thinner than the big archtops, not a trim thinline as the name might suggest. These had a single, rounded cutaway, and often came with very nice birdseye maple bodies, mahogany sides, a flat spruce top, and a cool tortoise pickguard with a pair of thin "lipstick"-style pickups. The necks were glued-in and bound, with white pearl block inlays in the fingerboard. Tuners were Kluson Deluxes.

An old-style threeway lever served as a pickup selector, and two volume and two tone controls rounded out the sonic options. An adjustable bridge was permanently mounted on two threaded studs; strings attached to a trapeze tail.

In 1957 the Thin Twin II with adjustable neck appeared.

The Thin Twin was a remarkably good guitar for its time. While the better necks were certainly thicker than most modern tastes allow — we're still in the Heavy Gauge Age here — they're very comfortable. The pickups, while hardly matching today's high-output electronics, are bright and clear, and handsomely aided by the extra wood inside, which combats feedback problems. By and large, the Kay Thin Twin is one of the great unsung heroes of this early American electric guitar era.

The Thin Twin lasted until the around '58. While it's impossible to date these with specificity, some useful guidelines that might help you place yours.

Necks. Some early Thin Twins had one-piece mahogany necks, but by '53 *most Kays* had three-piece mahogany necks with a maple center strip. Most Thin Twins provided for other brand names had (thicker) one-piece necks, often of basswood.

Headstocks. Kay Thin Twins had the normal, multi-curved Kay shape with a plastic veneer and binding. Guitars provided to other marketers began with this same shape, but by 1954 have a center-point design, and by '55, the binding and engraved designs have been replaced by silk-screened logos. Some have plain plastic veneers with no brand identification at all after '55. Thin Twins other than Kay included brands such as Old Kraftsman (Spiegel), Silvertone (Sears), Sherwood Deluxe (Montgomery Ward), and Orpheum.

Inlays. Thin Twins before 1954 have large pearl block inlays, whereas after that date they start to get smaller. In around 1955 the non-Kay brands had pearloid inlays, and later so did Kays.

Pickguards. Earliest Thin Twins have orange tortoise pickguard. By sometime in 1952 they were replaced by diagonally striped tortoise 'guards. These lasted until perhaps 1954 when the stripes become smaller and have a more zigzag pattern. By ca. 1958 Thin Twins have a black pickguard.

Knobs. Prior to 1955, Thin Twins have white Bakelite knobs with 12 bumps around the edge and the tip on the switch is white Bakelite. In '55 the knobs switch to white ribbed Bakelite and the tip on the switches to aluminum. At the very end these had skirt knobs. Obviously, knobs are the most easily changed guitar appointment and least reliable for dating, but if the other guidelines fit with the knobs, you may conclude they are original and confirm your date guesstimate.

(Left to Right) Ca. 1961 Kay Speed Demon K573. Ca. 1961 Kay Swingmaster K673 (photos: Gilbert Matossian).

Solidbodies and other '52 electrics

Three other Spanish electrics, two Hawaiian laps and one electric mandolin were offered in the '52 catalog. The K125 was Kay's first solidbody. This was a single-cutaway mini-Les Paul with a glued-in neck, humped head, hardwood body with faux curly top, sunburst, rosewood 'board, dots, adjustable bridge, cheap trapeze, a single Thin Twin-style pickup sitting on a large tortoise celluloid surround, and a Bakelite volume and tone sitting on a small tortoise celluloid strip, with a rhythm/lead tone switch ($49.50).

The K150 was basically a non-cutaway K34 with the Thin Twin pickup in the middle sitting on a celluloid surround, and Bakelite volume and tone controls sitting on the upper bass bout ($60). The K151 was a K1 with a flat, metal covered single-coil pickup tucked under the edge of the fingerboard, with a volume and tone control mounted on the top down on the lower bout ($92.50).

The K159 Hawaiian was the old familiar stepped body in an elaborate presentation. This had a bound triple-humped head, engraved bow-tie inlays, sunburst finish over a curly maple top, a single flat metal covered pickup on a fancy tortoise assembly, with Bakelite volume and tone ($75). The K156 Hawaiian was a student model pained in tan with a stenciled floral design, a simple celluloid pickup assembly with a thin metal covered pickup, volume and tone.

The K95 was the pear-shaped K64 mandolin with the Thin Twin pickup with volume and tone control mounted on the side on the waist ($60).

Three Kay high fidelity amplifiers were available in '52. The K600 ($145) was 18" x 24" x 10", covered in woven vinyl, with a 12" Jenson speaker, six tubes and 16-20 watts of output. The K615 ($157.50) was the same except for having a 15" Jenson. The K300 ($61.50) was a small amp with three tubes and an 8" speaker.

Kay Necks

A word about necks: you are likely to find a wide variety of neck profiles on old Kay guitars, ranging from fairly trim examples on Kay's own better guitars to, well, baseball bats on its lower end and on the guitars it provided to mass merchandisers.

Musical Instruments of Quality by KAY

KAY MUSICAL INSTRUMENT CO. • 1640 Walnut Street, Chicago 12, Illinois

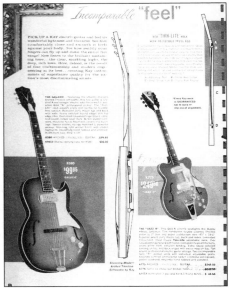

Incomparable "feel"

Incomparable response

Incomparable action

ELECTRIC BASSES

value

style

tone

NEW REVERB AMPLIFIER by KAY

2 in 1 package

ONE COMPACT UNIT *Gives you* A PROFESSIONAL AMPLIFIER PLUS "REVERBERATION"

Gives YOU THE NEW TOTAL SOUND ... "Band Shell" fullness with a stereo-like quality. Now you can get the same sound as the top pros — at a big savings, too!

BUILT-IN REVERB

$149.50

1961 Kay catalog; the Thinlines and acoustic instruments are the same as in the '60 catalog.

(Left to Right) Ca. 1961 Kay Jazz II K775 (photo: Gilbert Matossian). Ca. 1961 Old Kraftsman version of the Kay K775 Jazz II made for Spiegel (Don's Guitar & Music Center, Rapid Center, SD). Ca. 1961 Kay K8950 guitar probably made for Montgomery Ward (courtesy Bluebond Guitars, Philadelphia, PA).

Many of these larger necks were made of poplar, explaining the need for increased mass. And often, they've not survived the years as straight arrows. These thicker necks often turn off players used to the svelter shapes of Gibson, Fender or almost everyone else beginning in the 1960s. But, it's important to remember that most of these guitars are from before the age of steel-reinforced necks, where the wood alone was expected to carry the stress. And, as the late guitarmaker Gil Stiles once reminded me with a laugh, in the old days you only had one choice of string gauges: heavy. With no truss rod and a stiff pull from your Black Diamonds, the neck had to be pretty hefty. That the wood was not seasoned for eight years or so to guarantee stability is also fairly understandable when your talking about mass-produced guitars that often sold for far less than $25 new!

Truss rods

Anyhow, Kay had flirted with neck truss rods as early as 1936 with its electric amplifying guitars, and various higher end models were equipped with reinforcement off an on thereafter. By 1952 almost all new models featured a U-shaped reinforcement bar, non-adjustable. However, in 1955, Kay introduced its adjustable truss rod as standard equipment, at about the same time that the script logo began appearing in metal.

The Pro

In 1954, Kay introduced its next generation of electrics with the Kay Pro K172. This was a small-bodied, single-cutaway archtop with a 12$\frac{1}{2}$" lower bout measurement. This had the Kay triple-humped headstock with Kay shield logo, a curly maple body, a bound rosewood fingerboard with pearl block inlays, an adjustable bridge, and a pair of chrome-covered Hi-Fi pickups. This guitar cost about $185 and came in three finishes: Sunburst, Honey Blonde and Harewood Gray transparent.

This guitar was transmogrified into the third part of the Barney Kessel triumvirate in 1956 as the Barney Kessel Pro, but we get ahead of ourselves.

A companion "Pro" Model Electric Bass

K5965 also appeared probably about this same time. This was Kay's first electric bass guitar. It had the same body as the Kay Pro, triple-humped headstock and a single Thin Twin-style pickup mounted on a plastic surround. The volume and tone rested on another plastic strip on the lower bout. This bass lasted at least through the 1962 catalog, and was certainly out of the line by 1965.

Speed Demon necks

In around 1955, Kay's better guitars featured their patented Speed Demon necks. These were thin (for Kay) steel-reinforced with a lever adjustment mechanism housed in the heel of the neck and operated with a skate-key, similar to the Burns gearbox idea.

New '55 electric archtops

Two cutaway and two non-cutaway archtop electrics were introduced in '55. The K192 ($200) was the big 17" cutaway, basically the old K1, with a spruce top, curly maple body, a pair of Hi-Fi pickups, bound rosewood 'board with block inlays, the hooked jumbo pickguard, and two Bakelite volume and two tone controls mounted on the lower bout. This was available in sunburst, Honey Blonde and "gleaming metallic" Roman Gold.

The K152 was virtually the same guitar with one neck Hi-Fi pickup, available in sunburst mahogany ($137.50) and Honey Blonde ($147.50).

The K148 ($92.50) was the same as he old K151/K1, a non-cut archtop with a bound rosewood board, alternate single/double dots, one neck Hi-Fi pickup available in Glowing Walnut with Golden Sunburst or "New, Sparkling Metallic 'Butler' Silver" finishes.

The K130 ($57.50) was the old K150/K34, a dot-neck in Lustrous Metallic Gold with one wide flat-metal covered pickup in the middle of the top (no longer the Thin Twin) with one volume control.

Two single-cut, single-pickup, semi-hollow electric basses were offered, the K160

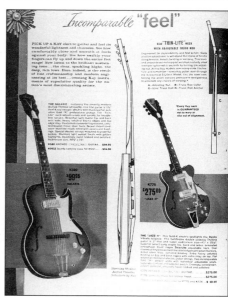

1962 Kay catalog; the low-end Thinlines and acoustic guitars, banjos and mandos.

Ca. 1961 Silvertone version of a Kay K6845 (courtesy Tinicum Guitar Barn, Ottsville, PA).

Electronic Bass Guitar ($192.50), with a regular bass guitar tuning, and the K162 Electronic Bass ($210) with tuning the same as a bass viol (G, D, A, E).

New '55 non-cut acoustic archtops

Most of the non-cutaway archtops continued on, but three new models appeared in 1955. The Kay K40 Spanish archtop ($85) was a 17" master size with spruce top, curly maple body, bound rosewood fingerboard and head (torch engraved), with three-piece tulip inlays, in mahogany sunburst or honey blonde. The Kay K35 Spanish super grand auditorium archtop ($37.50) was made of maple plywood, with a rosewood fingerboard and covered deluxe tuners, in violin brown sunburst. The Kay K32 Spanish super auditorium archtop ($29.50) was also

plywood with a walnut fingerboard and covered tuners, in shaded walnut sunburst. These lasted about a year through 1956.

New '55 solids

By '55 the old solidbody K125 was gone, replaced by the K142 and K136. The K142 ($125) was the same mini-Les Paul in what appears to be a unibody construction with copper finish, triple-humped head, script Kay logo, block inlays, large white pickguard, two wide metal-covered single-coils, vertically adjustable wooden bridge, trapeze, threeway lever, two volume and two tone controls on stacked Bakelite knobs. The K136 had one metal-covered pickup, dot inlays, a smaller pickguard, and a groovy spring green and white mist two-tone finish. These lasted until 1957.

'55 Hawaiians and amps

Two Hawaiian lap steels were still available in '55, the K155 Professional Electric Hawaiian Guitar ($110), a Lucite-covered baby with detachable legs, looking somewhat like a space shuttle, and the K157 Hawaiian Electric Guitar ($45), a green mist plastic-finished version of the same lap that had been around for the last 20 years or so. The K155 lasted only through '56, whereas the K157 made it till 1960, pausing to acquire a two-tone green Plextone covering in '57.

These electrics could be played through either the K600 ($200) Professional Amplifier (12" Jenson, 7 tubes, 20 watts), the

K615 ($225) bass amplifier (15" Jenson, 7 tubes), or the K300 ($64.50) 3-tube amplifier (8" speaker, green vinyl covering). These lasted through 1956.

Mid-'50s flattops

Three *new* jumbo flattops were introduced in 1955 (in addition to continuing some old standbys, like the K27, K24, K22 and K15), including Kay's first cutaway flattop. New was the K24 Professional Cutaway Flattop ($75), a 17" master size with spruce top, curly maple body, block inlays on a bound 'board, and belly pin bridge. The K18 ($49.50) was another cutaway with spruce top, curly maple body, triple-humped head, script logo, bound rosewood fingerboard, single/double dots, rectangular non-pin bridge, screwed on white pickguard, and golden brown finish with shading on the edges. The K12 was a super auditorium non-cut with spruce top, mahogany body, triple-humped head, dots, screwed on pickguard, rectangular pin-bridge, in natural. A K12-³/₄ was a ³/₄ size version. These all lasted only a year until '56, when numbering schemes (though not necessarily the guitars themselves) changed.

New '55 banjos

Three new banjo models debuted in '55, the K55, K51 and K50, all but one with the old asymmetrical headstock of the '30s. The K55 (symmetrical head, block inlays, curly maple resonator, chrome flange, $100) came in 5-string, tenor and plectrum

Ca. 1962 Kay K705 solid-state amplifier, top of the line. Ca. 1962 Kay K703 tube amplifier, a leftover from '61 with tubes and a redesigned grillcloth (photos courtesy Tinicum Guitar Barn, Ottsville, PA).

models. The K51 (Roman Gold resonator, flange, bound rosewood fingerboard, $75) came in 5-string and tenor. The K50 (curly maple resonator, "toast" brown finish, gold design on back, $49.50) came in 5-string and tenor. These lasted only until 1956.

Exit Kuhrmeyer

The Pro and cutaway flattops marked both the beginning and the end of an era. In 1955 Henry Kay Kuhrmeyer resigned after 33 years (according to press accounts) as President of Kay, selling his control of the company to a group of investors. Kuhrmeyer was feted at a luncheon in the Buckingham Room of Chicago's Congress Hotel on May 12, 1955. Max Targ of Targ & Dinner delivered the tribute. Kuhrmeyer received a two-piece set of luggage and planned to relax and travel. Unfortunately, his retirement was short lived, and, after a distinguished career and making so many contributions to the American music scene, Henry Kay Kuhrmeyer passed away one year later in 1956 at the age of 61.

Enter Katz

In 1955 presidency of the Kay Musical Instrument Company passed from Hank Kuhrmeyer to Sidney M. Katz, who was reportedly financed in part by Albert Pick of the Pick Hotel empire. In his farewell speech, Kuhrmeyer said, "Making and selling basses, cellos and fretted instruments requires a specialized knowledge of the business. Fortunately for all concerned, the right man came along — an aggressive, experienced young man who is determined to make Kay an even more important name in the music field."

Indeed, Katz was about to steer Kay in an entirely different direction. It is this later version of the Kay company — ultimately a pale reflection of the glory days under Kuhrmeyer — with which most guitar fans are familiar. Katz was a graduate of the

(Left to Right) Ca. 1962 Kay Swingmaster K672 (photo: Mike Newton). Ca. 1962 Kay Double Cutaway Solid Electric K300 (photo: Gilbert Matossian). Ca. 1962 Old Kraftsman version of a Kay Double Cutaway K592 (photo: Paul & Deb Grubich).

University of Chicago, and had previously an Executive Assistant at the Harmony Company. Katz would be assisted by Bob Keyworth, who'd already had 20 years in the music biz by '55, as Vice President and sales manager. Keyworth had joined Kay in 1944, coming from Sears, Roebuck, where he'd worked as a buyer, including during the brief period when Sears was getting guitars from Kay. Vice President in charge of production was Ted Rosenau, who had been supervising quality and quantity at Kay since 1927!

In a statement that falls into the "famous last words" category, Katz said, "No changes are contemplated in product, prices, or personnel. We intend to keep right on serving the same customers in the same Kay manner. The Kay formula, I know, has been a successful one. But I'm also convinced that complacency can be disastrous in the years ahead. So nothing will be taken for granted in making plans for the future." Though it didn't yet know it, the Kay Musical Instrument Company was now about to begin getting "face-lifts." In a thoroughly "modern" approach, by the way, a glamorous female model named "Kay" was used to pro-

mote the Kay line at the NAMM show, and conventioneers were invited to see "the gal" up in "Kay's room." Har, har, har. Hardly an approach one might imagine in the old days.

Face lift

Things quickly began to change under the new leadership. As a sign of things to come, Kay entered the endorsement game, not yet in the guitar domain, but in the banjo realm. Katz recruited "Mr. Banjo" Jose Silva to put his name to a redesigned line called the Jose Silva Banjo line. Silva was brought to the NAMM show in 1956 to demonstrate and promote Kay's new banjos, which featured a new exclusive device "which enables the player to attain a beautiful ringing, melodic tone or the traditional, sharp 'biting' banjo tone."

Actually there were three grades of Silvas introduced in '56, the plain Jose Silva Models, the Professionals, and the Artists. The Jose Silva Model K1000 5-String Banjo had chrome hardware, curly maple resonator, and pearlette blocks. The K1000T was a tenor, and the K1000P was a plectrum. The Jose Silva Professional Model K2000 5-

1962 J.C. Penney Fall/Winter catalog full of Kays.

String Banjo had chrome hardware, carved heel, pearlette resonator and pearlette blocks. It also came as the K2000T and K2000P. The Jose Silva Artist Model K3000 5-String Banjo had gold hardware, rosewood resonator, and mother-of-pearl blocks. Available as K3000T and K3000P.

Barney Kessel

Clearly Katz had different ideas about marketing Kay products than the more conservative resistance to annual "face-lifts" of the old Kuhrmeyer tenure. In any case, Katz had embraced the idea of employing glitz and of soliciting a big-name imprimatur, as he had done with Jose Silva banjos. Perhaps influenced by Gibson's smashing success with the Les Paul endorsement, the Katz administration decided to look for its own endorser. They settled on none other than the man who was voted "best jazz guitarist three years running in *Downbeat's* annual poll, Barney Kessel.

The process of snaring Kessel was wonderfully simple. Basically, in around 1956, Kay made a special version of the Kay Pro. Kay executives then took the guitar to a Chicago nite club where Kessel was playing, approached him at the bar during a break, offered him the guitar and coaxed him into endorsing a line of Kay guitars. It should be noted that while Kessel posed for

numerous publicity photos playing his namesake Kays, anecdotal evidence, at least, suggests that he never actually performed using Kay guitars. But never mind that, Kay had a big name endorser, just like Gibson.

The '56 Gold "K" Line

The result was the new Gold "K" Line, which debuted in late 1956 and marked a new stylistic presentation for Kay, one which many collectors hold in high esteem. These were fine archtop electric guitars sporting the new Gold K pickups, sometimes called "Kleenex box" pickups because of their patterned plastic covers, and the new "Kelvinator" extruded plastic headstocks.

There were three Barney Kessel models in the '57 Gold "K" Line, the Jazz Special, the Artist and the Pro.

The Barney Kessel Jazz Special was a full-sized (17"), single-cutaway jazz archtop guitar with either one (K8701, $350) or two (K8700, $400) Gold K pickups. These had somewhat large, goofy pickguards with Barney Kessel's name, fancy Melita adjustable bridges (like those found on Gretsches), bound ebony 'boards with split block and oval inlays, Grover Imperial tuners, and a fancy trapeze tailpiece. These could be had in sunburst or blonde finishes. A hardshell

case was an extra $32.50.

The Barney Kessel Artist was a slightly smaller archtop with a 15½" lower bout, bound rosewood fingerboard with pearl block inlays, a shorter 24¾" scale, and the Kelvinator headstock. The one-pickup K6701 cost $265; the two-pickup K6700 cost $300. Again, these were to be had in sunburst or blonde finishes.

The Barney Kessel Pro K1700 (two pickups) and K1701 (one pickup) were continuations of the old Kay Pro, now with a 13" body, Gold K pickups, Kelvinator headstock, Grover tuners and Barney Kessel pickguard. The K1700 came with a pair of pickups and cost $200; the K1701 had one pickup and cost $170. Both models came in sunburst or blonde finishes.

The Barney Kessels lasted through 1960, although beginning in that year they did not bear Kessel's endorsement.

Dreaded acoustic

One other new Kay guitar was introduced by Katz and Ko. in late '56, the K6000 Western Rhythm Guitar. This was Kay's first excursion into a dreadnought. At $175 it was pretty upscale, with a bound

Ca. 1962 Airline version of a Kay K592 with three Kleenex box pickups and no Bigsby (photo: Gilbert Matossian).

spruce top, rosewood body, maple neck, wide bound triple-humped head, ebony fingerboard, single/double dots, glued-on pickguard, and ebony belly pin bridge.

The Kessels and Western Rhythm were harbingers of things to come: they were the first Kay guitars (except for '54's "Pro" Model Electric Bass K5965) to bear a four-digit model numbers; in '57 all would switch to the new nomenclature.

Golden age

The most revered era of Kay commenced in 1957 as the so-called "Kelvinators" kicked in. The Kessels still paced the pack, but a host of new models debuted, many of which would hang around more-or-less till the end. It's important to note that we're still dealing with glued-in necks. Many of these new models would change over to bolt-on necks in the '60s. Except for the occasional leftover, all models now had four-digit numbers. New solidbodies appeared, but more importantly, so did a number of thinline hollowbody archtops.

Joining the Barney Kessels was the new archtop was the Kay Upbeat, a 17" single-cut archtop with a bound rosewood finger-

board and pearloid block inlays, Kelvinator headstock, big winged pickguard, trapeze tail, and "popular 'thin' body." This initially came in two versions, the K8990 with two Gold Ks ($189), and the K8980 with one Gold K. Three finishes were available, shaded walnut, blonde and jet black! At least some of these came with sparkle pickguards. In '58 the three-pickup Kay K8995 ($225) was added in '58. Both the K8995 and K8990 made it through '60, though by that time they'd acquired what's known as a half- or semi-Kelvinator headstock, a plainer version.

1957 marked the debut of the K6970 Swing Master, a thinline with a round single cutaway, bound rosewood fingerboard, single/double dots, winged pickguard, two humped metal covered pickups, and fancy trapeze with two crossbars.

1963 Kay Vanguard Model 704 amp, one of Kay's first transistorized amp (courtesy Bluebond Guitars, Philadelphia, PA).

The K6960 had one pickup. These would last until 1960, when they changed to bolt-on neck guitars.

The K6550 Pacer was a non-cut Spanish archtop electric with spruce top, curly maple body, triple-humped head, two humped pickups, bound rosewood 'board, and pick inlays. The K6540 was the same with one pickup. These lasted until 1960, when they were renumber as the K5550 and K5540.

The K6533 Value Leader was another single-pickup non-cutaway electric with triple-humped head, single/double dots, single pickup, and walnut finish. This lasted until '59.

Two new solidbodies replaced the earlier solids, the K4144 and K4140 Sizzler Solid Bodies. These were predecessors to the upcoming Solo King. Basically they were Les Paul shaped, but with a V-notch for the cutaway, with white angular pickguard with controls. The heads had a widely flared profile with a concave dip in the top. The fingerboard was maple, with black dots. The K4144 had two pickups, while the K4140 had one. Both came in black or brown "Plextone" finishes. These lasted only about a year until 1958. A natty black-and-white finished K1560 Professional Model Hawaiian console model replaced the old K155. This lasted until '60.

Name game

A passel of acoustic archtops remained

(Left) Ca. 1963 Kay Speed Demon K573 (courtesy Bluebond Guitars, Philadelphia, PA).
(Right) Ca. 1963 Kay Galaxie K580 (photo: Gilbert Matossian).

1964 Kay advertisement.

in the line in '57, most with new numbers, often suggestive of their forebears. The old K37 was repackaged as the K6437 All-Mahogany Arched Guitar, the K35 became the K6836 Big Value Leader, the K32 became the K6833 Super-Auditorium Special, the K21 became the K8921 Masterpiece, the K11 became the K8911 Rhythm Special, and the K1 became the K8901 Combo, all virtually identical. The K6950 and gorgeous K8921 lasted only until 1958, but the rest survived all the way through 1965.

Several other acoustic archtops debuted in late '57. The K6950 Cut-Away Leader had a round single cutaway with spruce top, curly maple plywood body, bound fingerboard, and dot inlays. This lasted only a year until '58. Three non-cutaways included the 17" K6838 Deluxe Arched Guitar with spruce top, curly maple plywood body, triple-humped head, bound rosewood 'board, and pick inlays. The K6858 Style Leader was made of all-maple plywood in sunburst finish, with a maple fingerboard and black dots. The K6868 Style Leader was the same with blonde finish with "graining." These all lasted until 1965.

Bushcuts

Flattops during the '57 makeover also included some oldies and newies. Recall

that at this time the "pop-culture" folk revival was in its infancy. Oldtimers included the K8224 Professional Cut-Away (the old cutaway K24) with spruce top, curly maple body, bound 'board, blocks, and an adjustable saddle; the K6118 Cut-Away (K18 in black or walnut); the K8110 Master Size Flattop (cf. K10, spruce top, mahogany plywood, parallelograms); and K8127 Solo Special (K27, 17" jumbo, spruce top, curly maple body, pearl blocks, new semi-Kelvinator head). The K8224 lasted till '58, the K6118 and K8110 till '60, the K8127 till '65.

New acoustics in '57 included the K6100 Country dreadnought (spruce, mahogany body, bound 'board single/double dots, till '65), K6116 Gleaming Super Auditorium Model (spruce top, maple plywood, bound 'board, single/double dots, sunburst, till '65), K5113 Plains Special auditorium-sized folk guitar (spruce top, mahogany plywood, dots, till '68), K113 Plains Special (3/4 size, till '65), K3500 Student Concert Model (spruce top, maple plywood, single/double dots), and two 15" trapeze-tailed bottom-enders, the K5160 Auditorium (maple plywood, painted blocks) and K1160 Standard (maple plywood, maple fingerboard, black painted blocks), both offered until '65. All

the new models except the K1160 (humped head) had a *new* center pointed head design.

Four new amps debuted in '57, all with black sides, white square "picture frame" fronts, swirly fabric grille, drawer pull handles. These included the K507 Twin Ten Special with seven tubes, two-10" speakers and about 20 watts output, the K505 Twin Eight Hi-Power Model with five tubes, two 8" speakers, 12 watts, the K503 Hot-Line Special with three tubes, 4 watts, and the K515 Heavy Duty Bass Amp with seven tubes, 15" speaker, and 15 watts. The guitar amps lasted through '61, the bass amp through '60.

This golden age of Kay basically lasted through the rest of the '50s unchanged. Many versions of these guitars were featured in Montgomery Ward catalogs, which offered some Harmony products, but a majority were Kays.

Swinging Sixties

The next big change in the Kay line occurred as the swinging '60s dawned. The Kessels remained, but minus their big-name endorsement. The big news was the introduction of the Thinline series of electrics.

The new Kay Thinlines were introduced at the beginning of 1960 and consisted of seven single-cutaway Les Paul-shaped gui-

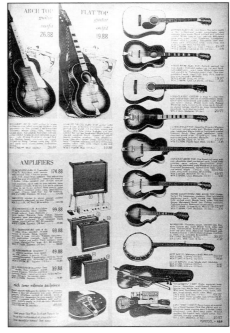

1964 Spiegel Spring/Summer catalog with Old Kraftsman guitars made by Kay.

tars and three matching amps. The guitars were subdivided into three groupings called the "Value Leader," "Style Leader," and "Pro Series." These were Kay's first bolt-neck guitars, to be followed in '61 by a massive redesign of many models to become bolt-ons.

The Value Leader guitars included three brown-to-yellow sunburst, maple plywood guitars with one pickup (#1961, $65), two pickups (#1962, $84.95) and three pickups (#1963, $99.95). These had steel-reinforced necks with maple fingerboards (a new development!), tortoise dot inlays, the old pointy Kay headstock, a moveable adjustable maple bridge, and plain trapeze tailpiece. These had a cool trapezoidal chrome-plated pickguard with a geometric design. The "newly-designed" pickups were flat, chrome-covered single-coils. Each pickup

(Left to Right) Ca. 1964 Airline three-pickup version of the Kay K592 (Blue Suede Shoe, Dallas TX). Ca. 1964 Kay K6533 (courtesy Tinicum Guitar Barn, Ottsville, PA). Ca. 1964 Silvertone 57K14136 version of the Kay Vanguard K321 (photo: Paul & Deb Grubich).

had volume and tone controls with bakelite knobs, with a chicken-beak rotary select on the multiple pickup models.

The two Style Leader guitars were basically the same with some "stylistic" enhancements. Both had double trapezoidal brushed copper pickguards with a geometric pattern. For these, the rotary select was moved up to the top pickguard. Bodies were of curly maple plywood, finished either in natural blonde or brown sunburst. Fingerboards were bound rosewood with dot inlays. The #1982 ($99.50) had two chrome-covered pickups, while the #1983 ($119.50) had three.

Two Pro Series guitars were offered, both with curly maple plywood bodies, in blonde or gleaming jet black. These had large plastic pickguards following the contour of the upper treble bout. Necks featured bound rosewood 'boards with pearlette block inlays. These had fancier trapeze tails, gold-topped plastic Gibson-style knobs, and pickups with the humped chrome covers. The pickup select was a chicken-beak on the upper bass bout shoulder. The #1992 ($139.50) had two pickups; the #1993 ($169.50) had three. All were available with a two-tone chipboard case ($10.50).

The Thinline guitars were joined in '60 by two basses, both with the single-cut hollowbody Les Paul shape and bolt-on necks with pointy heads. The K5961 ($79.95) a single metal pickguard design along the treble side, with one flat, metal-covered pickup at the neck, volume, tone, adjustable bridge, and trapeze. The K5962 ($79.95) was a nifty six-string bass version, meant to be tuned a full octave lower than a Spanish guitar.

These Kay Thinlines lasted in the Kay line through 1965, when they were replaced by more contemporary looking guitars in the '66 Seeburg catalog.

The ugliest guitar in the world

In 1960, after bringing us the lovely Kelvinator creations, Kay created what is indisputably the world's ugliest guitar ever, the Solo King. This is a totally demented guitar, often described as the State-of-Ohio-shaped body, which gets pretty close to the truth. The neck was integral to the body, appearing to be neck-through, though heaven knows there could be a glue joint. For a headstock the Solo King featured a six-in-line aberration which looks sort of like a meat cleaver. For a pickguard, this

sported natty mother-of-dinette sparkle formica. Best of all, the Solo King was finished in, well, let's be kind and spare four-letter adjectives, and call it a dark chocolate brown color. Affixed to this design *tour de force* were either one (K4101) or two (K4102) wide, flat, chrome-covered single-coil pickups. These are perhaps the only mitigating feature of the Solo King, offering that nice, clear tone often found on '50s single-coils.

There's a point where ugly turns the corner and actually becomes beautiful again. The Kay Solo King stops short of the turnaround. Even the frets are poorly seated, and any thought of reasonable intonation should be immediately dismissed. No, the Solo King, which was offered only one year, marks the nadir of the Kay company. Of course, you'd be a fool not to want one of these in your collection!

In 1961, by the way, the Solo King was redesigned with a rounded lower bout and sold through Montgomery Ward's mail-order catalogs. 9606M Solid Body Electric Cutaway Guitar had one pickup, while the 9607M had two. These were only offered through Wards, probably a thinly disguised attempt to dump them. The cosmetic

1965 Kay Vanguard K100 (note metal headstock logo).

makeover wasn't enough to save this baby and they were dead by '62.

Basso profundo

In 1960 the Kay Jazz Special Electric Bass K5970 joined the line. These were essentially semi-hollowbody double-cutaway bass versions of the Thin Twin with a semi-Kelvinator headstock, the old Thin Twin pickups, a cool '50s pickguard, volume, tone, Thin Twin-style bridge and trapeze tail. This was available in either blonde or jet black. The Kay Jazz Special Electric Bass lasted at least through the 1962 catalog. By the 1965 catalog, it was gone.

New acoustics

Five new acoustics were introduced in '60. The K8160 Solo Special was a 17" jumbo, with plywood body, sunburst finish, and trapeze tail. The K6120 Western Model was a dreadnought, with maple plywood body, walnut fingerboard, and dots. The K6130 Calypso Folk Guitar had a

(This Page and next page) 1965 Kay catalog with the bushwacker heads; the low-end Thinlines (last appearance) and acoustic instruments remain the same as the early '60s catalogs, only the prices have gone up.

spruce top, mahogany body, dots, and slothead. Two new classicals debuted, the K7000 Artist Model with spruce top, flamed maple body, and slothead; and the K7010 Maestro Model. All lasted until '65.

Two new 17" acoustic archtops bowed in '60, the cutaway K8950 Master Cutaway Model, and K8858 Master Value Leader, with maple fingerboard and tortoise dots. These, too, lasted till '65.

New mandos and banjos

Three mandolins were added in 1960, two electrics and one acoustic. the K390 Professional Electric Mandolin was a Venetian with spruce top, maple body and Thin Twin pickup, offered until '68. The K494 Electric Mandolin was pear shaped with spruce top, maple body, and one pickup. This lasted until 1966, in which year it was renumbered as the K495. The pear-shaped, maple plywood acoustic K460 Student Mandolin was renumbered as the K450 in '66, the last year of issue.

Two new banjos debuted in '60, the K1000 Artist Model 5-String Banjo, with maple plywood resonator, chrome flange, blocks, and arm rest, and the similar K1000T Artist Model Tenor Banjo.

Two new amps were added in '60, the K506 Vibrato "12," with 12" speaker, vibrato, six tubes, two channels, and 12 watts, and the K504 Vibrato Leader, with 8" speaker, vibrato, and 5 watts. Both lasted till '62.

Beginning of the downward slide 1961

In 1961 Kay introduced even more electrics to its line, including thin hollowbodies and more solids. It's really from this point on that Kay began to loose the creative vitality that marked its glory days as an archtop maker and took the first steps toward becoming the low-end commodity manufacturer most of us remember from the '60s. From 1961 on, *almost all Kay guitars had bolt-on necks.*

The new bolt-on necks were nowhere more evident than in Kay's '61 thinline electric line, which now held five different models. The old Swing Master was redone with a bolt-on neck, with the name contracted to Swingmaster and a new numbering scheme. The Swingmaster had a rounded cutaway horn, a laminated curly maple body, a maple neck, bound rosewood fingerboard with block inlays, the recently introduced center-pointed Kay headstock with script logo, a fancy trapeze tailpiece, and the Kessel-style pickguard. The K673 ($185) had three Gold K pickups, with three volume and three tone controls and a rotary select on the upper bass bout. The K672 ($159.50) had a pair of Gold Ks and a conventional threeway toggle select near the controls. Kay K671 had a single pickup. These lasted in the Kay line through 1965, after which they drop from sight.

New in '61 was the Kay Speed Demon,

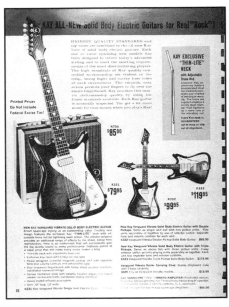

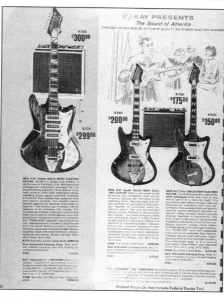

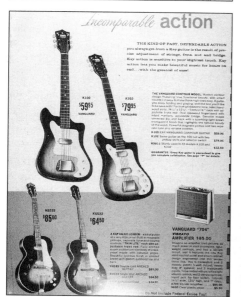

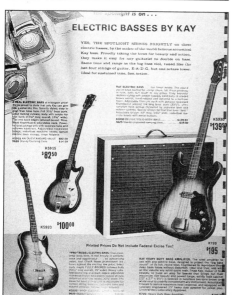

Ca. 1965 Kay Titan I K350.

a slightly downscale version with a pointed Florentine cutaway horn, arched spruce top and curly maple plywood body, center-pointed headstock with script logo and V chevrons, bolt-on neck, and large dot-in-laid rosewood 'board. The f-holes were three-part, with separated round holes on the ends. The K573 ($139.50) had a bound rosewood 'board, three of the older-style pickups with humped chrome covers and a chicken-beak rotary selector. The K571 ($92.50) had no binding on the neck and just one of the older pickups in the neck position. The Speed Demon also lasted through 1965, after which it was replaced by "groovier" options.

The Swingmaster and Speed Demon were offered with a curious optional plastic hard case described as being made of "Astramold high impact copolymer." Cost was $14.95. This was basically an early hardshell case made of injection molded plastic. By the mid-'60s this would be marketed in three versions and advertised as fitting the guitars of most major manufacturers.

Also new in '61 was the K775 Jazz II, a double-cutaway thinline archtop with a bolt-on Thin-Lite neck, semi-Kelvinator headstock, bound rosewood fingerboard with pearl line and quadrant inlays, a pair of Gold K pickups, two volumes and two tones, threeway toggle and a Bigsby, in sunburst or blonde ($249.50). The Jazz II lasted through the 1965 catalog; it was gone by 1966.

Also new in '61 was the K580 Galaxie (as in Ford, though not quite so cool). This was a down-sized thinline (15") with a single pointy Florentine cutaway, curly maple plywood top, bolt-on neck, the old pointed headstock, bound rosewood 'board with triangular "pick" inlays, cheapo four-part f-holes, moveable bridge, trapeze tail, a pointy slim pickguard and a single "Kleenex box" Gold K neck pickup, with volume and tone ($99.95). Like the Jazz II, this stayed around through 1965 and was gone by the '66 catalog.

Forward...

Kay also introduced two new solidbody electrics in '61, the Vanguards. These probably rank close to the Solo King for ugly design, with a dumpy slab offset double cutaway body, sort of a Simpsons' Jazzmaster, with a bolt-on neck, pointed head, a stylized "K" logo with a shield and block lettered KAY, a squiggly, Alamo-looking pickguard, and a chrome covered bridge/tailpiece assembly. The finish was sort of a milk chocolate brown sunburst. The K102 Vanguard ($79.95) had two of the flat, metal-covered single-coil pickups, threeway, two volumes and two tones. The K100 Vanguard ($59.95) had one pickup in the center.

The Vanguards, like so many other designs from this period, lasted through the 1965 catalog. However, the dumpy body shape would survive on in redesigned models that debuted in '66.

Only two electric archtops were represented in the '61 Kay line. These were a pair of sunburst non-cutaway archtops with spruce tops, curly maple bodies, glued-in necks, pointy headstocks, rosewood 'boards, alternating single/double dot inlays, and the flat, metal-covered pickups. The K6535 ($79.95) essentially took over for the old K148 with two pickups, a chicken-beak selector down by the pickguard, two volumes and two tones. The K6533 ($59.95) was a one-pickup version, the pickup now up at the neck instead of in the middle, as on older single-pickup archtops. These electric archtops lasted until '65.

Reverb power

The Kay "two-tone" amplifier line continued in 1961, enhanced by two new units, the K550 amp and K540 Reverb Power Pack. The K550 offered built-in reverberation, two 8" speakers, five tubes and 12 watts of output. The K540 Reverb Power Pack ($99.50), an outboard reverb unit with an 8" speaker and its own 3-watt amplifier to boost the reverb signal. The K540 hooked up directly to your amp speaker with two "alligator" clips!

These two-tone amplifiers lasted only through the year, and were replaced by an expanded, redesigned transistorized line in 1962.

Folk Boom acoustics (1961)

Kay acoustics continued pretty much as before. Despite the declining popularity, a new acoustic archtop was actually introduced in '61, the dotneck K6845 Mercury Arched Guitar made of curly maple plywood. Kay also introduced a third nylon-stringed acoustic in '61, the all-maple slothead K7020 Concerto Classic Guitar.

Ca. 1965 Kay Vanguard Solid Body Electric Guitar K331 without vibrato (photo: Paul & Deb Grubich).

Both of these new guitars lasted through 1965. One new banjo also debuted in '61, the K60 Folk Model 5-string Banjo with a maple plywood shell, 30 brackets and no resonator. The head was the old triple-humped variety with an oval Kay logo. This model lasted until the end in '68.

New for '62

Except for a couple new guitar models and a redesigned amp line, Kay guitars remained unchanged as the company moved into 1962.

New guitars included one hollowbody and one solidbody. The new for '62 hollowbody was the K592 Double Cutaway with Vibrato Tailpiece ($199.50). This was very similar to the old Kay Speed Demon except for having two sharply pointed Florentine cutaways, maple plywood body, a bolt-on neck with a rosewood faced pointy headstock, a "compass" K logo, bound rosewood 'board, triangular pick-shaped inlays, two humped metal covered pickups, two volumes, two tones, threeway chicken-beak select, pointy pickguard with a Kay music stand imprint, four-part f-holes, adjustable bridge, and what looks to be a Bigsby, but without the usual Bigsby name (unless it's retouched out of the

Ca. 1965 Silvertone version of the K321 with a six-in-line head (courtesy Blue Suede Shoe, Dallas, TX).

catalog photo). This had an adjustable truss rod, by the way, probably the first appearance of this feature.

The new solid was the K300 Double Cutaway Solid Electric ($139.50), an indication, said the copy, that Kay is "going places" fast! This was a slightly offset double cutaway more or less in a Strat shape. The top was curly maple, with bolt-on Thin Lite neck, adjustable truss, pointy headstock with semi-Kelvinator, bound rosewood fingerboard, pearlette blocks, twin humped metal covered pickups, and chrome covered bridge/tailpiece assembly similar to the Vanguards. The pickguard was a large tortoise affair with chicken-beak threeway, two volumes and two tones.

Space Age amplifiers (1962)

The Kay amplifier line got a total facelift in '62, as its new transistorized "space-age" amps debuted. Transistorized components began appearing on Magnatone amps in around 1960, but htese new Kay amps may just be candidates for being first all transistorized amplifiers!

Eight amps and a reverb unit were offered. In fact, except for cosmetics and the change from tubes to transistors, many of these remained identical to the previous two-tone line in terms of specs and features. The old charcoal and white vinyl was replaced by tan vinyl on the front and back edges (not the top) and a strip of brown vinyl down the middle of the sides and top. The new tweed grillcloth covered virtually the entire front and stretched over the top edge to the center strip which had either a metal or vinyl suitcase handle. The old 500 model numbers were upgraded to 700 designations.

The new top of the line was now the K708 Galaxie II amp ($300). This groovy piece sat on four removable, spindly tapered brass legs much like a Danish Modern pho-

(Left) Ca. 1965 Kay Swingmaster K672 (photo: Paul & Deb Grubich). (Right) Ca. 1965 Kay K5920 electric bass with mods and a missing 'guard (courtesy Arpeggio Music, Havertown, PA).

nograph or console television, or a good dinette! This had a 12" speaker, two channels, vibrato and 35 watts of output. Better yet, you could remove the amplifier chassis and set up the speaker as much as 25 feet away!

The K707 Galaxie I ($250) replaced the old K507 Twin Ten with a 12" speaker, two channels, vibrato and 35 watts. The K706 Vanguard "706" was next ($149.50) with 15" speaker, two channels, vibrato and 15-watt output. The K705 Vanguard "705" ($99.50) had a 10" speaker, vibrato and 10 watts. The K704 Vanguard "704" ($75) had an 8" speaker and 5 watts. The K700 Vanguard "700" ($59.95) had an 8" speaker and a "triple tone circuit!" The K703 Value Leader amplifier ($47.50) remained in the old styling, with tubes, 8" speaker and 4 watts. The K710 Reverb Power Pack Unit ($65) replaced the old tube unit and featured a four transistor amp to boost the signal. The large K720 Bass Amplifier ($195) with a 15" speaker rounded out the line.

These Kay space-age amps lasted through the '65 catalog. Seeburg redesigned the amp line in '66.

1965 Kay K6845 acoustic (courtesy Dave's Music, Winchester, IL).

Airlines and Silvertones

During the '60s Kay also produced variations on its guitars for the big mail-order houses Montgomery Ward and Sears, carrying the Airline and Silvertone brand names, respectively. These were mainly solidbodies, but can show up in almost any form. Typically, these will vary from standard Kay product, often sporting older necks/headstocks and/or older pickups. There's already so much to document here that we'll pass on trying to describe all these,

even if we could. Nevertheless, you can generally place one of these house-brand guitars by comparing specs to catalog Kays. They're usually not that far off.

Superplant

In '64 the British Invasion began and the world of music would never be the same. The Baby Boom had hit its stride, and it found its voice in playing guitars. Manufacturers could not keep up with demand. In June of 1964 Kay relocated to a new 100,000 square-foot superfactory in the Chicago suburb of Elk Grove Village, doubling its production capacity. By this time Kay was selling guitars to 45 different distributors who served as many as 7,000 retail outlets.

For the times, the Kay plant was quite modern, arranged for efficient — and mass — production. Two train cars of material could be unloaded at one time, inside in any weather (no small consideration in Chicago). A huge finishing system pumped 10 different finishes to 11 separate spraying booths. Huge laminating presses could produce 1,800 bodies a day! The mill room featured a new gang rip-saw which basically carved a completed neck on one pass through the equipment. Modular walls allowed the factory to grow or shrink depending on the need. Automated sanders, an on-site ma-

(This page and pages 159-161) 1966 Kay catalog under the Seeburg ownership.

chine shop, color-coordinated office furniture (!), even an employee cafeteria with hot and cold food vending machines to "spark morale" completed the picture.

Ironically, this fantastic new factory only had a few years of use in it.

Bushwhackers (1965)

Through the transition to the new manufacturing facility, Kay's line remained pretty much as before. The next major change for Kay occurred in 1965 when it introduced its guitars with the hip — or supremely ugly, depending on your point of view — "bushwhacker" six-in-line headstock and a bunch of new solidbody designs.

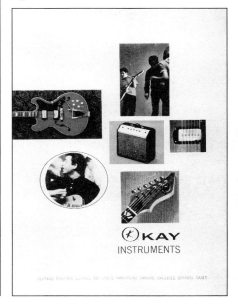

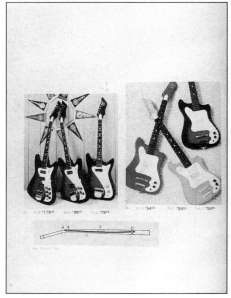

1956 Kay K142   1958 Kay K8990 Upbeat

1961 Kay K540 Reverb Power Pack

1960 Kay K4102 Solo King

Photo: Michael Tamborrino.

1963 Kay K573 Speed Demon and 1963
Kay Vanguard Model 704 Amplifier

Photo: Michael Tamborrino.

1965 Kay K350 Titan I

1966 Kay K682 Galaxie 11

Photo: Michael Tamborrino.

Ca. 1916 Maccaferri/Mozzani
Black Eagle lyre guitar

Ca. 1916 Maccaferri/Mozzani lyre guitar

Ca. 1916 Maccaferri/Mozzani lyre guitar

Photos: Michael Tamborrino.

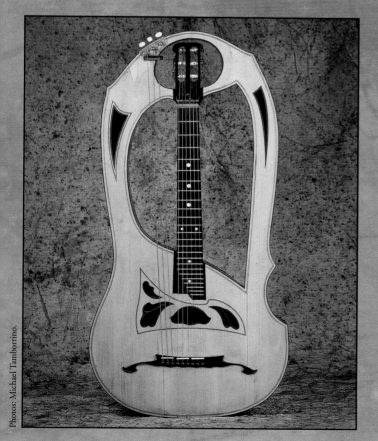

Ca. 1916 Maccaferri/Mozzani lyre guitar

Ca. 1916 Maccaferri/Mozzani lyre guitar

1988 Maccaferri/Monteleone classical guitar without sound chamber

Ca. 1984 Saga DG500

1988 Maccaferri/Monteleone classical guitar with sound chamber

Photos: Michael Tamborrino.

SOLID BODY ELECTRIC GUITARS

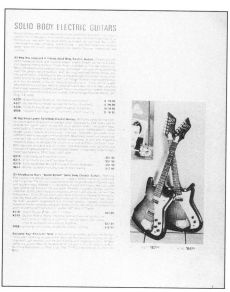

ACOUSTICAL ELECTRIC GUITARS

ELECTRIC BASSES

AMPLIFIERS

AMPLIFIERS

BASS AMPLIFIERS

FLAT TOP GUITARS

FLAT TOP GUITARS

FOLK GUITARS

COUNTRY FLAT GUITARS

COUNTRY FLAT GUITARS

CLASSIC GUITARS

SPECIAL FLAT TOP GUITARS

ARCH TOP GUITARS

MANDOLINS

UKULELES

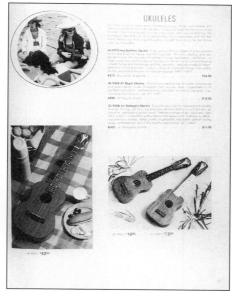

BANJOS

GUARANTEE

ADVANCE RELEASE

from **KAY MUSICAL INSTRUMENT CO.**
2201 West Arthur Avenue
Elk Grove Village, Illinois 60007

INTRODUCING THE K780 SELECT-A-RHYTHM® GUITAR AMPLIFIER

(Left) Ca. 1966 Kay Country II K6102 (courtesy Mike's Guitars, Etc., Erial, NJ). (Right) Ca. 1966 Titan II K355 with short-style vibrato (photo: Willie G. Moseley).

As previously mentioned, most of our old friends remained in the '65 line: the Jazz II, the old Swingmasters and Speed Demons, Galaxie, K300 solid, K592 Double Cutaway, Thinlines, the space-age amps, the acoustic archtops, flattops, mandolins and banjos, etc.

New for '65 were a redesigned solidbody electric line. These were primarily offset double cutaway guitars in various Strat-type variations, with contoured bodies and bolt-on necks, all sporting the new bushwhacker six-in-line head. This had a little point where the round Adam's apple of a Strat head would be, then a curve that looks sort of like a spatula ending in a dramatic, upward-turned point. Along the lower edge is an angled section like a sharpened knife or blade. The logo had the compass "K" in a circle with a block KAY underneath.

The old dumpy Vanguard line bore the brunt of the remake. Still in the line were the old K102 and K100, identical to the previous guitars. New were six other Vanguards with the new bushwhacker heads. Top of the line was the K333 Vanguard Vibrato Solid Body Electric Guitar ($119.95) with a rosewood 'board, triangular "pick" inlays, an angular hardwood body with a maple veneer top and back, a German-carve

bevel around the edges, cherry red sunburst finish, a simple adjustable saddle bridge, a Jazzmaster-style vibrato, large white pickguard, three of the flat, metal covered pickups, a chicken-beak selector, and three sets of volume and tone controls. The K332 ($99.95) was the same, with two pickups and a threeway toggle. The K331 ($79.95) had just one pickup. The K322 ($84.95) was basically the same as the K332 except it had a covered bridge/stop tailpiece assembly and alternating single/double dot inlays. The K321 ($64.95) was the comparable stop-tail version of the K331. Bottom of the line was the Kay Value Leader ($54.95), which still had the old frumpy Vanguard slab body and pickguard, basically a K100 with the new headstock and three groovy finishes, modern red (K310), soft teal blue (K311) and shaded walnut (K312). This last is the guitar held by the clean-cut teenager illustrated in Tom Wheeler's *American Guitars*, by the way.

New also in '65 were the Kay Artiste, Kay Apollo and Kay Titan I solidbodies. These had bodies which were more of a cross between a Strat and a Jazzmaster, with less extended horns. The lower side had an angled bevel while the upper waist had a dramatic indented contour. The cutaways were scalloped. The bolt-on necks had the bushwhacker heads and bound rosewood fingerboards. The Artiste K708 ($300) had a solid walnut body(!), the old split block-and-oval inlays, and three deluxe single-coil pickups with metal covers open in the center, with poles sitting on a black plastic insert. These deluxe pickups, by the way, look suspiciously like Japanese pickups, and probably mark Kay's first use of imported parts. The Artiste had an adjustable bridge with a unique cast Bigsby-style vibrato, half-body pick-

guard, chicken-beak select, and three sets of volume and tone controls. The Apollo K360 ($200) was almost the same except for solid block inlays, a solid mahogany body, two deluxe pickups and threeway toggle. The Titan I K350 ($150) was the same as the K360 except for having double parallelogram inlays and a trapeze tailpiece.

Three new electric bass guitars were in the line by '65. The K5930 Deluxe Solid Body Bass ($139.50) was a double-cutaway with a Stratish body like the K300 guitar. This had a Thin-Lite neck with basically a reverse-Bushwhacker headstock and no fingerboard inlays. A single humped metal-covered pickup sat in the middle, with a small blobby pickguard on which was engraved the compass K music stand, plus volume and tone controls. The K5920 Pro Model Electric Bass ($100) was a hollowbody single-cut-away, Les Paul-shaped bass with an arched curly maple top, no f-holes, same neck, head and pickup as the K5930, with a moveable bridge, trapeze tail and a Barney Kessel-style pickguard! The K5915 ($82.50) looked similar to the K5920 except it had the old pointy headstock, a flat top, and an old Vanguard-style pickguard assembly.

These marked the end of the second generation of leadership of the Kay company.

Ca. 1966 Kay Vanguard II K326 (photo: Paul & Deb Grubich).

Acquisition fever

Beginning in 1966, the Kay Musical Instrument Company began to change hands with rather startling frequency as the acquisition mania that had corporate America buying up other guitar companies like Fender and Gretsch also snared Kay in its grip.

Juke boxes

The guitar boom juggernaut of the late '50s and early '60s began to decelerate quickly in around 1965 as demand began to drop off. Maybe everyone already had a guitar! Perhaps seeing the writing on the wall, in late 1965 Sidney Katz sold the Kay Company to the Seeburg Corporation, headed by Louis J. Nicastro, the company perhaps most famous for its music juke boxes. Seeburg was in the process of acquiring a number of musical instrument properties at the time. Katz became head of Seeburg's musical instrument division, while Bob Keyworth became head of the Kay division. Seeburg would operate Kay for a bit less than two years.

In 1966, in celebration of the new ownership, the Kay line essentially weeded out all the old-fashioned guitars that had hung around since the beginning of the decade. The new-style solidbodies that had appeared in '65 were expanded, while the old Thinlines were trashed. The amplifiers were redone along a bit more conservative lines. And finally, the acoustics were given their first facelift in years, although they continued, in essence, to be the same ol' same ol'.

Seeburg solids

Remaining in the Kay line for '66 were the previous bushwhacker-headed Vanguards and the Artiste, Apollo and Titan solids, virtually unchanged except for new numbers, pricing and the occasional feature. The old dumpy Vanguard K102/103s remained as before as the Kay Value Leader series ($54.95), with one pickup and three finishes: red (K310), teal blue (K311) and walnut with golden highlights (K312). The angular double-cut Vanguards were now the Vanguard IIs, with one-pickup (K326, #79.95), two-pickup (K327, $99.95) and three-pickup (K328, $119.95) versions. The K708

Artiste returned as the Kay Artist K370 ($325), unchanged. The Apollo returned as the Kay Apollo II K365 ($200). The Titan was now the Kay Titan II K355 ($165).

Two new solidbody series joined the line. Just above the Value Leaders appeared the Speed Demon solidbodies, a transmogrific-ation of the venerable old hollowbodies with that name. Basically, these were the same as the angular-body Vanguard II except for having chrome-covered bridge/tailpiece assemblies instead of vibratos and dot inlays instead of the "picks." The K319 ($89.50) had two pickups, while the K318 ($64.95) had one pickup.

Just under the top-of-the-line Artist came the K400 Series Professional electric guitars. These were basically equal double-cutaway solids, actually fairly handsome in their own way, almost a softer version of the Gibson SG. These had an angled contour all along the perimeter and rounded horns. The lower bout had an angle somewhat like a Strat. These had bolt-on necks with the bushwhacker headstock, nattily done up in a two-tone finish. Fingerboards were bound with the triangular pick inlays flanked by two small rectangles, making them look like little tulips. All had a symmetrical pickguard in the center and the heavy-duty, Bigsby-style vibrato. The most interesting new feature was the appearance of a Melita Synchro-Sonic bridge, like those found on Gretsch guitars. The Professionals came with either two ($225) or three pickups ($250), in burnt orange (K400, K401), soft teal blue (K402, K403), gleaming white (K404, K405) and cherry red mahogany (K406, K407).

Seeburg acoustic-electrics

The old Kay hollowbodies were still reflected in the Seeburg line but with new names and features.

Our old friend the single Florentine cut-

(Left) Ca. 1966 Kay Galaxie II K683 (photo: Gilbert Matossian). (Right) Ca. 1966 Kay Concert Hall Style Series K561 (courtesy Tinicum Guitar Barn, Ottsville, PA.).

away Speed Demon had become the Concert Hall Style Series, in one pickup (K561, $69.95), two-pickup (K562, $87.50) and three-pickup (K563, $99.95) versions. This was finished in cherry red and had the new bushwhacker headstock, dots, the new pickups found on the solids (possibly imported), a large fin pickguard and new knobs on the controls.

The honored single round-horn cutaway Swingmaster was reborn as the Galaxie II, which, we should hasten to add, had nothing whatsoever to do with the previous Galaxie! These were substantially the same as of yore, with either two (K682, $129.50) or three (K683, $149.50) humped covered pickups. New was the bushwhacker head, a bound fingerboard with "pick" inlays, and a fancy Bigsby-style vibrato that looks Japanese. These, too, had large goofy pickguards, and came with a red-to-yellow sunburst.

The recently introduced K592 with the two pointy double-cutaways was changed into the K585 ($175). This now had the bushwhacker head, bound fingerboard with blocks, two new-style pickups, sunburst finish, the big fin pickguard and the probably imported vibrato.

The old Jazz II appeared transformed into

(Left) Ca. 1966 Kay Galaxie II K682. (Right) Ca. 1966 Kay K6858 (courtesy Bluebond Guitars, Philadelphia, PA).

the K625 (Cremona brown) and K626 (shaded cherry red) at $250. Replacing the rounded horns were points like the K585. A three-and-three head remained, the flatter version of the old pointed shape. The bound fingerboard had the "picks-and-rectangles" tulip design. A pair of rectangular metal-covered pickups, heavy cast Bigsby-style vibrato and the Melita bridge rounded this baby out.

The bottom of the line was a one-pickup, non-cutaway, full-bodied archtop, the K6530 ($64.50), which basically replaced the older K6533 except for the newer, flatter head and a larger, fin-style pickguard.

New was the K650 "PRO" Professional Model ($350), which was a sleek hollowbody variation on the previous K300 solidbody and one of Kay's most interesting thinlines in years. These had a narrow waist and rounded double cutaway horns. The body was a fiddle-back maple! The head was the flatter three-and-three, while the inlays were blocks. Otherwise this was very similar to the K625/626, with chrome-covered pickups, cast vibrato and Melita bridge.

Seeburg basses

Kay's bass line got a makeover in '66 with the Seeburg/Keyworth hegemony. Top of the line were the Finest Quality Professional Electric basses. These were solidbody bass versions of the Artist/Apollo/Titan body style, sorta Strat, with the deep waist contour. These had natural-finished mahogany bodies. The bolt-on necks had the bushwhacker head. The fingerboards had little rectangular inlays running along the top (bass) edge. Put me in a blindfold test and that would say "Teisco" to me, pardner. Pickups were the new metal with black insert variety, probably imported. The K5952 ($200) had two pickups, the K5951 ($175) had one.

Still in the line was the previous equal cutaway K5930, now renumbered to K5935 ($139.50), but otherwise unchanged except the very ugly and awkward reverse head was changed out for a bushwhacker on a "Teisco" neck.

Brand new was a series of maple plywood solid basses in the shape of a Fender Jazzmaster. These had non-contoured bodies with bound tops and backs. They also had groovy two-part pointy pickguards which looked a lot like Burns designs...or Japanese copies of Burns, which were beginning to be popular at the time. Necks were "Teisco" bushwhackers. These had either one ($99.50) or two ($125) chrome-covered humped pickups and came in burnt orange (K5921, K5922), striking white (K5923, K5924), or soft teal blue (K5925, K5926).

Finally, bottom of the bass line were the Value Leader solids ($79.50). These had the angular double-cutaway bodies of the old Vanguard with a bushwhacker head and dots running along the top edge of the fingerboard. They came in red (K5917), soft teal blue (K5918) or shaded walnut (K5919).

Seeburg amplifiers

Amps in '66 were given a whole new look. Gone were the Danish Modern legs in favor of a much more conventional mid-'60s look, with black vinyl coverings, grey grill cloth and front-mounted controls, all transistor, of course. These included the K765 ($400) Professional Piggyback with reverb, tremolo, 12" speaker and 100 watts. The K761 Professional ($275) was a combo version of the K765. The K766 ($250) was a 100-watt head to match the K767 Remote Column Speaker Enclosure ($165) with two 12" speakers. The K760 Value Leader Reverb and Tremolo ($149.50) offered a 12" speaker with 20 watts. The K756 Two Channel Tremolo ($125) had a 12" speaker and 20 watts, no reverb. The K755 Solid State Tremolo ($99.50) had an 8" speaker and 10 watts. The K754 Tremolo ($79.95) was a three-tube amp, an anomaly in this transistorized world. The K752 Value Leader ($49.95) was your basic 8" speaker and 5 watts. The K750 Budget Leader ($39.95) had an 8" speaker and a "big" sound!

Two bass amps were offered, the K770 Dual Purpose Guitar and Bass ($250) with a 15" speaker and 50 watts, and the K771 Value Leader Bass ($150) with a 12" speaker and 20 watts.

The K771 Reverb Power Pack Unit ($65) remained in the line, newly redesigned and fully solid state.

Seeburg flattops

Only one serious Kay jumbo remained in the line in '66, the K8130 Solo Special II ($150), essentially a repeat of the old K8127 Solo Special except for the flatter headstock, a regular rectangular pin bridge and a strange pointy pickguard.

Seeburg/Kay "folk" guitars, with Martin OM-style profiles, continued much as they had before except for the new flatter headstock and squarish pickguard. The K5113 Plains Special ($49.50) remained as before. The K6150 Golden Cherry Super Auditorium ($59.95) was basically the old K6116 Gleaming Super Auditorium.

New was the K6160 Deluxe Mahogany and Spruce ($75) had a solid spruce top, the weird pointy pickguard and "pick" inlays. Also new were the K6170 Deluxe with Glued On Adjustable Bridge (natural, $100) and K6175 (cherry). These had solid

Early Kay features

A useful way to track early Kay guitars is by headstock design, a method suggested and here illustrated by Mike Newton. This is not foolproof, because a lot of crossing over occurs, but it can be a help if you're trying to date an early Kay.

[Stromberg Venetian ca. 1925 to ca. 1932 [this should be reversed]

Kay Kraft asymmetrical ca. 1928 to ca. 1934, into the 1960s on some banjos and mandolins

Kay humped ca. 1937 to early '40s on cheaper models

Kay pointed ca. 1937 to early '40s on better models

Ca. 1927 to mid-'30s Stromberg Venetian fixed pin bridge

1920s Lyon & Healy Washburn fixed pin bridge

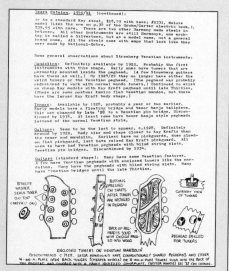

Anatomy of the Stromberg Venetian mandolin headstock with enclosed tuners

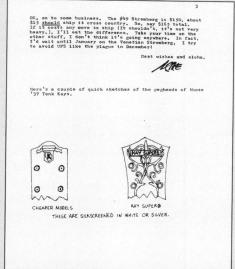

Late '30s silkscreened Kay logos

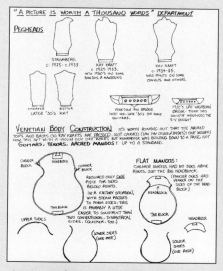

Anatomy of Venetian-body construction (Drawings by Mike Newton).

spruce tops, curly maple bodies, the pointy pickguards, block inlays, and a huge pin bridge.

Three other "folk" guitars graced the line. These had classical-style bridges but took steel strings. They had slotted headstocks with the plastic circle-K logo, and inlays near the top of the fingerboard. The K6140 Rhythm Special ($100) — its name borrowed from the early '50s K11 single-cutaway archtop — was quite handsome, with a white spruce top, curly maple body, bound rosewood fingerboard, rectangular inlays and a fancy, probably decal rosette. The K6135 (natural) and K6136 (red mahogany sunburst) were downscale versions ($79.95) with plywood bodies and dot inlays on the unbound 'boards.

A whole bunch of new dreadnoughts appeared in '66 under the banner of Country Flat Guitars. Top of the line was the very cool K6104 Professional Country Style ($175) with a double-bound spruce top, fiddleback curly maple laminated body, newer flat curved head, and bound rosewood 'board. Especially neat were the "bull horn"

inlays on the fingerboard, real inlaid rosette rings, a batwing pickguard and a glued-on pin bridge which looked for all the world like a bat in flight! The K6103 Western "Rich Bass" Model Blond Guitar followed ($99.50), a similar guitar except for having a rectangular pin bridge and the new "tulip" fingerboard inlays.

The K6102 Country II Model ($79.95) was a spruce and mahogany dreadnought with the plain pin bridge, fancy rosette decal, batwing pickguard, bound 'board and dots. The K6109 Western Plains Model ($59.95) was similar but with the classical-style bridge and no binding on the 'board. The K6105 Western Model with Steel Reinforced Neck ($39.95) had, well, a truss rod! This was a basic plywood model.

Three classicals continued vir-

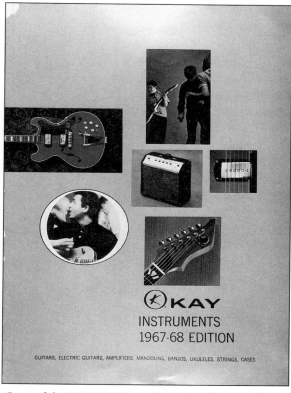

Cover of the 1967-68 Kay catalog under the new Valco ownership; otherwise the catalog is identical to the previous 1966 catalog.

Ca. 1967 Kay K6840 (courtesy Tinicum Guitar Barn, Ottsville, PA).

tually unchanged from '61 except for new numbers. The K7005 Artist II Classic ($89.50) replaced the old K7000 Artist. The K7008 Maestro II Classic ($59.95) replaced the old K7010 Maestro. The K7020 Concerto Classic remained as before, costing $4 more.

Budget Kay flattops continued with little but cosmetic changes as they had since '61. The K8165 Master Size Spanish ($45) was the old wonderful Kay jumbo shape previously known as the K8160, virtually identical except for twin white stenciled lines around the edges and soundhole, a larger, more squarish glued-on pickguard, a plainer trapeze tail and a metal chevron on the newer, flatter head. The K5160 Auditorium Size ($34.50) continued as before except the fingerboard had become painted black with painted white blocks, the pickguard (with a 16th note design) was painted on and the chevron adorned the head. The K4000 Student Concert Model ($39.95) was the old K3500 with the squarish pickguard and flattop head with chevron. The K1110 Slotted Head Standard ($29.95) was a downscale version of the old K6130 Calypso Folk Guitar, with a slothead and supposedly "convertible" between nylon and steel strings.

A number of specialty flattops were also

offered in '66, some with heritages going back in time. The K3900 ($49.50) was an all-mahogany tenor. The old ³/4 size K113 ($49.50) remained as before. The K7400 12-string ($100) joined the line with a spruce top, mahogany body, slothead, dots, batwing pickguard and a massive glued-on pin bridge. The K7950 Professional 12-String ($150) was an upscale version with curly maple laminated body and a bound fingerboard.

In '66 the archtop line had shrunk down to six basic models, almost painfully inferior to the glory days. The K8900 Master Cut-Away Arched Guitar ($100) was the only remaining cutaway with a spruce top and only maple laminated body. This had a bound rosewood 'board with the new tulip inlays, and the flatter rounded headstock. The K6440 Mahogany and Spruce Arched Guitar ($75) was next, with no cutaway and block inlays. The K6847 Spruce and Maple ($59.95) had four block inlays and a cherry finish. The K6840 Arched Guitar ($52.40) had a plywood body and sported a fake curly grain, plus the recent "pick" inlays. The K6835 Super Auditorium Special Arched Guitar ($44.95) was all

maple plywood with fake curl and a dark mahogany sunburst finish, with the old alternative single/double dot inlays. Finally, the Style Leader Arched Guitar ($39.95) was a gaudy plywood beast with fake curl all over which came in shaded dark brown (K6858), honey blond (K6868) or shaded reddish brown with golden sunbursts (K6878).

Kay banjos remained virtually unchanged in '66. The K90 Artist Model ($159.50) was the old K1000 Artist, available as 5-string, tenor and plectrum. The K52 Pro-

Ca. 1967 Silvertone version of a Kay Vanguard II K326 (photo: Paul & Deb Grubich).

fessional Model ($100) remained the same as before, in 5-string, tenor and plectrum. The K80 Long-neck Folk Banjo ($89.95) was a long-scale version of the old Folk Banjo. The K61 Folk 5-String ($69.95) was basically the old K60. The K75 Resonator Banjo ($65) was essentially the old K53, in 5-string or tenor. Lastly, the K65T Leader Banjo ($49.95) had a plywood shell and plastic head and there's not much more you can say about that!

Kay mandolins in '66 remained as before with some renumbering. The K390 Professional Electric Venetian mandolin remained as before, followed by the pear-shaped K495 Electric Mandolin, the old K494. The acoustic Venetian K345 was our old companion the K70, ancient scion of Joseph Zorzi and friends. The pear-shaped K465 Mahogany and Spruce Mandolin was the old K68 Concert. The K464 Value Special Arched Mandolin was the old K64 Value Special. The K450 Student Model Mandolin was the old K460 Student.

Finally, three ukes were offered, the K975 Baritone ($42.50), the K896 All Maple ($10.95) and the K900 All Mahogany ($13.95).

For all intents and purposes, that's all she wrote as far as American production of Kay guitars and other acoustic instruments goes. These American-made models would continue unchanged until the end. No new models would be introduced beyond this point.

Valco

In 1967, Valco, the company responsible for the National and Supro brands, descendants of the pioneering Dopyera brothers and George Beauchamp, bought Kay from Seeburg. Despite the enthusiasm of Valco President Robert Engelhardt that the merger would create the "most complete production facilities in the string instrument field," the union was the beginning of the end. From the notice of the event that appeared in the June 1967 *The Music Trades*, one almost gets the impression that Valco was after the big,

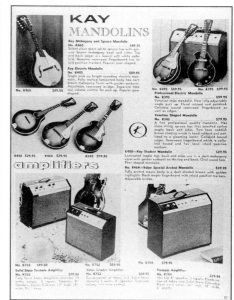

relatively new Kay factory.

Reportedly, Valco was interested in Kay's acoustic production capability. This is a curious little irony because, as you'll recall, way back in 1933 Kay made the mahogany-bodied El Trovador guitars for National, the predecessor of Valco.

The Kay line under this new Valco leadership was essentially unaffected. The 1967-68 Kay catalog, now published under the Valco imprimatur, was simply a reprint of the previous year's Seeburg/Kay catalog. The guitars made from 1966 on were the last American designs to come from the Kay company.

Supro/Kays

Valco's assertion of interest in Kay's acoustic production is supported by a Supro catalog from 1968-69, the end of the Valco line. All of the Supro acoustic guitars were identical to their Kay counterparts except for having Supro logos. Even the model numbers were unchanged, except for having an S rather than K prefix. "Supro" acoustics offered included the S6109, S6102, S7008, S7005, S5113, S6160, S6170 and S7900.

Three Kay archtops now bore Supro logos, two non-cutaways, the S6835 and S6840, and one cutaway, the S8900, all the same as their "K"-prefixed Kay equivalents.

Also in the Supro catalog were two thinline electrics: the two-pickup Clermont and three-pickup Stratford; three solidbody electrics: one-, two- and three-pickup Lex-

ington "Strats;" and one solid bass: the Taurus. These are almost certainly a combination of Japanese, Kay and probably Valco parts. The copy refers to their having Supro (!!) "Thin Line" necks, which suggests Kay necks (the thinlines have pointy Kay heads, while the solids have boar-snout six-in-line heads similar to Valco-made National-brand guitars as well as Custom Krafts built for St. Louis Music). However, the body styles look suspiciously Japanese, while vibratos are definitely of Japanese origin. Even the switches are now the little sliding variety mounted on small plastic plates, typical of Japanese guitars of the era. The pickups look as though they are the rectangular, metal-covered Supros seen on early Valco products; whether these are American or Japanese by this time is unknown.

The Kay banjos were also sold as Supros, the S75 and S52, the same as the K75 and K52.

Finally, in a nice poetic touch, three Kay mandolins bore the Supro name, the pear-shaped acoustic S464 (K464), plus the acoustic S345 (K345) and electric S395 (K390). These last two were the old familiar Venetian shape that traced its ancestry back to Kay's Roaring '20s and the Philip Gabriel and Joseph Zorzi.

It is not known if any Kay instruments were ever marketed as other Valco guitars, such as those bearing the National brand.

Not that it matters much. Time was running out fast.

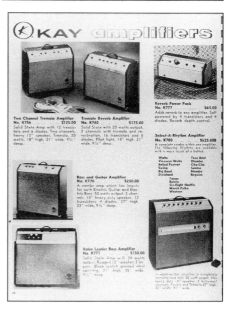

1968 Kay catalog, the last, a pastiche of previous catalogs.

Unfortunately, Valco ran into the Big Guitar Washout of the end of the '60s. It's often assumed that Kay and Valco were put out of business solely because of Japanese competition. The Japanese, so the wisdom goes, could build guitars much more cheaply than American firms. Certainly the Japanese manufacturers were tough competitors, and were a major factor, but the situation was a bit more complex. Throughout most of the '60s the demand for guitars kept well ahead of supply for both American and Japanese guitarmakers. Everyone could sell everything that could be made. This encouraged manufacturers, including Kay and its subsequent owners, to keep taking on more debt and keep pumping out the instruments as if there were no tomorrow. However, tomorrow would, of course, inevitably come as sure as the next day's sun.

For Valco, "tomorrow" came one year after purchasing Kay. Demand for guitars plummeted and in 1968, Kay/Valco went belly-up. Not that they were alone. There were a bunch of bankruptcies in Japan as well, and only the strongest companies survived. Harmony managed to struggle on for a few more years, but its sun set as well in the early '70s. For all intents and purposes, both Chicago's and America's role as the mass manufacturer of low-end instruments had come to an end.

In October of 1969, the assets of Kay and Valco were auctioned off. At least one of the companies represented at the auction was Alamo in San Antonio, Texas. Alamo bought truckloads of parts which ended up on the last examples of the Alamo brand.

Another purchaser was the large distributor Southland which also apparently bought bunches of leftover Kay stock because they were blowing out Kay guitars in an undated ca. 1968/'69 sale flyer. Southland was evidently not the only purchaser of remaining Kay inventory since there are reports of tons of New Old Stock hanging around in Chicagoland music stores well into the '70s. Apparently some Frankensteins were assembled for the auction, too, containing both Valco- and Kay-made parts, so if you encounter one of these, it may be unorthodox, but it could be kosher.

W.M.I. (Japanese Kays)

Among the assets which were auctioned off when Valco/Kay went under in '68 were the brand names held by the company. The venerable National and Supro brands, for example, were purchased by the suburban Chicago Strum & Drum, which also owned the Noble brand, once the property of Don Noble (who was known for having imported Italian Wandré guitars), and imported Japanese guitars carrying the Norma name. The National name was quickly applied to a line of Japanese copies of American guitars which were, at that very moment, just beginning to emanate from Japan. Indeed, one of the first Japanese "copy" guitars to be advertised in the United States was the National Big Daddy, a bolt-neck copy of the newly reissued Gibson Les Paul Custom (Big Daddy/Black Beauty) in 1970 (probably available before). The Supro name was never applied to any guitars.

Rights to the Kay name were purchased by W.M.I., another suburban Chicago outfit which at the time was known as Weiss Musical In-

Ca. 1958 Custom Kraft, a version of the Kay K4144 Sizzler made for St. Louis Music, here in cool sunbursts with tip of pickguard broken off (photo: Doug Lesho).

struments, but which had been founded originally by the import pioneer Jack Westheimer. W.M.I. was being run by the late Sil Weindling and Barry Hornstein, and is best known as the company responsible for importing the Teisco Del Rey guitars and Checkmate acoustic guitars and amplifiers, among other things. In fact, W.M.I. was reportedly the largest guitar company in the world at the time, selling somewhere between 40 and 50,000 guitars a month!

Under the W.M.I. ownership, parts of the Kay legacy were combined with W.M.I.'s own tradition, creating a steady focus on the low-end, beginner segment of the market. You'll recall that in the early days, Stromberg-Voisinet made guitars for the high end of the mass market. Through the Kuhrmeyer days Kay held down the middle of the pack, gradually shifting its focus more toward distributors and the trade. By the '60s Kay quality had definitely lowered to compete, to a great extent, with the Japanese for the beginner market, but through music retailers, not the big merchandisers like Sears and Montgomery Ward. It's a niche Kay continues to fill.

W.M.I. purchased the Kay name because it was interested in obtaining an entré into the music store market. Its previous success had been built on selling guitars to mass merchandisers and discount chains, including Sears and KMart. However, when it took Teisco Del Rey guitars into music stores, noses went up and no one would consider carrying the guitars. Rather than work on developing a new line and all the relationships with music retailers, W.M.I. took over Kay and gained access to the thousands of music store outlets available to that brand.

However, for now, the imported Teisco/Kay story will have to wait for another day...

Home at last

Although Kay made some cool and collectible guitars over its substantial history, it was never positioned as a high-end guitarmaker, and it never really competed with the professional powerhouses like Epiphone, Gibson, Gretsch and, later, Fender. Some of its better models do compare favorably with some of the lower-end guitars of those other makers, but that was never the point. Kay's mission was to supply the mass merchandisers and feed America's nearly insatiable appetite for guitars. However, from the many examples which still survive you'll find many excellent, even superb works of art.

And thus concludes this long and winding journey through the history of Kay guitars to its demise, just before it rose from the ashes as a low-end import imprimatur. From weird-shaped Groehsls, parlour Strombergs, Venetian Kay Krafts and the first "production" electric guitars and amps to the first "Silvertones," Kelvinator and bushwhacker headstocks, and '60s acquisition fever, it's been a great trip.

This chapter was written with indispensable contributions from Michael Lee Allen, Jim Dulfer, George Manno and Michael Newton.

Kay Guitars

Kay instruments have never featured meaningful serial numbers, so basically there is no way other than approximation to determine when a specific instrument was made. Electric instruments should have American-made potentiometers which are date-coded. That will give you the earliest date the guitar *could* have been made, but it could also be later. Since Kay was making lots of guitars, it's likely that the pot date is relatively close to the date of manufacture.

Obviously with a subject like Kay, with more than a hundred years of instruments and incomplete documentation, it's impossible to list every instrument ever produced, and, as usual, you should take the dates given here with a grain of salt. Nevertheless, this is the most complete listing of Kay guitars to date, and should provide an excellent starting point for dating any instruments you encounter.

Many of the guitars made by Stromberg-Voisinet were distributed by various major distributors using their own numbering schemes. These are listed as such because we have no other reference on the Stromberg designations, however, the model numbers are really those of the distributor and may identified differently by the manufacturer or other distributors. Note, for example, that some models as the Ward C748 is also listed as the D748 and E748, probably all the same guitar.

No attempt has been made to separate pressed and carved archtops, and all are listed as archtops, even though many, like the Kay Kraft Venetians and Arch Krafts, are very close to being flattops. Cutaway guitars are indicated, otherwise assume that the guitars are non-cutaways. Also, there may be a bit of redundancy implicit here, especially in the various guitars offered by distributors such as Tonk Brothers, Fischer, Continental and Montgomery Ward. Many of these may be the same or similar models, but without a Kay catalog as reference, it's pretty hard to discriminate between them.

Finally, models are listed separately when the names, specifications, or numbers change, even though they may actually be the same. For example, the early glued-neck Swing Masters and later bolt-neck Swingmasters share the same heritage, but are listed separately. This will be particularly the case toward the end of the Kay story, so be prepared for some additional redundance.

Dates Available	Instrument	Dates Available	Instrument	Dates Available	Instrument
Acoustic Flattop Guitars		1929	Ward D730 (Venetian, all-mah)	1929-30	Ward E805 "Two-in-One Guitar Outfit" (Hawaiian scene)
1918-21	Groehsl Guitars	1929	Ward D731 (Venetian, spr, gray pearloid)	1929-30	Ward E800 "Two-in-One Guitar Outfit" (birch)
1921-32	Stromberg Guitars	1929	Ward D845 Venetian Concertone Tenor Guitar (spr, mah, marquetry, banjo tp & hs)	1929-30	Ward E723 Students' Guitar (birch)
1925-26	Ward C748 Professional Concert Guitar			1929-30	Ward E727 Guitar (painted flowers)
1925-31	Ward C737 guitar	1929	Ward D817 "Serenader" Concert Size Guitar (spr, mah)	1929-30	Ward E905 Spanish Hawaiian Guitar (birch)
1925-26	Ward C738 Koa Wood Finish Hawaiian Guitar	1929	Ward D769 "Troubadour" Concert Guitar (spr, mah)	1929-30	Ward E560 (Venetian, Haw decal, mah)
1925-26	Ward C743 guitar	1929	Ward D748 Guitar (spr, rsw)	1929-30	Ward E731 (same as D731, gray pearloid)
1925-26	Ward C740 guitar	1929	Ward D736 Guitar (spr, mah)		
1925-26	Ward C742 guitar	1929	Ward D741 12-string Guitar (spr, mah)	1929-33	Fischer/Continental No. 2470 Venetian Tenor Guitar (pearlette fb, belly design)
1928-32	Stromberg/CMI No. 167 Spanish Guitar (spr, mah)	1929	Ward D800 "Two-in-One Guitar Outfit" (birch)	1929-32	Fischer/Continental No. 2472 Venetian Tenor Guitar (spr, pearlette body)
1928-30	Stromberg/CMI No. 67 Tenor Guitar (Venetian, spr, mah)	1929	Ward D723 Students' Guitar (birch)		
1928-35	Kay Kraft Style (Model) A Jumbo Guitar (mah)	1929	Ward D727 Guitar (painted flowers)	1930-31	Continental No. 2096 Guitar (Venetian, spr, pearlette)
1928-35	Kay Kraft Style (Model) B Jumbo Guitar (curly map)	1929	Ward D737 Spanish Hawaiian Guitar (spr, birch)	1931	Continental No. 2122 Guitar (Stromberg No. 34P, Concert, spr, birch, Ven hs)
1928-35	Kay Kraft Style (Model) C Jumbo Guitar (rsw)	1929	Ward D905 Spanish Hawaiian Guitar (birch)	1931	Continental No. 2108 Guitar (Stromberg No. 65M, all-mah)
1929-32	Stromberg No. 48 Venetian Tenor Guitar (spr, birch, Ven hs, pearlette fb)	1929-30	Ward E817 "Serenader" Concert Size Guitar (spr, mah)	1931	Continental No. 2104 Hawai-
1929-32	Stromberg No. 76 Venetian Guitar (spr, birch, Ven hs)	1929-30	Ward E748 Guitar (spr, rsw)		
1929-32	Stromberg No. 76T Venetian Tenor Guitar (spr, birch, Ven hs)				

Dates Available	Instrument
	ian Guitar (spr, mah, vine stencil)
1931	Regal No. 2106 Guitar (spr, mah, slothead)
1931	Regal No. 2110 Guitar (spr, rsw)
1931	Regal No. 2112 Guitar
1931-32	Stromberg No. 34P Spanish Guitar (spr, birch, pearlette fb, Ven hs)
1931-32	Stromberg No. 49 Spanish Gui-tar (spr, birch, pearlette fb, sq hs)
1931-32	Stromberg No. 65M Spanish Guitar (all-mah)
1931-32	Stromberg No. 65M Tenor Guitar (all-mah)
1931-32	Stromberg No. 60 Guitar (spr, mah, slothead)
1932-33	Continental No. 2111 Venetian Style Guitar (Stromberg No. 76)
c.1932-35	Fischer Guitar No. G-670 (Stromberg No. 48; Venetian, spr, mah, slot hs)
c.1932-35	Fischer Guitar No. G-680 (Grand Concert, all mah, Venetian hs)
c.1932-36	Fischer Handcraft Tenor Guitar No. G-860 (Grand Concert, all mah, asym hs)
c.1932-36	Fischer Venetian Tenor Guitar No. G-850 (Stromberg No. 76T; spr, birch, ebonized fb, checker binding, bakelite pg)
1933-34	S.S. Maxwell No. 728 Spanish F-hole Guitar (birch, pearloid snakehead, dk bn mah finish)
1933	National El Trovador Resophonic Guitar
1933	Hollywood Amplifying Guitar (Shireson Bros.)
1933-34	S.S. Maxwell Credenza Model Amplifying Guitar (f-holes, mah Shireson resonator cone, Targ & Dinner; some called Kay Kraft or Kay Deluxe)
1933-34	S.S. Maxwell Florenz Model Amplifying Guitar (f-holes,

Dates Available	Instrument
	spr, Shireson resonator cone, Targ & Dinner; some called Kay Kraft or Kay Deluxe)
1933-35	Oahu Style No. 60 De Luxe Jumbo (Haw curly map, symm hs, bound fb, vine inlay, pin br)
1933-36	Oahu Style No. 68B Jumbo (sb, symm hs, bound fb, dots, bakelite pg, gold stencil, pin br)
1933-35	Oahu Style No. 65m (all-mah, 3-hump symm hs, standard, checkerboard binding, pin br)
1934-35?	Arch Kraft No. 800 Auditorium (Spanish, all-birch, glued neck, dots, flat hs, trapeze)
1934-35?	Arch Kraft No. 802 Auditorium (Spanish, all-birch, adj neck, dots, flat hs, trapeze)
1934-35?	Arch Kraft No. 804 Auditorium (Spanish, all-mah, adj neck, dots, flat hs, trapeze)
1934-35?	Arch Kraft No. 805 Auditorium (Spanish, spr, mah, adj neck, dots, flat hs, trapeze)
1934-35?	Kay Kraft Deluxe Guitar K4 (Spanish, spr, birch)
1934-35?	Kay Kraft Deluxe Guitar K8 (Spanish, mah, birch)
1934	Kaywood No. 1 Amplifying Guitar (wood res plate, map)
1934	Kaywood No. 2 Amplifying Guitar (wood res plate, mah)
1934	Kaywood No. 3 Amplifying Guitar (wood res plate, curly map)
1934	Kaywood No. 4 Amplifying Guitar (wood res plate, rsw)
1935-36	Ward Spanish Auditorium flattop
1936-38	Oahu Style No. 66K Hawaiian (mah concert, symm hs, dots)
1936-38	Oahu Style No. 67K Spanish (mah, symm hs, dots)
1936-38	Oahu Style No. 65K Hawaiian (mah, symm hs, dots)
1936-38	Oahu Style No. 64K Spanish (mah, symm hs, dots)

Dates Available	Instrument
1936-38	Oahu Style No. 112K Tenor Guitar (spr, mah, asymm hs, pg, Venetian br)
1936-38	Oahu Style No. 23K Spanish (sb, pearlette fb, 3-humped slotted hs)
1936-37	Ward Kay-Kraft flattop (floral belly design)
1937-38	Oahu De Luxe Jumbo Style 68K Square Neck (African rw, symm 3-humped head, bound fb, vine inlays, pearl trim, pin br)
1937-38	Oahu De Luxe Jumbo Style 69K Round Neck (African rw, symm 3-humped head, bound fb, vine inlays, pearl trim, pin br)
1937-38	Oahu Jumbo Style No. 71K Square Neck (sb, symm hs, bound fb, dots, gold stencil, pin br)
1937-38	Oahu Jumbo Style No. 72K Round Neck (sb, symm hs, bound fb, dots, gold stencil, pin br)
1937-38	Oahu Style No. 53K Round Neck Spanish (mah, 3-humped slotted symm hs, dots)
1937-38	Oahu Style No. 54K Square Neck Hawaiian (mah, 3-humped slotted symm hs, dots)
1937-38	Continental No. 1121 Guitar (ribbed resonating wood diaphragm, f-holes)
1937-38	Kay/Continental No. 2092 Flattop (standard, birch, stiple map panel)
1937-38	Kay/Continental No. 2091 Flattop (diamond design/lyre sh)
1938-?	Kay K6 Auditorium Mahogany Spanish Guitar (spr, mah)
1938-?	Kay K2 Standard Spanish Guitar (mah)

Dates Available	Instrument
1939-?	Kay K8 Auditorium Mahogany Hawaiian Guitar (spr, mah)
1939-?	Kay K4 Auditorium Spanish Guitar (mah)
1939-40	Gretsch Grand Concert Size Spanish Guitar No. 20 (spr, mah jumbo)
1947-51	Kay K26 Artist Spanish Flattop (spr, mah)
1947-51	Kay K24 Artist Spanish Flattop (17", spr, curly map, blocks)
1947-56	Kay K22 Artist Spanish Flattop (17", spr, mah, small blocks)
1947-51	Kay K19 Super Grand Auditorium flattop (spr, curly map)
1947-51	Kay K16 Super Grand Auditorium flattop (spr, mah)
1947-51	Kay K14 Super Grand Auditorium flattop (spr, hardwood)
1947-51	Kamico No. 1150 Student Guitar (spr, birch)
1947-51	Kay K90 Resonator Guitar (spr, mah, National-Dobro resonator)
1947-50	Kay K91 Resonator Guitar (all mah, National-Dobro resonator)
1948	Rex Playboy Spanish flattop (Gretsch, 15" auditorium)
1948	Rex Playboy 3/4-size Ladies flattop (Gretsch)
1948	Rex Playboy Tenor flattop (Gretsch)
1948	Rex Royal Super Auditorium (mah, curly map grained, Gretsch)
1952-56	Kay K27 Jumbo Flattop (17", spr, curly map, blocks, belly br)
1952-56	Kay K23 jumbo flattop (17", spr, curly map)
1952-54	Kay K20 flattop (15 1/2", spr, curly map, sb)
1952-54	Kay K10 flattop (15 1/2", all mah, parallelograms, sb)
1952-56	Kay K15 Super Grand Auditorium flattop (15 1/2", spr, map, sb)
1952-56	Kay K15T Tenor flattop (15 1/2", spr, map, sb)

Dates Available	Instrument
1955-56	Kay K24 Professional Cutaway Flattop (cutaway, spr, curly map, blocks)
1955-56	Kay K18 Jumbo Flattop (1-cut, spr, curly map)
1955-56	Kay K12 Super Auditorium Flattop (spr, mah)
1955-56	Kay K12-3/4 3/4-size Flattop (spr, mah)
1956-58	Kay K6000 Western Rhythm dreadnought (spr, E Ind rw, eb fb)
1957-58	Kay K8224 Professional Cut-Away (K24, round 1-cut, spr, curly map, blocks)
1957-60	Kay K6118 Cut-Away (K18, round 1-cut, spr, curly map, bl or wal)
1957-60	Kay K8110 Master Size Flattop (cf. K10, spr, mah ply, parallelograms)
1957-65	Kay K6100 Country dreadnought (spr, mah, dots)
1957-65	Kay K8127 Solo Special (K27, 17" jumbo, spr, curly map, pearl blocks, semi-Kelvinator head)
1957-65	Kay K6116 Gleaming Super Auditorium Model (map ply, dots, sb)
1957-68	Kay K5113 Plains Special (spr, mah ply., dots)
1957-65	Kay K113 Plains Special (3/4 size, spr, mah ply., dots)
1957-65	Kay K5160 Auditorium (15", map ply., painted blocks)
1957-65	Kay K1160 Standard (15", map ply., map fb, black painted blocks)
1957-65	Kay K3500 Student Concert (14 1/2", spr, map ply., dots)
1960-65	Kay K8160 Solo Special (17" jumbo, ply, trapeze)
1960-65	Kay K6120 Western Model (dreadnought, map ply, wal fb, dots)
1960-65	Kay K6130 Calypso Folk Guitar (spr, mah, dots, slothead)
1960-65	Kay K7000 Artist Model

Dates Available	Instrument
	(classical, spr, flamed map, slothead)
1960-65	Kay K7010 Maestro Model (classical, slothead)
1961-65	Kay K7020 Concerto Classic Guitar (classical, all-map, slothead)
1966-68	Kay K8130 Solo Special II
1966-68	Kay K6150 Golden Cherry Super Auditorium
1966-68	Kay K6160 Deluxe Mahogany and Spruce (spr, picks)
1966-68	Kay K6170 Deluxe with Glued On Adjustable Bridge (natural spr, curly map, blocks)
1966-68	Kay K6175 Deluxe with Glued On Adjustable Bridge (cherry spr, curly map, blocks)
1966-68	Kay K6140 Rhythm Special (white spr, curly map, rectangles)
1966-68	Kay K6135 Rhythm Special (natural ply., dots)
1966-68	Kay K6136 (red mah sb ply., dots)
1966-68	Kay K6104 Professional Country Style (spr, fiddleback curly map ply., bull horn inlays)
1966-68	Kay K6103 Western "Rich Bass" Model Blond Guitar (spr, fiddleback curly map ply., tulip inlays)
1966-68	Kay K6102 Country II Model (dread, spr, mah, batwing pg)
1966-68	Kay K6109 Western Plains Model (dread, spr, mah, batwing pg)
1966-68	Kay K6105 Western Model with Steel Reinforced Neck (dread, ply.)
1966-68	Kay K7005 Artist II Classic
1966-68	Kay K7008 Maestro II Classic
1966-68	Kay K7020 Concerto Classic
1966-68	Kay K8165 Master Size Spanish (jumbo K8160)
1966-68	Kay K5160 Auditorium Size (painted white blocks, 16th note pg)
1966-68	Kay K4000 Student Concert

Dates Available	Instrument
	Model (K3500)
1966-68	Kay K1110 Slotted Head Standard (K6130 Calypso Folk Guitar)
1966-68	Kay K3900 Tenor (all-mah)
1966-68	Kay K113 3/4
1966-68	Kay K7400 12-string (spr, mah, slothead, dots, batwing pg)
1966-68	Kay K7950 Professional 12-String (curly map ply.)
1968	Supro S6109 (K6109 Western Plains Model, dread, spr, mah, batwing pg)
1968	Supro S6102 (K6102 Country II Model, dread, spr, mah, batwing pg)
1968	Supro S7008 (K7008 Maestro II Classic)
1968	Supro S7005 (K7005 Artist II Classic)
1968	Supro S5113 (K5113 Plains Special)
1968	Supro S6160 (K6160 Deluxe Mahogany and Spruce, spr, picks)
1968	Supro S6170 (K6170 Deluxe with Glued On Adjustable Bridge, natural spr, curly map, blocks)
1968	Supro S7900

Acoustic Archtop Guitars

Dates Available	Instrument
c.1927-32	Stromberg Venetian Guitar
1927-35	Kay Kraft Style (Model) A Venetian Guitar (mah)
1927-35	Kay Kraft Style (Model) B Venetian Guitar (curly map)
1927-35	Kay Kraft Style (Model) C Venetian Guitar (rsw)
1928-29	Ward D730 Venetian Hawaiian Guitar (mah)
1928-32	Stromberg Venetian Hawaiian Guitar (gray pearloid)
1928-29	Ward D731 Venetian Hawaiian Guitar (gray pearloid)
1928-29	Ward D845 Venetian Concertone Tenor Guitar (spr, mah)
1928-35	Kay Kraft Style (Model) A Ve-

Dates Available	Instrument
	netian Tenor Guitar (mah)
1928-35	Kay Kraft Style (Model) B Venetian Tenor Guitar (curly map)
1928-35	Kay Kraft Style (Model) C Venetian Tenor Guitar (rsw)
1929-30	Ward E560 Venetian Hawaiian Guitar (mah, decal)
1929-30	Ward E731 Venetian Hawaiian Guitar (gray pearloid)
1928-32	Stromberg Venetian Tenor Guitar (symm head)
1929-32	C.M.I. No. 67 Venetian Tenor Guitar
1930-32	Continental No. 2096 Venetian guitar
1930-32	Continental No. 2470 Venetian Tenor Guitar
1930-32	Continental No. 2472 Venetian Tenor Guitar (pearloid)
1933-35?	Arch Kraft No. 921 (K1) Tenor Guitar (Spanish, spr, mah)
1933-35?	Arch Kraft No. 920 (K2) Tenor Guitar (Spanish, spr, birch)
1933-34	Arch Kraft No. 778 Auditorium Size Archtop Guitar (F-holes)
1933-34	S.S. Maxwell No. 778 Auditorium Size archtop (waist f-holes, 14 fret, reddish bn)
1933-34	Marveltone Arch Kraft No. 778 Auditorium Size (f-holes, 14 fret neck, bl)
1934-35?	Arch Kraft No. 820 Grand Auditorium (Spanish, birch, adj neck, dots, sym hs, trapeze, 2-tone bn)
1934-35?	Arch Kraft No. 825 Grand Auditorium (Spanish, spr, mah, adj neck, dots, sym hs, trapeze)
1934-35?	Arch Kraft No. 830 Grand Auditorium (Spanish, spr, curly map, adj neck, pearl dots, sym hs, Grover De Luxe tuners, trapeze, 2-tone golden bn)
1934-35	Kay Kraft Deluxe Guitar K20 (Spanish, map)
1934-35	Kay Kraft Deluxe Guitar K25 (Spanish, mah)

Dates Available	Instrument
1934-35	Kay Kraft Deluxe Guitar K30 (Spanish, curly map)
1934-35?	Kay Kraft Deluxe Guitar K2 (Spanish, spr, birch)
1935-36	Ward Venetian Guitar (glued neck)
1935-36	Ward Spanish Archtop
1936-37	Ward Kay-Kraft Super-Auditorium carved archtop (spr, rsw)
1936-37	Ward Kay-Kraft Super-Auditorium carved archtop (spr, map)
1936-37	Ward Kay-Kraft Super-Jumbo archtop (spr, mah, steel reinforced neck)
1936-37	Ward Kay-Kraft Regular Super-Auditorium archtop (spr, map)
1936-37	Ward Kay-Kraft archtop (spr, birch)
1936-37	Ward Kay Kraft Super Auditorium Archtop (carved top)
1936-37	Ward Kay Kraft Super Auditorium Archtop (pressed top)
1936-37	Ward Full Grand Concert Archtop guitar (round soundhole)
1937-38	Tonk No.4315 Kay Superb Super Grand Archtop (curly map, vase-and-tendril, sym hs)
1937-38	Tonk No.4313 Archtop/Continental No. F-3 (pressed top, birch, koa-grained neck)
1937-38	Tonk No. 4311 Archtop/Continental No. 5400 (birch, lyre sh)
1937-38	Tonk Violin Style Guitar (symm. or cello head)
1936-38	Kay/Continental Normandie Archtop (curly map, metallic finish, reinforced)
1938-39	Kay K60 Television Model (super grand size, carved spr, flamed map, walnut brown sunburst, ribbon bridge)
1938-39	Kay K62 Television Model (super grand size, carved spr, flamed map, blonde, ribbon bridge)
1938-?	Kay K20 Super Auditorium

Dates Available	Instrument
	Archtop (all-Honduras mah, rsw fb)
1938-?	Kay K5 Auditorium Archtop (all-Honduras mah)
1939-?	Kay K25 Super Auditorium Archtop (spr, curly map)
1939-?	Kay K18 Archtop (spr, map)
1939-?	Kay K10 Archtop (spr, map)
1939-?	Ward Grand Auditorium Archtop (carved spr, curly map, checkerboard binding)
1939-?	Ward Grand Auditorium Archtop (spr, map)
1939-?	Ward Grand Auditorium Archtop (spr, mah)
1939-?	Ward Grand Auditorium Archtop (spr, map)
1939-?	Ward Grand Auditorium Archtop (birch)
1941-42	Sears Silvertone Super-Artist (Television)
1941-42	Sears Blonde Silvertone (Grand Auditorium, spr, curly map)
1941-42	Sears Silvertone Crest (Grand Auditorium, spr, curly map)
1941-42	Sears Silvertone DeLuxe Playtime (Auditorium, spr, map)
1941-42	Sears Silvertone Blond Playtime (Auditorium, spr, curly map)
1941-42	Sears Silvertone Prep All Maple (Auditorium, map)
1941-42	Kay Professional archtop (spr, map, later Artist)
1945-46	Kay Professional archtop (carved spr, curly map, blond)
1945-46	Kay Imperial (carved spr, flamed map, sb)
1947-51	Kay K48 Master Size Artist Archtop (17", carved spr, curly map, split blocks/ovals, sb or bl)
1947-51	Kay K46 Master Size Artist Archtop (17", carved spr, curly map, line & quadrants)
1947-51	Kay K44 Artist Archtop (17", spr, curly map, blocks)
1947-51	Kay K42 Master Size Archtop

Dates Available	Instrument
	(17", spr, curly map)
1947-51	Kay K39 Super Grand Auditorium Arched Guitar (spr, curly map)
1947-51	Kay K36 Super Grand Auditorium Arched Guitar (mah)
1947-56	Kay K34 Super Grand Auditorium Arched Guitar (spr, hardwood)
1947-51	Kamico No. 8457 Master Size Guitar (spr, map, oval sh)
1947-51	Kamico No. 5429 Auditorium Maple Guitar (spr, map, f-holes)
1948	Rex Lancer Auditorium Archtop (mah)
1948	Rex Aragon Super Auditorium Archtop (spr, curly map)
1948	Rex Royal Super Auditorium Archtop (mah, curly map grained)
1952-54	Kay K45 Professional Master Size Archtop (17", spr, curly map, blocks, blond)
1952-56	Kay K43 Master Size Archtop (17", spr, curly map, sb)
1952-56	Kay K37 Spanish archtop (15¹/2", mah)
1952-56	Kay K37T Spanish Tenor archtop (15¹/2", mah)
1952-56	Kay K30 Spanish archtop (map)
1952-56	Kay K1 archtop (cutaway, 17", carved spr, curly map,sub)
1952-56	Kay K21 Cut-Away Professional archtop (master size 17", carved spr, curly map)
1952-56	Kay K11 Rhythm Special archtop (cutaway, spr, curly map, sb or blond)
1955-56	Kay K40 Spanish archtop (17", spr, curly map, 3-pc tulip inlay, sb, blonde)
1955-56	Kay K35 Spanish archtop (map ply)
1955-56	Kay K32 Spanish archtop (ply)
1957-65	Kay K6838 Deluxe Arched Guitar (17", pick inlays)
1957-65	Kay K6437 All-Mahogany

Dates Available	Instrument
	Arched Guitar (old K37, all mah, dots)
1957-65	Kay K6836 Big Value Leader (old K35, map ply, dots)
1957-65	Kay K6833 Super-Auditorium Special (old K32, map ply, spr-grained top, wal. fb)
1957-66	Kay K6858 Style Leader (map ply, sb)
1957-66	Kay K6868 Style Leader (map ply, blond graining)
1957-58	Kay K6950 Cut-Away Leader (round 1-cut, spr, curly map ply, bound fb, dots)
1957-58	Kay K8921 Masterpiece (old K21, round 1-cut, spr, fiddleback map, ribbon br, fancy tp, bound fb, split blocks, sb or blonde)
1957-60	Kay K8911 Rhythm Special (old K11, round 1-cut, spr, curly map, bound fb, line & quadrants, sb or blond)
1957-58	Kay K8901 Combo (old K1, round 1-cut,l spr, curly map, bound fb, blocks)
1960-65	Kay K8950 Master Cutaway Model (1-cut 17" K1)
1960-65	Kay K8858 Master Value Leader (17" jumbo, map fb, tortoise dots)
1961-65	Kay K6845 Mercury Arched Guitar (curly map ply, dots)
1966-68	Kay K8900 Master Cut-Away Arched Guitar (spr, map ply., tulips)
1966-68	Kay K6440 Mahogany and Spruce Arched Guitar (non-cut, blocks)
1966-68	Kay K6847 Spruce and Maple (cherry non-cut, blocks)
1966-68	Kay K6840 Arched Guitar (ply., fake curly grain, picks)
1966-68	Kay K6835 Super Auditorium Special Arched Guitar (map ply., fake curl, dots)
1966-68	Kay K6858 Style Leader Arched Guitar (shaded dark brown ply., fake curl, dots)

Dates Available	Instrument
1966-68	Kay K6868 Style Leader Arched Guitar (honey blond ply., fake curl, dots)
1966-68	Kay K6878 Style Leader Arched Guitar (shaded reddish brown/golden sunburst ply., fake curl, dots)
1968	Supro S6835 (K6835 Super Auditorium Special Arched Guitar, map ply., fake curl, dots)
1968	Supro S6840 (K6840 Arched Guitar, ply., fake curly grain, picks)
1968	Supro S8900 (K8900 Master Cut-Away Arched Guitar, spr, map ply., tulips)

Electric Hollowbody Guitars

Dates Available	Instrument
1928-29	Stromberg Electro Guitar (Spanish or Hawaiian)
1928-29	Stromberg Electro Tenor Guitar (Venetian)
1936-37?	Ward Electric Amplifying Guitar (curly map)
1937-38	Oahu Volu-Tone (flattop, no sh, symm hs, large rect pu probably non-Kay)
1939-?	Kay Spanish Electric Guitar (Super Grand archtop, map, 1 neck pu)
1939-42	Oahu Valencia Spanish Electric Guitar No. 303K (Super Grand f-hole archtop, spr, map)
1947-51	Kay F451 Electric Spanish Guitar (1 pu, 17", spr, curly map/mah, sb)
1947-51	Kay F453 Electric Spanish Guitar (1 pu, 17", spr, curly map/mah, shaded brown)
1947-51	Kay K160 Spanish Electric Guitar (spr, curly map, 17", 1 slanted pu)
1952-58	Kay K161 Thin Twin Spanish Electric Guitar (cutaway, semi-hollow, 15", 2 pu, spr, birdseye map/mah)
1952-54	Kay K150 Spanish Electric archtop (K34 w/1 pu)

Dates Available	Instrument
1952-54	Kay K151 Spanish Electric archtop (K1 w/1 pu)
1954-56	Kay K172 Pro Spanish Electric Archtop (cutaway, 2 pu, 12 1/2", curly map, sb, blond and transparent gray; Barney Kessel Pro in '57)
1955-56	Kay K192 Spanish Electric archtop (cutaway, 2 pu, spr, curly map, sb, blond, metallic gold)
1955-56	Kay K152 Spanish Electric archtop (cutaway, 1 pu, spr, curly map, sb mah, blond)
1955-56	Kay K148 Spanish Electric archtop (K151, 1 pu, walnut sb, metallic silver)
1955-56	Kay K130 Spanish Electric archtop (K150, 1 pu, metallic gold)
1956-60	Kay K8701 Gold K Line Barney Kessel Jazz Special (cutaway, 17", 1 pu, Kelvinator, Melita br., sb or blond; Kessel name dropped in '60)
1956-60	Kay K8700 Gold K Line Barney Kessel Jazz Special (cutaway, 17", 2 pu, Kelvinator, Melita br., sb or blond; Kessel name dropped in '60)
1956-60	Kay K6701 Gold K Line Barney Kessel Artist (cutaway, 15 1/2", 1 pu, Kelvinator, sb or blond; Kessel name dropped in '60)
1956-60	Kay K6700 Gold K Line Barney Kessel Artist (cutaway, 15 1/2", 2 pu, Kelvinator, sb or blond; Kessel name dropped in '60)
1956-60	Kay K1701 Gold K Line Barney Kessel Pro (cutaway, 13", 1 pu, Kelvinator, sb or blond; Kessel name dropped in '60)
1956-60	Kay K1700 Gold K Line Barney Kessel Pro (cutaway, 13", 2 pu, Kelvinator, sb or blond; Kessel name dropped in '60)

Dates Available	Instrument
1956-60	Kay K8990 Gold K Line Upbeat (cutaway, 17", 2 pu, Kelvinator, sb, blond or black)
1956-59	Kay K8980 Gold K Line Upbeat (cutaway, 17", 1 pu, Kelvinator, sb, blond or black)
1956-60	Kay K6970 Swing Master (round 1-cut thinline, glued, bound fb, 2 pu)
1957-60	Kay K6960 Swing Master (round 1-cut thinline, glued, bound fb, 1 pu)
1957-60	Kay K6550 [K5550 in '60] Pacer (non-cut, picks, 2 pu)
1957-60	Kay K6540 [K5540 in '60] Pacer (non-cut, picks, 1 pu)
1957-59	Kay K6533 Value Leader (non-cut, dots, 1 pu)
1958-60	Kay K8995 Gold K Line Upbeat (cutaway, 17", 3 pu, Kelvinator, sb, blond or black)
1960-65	Kay #1961 Thinline Series Value Leader (hollow cutaway, bolt, 1 pu, ply)
1960-65	Kay #1962 Thinline Series Value Leader (hollow cutaway, bolt, 2 pu, ply)
1960-65	Kay #1963 Thinline Series Value Leader (hollow cutaway, bolt, 3 pu, ply)
1960-65	Kay #1982 Thinline Series Style Leader (hollow cutaway, bolt, 2 pu, curly maple ply, copper pg)
1960-65	Kay #1983 Thinline Series Style Leader (hollow cutaway, bolt, 3 pu, curly maple ply, copper pg)
1960-65	Kay #1992 Thinline Series Pro (hollow cutaway, bolt, 2 pu, curly maple ply, plastic pg)
1960-66	Kay #1993 Thinline Series Pro (hollow cutaway, bolt, 3 pu, curly maple ply, plastic pg)
1961-65	Kay K673 Swingmaster (round cutaway thinline, bolt-neck, 3 pu)
1961-65	Kay K672 Swingmaster (round

Dates Available	Instrument
	cutaway thinline, bolt-neck, 2 pu)
1961-65	Kay K671 Swingmaster (round cutaway thinline, bolt-neck, 1 pu)
1961-65	Kay K573 Speed Demon (pointed cutaway thinline, bolt-neck, 3 pu)
1961-65	Kay K572 Speed Demon (pointed cutaway thinline, bolt-neck, 2 pu)
1961-65	Kay K571 Speed Demon (pointed cutaway thinline, bolt-neck, 1 pu)
1961-66	Kay K775 Jazz II (2-cut thinline, bolt, semi-Kelvinator, 2 pu, Bigsby, sb or blond)
1961-66	Kay K580 Galaxie (1-cut thinline, 1 Kleenex pu, curly map ply, bolt, pick inlays)
1961-65	Kay K6535 (non-cut, spr, curly map, 2 pu)
1961-65	Kay K6533 (non-cut, spr, curly map, 1 pu)
1962-66	Kay K592 Double Cutaway with Vibrato Tailpiece (2-cut Florentine, map ply., bolt, picks, 2 pu, Bigsby)
1966-68	Kay K561 Concert Hall Style Series (hollow 1-cut Florentine, bolt-on, bush-whacker hs, 1 pu)
1966-68	Kay K562 Concert Hall Style Series (hollow 1-cut Florentine, bolt-on, bush-whacker hs, 2 pu)
1966-68	Kay K563 Concert Hall Style Series (hollow 1-cut Florentine, bolt-on, bush-whacker hs, 3 pu)
1966-68	Kay K682 Galaxie II (hollow round 2-cut, bolt-on, bush-whacker hs, picks, 2 pu, Bigsby-style vib)
1966-68	Kay K683 Galaxie II (hollow round 2-cut, bolt-on, bush-whacker hs, picks, 3 pu, Bigsby-style vib)
1966-68	Kay K595 Double Cutaway

Dates Available	Instrument
	with Vibrato Tailpiece (2-cut Florentine, map ply., bolt, bushwhacker hs, blocks, 2 pu, Bigsby)
1966-68	Kay K625 (Cremona brown 2-cut thinline, picks/rectangles, 2 pu, Melita, Bigsby-style)
1966-68	Kay K626 (Shaded cherry red 2-cut thinline, picks/rect-angles, 2 pu, Melita, Bigsby-style)
1966-68	Kay K6530 (non-cut full arch-top, 1 pu)
1966-68	Kay K650 "PRO" Professional Model (round 2-cut, fiddle-back maple, blocks, 2 pu, Melita, Bigsby-style)
1968	Supro Clermont thinline elec-tric (Kay neck, 2 pu, Japanese and Valco parts)
1968	Supro Stratford thinline elec-tric (Kay neck, 3 pu, Japanese and Valco parts)

Electric Solidbody Guitars

Dates Available	Instrument
1952-55	Kay K125 Spanish Electric Solidbody Guitar (cutaway, 1 pu, hardwood, sb)
1955-57	Kay K142 Spanish Electric solidbody (cutaway, 2 pu, cop-per)
1955-57	Kay K136 Spanish Electric solidbody (cutaway, 1 pu, spring green & white mist)
1956-58	Kay K4144 Sizzler Solid Body (1-cut, glued, flared 3/3 hs, map fb, bl dots, 2 pu, blk or bn Plextone, wh pg)
1956-58	Kay K4140 Sizzler Solid Body (1-cut, glued, flared 3/3 hs, map fb, bl dots, 1 pu, blk or bn Plextone, wh pg)
1960	Kay K4102 Solo King (State-of-Ohio, 2 pu, bn)
1960	Kay K4101 Solo King (State-of-Ohio, 1 pu, bn)
1961	Ward 9606M Solid Body Elec-tric Cutaway Guitar (rounded State-of-Ohio, 1 pu, bn)

Dates Available	Instrument
1961	Ward 9607M Solid Body Elec-tric Cutaway Guitar (rounded State-of-Ohio, 2 pu, bn)
1961-66	Kay K102 Vanguard (offset 2-cut solid, bolt, 2 pu)
1961-66	Kay K100 Vanguard (offset 2-cut solid, bolt, 1 pu)
1962-66	Kay K300 Double Cutaway Solid Electric (offset 2-cut, curly map, bolt, semi-Kelvinator hs, blocks, 2 pu)
1965	Kay K333 Vanguard Vibrato Solid Body Electric Guitar (off-set 2-cut, 3 pu, bushwhacker hs, pick inlays, Ger carve)
1965	Kay K332 Vanguard Vibrato Solid Body Electric Guitar (off-set 2-cut, 2 pu, bushwhacker hs, pick inlays, Ger. carve)
1965	Kay K331 Vanguard Vibrato Solid Body Electric Guitar (offset 2-cut, 1 pu, bush-whacker hs, pick inlays, Ger. carve)
1965	Kay K322 Vanguard Solid Body Electric Guitar (offset 2-cut, 2 pu, bushwhacker hs, dots, Ger. carve, stoptail)
1965	Kay K321 Vanguard Solid Body Electric Guitar (offset 2-cut, 1 pu, bushwhacker hs, dots, Ger. carve, stoptail)
1965-66	Kay K310 Value Leader (mod-ern red offset 2-cut, 2 pu, bush-whacker hs, dots, stoptail)
1965-66	Kay K311 Value Leader (teal blue offset 2-cut, 2 pu, bush-whacker hs, dots, stoptail)
1965-66	Kay K312 Value Leader (shaded walnut offset 2-cut, 2 pu, bushwhacker hs, dots, stoptail)
1965	Kay K708 Artiste (walnut Jazz-Strat, 3 pu, bushwhacker hs, split block/ovals, vib)
1965	Kay K360 Apollo (mah Jazz-Strat, 2 pu, bushwhacker hs, blocks, vib)
1965	Kay Titan I K350 (mah Jazz-

Dates Available	Instrument
	Strat, 2 pu, bushwhacker hs, 2 parallelograms, trapeze)
1966-68	Kay K360 Artiste (walnut Jazz-Strat, 3 pu, bushwhacker hs, split block/ovals, vib)
1966-68	Kay Apollo II K365 (mah Jazz-Strat, 2 pu, bushwhacker hs, blocks, vib)
1966-68	Kay Titan II K355 (mah Jazz-Strat, 2 pu, bushwhacker hs, 2 parallelograms, trapeze)
1966-68	Kay K319 Speed Demon (solid Jazz-Strat, bolt-on, bushwhacker hs, 2 pu dots, stoptail)
1966-68	Kay K318 Speed Demon (solid Jazz-Strat, bolt-on, bushwhacker hs, 1 pu dots, stoptail)
1966-68	Kay K400 Professional (burnt orange 2-cut, bolt-on, bushwhacker hs, picks, 2 pu, Melita bridge, Bigsby-style vib)
1966-68	Kay K401 Professional (burnt orange 2-cut, bolt-on, bushwhacker hs, picks, 3 pu, Melita bridge, Bigsby-style vib)
1966-68	Kay K402 Professional (soft teal blue 2-cut, bolt-on, bushwhacker hs, picks, 2 pu, Melita bridge, Bigsby-style vib)
1966-68	Kay K403 Professional (soft teal blue 2-cut, bolt-on, bushwhacker hs, picks, 3 pu, Melita bridge, Bigsby-style vib)
1966-68	Kay K404 Professional (gleaming white 2-cut, bolt-on, bushwhacker hs, picks, 2 pu, Melita bridge, Bigsby-style vib)
1966-68	Kay K405 Professional (gleaming white 2-cut, bolt-on, bushwhacker hs, picks, 3 pu, Melita bridge, Bigsby-style vib)
1966-68	Kay K406 Professional (cherry red mahogany 2-cut, bolt-on, bushwhacker hs, picks, 2 pu, Melita bridge, Bigsby-style vib)
1966-68	Kay K407 Professional (cherry red mahogany 2-cut, bolt-on, bushwhacker hs, picks, 3 pu, Melita bridge, Bigsby-style vib)

Dates Available	Instrument
1968	Supro Lexington solidbody (Valco neck, 1 pu, Kay and Japanese parts)
1968	Supro Lexington solidbody (Valco neck, 2 pu, Kay and Japanese parts)
1968	Supro Lexington solidbody (Valco neck, 3 pu, Kay and Japanese parts)

Electric Hawaiian Guitars

Dates Available	Instrument
1928-29	Stromberg Electro Hawaiian Guitar (Venetian)
1936-37	Ward All-Metal Hawaiian Model electric (cast aluminum)
1937-40	Oahu No. 229K Tonemaster Hawaiian Electric (mah, symm 3-hum hs, oval logo, horseshoe pu; plain pu by '38; center-peaked hs, stencil logo by '39)
1937-40	Oahu No. 363K Diana Hawaiian Electric (mah, gold leaf, symm 3-hum hs, oval logo, horseshoe pu; plain pu by '38; center-peaked hs, stencil logo by '39)
1939-?	Kay Hawaiian De Luxe Model (stair-step body, all mah, 1 pu, vol/tone)
1939-?	Kay Hawaiian Standard Model (Spanish/pear shape, all mah, 1 pu, vol/tone)
1939-40	Gretsch Electromatic Hawaiian lap steel (mah, Harlin 6-in-line tuners)
1940-41	Sears #2307 Hawaiian lap steel
1940-41	Sears #2331 Hawaiian lap steel
1945-46	Kay Hawaiian DeLuxe Model
1947-49	Kay F461 Electric Hawaiian Guitar (1 pu, mah/curly map, brown sb)
1947-49	Kay F463 Electric Hawaiian Guitar (stepped body, 1 deluxe pu, mah/curly map, brown sb)
1951-54	Kay K159 Hawaiian Electric Guitar (curly map top, Kay handrest, tapered body)
1952-56	Kay K156 Hawaiian Electric (student)

Dates Available	Instrument
1955-56	Kay K155 Professional Electric Hawaiian Guitar (lucite, legs)
1955-60	Kay K157 Hawaiian Electric Guitar (green mist plastic; 2-tone green Plextone in '57)
1957-60	Kay K1560 Professional Model Hawaiian (blk & wh, legs)

Bass Guitars

Dates Available	Instrument
1938-60s	Kay upright acoustic basses and cellos
1954-65	Kay K5965 Pro Model Electric Bass (cutaway, 1 pu, 12^1/^{2}")
1955-56	Kay K160 Electronic Bass Guitar (cutaway, 1 pu)
1955-56	Kay K162 Electronic Bass (cutaway, 1 pu, bass viol tuning)
1960-64	Kay K5970 Jazz Special Electric Bass (blk or blond)
1960-65	Kay K5961 Thinline Bass (hollow cutaway, bolt, 1 pu)
1960-65	Kay K5962 Thinline Bass (hollow cutaway 6-string, bolt, 1 pu)
1965-66	Kay K5930 Deluxe Solid Body Bass (equal 2-cut, bolt-on, rev Bushwhacker hs, 1 pu)
1965-66	Kay K5920 Pro Model Electric Bass (1-cut hollow, curly map archtop, rev Bushwhacker hs, 1 pu)
1965-66	Kay K5915 Pro Model Electric Bass (1-cut hollow, 1 pu)
1966-68	Kay K5952 Finest Quality Professional Electric bass (offset 2-cut, bolt-on, Teisco bushwhacker hs, 2 pu)
1966-68	Kay K5951 Finest Quality Professional Electric bass (offset 2-cut, bolt-on, Teisco bushwhacker hs, 1 pu)
1966-68	Kay K5935 Deluxe Solid Body Bass (equal 2-cut, bolt-on, Teisco bushwhacker hs, 1 pu)
1966-68	Kay K5921 Solid Body Bass (burnt orange offset 2-cut, map ply., 1 pu, bolt-on, Teisco bushwhacker hs)
1966-68	Kay K5922 Solid Body Bass

Dates Available	Instrument
	(burnt orange offset 2-cut, map ply., 2 pu, bolt-on, Teisco bushwhacker hs)
1966-68	Kay K5923 Solid Body Bass (striking white offset 2-cut, map ply., 1 pu, bolt-on, Teisco bushwhacker hs)
1966-68	Kay K5924 Solid Body Bass (striking white offset 2-cut, map ply., 2 pu, bolt-on, Teisco bushwhacker hs)
1966-68	Kay K5925 Solid Body Bass (soft teal blue offset 2-cut, map ply., 1 pu, bolt-on, Teisco bushwhacker hs)
1966-68	Kay K5926 Solid Body Bass (soft teal blue offset 2-cut, map ply., 2 pu, bolt-on, Teisco bushwhacker hs)
1966-68	Kay K5917 Value Leader (red offset 2-cut solid, 1 pu, bolt-on, bushwhacker hs)
1966-68	Kay K5918 Value Leader (soft teal blue offset 2-cut solid, 1 pu, bolt-on, bushwhacker hs)
1966-68	Kay K5919 Value Leader (shaded walnut offset 2-cut solid, 1 pu, bolt-on, bushwhacker hs)

Mandolins

Dates Available	Instrument
1890-21	Groehsl Mandolins
1921-32	Stromberg Mandolins
1925-26	Ward C753 flatback mandolin
1925-26	Ward C753 flatback mandolin
1928-29	Ward D766 Venetian Mandolin (mah)
1928-29	Ward D833 Venetian Mandolin (mah)
1928-29	Ward D835 Venetian Mandolin (rsw)
1928-29	C.M.I./Stromberg Electro Mandolin (Banjolin?)
1928-32	C.M.I./Stromberg No. 600 Mandolin (Venetian, spr, mah; Epi hs in '32)
1928-32	Stromberg Venetian Mandolin (symm. head)
1928-35	Kay Kraft Style (Model) A Venetian Mandolin (mah)

Dates Available	Instrument
1928-35	Kay Kraft Style (Model) B Venetian Mandolin (curly map)
1928-35	Kay Kraft Style (Model) C Venetian Mandolin (rsw)
1929-30	Ward E766 Venetian Mandolin (mah)
1929-32	Fischer/Continental No. 2230 Venetian Mandolin (flatback, birch)
1929-32	Fischer/Continental No. 2232 Venetian Mandolin (flatback, mah)
1930-32	Continental No. 2230 Venetian Mandolin
1930-32	Continental No. 2232 Venetian Mandolin
1931?-39	Kay Kraft Model A Venetian Mandola (spr, mah)
1931?-39	Kay Kraft Model A Venetian Mando-Cello (spr, mah)
1932	Stromberg No. 75 Venetian mandolin (spr, mah, sq hs)
1932	Stromberg No. 76 Venetian mandolin (spr, birch, Epi hs)
1932	Stromberg No. 450 Venetian mandolin (spr, birch, Epi hs)
1932	Stromberg No. 750 Venetian mandolin (spr, rsw, Epi hs)
1932-33	Continental No. 2221 Venetian Style Mandolin (all mah)
1932-33	Continental No. 2227 Venetian Shaped Mandolin (spr, mah, checker binding)
1932-35	Fischer No. G-355 Venetian (spr, birch, checker binding)
1932-35	Fischer No. G-335 "The Milano" (Venetian, all mah)
1932-35	Fischer No. G-325 "The Patrician" (pear, all mah)
1933-34	Arch Kraft No. 1515 Mandolin (Venetian, mah, asym hs)
1933-34	Arch Kraft No. 1514 Mandolin (Venetian, birch, asym hs)
1936-37	Ward Kay-Kraft Venetian mandolin (f-hole)
1936-37	Ward Kay-Kraft Venetian mandolin (roundhole)
1937-38	Continental No. 2225 Venetian Mandolin (mah)

Dates Available	Instrument
1937-38	Continental No. 2224 Venetian Style Mandolin (birch)
1939	Grossman Winton Venetian Model Mandolin No. 4009 (birch, asym head)
1939-66	Kay Model K70 Venetian Mandolin (f-hole, spr, curly map; K345 in '66)
1939-42?	Kay Model K68 Venetian Mandolin (Honduras mah)
1939-50	Kay Model K66 Venetian Mandolin (spr, mah; K66 1/2 by '50)
1939-50	Kay Model K61 Venetian Mandolin (mah; K61 1/2 by '50)
1939-42?	Kay Model K30 Venetian Mandolin (mah, oval sh)
1939-42?	Kay Model K71 Mandolin (pear, birch)
1939-42?	Kay Model K72 Mandolin (pear, spr, hardwood)
1939-50	Kay Model K73 Mandolin (pear, spr, curly map)
1941-42	Sears Silvertone Professional Mandolin (Venetian, spr, map)
1952-60	Kay K72 Venetian Mandolin (spr, curly map)
1952-66	Kay K68 Concert Mandolin (pear, spr, curly map; K465 in '66)
1952-66	Kay K64 Value Special Mandolin (pear, map; K464 in '66)
1952-60	Kay K95 Electric Mandolin (pear K64 w/ 1 pu)
1956-60	Kay K74 Venetian Mandolin
1960-68	Kay K390 Professional Electric Mandolin (Venetian, spr, map, Thin Twin pu)
1960-66	Kay K494 Electric Mandolin (pear, spr, map, 1 pu; K495 in '66)
1960-66	Kay K460 Student Mandolin (pear, map ply.; K450 in '66)
1966-68	K495 Electric Mandolin (K494, pear, spr, map, 1 pu)
1966-68	K345 Venetian (K70, spr, curly map)

Dates Available	Instrument
1966-68	K465 Mahogany and Spruce Mandolin (K68 Concert; pear, spr, curly map)
1966-68	K464 Value Special Arched Mandolin (K64 Value Special; pear, map)
1966-68	K450 Student Model Mandolin (K460 Student; pear, map ply)
1968	Supro S464 Value Special Arched Mandolin (K464, Value Special; pear, map)
1968	Supro S345 Venetian (K345, spr, curly map)
1968	Supro S395 Professional Electric Mandolin (K390, Venetian, spr, map, Thin Twin pu)

Banjos

Dates Available	Instrument
1918-21	Groehsl Banjos
1921-32	Stromberg Banjos
1925-26	Ward C770 Orchestra Tenor Banjo
1925-26	Ward C753 Melody King Banjo
1925-26	Ward C765 Tenor Banjo
1925-26	Ward Popular Tenor Banjo
1928-29	Stromberg Electro Banjo
1928-29	Stromberg Electro Tenor Banjo
1928-29	C.M.I./Stromberg No. 51 Tenor Banjo (20 brackets, mah res, diamonds)
1929	Ward D757 "Super Deluxe" Banjo
1929	Ward D696 "Melody King" Banjo
1929	Ward D762 "Syncopator" Tenor Banjo
1929	Ward D842 Tenor Banjo Outfit
1928-37	Kay Kraft Style (Model) A Tenor Banjo (mah res)
1928-37	Kay Kraft Style (Model) B Tenor Banjo (curly map res)
1928-37	Kay Kraft Style (Model) C Tenor Banjo (rsw res)
1928-37	Kay Kraft Style (Model) A Plectrum Banjo (mah res)
1928-37	Kay Kraft Style (Model) B Plectrum Banjo (curly map res)

Dates Available	Instrument
1928-37	Kay Kraft Style (Model) C Plectrum Banjo (rsw res)
1928-39	Kay Kraft Style (Model) A Banjo-Mandolin (mah res)
1928-37	Kay Kraft Style (Model) B Banjo-Mandolin (curly map res)
1928-37	Kay Kraft Style (Model) C Banjo-Mandolin (rsw res)
1928-37	Kay Kraft Style (Model) A 5-String Banjo (mah res)
1928-37	Kay Kraft Style (Model) B 5-String Banjo (curly map res)
1928-37	Kay Kraft Style (Model) C 5-String Banjo (rsw res)
1952-68	Kay K52 5-String Banjo (mah res, nickel, 20 br)
1952-68	Kay K52T Tenor Banjo (mah res, nickel, 20 br)
1952-56	Kay K52BM Banjo Mandolin (mah res, nickel, 20 br)
1952-68	Kay K54 5-String Banjo (curly map res, nickel, 16 br)
1952-68	Kay K54T Tenor Banjo (curly map res, nickel, 16 br)
1952-56	Kay K54BM Banjo Mandolin (curly map res, nickel, 16 br)
1952-68	Kay K53 5-String Banjo (open back, map rim)
1952-68	Kay K53T Tenor Banjo (open back, map rim)
1952-56	Kay K53BM Banjo Mandolin (open back, map rim)
1955-56	Kay K55 5-String Banjo (curly map res, chrome)
1955-56	Kay K55T Tenor Banjo (curly map res, chrome)
1955-56	Kay K55P Plectrum Banjo (curly map res, chrome)
1955-58	Kay K51 5-String Banjo (met. gold res)
1955-58	Kay K51T Tenor Banjo (met. gold res)
1955-56	Kay K50 5-String Banjo (curly map res, gold design)
1955-56	Kay K50T Tenor Banjo (curly map res, gold design)
1956-57	Jose Silva Model K1000 5-String Banjo (chrome hdw,

Dates Available	Instrument
	curly map res, pearlette blocks)
1956-57	Jose Silva Model K1000T Tenor Banjo (chrome hdw, curly map res, pearlette blocks)
1956-57	Jose Silva Model K1000P Plectrum Banjo (chrome hdw, curly map res, pearlette blocks)
1956-57	Jose Silva Professional Model K2000 5-String Banjo (chrome hdw, carved heel, pearlette res, pearlette blocks)
1956-57	Jose Silva Professional Model K2000T Tenor Banjo (chrome hdw, carved heel, pearlette res, pearlette blocks)
1956-57	Jose Silva Professional Model K2000P Plectrum Banjo (chrome hdw, carved heel, pearlette res, pearlette blocks)
1956-57	Jose Silva Artist Model K3000 5-String Banjo (gold hdw, rw res, mother-of-pearl blocks)
1956-57	Jose Silva Artist Model K3000T Tenor Banjo (gold hdw, rw res, mother-of-pearl blocks)
1956-57	Jose Silva Artist Model K3000P Plectrum Banjo (gold hdw, rw res, mother-of-pearl blocks)
1960-68	Kay K1000 Artist Model 5-String Banjo (map ply. res, chrome flange, blocks, arm rest)
1960-68	Kay K1000T Artist Model Tenor Banjo (map ply. res, chrome flange, blocks, arm rest)
1961-68	Kay K60 Folk Model 5-string Banjo (map ply. shell)
1966-68	Kay K90 Artist Model 5-String Banjo (K1000 Artist)
1966-68	Kay K 90 Artist Model Tenor Banjo (K1000 Artist)
1966-68	Kay K90 Artist Model Plectrum Banjo (K1000 Artist)
1966-68	Kay K52 Professional Model Plectrum Banjo
1966-68	Kay K80 Long-neck Folk Banjo (long-scale Folk Banjo)

Dates Available	Instrument
1966-68	Kay K61 Folk 5-String (K60)
1966-68	Kay K75 5-string Resonator Banjo (K53)
1966-68	Kay K75 Tenor Resonator Banjo (K53)
1966-68	Kay K65T Leader Banjo (ply. shell, plastic head)
1968	Supro S75 5-string Resonator Banjo (K75)
1968	Supro S75 Tenor Resonator Banjo (K75)
1968	Supro S52 Professional Model 5-String Banjo (K52)
1968	Supro S52 Professional Model Tenor Banjo (K52)

Amplifiers

Dates Available	Instrument
1928-29	Stromberg amplifier (d.c., 3 input)
1936-37?	Ward Amplifier (5 tubes, Kay?)
1939-?	Kay amplifier (lt bn tolex, vert stripes, 2 ch, 8-10w)
1939-?	Kay amplifier (plain tolex, 2 inputs, 6-8w)
1939-42	Oahu De Luxe Amplifier
1939-42	Oahu Standard Amplifier
1939-40	Gretsch Electromatic amplifier
1945-46	Kay amplifier (Art Deco, 8-10w)
1947-51	Kay No. F475 High Fidelity Amplifier (12", 5 tubes)
1952-56	Kay K600 High Fidelity Amplifier (12" Jenson, 6 tubes, 16-20w)
1952-56	Kay K615 High Fidelity Amplifier (15" Jenson, 6 tubes, 16-

Dates Available	Instrument
	20w)
1952-56	Kay K300 High Fidelity Amplifier (8", 3 tubes)
1957-61	Kay K507 Twin Ten Special (2-10", 7 tubes, 20w)
1957-61	Kay K505 Twin Eight Hi-Power Model (2-8", 5 tubes, 12w)
1957-61	Kay K503 Hot-Line Special (3 tubes, 4w)
1957-60	Kay K515 Heavy Duty Bass Amp (15", 7 tubes, 15 w)
1960-62	Kay K506 Vibrato "12" (12", vib, 6 tubes, 2 channels, 12w)
1960-62	Kay K504 Vibrato Leader (8", vib, 5w)
1961-62	Kay K550 (2-8", 5 tubes, 12w, reverb)
1961-62	Kay K540 Reverb Power Pack (8", 3w amp)
1962-65	Kay K708 Galaxie II Amplifier (transistors, 12", vib, 35w, separate chassis/speaker)
1962-65	Kay K707 Galaxie I Amplifier (transistors, 12", vib, 35w)
1962-65	Kay K706 Vanguard "706" Amplifier (transistors, 12", vib, 15w)
1962-65	Kay K705 Vanguard "705" Amplifier (transistors, 10", vib, 10w)
1962-65	Kay K704 Vanguard "704" Amplifier (transistors, 8", 5w)
1962-65	Kay K703 Value Leader Amplifier (transistors, 8", 4w)
1962-65	Kay K700 Vanguard "700" Amplifier (transistors, 8", triple tone circuit)

Dates Available	Instrument
1962-65	Kay K710 Reverb Power Pack Unit (4 transistor amp)
1962-65	Kay K720 Bass Amplifier (15")
1966-68	Kay K765 Professional Piggyback (12", 100w, rev, trem)
1966-68	Kay K761 Professional (combo, 12", 100w, rev, trem.)
1966-68	Kay K766 (100w head)
1966-68	Kay 767 Remote Column Speaker Enclosure (2-12")
1966-68	Kay K760 Value Leader Reverb and Tremolo (12", 20w)
1966-68	Kay K756 Two Channel Tremolo (12", 20w)
1966-68	Kay K755 Solid State Tremolo (8", 10w)
1966-68	Kay K754 Tremolo (3-tubes)
1966-68	Kay K752 Value Leader (8", 5w)
1966-68	Kay K750 Budget Leader (8")
1966-68	Kay K770 Dual Purpose Guitar and Bass (15", 50w)
1966-68	Kay K771 Value Leader Bass (12", 20w)
1966-68	Kay K771 Reverb Power Pack Unit (solid state)

Other Instruments

Dates Available	Instrument
1925-26	Ward C786 Tenor Banjo Ukulele
1925-26	Ward C780 Banjo Ukulele
1929	Ward Banjo-Ukulele
1957	Kay K5 Banjo Uke
1966-68	Kay K975 Baritone Ukulele
1966-68	Kay K896 All Maple Ukulele
1966-68	Kay K900 All Mahogany Ukulele

Kay headstock gallery

This is not meant to be any sort of comprehensive representation of Kay headstocks, but it will give you a photographic flavor of the variety available.

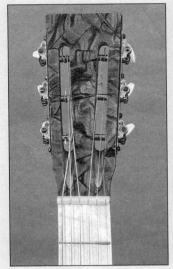

1932 Stromberg #49

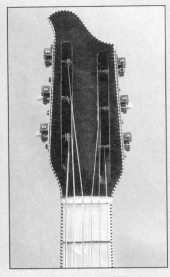

1932 Stromberg #76 Venetian

Ca. 1933 Asymmetrical Kay Kraft Model B

Ca. 1934 Recording King

1938 Humped Kay Violin Archtop

1937 Center Peaked Oahu No. 229K Tonemaster

Ca. 1939-41 Oahu Diana (courtesy Tinicum Guitar Barn, Ottsville, PA)

Ca. 1939-41 Oahu Diana (courtesy Tinicum Guitar Barn, Ottsville, PA)

1941 Pointed Silvertone Crest

Late '40s Triple Humped K23 (courtesy Bernunzio Vintage Instruments, Penfield, NY)

Late '40s Sherwood Deluxe K23 (courtesy Bernunzio Vintage Instruments, Penfield, NY)

Ca. 1948 Sherwood Deluxe/
Kay No. F451 (photo: Gilbert
Matossian)

Ca. 1952 Kay K21 (photo:
Gilbert Matossian)

1954 Kay K161 Thin Twin

1953 Spiegel Old Kraftsman
(photo: Mike Newton)

1956 Sears Silvertone (photo:
Mike Newton)

Ca. 1955 Kay K11B (photo:
Gilbert Matossian)

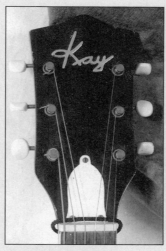

Ca. 1957 Kay K571 (photo:
Richard Nesdale)

Ca. 1957 Kay K6533 Value
Leader (courtesy Society Hill
Loan, Philadelphia, PA)

1958 Kay Upbeat K8995 with
three pickups and gold hardware
(photo: Gilbert Matossian).

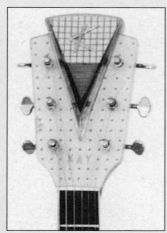

Ca. 1959 Kelvinator Kay Jazz
Special (courtesy SteveJohnson,
photo: Jay Scott)

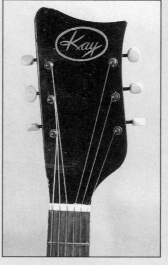

1960 Kay K4102 Solo King

1963 Kay K573 Speed Demon

Ca. 1963 Kay K300 (photo: Gilbert Matossian)

Ca. 1963 Kay K6535 (courtesy Society Hill Loan, Philadelphia, PA)

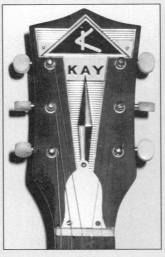

Ca. 1963 Kay Vanguard K102 (photo: Gilbert Matossian)

Ca. 1965 Kay K5920

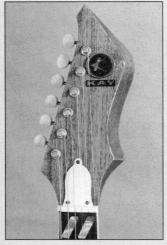

1965 Bushwhacker Kay K350 Titan I

1966 Kay K682 Galaxie II

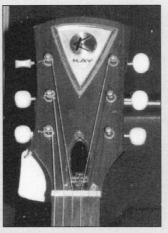

Ca. 1966 Kay Country II K6102 (courtesy Mike's Guitars, Etc., Erial, NJ)

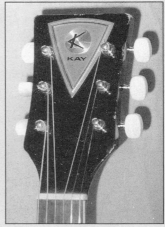

Ca. 1966 Kay K6858 (courtesy Bluebond Guitars, Philadelphia, PA)

Ca. 1966 Kay K6878

Ca. 1967 Kay K6109 (courtesy Society Hill Loan, Philadelphia, PA)

Maccaferri
GUITARS

Italian Classics to Fantastic Plastics

Drop the name "Maccaferri" to most guitar buffs and more than likely the response will involve plastic guitars and, if you're lucky, something about Django Reinhardt. For a lifetime's devotion to music that literally spanned almost the entire 20th Century, such a reduction might be viewed as sadly ironic. On the other hand, given the creative genius that infuses Mario Maccaferri's brilliant career, including his remarkable plastic guitars, it may just be the greatest tribute of all.

Whether or not you agree with such enthusiasm for Maccaferri's plastic guitars, the fact remains that Mario Maccaferri lived a long full life and achieved far more than most could dream in the pursuit of his passions, passions which never strayed far from music.

A lot of parts of the Maccaferri story have been related over the past few years, mostly focusing on his early contributions, often at the expense of the less politically correct plastic parts. However, like most good yarns, the story of the guitars which endeared the late famous and indefatigable luthier Mario Maccaferri to guitar lovers has a lot more to it than just some remarkable plastic fabrication. Indeed, the tale of Mario

Maccaferri is one full of amazing artistic, business and engineering achievement, and not a little romance and adventure woven

A very early ca. 1916 photograph of the young Mario Maccaferri probably taken at about the time the Mozzani/Maccaferri lyre-guitars were made (courtesy Maria Maccaferri).

into its twists and turns. Here, for the enjoyment of guitar aficionados, is the full Maccaferri story, complete with some brief forays into 19th Century guitar history, and including a detailed accounting of the plastic guitars.

Origins in the Po River valley

The beginnings of the Maccaferri story go back to the dawn of the century — or before — in northeastern Italy. Mario Maccaferri was born on May 20, 1900, in the town of Cento, which lies in the plains along the Po River halfway between Bologna and Ferrara, an area fertile with guitar activity. Mario was one of seven children, the son of Erminio, a carpenter, and Demetria Maccaferri. He attended school until the age of nine, whereupon, diploma in hand, he held various jobs including dish washer and apprentice carpenter. Fortunately for us and the world, such career paths were quickly abandoned by the youthful Maccaferri for the call of music. In 1911, several years before Europe would erupt in the War To End All Wars not that far from Maccaferri's home,

For comparison, a much bulkier ca. 1911 Gibson Harp Guitar (courtesy Gravity Strings, St. Louis, MO).

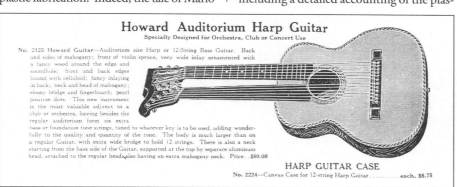

Howard Auditorium Harp Guitar
Specially Designed for Orchestra, Club or Concert Use

No. 2125 Howard Guitar—Auditorium size Harp or 12-String Bass Guitar. Back and sides of mahogany; front of violin spruce, very wide inlay ornamented with a fancy wood around the edge and soundhole; front and back edges bound with celluloid; fancy inlaying in back; neck and head of mahogany; ebony bridge and fingerboard; pearl position dots. This new instrument is the most valuable adjunct to a club or orchestra, having besides the regular auditorium form six extra bass or foundation tone strings, tuned to whatever key is to be used, adding wonderfully to the quality and quantity of the tone. The body is much larger than on a regular Guitar, with extra wide bridge to hold 12 strings. There is also a neck starting from the bass side of the Guitar, supported at the top by separate aluminum head, attached to the regular head, also having an extra mahogany neck. Price..$80.00

HARP GUITAR CASE
No. 2224—Canvas Case for 12-string Harp Guitar...........each, $8.75

A Howard Auditorium Harp Guitar from the 'teens (courtesy Michael Lee Allen).

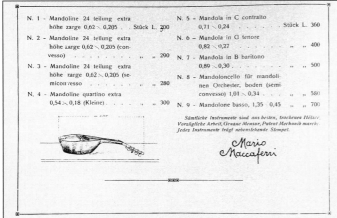

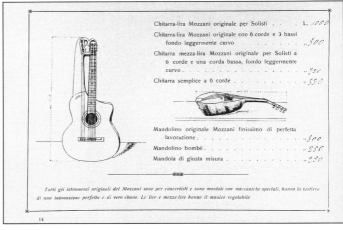

(This page and next page) 1926 Valeriano Rovinazzi catalog including Mozzani and Maccaferri instruments (courtesy Maria Maccaferri).

he was apprenticed to guitarist and luthier Luigi Mozzani, who had established a school of lutherie in Cento.

Luigi Mozzani

To understand the achievements of Mario Maccaferri we have to know at least something about Luigi Mozzani, one of guitardom's unsung heroes, and touch on a nexus of long-standing technical and political issues related to guitars, all of which you directly tap into when you pick up a Maccaferri plastic guitar!

Luigi Mozzani was born in Faenza, Italy, on March 9, 1869. He was drawn to the guitar early on and began studying music under Professor Castelli at the Conservatory of Music in Bologna.

That interest in guitars should occur here was no accident. Bologna was a busy center of guitarmaking and had been the home of another famous Italian guitar virtuoso, Zani De Ferranti (1802-1878), who had resettled

into his birthplace following a successful European career as a classical guitarist. Another name associated with this region of northern Italy is the guitarist and composer Luigi Legnani, who had been born in Ferrara in 1790, and who maintained a long friendship with the great violinist (and guitarist) Nicolo Paganini, touring the Continent and for some time sharing his home in nearby Parma with the fiery fiddler. During his career, Legnani had been associated with Johann Stauffer in Vienna, the legendary luthier who trained C.F. Martin. Legnani died in 1877, after devot-

ing much effort to the problem of guitar construction, in Ravenna, Italy.

Mozzani, following an aborted start as an oboist in a traveling orchestra, which toured North America in the 1890s, switched to classical guitar and began a celebrated concert career. Based in Paris,

Ca. 1920s shot of Mario Maccaferri and another unknown guitarist playing lyre-guitars in duo (courtesy Maria Maccaferri).

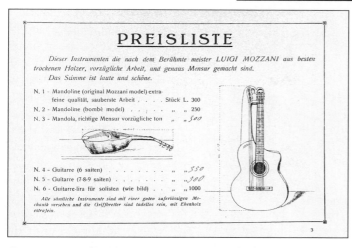

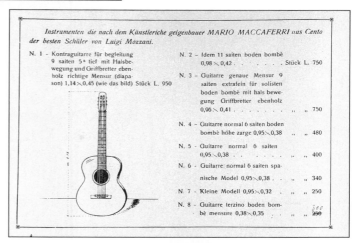

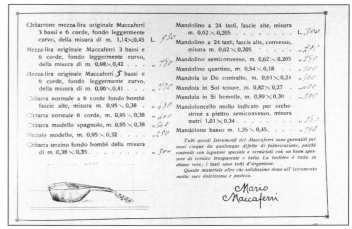

Mozzani concertized throughout Europe and became a much sought-after teacher in fashionable Parisian society. He was a well-published composer, as well.

Like many another guitarist at this time, Mozzani became increasingly dissatisfied with the limitations of then current guitar design, and turned his attention to lutherie. This was an era when classical guitars were often relatively small-bodied, figure-8-shaped "parlour" guitars with simple transverse bracing and bearing gut strings. No way to fill Lincoln Center. This is the situation which the renowned luthier Jose Antonio Torres and others had been addressing in Spain. Eventually, Mozzani moved back to his homeland to study guitar construction, finally establishing lutherie schools in Cento, Bologna and Rovereto in around 1908. Cento was home to other luthiers, including Carlo Carletti and Orsolo Gotti.

Aside from the fact that Mario Maccaferri would become his star pupil, two other issues attach themselves to Mozzani which relate here: playing technique and instrument construction.

Mozzani and the thumbpick

The first is the question of classical guitar technique, which was a hot issue among guitarists desiring to be heard by serious audiences of the day.

Actually, the technical issue in question dated back a century earlier (if not much longer, if truth were ascertainable), and involved *fingernails*. Modern classical guitarists generally play using a technique promoted by Andres Segovia, striking the strings with a combination of carefully shaped fingernails and the flesh of the tips of the fingers. This was not always so.

Sor vs. Aguado

Among the technical debates which engaged the attention of early classical guitarists was whether the guitar should be played with fleshy fingertips or with the fingernails. Advocating the former position was the great Spanish virtuoso/composer Fernando Sor, who participated in a public argument

Ca. 1923 photo of the seven mandolins offered by Mario Maccaferri (courtesy Maria Maccaferri).

(Left) Mario Maccaferri in 1926 playing a lyre-guitar by his teacher Luigi Mozzani (courtesy Maria Maccaferri). (Right) Another view of Mario Maccaferri in 1926 using Eddie Van Halen two-handed technique on a Mozzani lyre-guitar (courtesy Maria Maccaferri).

An ancient tradition

It's tempting to see harp (or lyre) guitars as aberrations of the Industrial Revolution, with its fixation on mechanical excess, but, in fact, they're really descendants of a heritage stretching back at least to the early 1500s, and probably earlier.

The ancestors of the harp guitar date, as far as is known, to the 16th Century and involve the popularity of the guitar's cousin, the lute. At that time, the lute was used in lute ensembles and, increasingly, as a continuo instrument (basically an accompaniment role usually taken by keyboards). Both these contexts required a wider frequency range than was then available on the lute itself, and a class of larger bass lutes called *archlutes* was developed, probably in Northern Italy, which has historically been a primary center of European lutherie. Archlutes had a regular lute fingerboard plus extra free-standing bass strings attached to a second pegbox, usually growing out of the side of the regular head like a Siamese twin. Examples of these archlutes included the theorbo, a five foot long lute with a four course neck and eight

with another famous Spaniard, Dionisio Aguado, who favored use of the nails. (Later in his career Aguado compromised and switched to using a nailless thumb on the bass.) This technical disagreement continued through the 19th and into the early 20th Century, even after Francisco Tarrega solidified modern technique, with Tarrega's pupils Miguel Llobet and Emilio Pujol advocating nails and flesh respectively.

Mozzani's solution to this technical dilemma was novel. He performed — and taught — using fingernails on the fingers and a metal thumbpick, pretty much like those in use today by some bluegrass musicians. This was the technique which Mozzani's student, Mario Maccaferri, would learn. Maccaferri would eventually go on to build his respected European classical concert career using a thumbpick, but we get ahead of ourselves.

Mozzani and the lyre-guitar

The second matter important to the Mozzani/Maccaferri connection involved experiments in guitar construction. Mozzani was a tireless innovator and held many patents, but perhaps he is best re-

membered as an advocate — along with his disciple Maccaferri — of the guitar-lyre or lyre-guitar, a large, often spectacular instrument which combined a standard guitar with an extended bass-side soundboard and a number of extra, non-fretted bass strings extending the bass register downward.

Mozzani was not, of course, the inventor of these strange beasts. Indeed, these guitars are seen in both Europe and the United States in the 19th and early 20th centuries. Perhaps the best known versions of these in the United States were the *harp* guitars made by Gibson, Christopher Knutsen and the Larson Brothers (whose creations were sold under the Dyer brand name and played by folklorist Richard Dyer-Bennet).

Early '30s photo of Mario Maccaferri playing a nine-string lyre-guitar (courtesy Maria Maccaferri).

Ca. 1928-29 catalog of Professor Mario Maccaferri (courtesy Maria Maccaferri).

extra bass strings (15 or 16 strings), the theorbo lute, with an eight course neck and six free bass strings (21 strings in all), and the chitarrone, a six foot long variant on the theorbo lute, some examples of which had steel and brass strings instead of the usual gut.

Archlutes lasted well into the 1700s when the lute fell out of favor, to be replaced by the up-and-coming guitar. Curiously, the bowl-backed lute was absorbed into a rage for *lute guitars* at the end of the 18th Century (basically lutes with guitar necks), while the idea behind the archlutes transmogrified into the concept of harp or lyre guitars. Many of the harp guitars seen from the 1800s were more or less conventional gut-string flattops with Siamese twin headstocks and a second "unfretted" neck which served as a support beam to carry the tension of the extra strings. The famous French composer Camille Saint-Saens, who was also a

fan of guitars and mandolins, played a harp guitar, for example.

The lyre guitars of Mozzani and later Maccaferri (which were developed in around 1916 when Mario Maccaferri was still

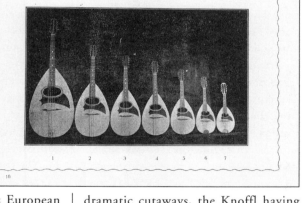

a teenager) fall within this European archlute/harp guitar tradition. Indeed, Mozzani had been studying harp guitars by several other European luthiers when he developed his ideas, including some quite similar to his own designs made by Schenck in Vienna, as well as another version built by a luthier named Raab in Munich. The Schenck harp guitars and another guitar that interested Mozzani by man name Knoffl, also of Vienna, had

dramatic cutaways, the Knoffl having *double* cutaways. Most centers of European guitarmaking had harp guitar traditions by the time of Mozzani.

Like most other harp guitars (inspired by the archlutes before them), Mozzani and Maccaferri lyre guitars feature a conventional six-string guitar neck with (in most cases) the addition of extra, unfretted bass strings below the sixth string, attaching to a separate peghead. However, they

(Left) 1932 photo of Mario Maccaferri playing one of his classicals; note the split saddles (courtesy Maria Maccaferri). (Right) The young artiste: Mario Maccaferri from the late '20s (courtesy Maria Maccaferri).

also have some very distinctive design ideas.

Art Nouveau works of art

The Mozzani/Maccaferri lyre guitars are spectacular instruments with many curious features. They may have been designed for steel strings, like their American counterparts. However, they also have classical-style slotted headstocks (based on Mozzani's design) and were played by Maccaferri, as long as anyone can remember, with either gut or nylon strings.

Except for unusual examples like the six-string shown here, the Mozzani/Maccaferri lyre guitars are basically nine-string guitars, with only three additional sub-bass strings. Recalling their ancient archlute origins, lyre guitars were intended to allow the playing of lute repertoire on a guitar. Few lute pieces require more than nine courses.

The elaborate pin bridges on these guitars illustrate another feature on which Mario Maccaferri would rely for most of his guitarmaking career: an articulated saddle. To compensate for the different string gauges, these were divided into three segments.

The most obviously distinctive feature of the lyre guitar is the spruce soundboard ex-

tension, which usually include dramatically extended upper and lower horns which stretch up to the headstock. These horns include extensions of both soundboard and body. Soundholes involve a variety of interesting patterns (anticipating Ovation by some 60 years) placed between the neck and the bridge. The upper table extension and the odd-shaped soundholes were features found on the Schenck instruments, by the way. As seen here, these "wings" attach to the six-string headstock just above the nut, often then completely surrounding the slotted head.

In addition, these tops are often decorated with Art Nouveau designs, sometimes carved into the wood and colored, sometimes just painted on. The most spectacular of these is the Black Eagle, with the upper horn transformed into a feathered wing.

The bodies of these lyre-guitars consist of either figured maple or burled walnut, carved on the back with an outer curved relief not dissimilar to what is known as the "German carve."

Curious bolt-on necks

But the most interesting technical features of the Mozzani/Maccaferri lyre guitars are

the necks. Several of these guitars had *solid* ebony necks. Their profile was extraordinarily thin for the time, around $^3/_4$" thick at best. Most curious of all, they were *bolted* on. A regular slotted headstock was bolted to the upper horn connection, while the heel was bolted to the body. As a result, the neck was uniformly thin all the way up the scale, for very contemporary easy access.

Furthermore, the heel of the neck was connected with two bolts which attached to the heel block in a small open cavity accessible from the back. Through this cavity the neck-tilt angle — and therefore the action — could be adjusted. Again, the idea of bolting on necks and devising a neck-tilt mechanism went back to the early 19th Century, at least. Even early Martin guitars had adjustable necks which used a clock-key. The solution employed by Mozzani and Maccaferri is reported to have been adapted from some prior German designs.

As on classical guitars, these lyre guitars have nice, wide, fairly flat ebony finger-

Mario Maccaferri with one of his experimental guitars--connected to organ pipes--in Paris during the early '30s (courtesy Maria Maccaferri).

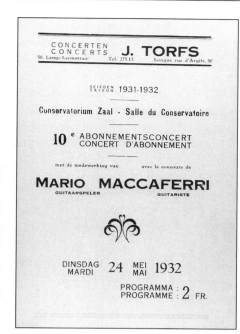

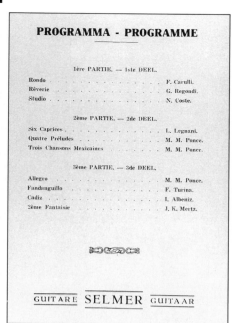

Program from a Maccaferri concert given on May 24, 1932 (courtesy Maria Maccaferri).

boards. They tend to have excellent bass response and well-defined trebles. Despite appearances, they balance remarkably well on the leg and are well-designed for playing.

Some of these lyre guitars were deliberately left unfinished because Maccaferri was interested in getting the pure sound of the

Ca. 1931-32 publicity photo of Chappie D'Amato (nice shoes!) with his new Maccaferri-designed Selmer guitar (courtesy Maria Maccaferri).

wood without the interference of the finish.

Compared to American designs

As mentioned, the Mozzani/Maccaferri lyre guitar had analogs in American guitarmaking, though it's pretty hard to draw much of a conclusion about influences. Lutherie has always been a small world, and there were frequent direct contacts between the U.S. and European makers at least up until World War II. During Mozzani's prime years, for example, Chicago's Lyon & Healey routinely recruited young luthiers from the Italian shops that provided its violins.

Gibson was building harp guitars before Mozzani, however, there is little relationship. Gibson's harp guitars, which appeared as early as the turn of the century, featured carved, arched tops and backs, a Siamese twin headstock, with the second head usually supported by a wooden support bar (and

sometimes a second metal one),and anywhere from nine to thirteen bass strings, with ten, as found on the Style U, being the most common (16 strings total). The Gibson mechanism for supporting the extra bass strings was similar, at least conceptually speaking, to the tack taken by the majority of makers in Europe with a second supporting neck. Generally speaking, Gibson harp guitars were mainly intended for use in mandolin orchestras and other such string bands.

Somewhere in between the Gibson archtop design and the flattop of Knutsen and the Larsons was another curious guitar called the Howard Auditorium Harp Guitar (or 12-String Bass Guitar) from early in the century. This was a large flattop with a spruce top (rope binding and rosette) and mahogany body. It had six normal strings on a regular neck, with slothead and ebony 'board, attaching to a large ebony pyramid-style pin bridge with twelve pins. A second mahogany neck attached to the bass side of the guitar and extended to an "aluminum" head which attached to the regular head. This neck was fretless with an ebony 'board, and carried a second six strings. The second head, by the way, was flat with banjo-style tuners arranged in a "reverse diagonal" pattern from treble to bass.

Another early '30s publicity photo of Al Bowlly and his Maccaferri-designed Selmer guitar, plus a pretty neat microphone (courtesy Maria Maccaferri).

The design reportedly patented by Washington State luthier Chris Knutsen in 1898 featured a flat top with a long arm extension of the guitar body and top stretching from the upper shoulder to a second headstock, which only joined the six-string head with a little bracket. Again, there is no suggestion of any connection with Mozzani.

The Larson Brothers' design was based on Knutsen's idea and featured flat tops and backs (probably slightly "stressed," with a slight curve to the "flat" top obtained by bending, not carving, the method preferred by the Larsons) and either five or six extra bass strings (11-12 strings total), and debuted in around 1912. The Larson harp guitar also featured the long arm extension of the guitar body and top. As mentioned, these guitars were sold as Dyers and often found use in vocal accompaniment.

In a curious aside, Martin built a harp guitar for a New York doctor in 1914. This was based on several examples which the good doctor had obtained from a Turkish guitarist name Dubetz. One of these originals is shown in Mike Longworth's *Martin Guitars: A History* (4 Maples Press, Inc., 1988), and it appears to be a Mozzani! The Martin "copy" was not an exact one, apparently, but featured a number of differences specified by the purchaser. In this one unusual case we can document a direct influence from Mozzani to Martin!

Swan song

Not long after the Mozzani-Maccaferri lyre-guitars were built, Mario Maccaferri would strike out on his own, frequently performing on the lyre guitar. The exposure his concertizing afforded these guitars was to no avail. Demand for harp and lyre guitars, never blistering hot, had pretty much cooled down by the 1920s, and Mario's advocacy was pretty much a voice crying in the wilderness. Today, guitar players who feel the need for additional string courses usually play seven-string guitars or, if you're Narcisco Yepes, ten-string monsters. Harp guitars are still being made today by individual luthiers, however, contemporary market for these strange birds has more to do with collecting than performance. In any case, the beautiful Art Nouveau lyre-guitars by Luigi Mozzani and Mario Maccaferri stand as some of the most elegant examples of this ancient and noble breed.

A Selmer Modèle Hawaienne from circa 1932-33, complete with internal resonator, pickguard added (courtesy Vintage Instruments, Philadelphia,

Following a long and fruitful career which yielded many patents for the ingenious guitarist and luthier, Luigi Mozzani passed away in 1943.

This probably feels like a meandering picaresque novel by now, but this rather lengthy diversion sets the stage and brings us back again to the main narrative of Mario Maccaferri.

Mozzani and Maccaferri

Young 11-year-old Mario Maccaferri joined Mozzani's school in 1911 as an apprentice and rose to become Mozzani's premier disciple, learning to make guitars, violins and mandolins and eventually supervising other apprentices. Accounts differ about Maccaferri's tenure with Mozzani. Although he was listed as "Senior Instructor" for Mozzani from 1920 to 1928, confirming a continued relationship as a technical advisor, Maccaferri actually struck out on his own in around 1923. And indeed, Maccaferri advertised himself as a maker of all fretted instruments after 1923, offering nine different guitar

Another 1930s photo of Chappie D'Amato playing a Maccaferri-designed Selmer guitar (courtesy Maria Maccaferri).

models, seven various mandolins, as well as violins and cellos.

A telling comparison between the work of Maccaferri and his master, Mozzani, can be seen in a 1926 catalog from Valeriano Rovinazzi of Bologna, who specialized in high-quality guitars, including those of Mozzani and Maccaferri, as well as those by other luthiers including Dall'Osso Umberto of Bologna (who had studied with the Fornasari brothers of Bologna) and Balboni (a student of Mozzani).

Perhaps the most obvious difference is in the side-by-side photographs of Mozzani and his disciple. Both are pictured with their lyre-guitars. Mozzani's has double neck/soundboards on either side of the regular neck, a symmetrical homage to Art Nouveau. Maccaferri's interpretation is much cleaner, more modern, with a single, understated neck (painted black to minimalize it's visual impact), clearly pointing toward the future.

Six Mozzani instruments were offered. No. 1 was a mandolin, "original Mozzani model," No. 2 a mandolin, No. 3 a mandola, No. 4 a six-string guitar, No. 5 a guitar with seven, eight or nine strings, and No. 6 a lyre-guitar with a single extra neck and a cutaway, very like Maccaferri's own of a few years later. Mozzani is reported to have been making cutaways as early as

1908, so there's little doubt where this feature came from. Also like Maccaferri's later instruments, Mozzani's mandolins had flat backs. These were actually more like bowl-backs with the back round part cut off and flattened out rather than like the better known Venetian-style mando.

Eight Maccaferri instruments were listed. No. 1 was a Contraguitar with nine strings, No. 2 was similar with eleven strings, No. 3 was a nine-string guitar, No. 4 was a regular six-string with a cutaway, No. 5 was a regular six-string, No. 6 was a six-string Spanish model, No. 7 was a small-bodied guitar, and No. 8 was a terz guitar. The artwork illustrates one of Maccaferri's regular six-strings, which has a 20-fret neck and the typical Maccaferri tapered slotted headstock. While no other descriptions or illustrations are available, these are no doubt very similar to those which appeared a few years later in Maccaferri's own catalog.

The 1929 line

A later snapshot of Maccaferri's creations after he had established himself more independently can be seen in a Professor Mario Maccaferri catalog of "Premiata Liuteria" from around 1928-29 when Maccaferri was in Cento, Italy. Showing a picture of Mario with a lyre-guitar and touting

The finishing cabinet at the Selmer factory ca. 1932 surrounded by Maccaferri-designed guitars (courtesy Maria Maccaferri).

his prizes, this advertised his offerings of guitars, mandolins, mandolas, violins, violas and violincellos. Among the technical features discussed were his methods for forming mandolin backs, his compensated bridge saddles, the construction of the headstocks on his lyre-guitars, and his already trademark deep horizontal guitar cutaway for greater fingerboard access.

Maccaferri's ca. '28-29 catalog featured four lyre-guitars and four Spanish guitar models.

Of the lyre-guitars, Model No. 1 Chitarrone was the largest, a nine-string with a jumbo body, a wide, almost squarish lower bout, a round soundhole and the deep cutaway. This had the regular six-string neck with slotted headstock and the second neck/soundboard extension for an additional three strings. Models No. 2 Chitarra and No. 3 Chitarra were virtually the same, with slightly smaller bodies, except for having either nine or eleven strings, respectively. Model No. 5 Chitarra was a nine-string non-cutaway version, curiously enough, with no extra neck/soundboard extension. Instead, this simply had the Siamese twin headstock and free-standing strings which sort of hung in the air above the regular fingerboard. All had 20 frets, with the cutaway joining the neck at the 17th fret.

Of the Spanish guitars, Model No. 5 was a regular guitar with the single cutaway,

A 1930s publicity photo for Gino Bordin and his Le trio Havaien, with Stefano Giovanni on archtop, Bordin on what appears to be a Vega lap steel, and Vincenzo De L on a Selmer guitar (courtesy Maria Maccaferri).

Mario Maccaferri with a broken hand in 1933 (courtesy Maria Maccaferri).

similar to the Models No. 2 and 3. It did not, of course, have the extra strings, neck or bridge. This had a pin bridge. The Model No. 6 was a standard non-cutaway version of the Model No. 5 lyre-guitar, with typical classical shape and dimensions. Model No. 7 was a much narrower guitar, with both bouts thinner and almost rectangular, more like a parlour guitar. Model No. 8 was a terz guitar which returned to the typical classical shape but with much smaller body dimensions. All had tapered slotted headstocks which would characterize most of Maccaferri's acoustics.

Maccaferri's mandolin/mandola line consisted of the seven eight-string (four course) models, Nos. 1-7, going from a huge No. 1 to a mini No. 7. No. 1 was the Mandolone, No. 2 the Mandoloncello, No. 3 the Mandola baritono, No. 4 the Mandola tenore, No. 5 the Mandola soprano, No. 6 the Mandolino (available in two tunings), and No. 7 the Quartino. They were virtually identical in appointments, with slotted heads and a natty sort of quarter-moon pickguard, and presumably one or the other of Mario's flat or slightly arched backs, direct descendants of Mozzani's designs. Interestingly, Maccaferri provided the actual tuning of each of these instruments at the back of his catalog.

Gold Medals

Clearly Maccaferri had learned his craft well, because in 1926 he won gold medals for his violins at both the Esposizione Internazionales in Rome and Montecatini, another gold medal at the Fiume exposition of 1927, and 2nd place and honorable mention in violin making at the 1927 Concorso Nazionale di Liuteria, indetto dalla R. Filamonica Romana, in Rome. A promising career as a luthier loomed, but that was not the only path Mario was pursuing.

Professor of Guitar and Music

While Maccaferri studied lutherie at Mozzani's school, he also applied himself to learning classical guitar performance, and it was as a concertizing guitarist in the long northern Italian tradition that he intended to build his career.

Actually, Mario was pressed into service as a musician, as he related in an interview conducted by George Clinton for England's *Guitar Magazine* (January 1976). There Maccaferri describes being "chosen" at age 12 by Mozzani — himself a composer and reportedly talented performer *in private* — to take guitar lessons and, spending a year in the first position, hating every minute of it. Finally, Mozzani began to show the youngster chords, and Maccaferri was converted. According to Maccaferri, by the way, Mozzani did not attempt to proselitise Maccaferri to the use of a thumbpick, but Mario simply saw his master do it and fol-

A ca. 1933-34 Selmer Modèle Jazz (photo: Stan Jay, Mandolin Brothers, Staten Island, NY).

lowed suit. It was this use of a thumbpick which allowed Maccaferri to keep his thumb parallel to the strings (as opposed to diving into them with the thumbnail) and he was apparently able to develop a remarkably facile tremolo technique. Mario himself described it as being *a-m-i-a-m-i-p*, with the thumb remaining independent of the fingers, unlike, for example, Segovia's version, which employed the more common moves, *p-a-m-i-p-a-m-i*.

In 1916 Mario Maccaferri began studying music at the Conservatory of Music in Sienna. Maccaferri began to build his reputation as a performer by giving recitals from 1920 — some reports say as early as 1919 — until 1923, while he was still with Mozzani. Mario has stated that he didn't view these early performances as laying a foundation for a professional touring career. Indeed, he was (as many other personalities associated with guitars would be; cf. Wandre Pioli and Paul Bigsby), more interested in motorcycles.

The turning point came in 1926. In that year Maccaferri was named "Professor of Guitar and Music" from the Conservatory in Sienna and saw the young up-and-coming virtuoso Andres Segovia in Milan. Segovia's performance inspired a competitive reaction in the

Mario Maccaferri as the Unknown Guitarist during a mid-'30s French cabaret performance (courtesy Maria Maccaferri).

Beginnings of the form

A rare chance to see Mario Maccaferri's early lutherie — a preview of his later, better known Selmer guitars — is afforded by the example shown here of a 1925 Maccaferri Model No. 4. The label says Mario Maccaferri, Cento, and is signed by Maccaferri and presented to Professor Enzo. This had a jumbo-sized body with a wide lower bout and the trademark almost horizontal cutaway. The two-piece walnut neck had a very flat heel and a center-peaked slotted headstock. The back was made of walnut and featured an arch which was almost like a "German carve," but not so pronounced. The heel came down flush to the back and the back was cut with a little extension which covered the bottom of the heel like a cap.

The fingerboard was 21 frets in ebony with dots. The upper registers extended over the soundhole, the 21st fret being a short one for just the first two strings. A rough feature is that the slot for the 21st fret was actually cut into a little piece of 'board under the sixth string, but had no fretwire. The top of this guitar was spruce, the round soundhole inlaid with a multi-striped rosette. The bridge was a wide ebony affair which sat on two feet and was adjustable. A small pickguard sat under the strings and was inlaid with an elaborate lyre and floral design. The tailpiece was a bent metal trapeze as found on later Maccaferris.

1925 Maccaferri Model No. 4 (courtesy Jacques Mazzoleni, Guitar Network, White Hall, MD).

young Maccaferri, who felt he could play everything Segovia had in the concert. The following day he visited a concert promoter, who, of course, didn't know Mario from Adam. However, Mario was confident and the promoter asked for references. Mario gave him some names of people from the Conservatory of Bologna and a music critic Mario knew. The promoter checked the references and three months later Mario Maccaferri was playing the same Milanese hall Andres Segovia had played. Maccaferri's program included Sor's "Sonata No. 22 in C," some selections by Napoleon Coste, Mozzani, Granados, Bach's "Prelude, Gavotte and Courante," Tarrega's "Capricho Arabe," Chopin's "Nocturne No. 9," and Mertz's "Fantasia No. 3." The critics were quite flattering, except for one who lambasted the Chopin transcription, and a fellow name Mussolini who thought the packed house contained too many "peasants."

Within the year Mario had begun touring throughout Europe, performing as "Professor Maccaferri."

Maccaferri in London

Early on in Maccaferri's performing career he was fortunate enough to be introduced to Arturo Toscanini at La Scala. Mario played for him and Toscanini was impressed, and gave the young guitarist some valuable tips which Mario incorporated into his performances.

It was during this period that Maccaferri met and became friends with Andres Segovia. Indeed, the first meeting was with his mentor Luigi Mozzani. Maccaferri recalled not being very impressed with Segovia's guitar, a Ramirez. However, the two guitarists became quite friendly thereafter.

During these early days of the century, Maccaferri was regarded by contemporaries as being on a par with the late Segovia, ranking right behind the Maestro in popular appeal in European guitar circles. Had

English guitarist Louis Gallo, with a Maccaferri classical guitar (courtesy Maria Maccaferri).

events not transpired as they did, we might today regard the two as seminal influences on modern classical guitar, but history, for bettor or worse, had other things in mind.

A glimpse of the kind of music Mario played can be had from a program for a concert he performed on May 24, 1932. The concert was divided into three sets. The first consisted of "Rondo" by Fernando Carulli, "Reverie" by Regondi and "Studio" by Napoleon Coste. The second part consisted of "Six Caprices" by Luigi Legnani, "Quatro Preludes" by Manuel Maria Ponce, and "Trois Chansons Mexicaines" by Ponce. The finale included "Allegro," again by Ponce, "Fandanquillo" by Frederico Turina, "Cadiz" by Isaac Albeniz, and "2eme Fantasie" by J.K. Mertz. This is a carefully paced program that includes serious repertoire and some of the very latest compositions of the time. This is not the program of a dilettante!

A record

At some point during this period Mario recorded and released some recordings. How many discs were recorded and released is unknown, but we have at least one example released by the Columbia

Gramaphone Co. Ltd. of London. Otherwise known as the famous Columbia record company. These two sides were "Fabriqe en France pur Couesnon & Co., Paris," which suggests that Mario probably laid these down while in Paris. The A side was devoted to Maccaferri's mentor Luigi Mozzani, featuring his "Aria Con Variazioni" [(L 1496) D 19186], backed with "Le Régiment Qui Passe" by Sconosiuto [(L 1499) D 19186].

Relocation

One of Professor Maccaferri's concert tour stops was in London, where he performed at prestigious Wigmore Hall. Like so many classical guitarists before him, he found London a receptive home, and decided to settle there, performing and teaching guitar.

During this period, Maccaferri performed on a variety of instruments, often built by himself. Among the instruments Maccaferri played were his nine-string lyre-guitars. At least one of these guitars had seven strings on the neck, with two additional bass strings, however, this proved difficult to adjust to, and Mario went back to the more common six and three combination. One of his treasured pieces was the Sor's beautiful "Mozart Variations." His performances were reportedly infused with his strong, romantic personality.

It was also during this period in London that Maccaferri began to work out some new ideas about guitars and build prototypes,

some of which would eventually become legends in guitardom, and mark a portentous change of direction for the still young Maccaferri.

A free-standing guitar

One of Maccaferri's novel ideas was not exactly new, but curious enough to relate. Maccaferri is reported to have once told Segovia that he found playing classical guitar rather undignified and that a classical

(French stamp) 1993 French stamp commemorating Belgian gypsy jazz guitarist Django Reinhardt known for playing Selmer guitars, though mostly the post-Maccaferri design (courtesy Michael Lee Allen).

guitarist looks "like a monkey scratching his belly," an amusingly accurate observation! It was Mario's idea that a guitarist ought to be able to stand up in front of an orchestra as a soloist. To that end, in 1931 he invented a free-standing guitar. Resting on a stand, the guitarist was free to play standing up. In the interest of increased

Mario Maccaferri ca. 1949-50 at the publicity event announcing his new plastic uke (courtesy Maria Maccaferri).

sound, this instrument was a resonator guitar. It had a floating membrane soundboard mounted on an L-shaped body which ended in a bunch of different-sized resonator tubes. Whether or not this guitar ever made it to performance is unknown, but it does seem to be a long way around to a guitar strap!

Curiously enough, the guitarist Dionisio Aguado had invented a stand to hold a guitar almost a century earlier, though without the resonators.

Another of Mario's experiments included a lyre-guitar with seven strings on the fingerboard and an additional five unfretted bass strings. However, Maccaferri will be most remembered for his work with six-string guitars during this period of his life.

The sound chamber

Clearly, Mario — like almost every other progressive luthier at the time — was thinking hard about increasing the sound volume of the guitar. This experimentation led to the development for which Maccaferri's wooden guitars are best known: the internal sound chamber. While most folks refer to this device as a "sound chamber," Maccaferri's patents called it an "internal resonator."

Basically, Mario's idea was to isolate the vibrating back of the guitar's sound chamber from the damping effects of the "monkey's belly," as the guitarist clutched the instrument to the abdomen. To address this, Maccaferri built a separate sound chamber inside the guitar body, which attached to the top along the edges. A reflector plate was mounted diagonally above the soundhole to project the resulting sound outward.

Selmer & Cie

Through his contacts in London's music world Maccaferri was introduced to Ben Davis, the director of the London office of Selmer & Cie. Davis and his brother ran the Selmer franchise in England, and reportedly were interested in capitalizing on the popularity of Eddie Freeman, a jazz guitarist who played a plectrum guitar. Selmer, at the time, was primarily a maker of wind

instruments built in France. The Davis brothers and Maccaferri talked about Maccaferri's guitarmaking ideas, and talked Selmer into undertaking the making of guitars. It was through this connection that, in 1931, Selmer asked the "Professor" to design a line of guitars for it, which Maccaferri proceeded to do.

Basically, Selmer authorized Maccaferri to do what was necessary to set up a guitar operation, which he did in a remarkably short period of time. A part of the challenge was to develop not only classicals, Mario's first love, but also steel-stringed guitars.

Reportedly Maccaferri set about researching steel-stringed guitars, exploring jazz, which was not to his taste. Nevertheless, Maccaferri adapted his classical designs to steel strings.

Maccaferri's official relationship with Selmer was actually relatively brief, lasting approximately from 1931 to 1933. Dur-

Mario Maccaferri playing one of the Mozzani/Maccaferri lyre-guitars in the 1950s (courtesy Maria Maccaferri).

Label for Maccaferri Reeds from French American Reeds Manufacturing Company during its Broadway tenure (courtesy Michael Lee Allen).

ing that time, Maccaferri exhibited his genius as an equipment designer, personally designing and building the jigs, fixtures and machines needed to produce his guitar designs at the Selmer facility in Mante La Ville, a Parisian suburb. Maccaferri then proceeded to build the first prototypes. Once the specifications for the guitar line

were established, Mario hired the craftsmen to build his Selmer guitars.

New ideas

The guitars Maccaferri designed for Selmer were based on his experience with Mozzani and the designs he'd worked on in London, including the internal sound chamber (which Maccaferri patented) and several other innovations. Among these new ideas were the first sealed, lubricated, self-contained tuning gears, a concept which is now commonplace on almost all new guitars, although self-contained tuner units had been an idea evolving from the 19th century, at least.

The cutaway on these guitars was a dramatic right-angle rounded cut on the treble side, an idea derived from his work with Mozzani. Another feature included a slotted headstock, a design also derived from Mozzani. Like most guitars of the era, the neck joined the body at the 12th fret. Fingerboards were dot-inlaid and featured zero frets. Fingerboards had a small extension over the soundhole to give the

Mario Maccaferri in his office circa late '40s (courtesy Maria Maccaferri).

treble string a two-octave range. All of these had multiple-bound solid spruce tops which were technically "flat," but which were glued down over slightly curved braces, making them slightly curved, similar to the stressed tops on Larson Brothers guitars. Most came with rosewood laminate bodies, with only a few, including at least one harp-guitar, having solid mahogany bodies. Some time after Maccaferri left off his association with Selmer a number of these guitars are reported to have been built with American birdseye maple bodies.

Maccaferri's unique internal sound chamber was standard, and was tied to a large "D"-shaped soundhole with wide marquetry rosettes. The internal sound chamber turned out to be a commercial failure, especially on the steel-stringed guitars, which marked the wave of the future. Many owners disassembled the sound chamber, which apparently did not stand up well to the stresses of steel strings. Even though the chamber was supposed to be standard, quite a number of examples are seen without this feature.

The first production Maccaferri-designed Selmer guitars appeared in 1932. In 1933, once production was self-sufficient, Maccaferri left the Selmer operation and returned to his concert career, a move that, according to later accounts, had been mutually agreed upon by both parties, although, as we shall see, another event in-

tervened to hasten the departure.

The Selmer/Maccaferri guitars

Basically, there were six different Selmer guitar models, which Selmer touted in its catalog as being by Mario Maccaferri, a man who, said the copy, displayed "astonishing adaptability, both as a performer and designer of guitars." The Maccaferri-designed Selmer guitar line consisted of the Modèle Espagnol, Modèle Concert, Modèle Orchestre, Modèle Jazz, Modèle Hawaienne, and a plectrum called the Guitare Eddie Freeman.

The **Espagnol** or Spanish model was a small-bodied gut-string flattop with a classical-style bridge and a round soundhole. Notable about this design was a split two-piece saddle, a feature typical of both Mozzani and Maccaferri guitars, which offered improved intonation between treble and bass strings.

The **Concert** had a bigger body more often associated with Maccaferri and Gypsy jazz guitar legend Django Reinhardt (more on that subject soon). This had a flat top, single cutaway and the "D" soundhole. It too had a classical-style glued-on bridge (split saddles) and was intended for gut strings.

The **Orchestre** was a single cutaway steel string guitar which came with either a round or a D soundhole. This model name was often applied to custom made instruments. Early versions of this guitar had a floating bridge which made contact with the top all along the bottom, though later examples had a bridge with two feet and an open center, similar to other designs of the times. All Orchestres had a special tail-

(Left) A dapper Mario Maccaferri from about the time of the plastic guitars (photo: King Studios, N.Y.C.; courtesy Maria Maccaferri). (Right) Mario Maccaferri at his drafting table circa late '40s (courtesy Maria Maccaferri).

piece (which would come to signify later Maccaferri guitars).

The **Jazz** was another Maccaferri body with a cutaway designed for steel strings. It had the typical D soundhole and a floating bridge centered between two "mustaches."

The **Hawaienne** was basically the Jazz outfitted with a bigger neck and raised nut for steel playing. This was typically non-cutaway. A seven-string version was optional.

The **Eddie Freeman** guitar was a four-string plectrum built for an American-born jazzman by that name popular in England and one of the indirect inspirations for Selmer guitars. Freeman, a former banjo player in jazz big bands, like many of his contemporaries switched over to four-string plectrum guitars once the guitar began to supplant the banjar in popularity. This was designed for a plectrum tuning, (low to high) C, G, B, D, not the usual upper four strings of a guitar as on tenor guitars. The body was full-size, not the smaller body seen on later Selmer tenor guitars. This was intended to give the guitar more cut-through in the rhythm section. Most of these were sold to the London distributor who started

the Maccaferri ball rolling. Not long after the Freeman model was introduced, the taste in music changed again, and many of these were later converted to six-string guitars, with widened necks and fingerboards.

Selmer also produced some smaller-bodied tenor guitars, with the upper four strings of a six-string guitar.

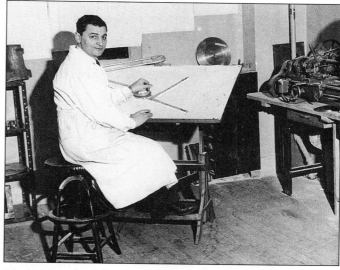

Mario Maccaferri's "work station" circa late '40s (courtesy Maria Maccaferri).

Rare birds

Production of the Maccaferri-designed Selmers began in 1932 and lasted until around 1934, at the latest, by which time at least 335 genuine Maccaferri-designed guitars had been built. These guitars all had headstock logos including both the Selmer and Maccaferri names and bore labels reading "Fabriqué en France sous la direction technique de M. Maccaferri, Selmer & Cie, Paris." The majority of these Maccaferris were steel stringed guitars, rather than the classicals which were his true love. Apparently the Jazz, as *described*, was relatively rare, though a fair number of guitars matching both the Orchestre and Freeman descriptions were actually labelled as being "jazz" models.

A word on the internal sound chamber. A good number of guitars were equipped with them. Those who have played good examples of these guitars report that they were clear, crisp, well balanced and loud. They were also not significantly superior to guitars without them. In addition, the sound chambers frequently came loose from the anchorages to the body, and began to rattle

and buzz, causing many owners to have them removed.

Separation

For better or worse, Maccaferri's relationship with Selmer ended in a dispute regarding their contractual agreement, although some have suggested that the commercial failure of Mario's internal resonator may have been a contributing factor. Reasons for the disagreement reflect Mario Maccaferri's temperamental personality and his strong sense of moral rectitude. There are, by the way, a number of speculative accounts of this story in print, but this is the version related by Mario himself, as told by his wife Maria.

One evening at Maccaferri's apartment in 1933, shortly after the intense activity of setting up the Selmer guitar factory was through, Mario decided to read the contract he'd signed, like most folks, without reading the fine print. There in the little type at the bottom was a zinger. According to the contract, Selmer could terminate Mario without cause or notice. This was a moral offense not to be brooked.

The following day Maccaferri went in to see Henri Selmer and confronted him with the termination clause. As Mario used to relate the event, he pointed to the clause and told Selmer "You won't have to do that, because I'm leaving now."

With a look of apprehension in his eyes,

Mario Maccaferri and a pair of stewardesses on their way to donate plastic ukes to the Boy's Town of Italy (photo: Al Hauser; courtesy Maria Maccaferri).

An early '50s publicity still with Mario, Les Paul and Mary Ford (courtesy Maurice J. Summerfield).

Mr. Selmer put his hand on Mario's shoulder and asked, "What are you going to do now?" Beneath this ominous question was the fear that Maccaferri was going to set up a competing guitar manufacturing operation.

Asked Selmer with some trepidation: "Are you going to make guitars?"

Mario thought for a moment. Then he looked Selmer in the eye and replied: "No, I'm going to make *reeds*, because I have a new idea about that, too!" Reed-making was another major Selmer business endeavor.

And that's just what Mario set about to do.

In the meantime, Maccaferri resumed his concertizing.

The oval soundhole

By 1934, with Mario departing, the Selmer Paris factory had made major alterations to the popular Jazz design. By that time the 12-fret guitars had acquired an oval soundhole (no trace of the internal resonator). It's possible that the oval soundhole design was adopted to differentiate Selmers from the Maccaferri design. The earlier Maccaferri D design was intended to augment the effect of the internal resonator. Maccaferri himself always believed the oval soundhole was changed to accommodate a new electric pickup, which would not fit the D soundhole, although the pickup in question was not probably related to Selmer. The pickups in question were actually developed by Stimer in around 1950, and were heartily endorsed by Django Reinhardt, inspiring some folks to install them, and accounting for examples of the oval soundhole found with screw holes. The Stimers actually were designed to attach with non-invasive clips, but some were screwed on.

Shortly thereafter the neck was changed to a 14-fret design, which necessitated changes in the bracing to accommodate a different bridge placement. This design was fairly long in coming, since American guitarmakers had — with the help of Italian immigrant luthiers — already discovered the idea years before.

Production of Selmer guitars continued more or less until the company's closure in 1952 (minus the World War II years, of course). According to factory logs, only between 996 and 998 guitars were ever produced. Django Reinhardt always endorsed all Selmer guitars. For a little extra fee, some featured gold-leafed "Mod. Django Reinhardt" on the headstock, but this was a financial consideration, not necessarily proof of Django's endorsement.

Django Reinhardt

Which brings us to the subject of Django Reinhardt. According to modern guitar legend, Mario Maccaferri was "Django's guitar designer." In fact, this is only tangentially the case. Maccaferri actually never met Django, and, indeed, as a classical guitarist, was not familiar with the great jazzman's music. Selmer guitars, with their excellent construction and sound, however, were Django's main choice of guitar during the '30s, and his first one happened to be a D-hole Maccaferri, *sans* sound chamber, by the way. When the Jazz model was redesigned, Django changed to this new guitar and owned four for the rest of his career, including one which he considered his main axe. Thus, it is stretching the point to argue too strong a connection between Mario and Django.

Mario Maccaferri getting down with popular guitarist Harry Volpe at the introduction of the plastic guitars (courtesy Maria Maccaferri).

A publicity shot of Mario Maccaferri with his new plastic guitar and an unknown model in 1953 (photo: Bruno of Hollywood, NYC; courtesy Maria Maccaferri). (Right) Maccaferri, Volpe and Rey De La Torre at the introduction of the plastic guitar (courtesy Maria Maccaferri).

The movies and the accident

As mentioned, upon leaving the company of Selmer in 1933, Mario Maccaferri resumed his successful concert career, venturing upon a tour that took him to Berlin, Hamburg, Cologne, Brussels, Antwerp, London and Paris.

It was after this final tour as the classical Professor that Maccaferri in Paris and his

Mario Maccaferri playing his new creation, the G-30 plastic guitar, in the early '50s (courtesy Maria Maccaferri).

life took a dramatic, unexpected turn.

Back in Paris, in what would prove to be a history-changing event, Mario Maccaferri was offered a bit part in a movie, "La Fille du Lak," starring Simone Simone. Mario's role involved playing guitar in a canoe scene. Filming was done in July of 1933 and it was hot. The cast took a break and went swimming at the swimming pool at the Pathe Nathan Studio in Joinville. While diving into the water, the "break" turned into a real one. Mario collided with one of the other swimmers and fractured his right hand, so vital to classical technique.

Alas, the break never healed properly, and essentially, Maccaferri's career as a concert classical guitarist (and movie star) was ended.

Fortunately for Maccaferri and the world, the guitarist and luthier had plenty other cards up his sleeve which would inform the direction of the remainder of his career.

The Unknown Guitarist

Maccaferri's unfortunate hand

accident didn't actually end his performing days, just his public classical playing. The hand injury meant that he couldn't play his classical repertoire up to the standards to which he was accustomed. Mario did, however, continue to play popular music gigs in Parisian cafes. But, because he felt his playing was not up to his former glory, Maccaferri performed wearing a mask and billed himself as "The Unknown Guitarist."

Maccaferri had not neglected his pledge about making reeds, however.

A wife and business partner

It was during this period of the late '30s in Paris that Mario met his future wife Maria Centuori. Maria had been born in Foggio, Italy, in 1920 and as a young girl had moved to Paris, where she was raised and went to school. Mario and Maria met in Paris, fell in love, and were married in 1937, when Maria was 16 years old. Maria would stay with Mario throughout the rest of his life, contributing to his success in a dual role as the proverbial devoted wife and as a shrewd partner who helped run the hands-on day-to-day operations of the Maccaferri businesses. At the time of this writing, Maria Maccaferri continues to

Hubba, hubba! Another unknown model showing off the curves of the new Maccaferri plastic guitar (courtesy Maria Maccaferri).

operate the French American Reeds Company, which the two of them established while in Paris.

French American Reeds

During his brief association with Selmer, Maccaferri had had the opportunity to observe the reed manufacturing process, which involved cutting the raw cane with metal cutters. He also had observed many a wind instrument player struggling with warped reeds. Maccaferri had a better idea about how to improve both these circumstances.

Maccaferri got the idea that he could cut reeds using diamonds instead of metal and cut them in such a way as to counteract warping. He was acquainted with a jeweller named Pierre Rosier whom he consulted regarding making the diamond cutters. He then designed and built a clever machine which cut and trimmed the reed blanks using two simple hand motions. The result was the warp-resistant Isovibrant reed, a superior design for which he received a patent.

In 1939, Mario and Maria Maccaferri set up the French American Reeds Manufacturing Company in Paris, began compet-

ing with Selmer in Europe, and exporting reeds to the U.S. (where they were distributed by Broadus). While Mario handled design and marketing, his young wife Maria took over managing production and the business side of things.

America

Maccaferri's reed success soon caught the attention of the American outfit Gratz and Company, which approached him about becoming a partner. To that end Gratz brought the Maccaferris to New York. It was 1939, time of the New York World's Fair.

Maria Maccaferri remembers this introduction to New York vividly. The representative of Gratz installed the Maccaferris, with their new baby daughter, in a seedy hotel on Third Avenue. The first night, the baby was disturbed, and when Maria turned on the light, she saw bugs in bed with her young daughter. She proceeded to close up their luggage and took her baby out into the hallway where they spent the night in a chair. The next day they relocated to a decent hotel.

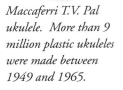

Maccaferri T.V. Pal ukulele. More than 9 million plastic ukuleles were made between 1949 and 1965.

The bed bugs were an inauspicious sign. The Gratz offer, as it turned out was a 51-49% deal. Maccaferri, who'd quit Selmer just because of an unexercised contract clause, asked if they thought he was stupid. It was *his* machinery and his reeds. The deal was off.

But Maccaferri did get to see the New York World's Fair, and that got him interested in a new material: plastic. Indeed, he quickly became convinced that this miracle substance would be the future of America. He was, of course, prophetically correct. It was this experience that inspired him to develop a cane reed impregnated with plastic, further stabilizing the device. Plastic would soon play a huge role in Mario Maccaferri's life.

However, world events were soon intervene, offering yet another opportunity for Maccaferri to demonstrate his "adaptability."

Escape

In 1939, Europe was staring down the barrel of world conflagration in the face of the Nazi Blitzkrieg. In particular, the bead had been taken on France, but a political agreement created a brief sense of false security. Leaving his wife and daughter in the safety of America, Maccaferri took advantage of the lull and returned to Paris to check on the reed busi-

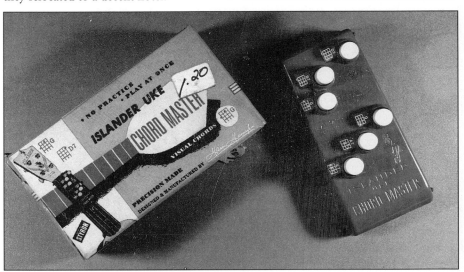

Maccaferri Chord Master, a groovy little device which attached to a uke with rubber bands and allowed playing chords by pushing buttons (courtesy Music City, Newark, NJ).

ness. Fearing what might be coming, Maccaferri packed up two reed-cutting and two shaping machines and shipped them off to New York.

That's when a call from an old friend in the Foreign Office came, advising him that the truce was off and to leave post haste. The Germans were about to take Paris. Departure might already be impossible. Maccaferri beat it to the docks only to find the harbor blockaded by German warships and the last ship allowed to leave, the *Ile de France*, loading passengers, with no more tickets available.

The story of Maccaferri's escape from France has been often related, but here is a direct account by Maccaferri relayed to Michael Dresdner in a 1982 story.

"I went down to the French Line, which was in the same building as the Embassies, and saw a line of people circling more than two blocks. 'What am I going to do,' I thought? At that time, I was wearing glasses — I didn't need them, but I thought they looked good — and sported a small mustache, a dark suit and a Homburg [hat]. I knew I had to get in there, so I went to a place where they rented limos, hired one, and gave the chauffeur a $20 tip in advance. I told him, 'Take me to the French Line. Drive right up to the entrance, get out of the car, open the door for me and salute me.' When I got out carrying my briefcase, the two guards rushed over and saluted me, and I walked right inside.

"The room was empty, just columns and a skylight, and I thought: 'What the hell am I going to do now?' So I stood by one of the columns as if I were waiting for someone and watched as one man passed by a few times, going from one office to another. So I called him over. I had $10,000 in my pocket. I said to him, 'I'll give you ten thousand dollars if you get me on that god-damned boat. I'm going to stay right here, so make up your mind.'

"Anyhow, I got on the boat. When I got here [to New York], the Customs agent asked me if I had any money. I told him, 'Yes, I have three dollars in my pocket.' He said, 'What do you think you are going to do with only three dollars?' I said, 'I'm going to see my wife and baby, and then I'll think about it.'"

Back in New York, of course, Maria Maccaferri was worried to death about her husband's safety. She was, of course, totally unaware of Mario's adventure in progress. However, once the *Ile de France*

A collection of Maccaferri plastic instruments: G40 guitar, Roco guitar, Islander uke, Sparkle Plenty Ukette, T.V.Pal uke, ShowTime guitar, G30 guitar (photo: Ron Caimi).

reached American-controlled waters and radio silence could be broken, Mario sent Maria a telegram announcing simply: "I'll be home tomorrow." You can imagine her excitement! She grabbed the baby, squeezing her and dancing around their apartment for joy.

The Bronx

Maccaferri's first thought upon returning to America was to visit a friend who made French Horns. In typical fashion, Mario observed the manufacturing process and devised some ways to improve the quality of the products while decreasing the cost of production. Maccaferri stayed with his friend's business for a few months, whereupon he struck out on his own again. Taking the reed machines he'd had the foresight to send ahead of him from France, Maccaferri opened up his first factory at 1658 Broadway in New York in December of 1939 and the French American Reeds Manufacturing Company resumed making reeds. After some time at this site, French American Reeds rented space in the Roseland Building on 50th Street in the Bronx, eventually buying the building and expanding at that location, where it spent close to four decades. In the late '80s the city was interested in purchasing the Bronx location and the operation was moved to the next-door suburb of Mount Vernon, New York. As before, Mario served as the

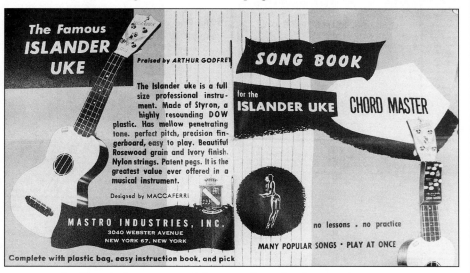

Instruction booklet which accompanied the Maccaferri Chord Master (courtesy Music City, Newark, NJ).

Another Maccaferri T.V. Pal ukulele with a "rosewood" body (photo: Ron Caimi).

idea and marketing person, while Maria supervised production and ran the business.

Maria Maccaferri is often asked what it was like being both Mario's wife and business partner. Her answer is simple: "when we were at home, I was his wife; when we were at the office, he was 'the boss.'"

Benny Goodman et al

Initially, Maccaferri's reed manufacturing company continued making the improved reed design Maccaferri had developed in France.

Following what emerges as a life-long gift of being in the right places at the right times (combined with his own creative genius), Maccaferri took some examples of his reeds to a Benny Goodman performance in Manhattan. Backstage, Mario got to meet Goodman and gave him the reeds. Goodman found them great and visited Mario at his shop the next day, eventually becoming a good friend.

Soon all the top musicians were beating a path to Maccaferri's door, calling Mario "Dr. Maccaferri," because he always wore a white lab coat at work, and bringing him their instruments to fix. By around 1940,

Maccaferri's reeds — known as "My Masterpiece" — were endorsed by both the famous and now forgotten stars of the day, including Goodman and his sax players (Bus Bassey, Buff Estes, Toots Mondelo, Jerry Jerome), Jimmy Dorsey, Eddie Miller and Irv Fazola of Bob Crosby's Band, Sal Franzella, Jr., Spud Murphy, Gil Rodin, Edmund C. Wall, Arthur Rollini, Bernie Donacio, Les Robinson and Gene Krupa's sax players (Sam Musiker, Clint Newbury, Bob Snyder, Sam Donahue). Throughout Maccaferri's entire involvement with instrument-making, all professional endorsements were given free-of-charge, never with a payment.

Indeed, the war presented a great opportunity. European manufacturers were unable to make reeds, leaving Maccaferri almost in sole control of the field. He received the contract to supply reeds to the American Armed Forces bands.

To help meet the demand, Maccaferri needed more machines, but couldn't obtain new parts because of the war effort. Following his innovative inventor's heart, Mario managed to build more machines by adapting other available machinery to serve his needs. These machines are still in use

to this day.

Plastic

During World War II, the supply of canes used for making the reeds, largely grown in France, evaporated. Maccaferri, employing his legendary "adaptability," came up with a solution using the newly emerging material which had already caught his attention: plastic.

In around 1944, Maccaferri's military contract allowed him to obtain injection molding equipment at a time when most other companies were required to convert operations to producing war items. Maria Maccaferri recalls that the equipment was so big that it wouldn't fit in the elevator at the Roseland building, so the street was blocked, a crane brought in and a window removed so the machinery could be moved into the building. Plastic for the new machinery was provided by Dow and Monsanto.

Working with his new injection molding equipment, Maccaferri figured out how to replicate the cane reed using plastic. Initially the music industry scoffed at the idea that one could manufacture acceptable reeds from plastic, but, of course, the joke

(Left) 50s Maccaferri Islander ukulele. (Right) 50s Maccaferri Sparkle Plenty Ukette (photos: Ron Caimi).

was on the nay-sayers. Indeed, Mario's good friend Benny Goodman quickly became a fan of the plastic reeds and began using them, spearheading their rapid acceptance by many Big Band stars.

Maccaferri's wartime success put him in a strong position for becoming the dominant provider of reeds in the post-war era. Following the war, Maccaferri attempted to obtain French cane again, but, to his dismay, found that he had been wrongly named as a German collaborator, unwelcome in France. It took some time to clear up this misunderstanding, but eventually Maccaferri's name was cleared and he set up a French arm of his operation.

Clothespins

As successful as Maccaferri's reeds were, though, it was a much more prosaic product which would come from Maccaferri's newfound expertise in plastics and make his fortune: clothespins.

The story of the plastic clothespin is classic Maccaferri. As Maria recalls the tale, the Maccaferri family used to take a holiday in the country during the summer. In the summer of 1944, upon arriving at their vacation home, she noticed that there were not enough clothespins, so she asked

Headstock of the G30 guitar. Note the banjo-style "planetary" gears.

Mario to go into the village to buy some more clothespins. When Mario asked the shopkeeper about clothespins, he was told that there were no clothespins to be had. It was wartime. Well, here was another dilemma to be solved. As usual, Mario had an idea.

When Mario returned home, he told Maria that he was going back to the plant and would be back soon. At the factory, Maccaferri took a sheet of lucite plastic and cut out six plastic clothespins of the solid, two-legged variety. He returned and pre-

sented them to Maria, who proceeded to use them to hang out a silk slip. Unfortunately, the gripping ridges put a hole in the slip. Mario went back the next day and corrected the problem, and the plastic clothespin was born.

Maccaferri began to market his novel device and was wildly successful. Because of the war, it was virtually impossible to obtain any consumer goods, and the public was eager to buy anything, including plastic clothespins. Eventually, millions of these would be made each day. In fact, they could not even find the time to package them. Some New York retail outlets would drive to the factory each day with their own steel drums and have them filled with plastic clothespins.

As a result of the success of the plastic clothespins, in 1944 or '45, the Maccaferris spun off a subsidiary of the French American Reeds Manufacturing Company called the Mastro Plastics Corporation. This was the manufacturing entity which produced all of Maccaferri's plastic creations. Throughout the '50s French American Reeds was generally identified as the parent company of Maccaferri instruments, however, by the '60s instrument manufacturing was identified as being part of Mastro Industries, Inc.

From clothespins to wall tiles

The humble two-foot clothespin eventually led to hinged clothespins, plastic spring clamps and a vast plastics empire which would make everything from tape dispensers to clothes hangers, acoustical ceiling tile and even a motorized fishing lure!

In any case, once World War II was over, consumer goods again became available, and the plastic clothespin business dropped off. That was fine, because Mario Maccaferri was turning his attention to his next project: plastic tiles.

One day an Italian machine was brought in to make plastic wall tiles, but it didn't work, and the tiles didn't even have bevels

Mid-'50s Maccaferri G30 guitar, the flattop version with the integral bridge/tailpiece assembly. The plug at the bottom of the top covers the screw neck-tilt adjustment.

on the edges. Mario and his engineers fixed the machine and improved the design, which led to the production of millions of those plastic kitchen and bath tiles that decorated the post-war suburban building boom.

While ultimately the seeds of Mario Maccaferri's successes lay in his native genius and unrestrained impulse to invent, the specific roots of Maccaferri's plastics empire came from music, the reed solution. So it's not surprising — and completely fitting — that, in true Hegelian fashion, Maccaferri's career should synthesize clothespins with musical instruments.

The plastic uke

Maccaferri's first foray into complete plastic instruments began with an unlikely candidate, the plastic ukulele, which would become yet another business triumph, inexorably tied to the name Arthur Godfrey. A number of accounts of this part of the Maccaferri saga have been published, but this is the official version. Contrary to what some have reported, the plastic uke was

Ca. 1953 Maccaferri G30 guitar. This variant has the extra plain metal trapeze tailpiece, although this appears to be either an added stress reliever or purely decorative (photo: Ron Caimi).

entirely Maccaferri's idea, and not suggested by Arthur Godfrey.

Mario got the idea for a plastic uke during the late 1940s. However, he had one big problem: insufficient capital to start his project. Through his connections with music distributors, Maccaferri knew Charlie Sonfield, whom he'd met at C. Bruno. Sonfield had become an executive at RCA. Maccaferri approached Sonfield with his idea and asked for a $5,000 loan. But, added Maccaferri in an important caveat, he couldn't guarantee that the plastic uke idea would fly, or that he could repay the loan. Sonfield gave Maccaferri the money. In return, Mario promised Sonfield the profits from the first 100 cases shipped each week. Sonfield would eventually make a pile of money on his investment!

Mario Maccaferri invented the Islander plastic ukulele, patterning it after Martin's style O uke, in 1949.

Arthur Godfrey

Enter Arthur Godfrey. The carrot-topped, befreckled Godfrey, you'll recall, had built an enormously successful career as a network radio entertainer and had just embarked on an equally impressive achievement as a trailblazing television show host. Indeed, Godfrey has the unique distinction of simultaneously having had two of the top-rated shows during network TV's early years. "Arthur Godfrey's Talent Scouts" debuted on CBS in December of 1948, followed in January of '49 by "Arthur Godfrey and His Friends." Among the talents introduced to American audiences through Godfrey's programs were names such as the Chordettes, Julius LaRosa, Pat Boone, the McGuire Sisters, Steve Lawrence, Tony Bennett, Rosemary Clooney, Connie Francis, Al Martino, Leslie Uggams, the Diamonds, Roy Clark and Pasty Cline (Elvis Presley and Buddy Holly didn't make it through auditions!). These programs rode high in the ratings through the early '50s.

Godfrey's shows, as were all TV shows in those early days, were directly linked to their sponsor, Lipton Tea, and Godfrey would always appear sipping his tea and plugging its pleasures between acts.

Closeup of the heel/neck joint of the Maccaferri G40.

Typical of Godfrey's down-home style was a refusal to promote any product he didn't believe in. A part of Godfrey's act was displaying a self-deprecating sense of humor and performing mostly comedy songs on a ukulele. Indeed, from April through June of 1950, Godfrey even had a CBS network show teaching how to play the ukulele!

Hawaii

The plastic uke was, again, right for the times. The uke was riding a crest of popularity mainly due to its associations with Hawaiian music, which had an amazing run of sustained popularity stretching from the 'Teens through the early '50s, a remarkable run of popularity rivalled perhaps only by rock and roll in this century. Godfrey's championing of the uke gave it new life, and it was a major money maker for music stores beginning to salivate at the massive numbers of children that were making up the now fabled post-war Baby Boom. Indeed, as one of those earliest Boomers, I recall the Arthur Godfrey TV show and my first instrument in about 1951 or '52 was a little blue University of Michigan ukulele, which I quickly mastered, leading to decades of subsequent demented guitaromania.

Anyhow, by one means or another Godfrey got ahold of one of Maccaferri's early plastic ukes and gave it a plug on his TV show. To paraphrase, he said: "Hey, there's this guy named 'Mac-a-something' [mispronounced the name] in the Bronx who's making these plastic ukuleles and they're very good. In fact, you even get a nickel back because they only cost $5.95."

The following day, the Maccaferris were swamped with phone calls from people wanting Islander Ukes, so many that in exasperation Mario refused to allow the phone to be answered any more.

9 million ukes

Maccaferri uke production had begun in 1949 and by the end of the run in 1969 tallied more than 9 million plastic ukulele sales.

Awhile later, Mario got a phone call from Arthur Godfrey himself requesting a couple dozen plastic ukes for a party he was throwing at Miami's Kennilworth Hotel. Godfrey wished each guest to have a plastic uke.

Maccaferri got on a plane and flew the ukes down personally. This was the first time he and Godfrey actually met.

Dow Styron

There are a number of fascinating aspects to these little gizmos.

For one thing, they represent early experiments in complex injection molding and use of Dow Chemical Company's new miracle plastic, Styron. Styron was both sturdy and resilient. It could be molded in almost any shape desired, and was capable of being almost endlessly colored. Maccaferri applied for and eventually received at least six patents on the manufacture of these instruments which by 1954 gave him complete patent protection for plastic ukes. As you might expect, such a successful product was quickly imitated by companies such as Eminee, but once Maccaferri held the patents, all other plastic ukes were supposed to be licensed.

For another thing, Maccaferri's plastic

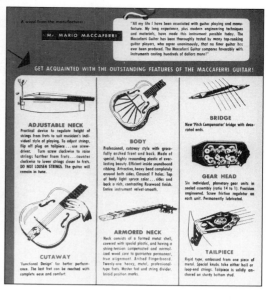

Flyer that accompanied the Maccaferri G guitars.

Ca. 1953 Maccaferri G40 guitar, the archtop version with elaborate trapeze tailpiece.

ukes sounded and played pretty darned good for a $5.95 instrument. Curiously enough, the molding process allowed intonation to be consistently correct. The ukes' top was an ivory color, while the body could be colored, including with a more or less woodgrain effect.

The Islander line

By November of 1951 the Maccaferri Islander uke line included three instruments, "For Happy Moments!" the original Islander, "the UKE Arthur Godfrey made famous," at $5.95, the Islander Deluxe at $7.95, and the Sparkle Plenty Islander Ukette at $2.98. The Islander was a standard uke which came packaged with a book by Jack O'Brian, *Godfrey the Great: The Life Story of Arthur Godfrey*, an instruction and song book by May Singhi Breen, an all-weather polythene bag, felt pick and key adjuster. The Islander Deluxe had a slightly larger body, a fingerboard that extended an extra three frets on the treble side, "metalized frets," and special patented tuning pegs. It, too, came with the books. The Ukette was a small-scale (!) uke for small children and came with an instruction book with songs for children. The Sparkle Plenty moniker, by the way, was another curious example of marketing pizazz. Sparkle Plenty was a comic strip character whose name was licensed from the Chicago Tribune.

In addition to the three ukes, there was also the Islander Visual Chordmaster that could be had for a buck. This was an attachment secured to the fingerboard by rubber bands which featured little buttons with chord names. Press a button and the strings were automatically stopped down, turning the uke into sort of an autoharp.

By April of 1952, improvements in production efficiency (and no doubt competition from knock-offs), allowed Maccaferri to slash the price of the Islander from $5.95 to $3.95, without cutting dealer margins. As reported in *The Music Trades*, "all Islander Ukuleles are still hand finished by master craftsmen."

Godfrey and the lawyers

One final word about the Arthur Godfrey connection. The Islander Deluxe was originally intended to be the Arthur Godfrey model. However, just before the idea was to be presented to Godfrey, on the air Arthur trashed a uke being sold by a big retail chain. He was eventually sued by the retailer and lost over the incident. The Maccaferris' lawyer recommended that the potential liability from Godfrey's freewheeling opinions was too great a risk to take, and the uke became simply the Islander Deluxe.

Over the years Maccaferri desired to repay Godfrey for the incredible boost to business the entertainer's endorsement in-

(Left) Ca. 1954 Maccaferri G16 Islander Guitar. (Right) Mid-'50s Maccaferri ShowTime Guitar (photo: Ron Caimi).

spired, but he refused to take any recompense. Once Mario even rolled up a bunch of $100 bills and put them into an expensive cigarette case and sent them to Arthur, but Godfrey sent the gift back.

The plastic guitar

Like the plastic clothespin before it, however, the plastic ukulele was merely a stepping stone to Maccaferri's higher ambition of making a plastic guitar. Let's face it, ukes hardly represent a great sonic challenge, but making a guitar out of Dow Styron? That's something else altogether!

The Maccaferri plastic guitar officially debuted in the Spring of 1953, although it was probably commercially available in '52, since both the flattop and archtop appear in the '52 Targ & Dinner jobber catalog. The introduction festivities were extensively covered by *The Music Trades* in May of '53, which reported a press luncheon thrown by Dow Chemical for Mario Maccaferri at the Waldorf-Astoria hotel in New York on April 29, 1953.

Described in glowing terms — lunch must have been great — Maccaferri introduced two guitars and emphasized the re-

sources and cost of developing his new guitars. Indeed, Amos Ruddock of Dow's plastic merchandising department indicated that the project took two years of testing various formulations of Styron and another Dow plastic called Ethocel and that tooling up cost around $350,000.

The Music Trades quoted Maccaferri's speech at length. While referring to a painting of legendary violinmaker Antonio Stradivarius working at his bench with a few simple tools, Maccaferri remarked, "A like painting symbolizing such craftsmanship today would have to suggest the following elements: 1. Some idea of the enormous industrial resources and scientific know-how of America today; 2. Not one genius, but a dozen of them; 3. The pile of money necessary to accomplish the task."

After citing famous musicians and composers, particularly Paganini, who played the guitar for their own personal enjoyment and wrote music for it, Maccaferri continued, "I have always promised myself that one day I would make a good guitar at a popular price. I had no idea that I would end up by making a plastic guitar. But when I realized that plastic would offer me the

chance to make a perfect instrument with none of the shortcomings known in the wooden guitar, it did not take long to decide and satisfy my life's ambition. So, I went to work.

"Often in my lifetime of playing guitar, I have had disappointments in its performance. On many occasions I would find the instrument's neck warped or the fretting defective, or the body of the instrument expanded or contracted, caused by humidity or dryness; thus making my guitar simply unplayable. Anyone playing the guitar knows what I mean.

"Although today's fine wooden guitars are the result of 300 years of guitar making experience, I do not hesitate to say that our 1953 all-plastic guitar compares favorably with any wooden guitar made.

"This all-plastic guitar wasn't an easy job, as you will understand. We had a lot of engineering problems and it represents quite a costly venture for us, but the Dow Chemical Company came up with suitable materials and we overcame the other problems. To this instrument we have applied all the improvements that guitar players have been seeking in it for many years. It has beauty and it is easier to play — it pro-

Ca. 1956 Roco classical, a relatively rare budget version of the ShowTime.

Ca. 1953 Maccaferri G-40 archtop.

Photo: Michael Tamborrino.

1960s Maccaferri T.V. Pal and Mastro plastic electric flattop guitars

1960s Mastro prototype plastic "solidbodies" with Mastro H-1 1 amplifiers

1960s Maccaferri acoustic, plastic body/neck, wood top

1960s Maccaferri prototype solidbody electric guitars

Photos: Michael Tamborrino.

1954 Maccaferri G16 Islander Guitar.

Ca. 1956 Roco (Maccaferri) classical guitar

1953-55 Maccaferri T.V. Pal Ukulele

Ca. 1960s Maccaferri Mastro River Show Boat toy banjo

Photos: Michael Tamborrino.

1963 Martin F-65

Photos: Michael Tamborrino.

1979 Martin EM-18

Photo: Michael Tamborrino.

Groovy Martin GT-70, GT-75, mysterious GT Bass (which is not mentioned in Longworth's book) and Martin SS140 amplifier

Ca. 1987 Martin Stinger SSL-20

Veleno
GUITARS
FINISH SAMPLES

Real Gold Plating (not shown)

Chrome Plating (not shown)

Polished Aluminum (same appearance as Chrome)

RED ANODIZE

GOLD ANODIZE

BLUE ANODIZE

GREEN ANODIZE

EBONY ANODIZE

SUPER FINISH

ANODIZE AND SUPER-FINISH ARE NON-CONDUCTIVE

Veleno Instrument Company
8122 - 15th Way North
St. Petersburg, Florida 33702

Color chart for Veleno guitars

Photo: Michael Tamborrino. Chart courtesy of John Veleno.

Ca. 1970-71 Veleno Original #4, the
first Traveler #001 both made for Mark
Farner, and ca. 1974 Original #115
(courtesy of Barney Roach).

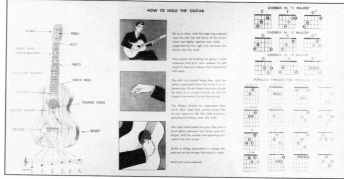

Guitar method that accompanied many Maccaferri guitars.

duces music in perfect pitch, and it has good tone and plenty of it. And this all-plastic guitar is not subject to any of the short-comings mentioned earlier."

Heavyweight support

While Arthur Godfrey was a great en-dorser of Maccaferri's Islander Ukulele, it might surprise you to learn that Maccaferri brought his plastic guitar to the world bear-ing the endorsements of none other than classical maestros Andres Segovia, his old friend from the '20s, and Rey De La Torre, and pop-jazz great Harry Volpe. De La Torre and Volpe attended the luncheon and performed on Maccaferri guitars, making the guitar "speak for itself," after which Maccaferri himself was prevailed upon to toss off a "lively Neapolitan melody with skill and dexterity."

Indeed, Mario recollected the dem-onstration for Segovia which garnered his endorsement. Mario took his new guitar to Segovia's apartment in New York. Segovia lay down with his feet up on a chair, encouraging Maccaferri to play until five in the morning. Segovia then came down to see the factory. Segovia endorsed Maccaferri's plastic guitar, although the fac-tory visit ended up in a royal row, regard-ing another instrument. At the time Mario had developed a guitar with a wood top and f-holes. Mario recognized that the mag-netic pickup was quite effective, but that it didn't work on nylon strings. He devised what was a sort of hybrid approach, with a condenser at the bridge and strings which had been "metalized," coated with lead and a gluing agent. These were then detected with electric fields above and below, sent

to a pre-amp and out the guitar. Segovia loved the sound, but objected to the "com-mercialized, Americanized" look, with f-holes and the cutaway, preferring a "classi-cal Spanish" look.

G30 and G40

The two guitars Maccaferri introduced at the Waldorf were described as "full, mas-ter size instruments," "the flat-top, arched bottom, cutaway model retailing at $29.95; and the DeLuxe Arched Top at $39.95." While the denomination is strange, it's these

Plastic case for Maccaferri Strings, which were never produced (courtesy Maria Maccaferri).

which would quickly be known as the G30 and G40, respectively. Both had similar, Selmer-like shapes with the Maccaferri square cutaway, the former with a flat top, the latter with an arched top (although the differences in degree of "arch" between the two models is minimal, at best). Pictured in the article are Maccaferri and Volpe get-ting down with a pair of plastics, Maccaferri

on a G30, and Volpe holding a striking ver-sion of what looks like a G40 with an ivory (a.k.a. "maple") fingerboard. These are quite remarkable pieces of technology, each composed of more than 100 separate parts, not all plastic, to be truthful.

Both had fancy headstocks with Maccaferri's patented planetary tuning machines. These were "banjo" style tuners with a 14:1 ratio, a patented design usingthree interlocking gears. The G30 had a molded in bridge assembly to which the strings attached and a separate plastic saddle glued in. The G40 had a glued-on arch-top-style bridge and a fancy trapeze tail-piece. Both had two f-holes. Curiously enough, wooden struts were glued under the tops. The tops were ivory, the sides and backs done up in a swirled reddish-brown rosewood color. Both were, by the way, *steel*-stringed guitars, not ny-lon stringed instruments like the Islander ukes. One point to note: early G30s had only the molded bridge assembly. Some time later a plain metal trapeze tailpiece was added. This did not serve as the anchor for the strings, but either as some sort of added support for the bridge assembly or as merely decoration.

The most curious design elements con-cerned the neck. The neck was bolted on the guitar in an early version of a slightly cutaway heel. The outside of the neck con-sisted of two pieces of plastic, the outer back and the fingerboard. The fingerboard bore actual frets and white position markers (which are actually part of the back and help align the parts). Inside there's a metal sheath, referred to as an "armored neck," and at the core a piece of wood. This de-

Plastic '50s Flamingo Ukulele by Mastro competitor Emenee, endorsed by Arthur Godfrey.

sign was guaranteed never to warp.

Already we've described a pretty interesting bit of guitar design, but wait, there's more! This neck was essentially a neck-through design. The inner core ran all the way through the body to the endpin. There it was notched and had a threaded bolt running perpendicular to it. This bolt had a couple nuts above and below the neck core and was slotted. By removing a metal plug from a hole on the top of the guitar down at the bottom of the lower bout, you can use a screwdriver and basically adjust neck tilt and therefore action by tightening or loosening this bolt!

Ok, we have a plastic guitar with a warp-proof neck, perfect intonation, adjustable action and pretty natty faux-rosewood looks. Let's cut to the chase. How does it sound? Well, beauty is in the ear of the beholder, but in my opinion pretty good, indeed. The tone is not really like a typical wood sound. In some ways it's sort of like an acoustic variant of the Strat's out-of-phase sound, kind of funky. In a good one, the balance and sustain are quite remarkable. Of those I've personally played, I've found the newer ones to have better sound, and I prefer the tone of the flattop G30 to the more upscale archtop G40. If I were a recording artist, I'd consider a G30 as an indispensable part of my studio arsenal, and would never apologize for the tone.

With all the fuss over the introduction of Maccaferri's plastic guitars, they went over among guitarists, well, like a plastic guitar. Guitar players, as you know, are a pretty conservative lot when it comes to instruments, and the Maccaferris probably were never able to shed the "toy" image. Actually, the guitar may have been done in by a minor design flaw in the earliest versions. According to Maria Maccaferri, some of the heads began to warp under the stress. Mario corrected this design error quickly, and the majority did not have this problem, but Maria suspected that this is what gave the plastic guitars a "black eye," as she put it. Production went along quite briskly for a couple years, however, at some point Mario's plastics came in for some rough criticism by guitar critics, possibly due to the old head problem. Rather than fight the negative comments, Mario simply decided to abandon his project midstream. He just put an end to production, leaving hundreds and hundreds of unassembled guitars. Maria recalls assembling many of the last instruments herself, after Mario had washed his hands of the matter. Many parts remained unassembled decades later. Maria did not recall just when production was halted on the G30 and G40, but thought it might have been around 1958, though it could possibly have been much earlier, as early as 1955 or '56.

More toys

Despite the luke-warm reception of the plastic guitars, Maccaferri forged ahead with his plastic instrument empire. In the Winter of 1953 the Islander Baritone Ukulele was added to the line, just in time for the holiday season.

In a February 1954 ad in *The Music Trades*, the Maccaferri line included the new Islander Baritone Ukulele ($12.95), the G30

($35.95 with case) and G40 ($45.95 with case) guitars, the U150 Islander Ukette ($1.00), the C100 Chordmaster attachment, the U400 Islander Ukulele ($3.95), the U600 Islander DeLuxe Ukulele and MU25 Midget Uke ($.25). Both Islander Ukes came in a "Combination" package (UC500 for $4.95 and UC700 for $6.95); just what that combination consisted of is unknown, but was probably the Chordmaster and accessories, as before.

In an undated catalog supplied by Michael Lee Allen, probably from around this time based on pricing, the Maccaferri uke line consisted of the Islander uke ($4.50 alone, $5.70 with Chordmaster, books and accessories), the T.V. Pal, a stripped down version of the Islander ($1.75), the Islander DeLuxe ($5.95), and the Islander Baritone ($12.95).

The Islander Guitar

Also introduced in February of 1954 was the No. G16 "Popular-Priced" Islander Guitar. This was basically a standard non-cutaway acoustic flattop, slightly smaller than the cutaway G30 and G40. This was 35" long, 13" wide and 4¹/₂" deep. It had a round soundhole with a plastic lattice ro-

Ad for the Islander Uke and Ukette and T.V. Pal Baritone Uke in the '58 David Wexler catalog.

sette of semi-circles. The G16 had a little black plastic pickguard. The bridge unit was the same as the G40 archtop, with the fancy stamped metal trapeze tailpiece. The headstock was a slightly tapered three-and-three with an open book top and planetary tuners. The top and headstock face were ivory, which the body and neck were ebony with gold swirls. The fingerboard was "ebony" with white dots arranged in an alternating one-and-two pattern. The neck was actually molded onto the body, like other less expensive Maccaferri plastics, but also had curious, unique features. The neck, which was hollow, was reinforced with two roughly $^1/_2$" by $^1/_8$" aluminum rods along either side of the channel. Furthermore, this reinforcement structure was anchored in the heel and abutted a contraption with a large screw aimed toward the soundhole. Putting a screwdriver into the soundhole and tightening the set screw allowed the tilt of the neck, and hence the action, to be adjusted. Pretty clever.

The coolest thing about the G16 was the choice of finishes. It could be had with mahogany grain body, ivory top and ebony fingerboard, with mahogany grain body and top with an ivory fingerboard, and with an

(Left) Competing ca. '50s Carnival Varsity plastic uke, not made by Mastro. (Right) Competing ca. '50s Carnival Combo Guitar (actually a uke) in original packaging plus a red plastic Mickey Mouse uke, neither made by Mastro (Photos courtesy Tinicum Guitar Barn, Ottsville, PA).

ebony grained body and top with ivory fingerboard. These had the typical Maccaferri headstock with planetary tuners.

The classic Maccaferri G30, G40 and G16 plastic guitars were kept in the catalog until the instrument business was ended in 1969, even though production had long since ceased. The Maccaferris' typical approach was to make a large batch of products and then inventory them until more were needed. How many of these guitars were actually produced over the years is impossible to tell, but there were quite a few sold, although certainly not approaching the 9 million uke mark. A huge cache was discovered in a warehouse in the early '80s and these were quickly sold to collectors. When the remaining assembled stock was liquidated in the early '90s, nearly 5,000 instruments were still available.

The Romancer

In June of 1957 Maccaferri introduced the Romancer Classic Style Guitar, No. R20. This was advertised as a "standard-size" guitar, 35" long,

13" wide and $4^1/_2$" deep. It featured Maccaferri's patented planetary tuners and fancy headstock. The body and neck had now become a single molded unit, more like the ukuleles than the elaborate G30/G40/G16s designs. The copy alludes to "Wood-armoured neck and body," which we can presume to mean there was wood reinforcement inside the neck and probably wooden struts. The neck and body were made of "grained ebony" plastic, while the top and fingerboard were ivory, silk-screened with decorations. The body had music staves looking like ribbons and five different musical scenes of teens getting down. One was a trio (a la Kingston), two guys solo, a little jazz combo with a piano (a la Nat King Cole?), and a guy and gal duo. The position markers on the fingerboard were little pictures. The Romancer came with a rope strap, guitar method and pick, "very easy to play, and luxuriously finished — the ideal guitar for any type of music — from classical to popular, folksong, Calypso, Rock 'n Roll, etc."

ShowTime

Among the later plastics was the

1961 Targ & Dinner catalog ad for the T.V. Pal Uke and Baritone Uke and the Islander Uke with the Visual Chordmaster.

(Left) Mario Maccaferri and Maurice J. Summerfield trying out the new CSL "Gypsy" guitar in New York in January of 1975. (Right) Mario Maccaferri in around 1975 playing a Selmer-style classical; note he still uses a thumbpick (Photos courtesy Maria Maccaferri.

ShowTime classical guitar, a nylon-stringed axe with teen scenes which, based on the look of the teens is probably circa 1959-60 vintage. This looks to be another iteration of the Romancer. Although the headstock contains Maccaferri's trademark planetary tuners, this guitar has a molded neck attached to the body similar to the Romancer. Instead of inlaid metal frets, this has plastic frets molded into the fingerboard and painted silver. Despite this unflattering description, again the tonal response is quite good. Hey, it isn't a Ramirez, but for what it is, a plastic classical, it has a distinctive character.

Market testing

It was at about this time, during the later '50s, that Mario Maccaferri did some marketing experimentation. Getting advice that he should lower his prices, he tried floating several plastic guitar models with brand names other than Maccaferri. These included the Roco brand and the Mastro brand. The Roco guitar was basically a nylon-stringed variant on the Islander, with the G30 bridge, not the G40, molded frets (like on the ShowTime), a single row of dots on the "ebony" 'board, and some all-plastic, friction-style banjo tuners. The Roco had the same neck-tilt adjustment as the Islander.

These excursions into alternative brands did not go well, and very few of these instruments were ever produced, so if you encounter one, it's pretty rare.

Electrics

Among the many whimsical plastic Maccaferri designs of this era was a brief early '60s excursion into electric guitars with the small Maestro electric tenor guitar. This guitar had four strings and a short $18^{1}/_{4}$" scale, and contained its own battery-powered amplifier. Strings attached either to a trapeze tailpiece or onto the bridge, as the player desired. The Maestro had one single-coil pickup at the lead position. Tuners were the basic open-backed variety.

Maccaferri did a fair amount of experimentation on electrics, although these would never be his forte. Shown on page 208 is a "Strat" which was a one-off experiment which Mario had made in Italy at an enormous expense. This was a terribly complex guitar with a wicked vibrato design and tons of knobs. It even offered alternative mono or stereo output. This strange beast, alas, never made it to market.

Sometime during this period Maccaferri

Shiro Arai, Mario Maccaferri and Paco Pena in London, 1975 (courtesy Maurice J. Summerfield).

also added various plastic horns to his repertoire.

Introducing the Beatles...

The last notice of Maccaferri's instruments occurred in the July, 1964, *The Music Trades*, in which the new "Beatles" line was discussed. The company was now identified as Mastro Industries, Inc. Introduced in March of '64, significantly at the Toy Show in New York, the Beatles line marked a final burst of success for the Maccaferri plastic instrument venture. Maccaferri had obtained the exclusive U.S. license to market official instruments using The Beatles name.

Included were four Beatle guitar models made of "Beatle Red" and "Beatle Orange" injection molded polystyrene plastic bodies. The ivory tops included brown printed portraits of the Fab Four with reproductions of their signatures. Two four-string tenor guitars were offered, the Jr. Guitar and the Four Pop, and two small-bodied six-strings, the Yeah Yeah and the Beatle-ist. Construction appears to be similar to that of the ShowTime. Each came with instructions, song book and a pick.

The Mastro Beatle line also included a set of Ringo Drums, plastic bongo drums and a plastic banjo. There was also a miniature Pin-Up guitar which was a 5" replica of the real Beatle plastic guitar!

According to the article in *The Music Trades*, Mastro had already shipped 500,000 of the Beatle guitars and was pro-

jecting two million by the end of the year. Whether or not Maccaferri ever met that projection is unknown, but Beatlemania, too, began to spread out and change quickly as the fans grew older and the pace of the decade picked up.

1965 plastics

A good picture of the mature Maccaferri Mastro line can be seen in the 1965 catalog. Top of the line were the G-40 archtop and G-30 flat top, followed by the Showtime No. 1020 (sans decoration) and Romancer No. 1010. By this time both the Showtime and the Romancer had the neck design that featured a tension screw inside the body at the heel accessible with a long screw driver. Tightening or loosening the screw changed the neck tilt and therefore the action.

Also available were the G-16 Islander Guitar, the 35" Mastro G-10 Guitar with armoured neck, and the 31" Mastro G-5 Guitar.

In addition, there were two versions of the 30" nylon-stringed Sonora Guitars No. 727. The A-SH was in a marbled woodgrain color, while the IC was in cream and black. Under these were the No. 500 TV Pal Guitar in two colors (PIC) or woodgrain (A-SH). The No. 775 Western Guitar featured singing cowboys, bucking broncos, boots and saddles on the front.

Still in the line were a small Maestro electric six-string and tenor guitars. The GTA-

(Above and next two pages) 1965 Mastro catalog (courtesy Maria Maccaferri).

5 Electric Guitar was a 32" woodgrain-colored non-cutaway acoustic with a small humbucker attached near the bridge. The wiring came out the treble side through a tube into a small housing with a volume control and jack for a mini-plug. The CT GTA-5 Tenor Cutaway Electric Guitar was basically a four-string version, with the optional string attachment at the tailpiece or bridge. These guitars had a new patent-pending design which featured a rigid metal beam which ran through the guitar from the nut to the heel, detouring toward the back once inside the body. Both were played through the matching TA-5 Mastro Amplifier, a small 5-watt portable transistor amp with a 6" speaker, operating off two 9-volt batteries.

The recently introduced Beatle line was also available, of course. Beatles guitars included the 30½" Beatle-Ist Guitar (No. 340), the 22" Beatles Yeah-Yeah Guitar (No. 330), the 21" Beatles Four Pop Guitar (No. 320, four-string), and the 14½" Beatles Jr. Guitar (No. 300). The 22" Beatles Banjo (No. 350) was offered, as were the Beatles Ringo Snare Drum (No. 380), the Beatles Beat Bongo (No. 360), the Beatles Big Beat Bongo (No. 370), and the Mastro Beatles "Pin-Up" Guitar, miniature guitars you could clip on your shirt. All had portraits and signatures of the Fab Four on the front.

Mario Maccaferri in 1975, with Maurice Summerfield, Louis Gallo and Ray Gallo (courtesy Maurice J. Summerfield).

GOLD TRUMPET

GOLD SAXOPHONE

GOLD CLARINET

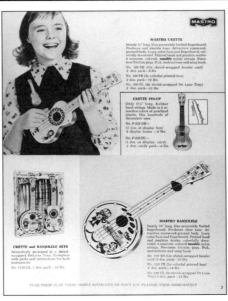

MASTRO UKETTE

UKETTE PIN-UP

MASTRO BANJOLELE

UKETTE and BANJOLELE SETS

TUNE THEM! PLAY THEM! SIMPLE INSTRUCTIONS HAVE YOU PLAYING THEM IMMEDIATELY

MASTRO

TV PAL UKE

TV PAL UKE with AUTOMATIC CHORDMASTER

VISUAL CHORDMASTER

TV PAL CUTAWAY TENOR GUITAR

MASTRO UKE

MASTRO JR. GUITAR

MASTRO

SQUARE DANCE FIDDLE

STRADIVARIUS VIOLIN

MASTRO

SAXOPHONE

TRUMPET

CLARINET

MASTRO

SONORA GUITAR

SONORA TWO-COLOR GUITAR

MASTRO

SHOWTIME GUITAR

ROMANCER GUITAR

MASTRO

BEATLES
MUSICAL INSTRUMENTS

EXCLUSIVE U.S.A. LICENSEE
TO MANUFACTURE
BEATLES MUSICAL INSTRUMENTS

BEATLES GUITARS

BEATLE-IST GUITAR

BEATLES YEAH-YEAH GUITAR

BEATLES FOUR POP GUITAR

BEATLES JR. GUITAR

BEATLES BANJO

Full-size 22" banjo-uke with perfect pitch. Accurately fretted fingerboard has engraved position marks. Weatherproof head. Tension rods. Patented tuning keys. Pick and song book. On shrink-wrapped colorful card.

No. 350 G½—½ doz. pack—12 lbs.

BEATLES BONGOS

Weatherproof head . . . always in tune. Permanently stretched for maximum resonance and quick response. Non-slip foam discs on sides. Simple-to-follow instruction booklet. In eye-appealing display merchandiser.

No. 360 PDB—
BEAT BONGO
[Height 5¼", heads 5" and 5½"]. ½ doz. pack—50 lbs.
No. 370 FDB
BIG BEAT BONGO
[Height 6¼", heads 6½" and 7¼"] ½ doz. pack—15 lbs.

BEATLES RINGO SNARE DRUM

Full size 14" x 6½", snare drum with brilliant tone quality and deep resonance. Golden hoop and attachments, red, gold-sparkled shell. Adjustable tension rods. On and off snare mechanism. Abrased bar for brush effects. Adjustable steel tripod stand. Balanced wood drum sticks. Simple instruction booklet. Packaged in colorful portable case.

No. 200 PCC—½ doz. pack—32 lbs.

MASTRO BEATLES "PIN-UP" GUITAR

Miniature of the popular Mastro Beatles playing guitars. Only 5" with built-in clip. Beatles' likenesses printed on face.

No. P5-DB
DISPLAY BOX
2 dozen guitars in box. Packed 6 boxes to carton.
No. P5-DC
DRM-UP CARD
1 dozen guitars to a card.
Packed 1 dozen cards to carton—6 lbs.

MASTRO TV PAL CUTAWAY BARITONE UKE

Features professional cutaway with extended precision fingerboard, precision patented keys for fine tuning. 2 nylon and 2 nylon wound strings. Grained ebony color body with contrasting ivory color finished face. Face and head decorated in two-color Hawaiian scenes. Size 29½". Pick, instructions and song book. In shrink wrapped Deluxe Tray.

No. 610 DL—½ doz. pack—16 lbs.

ISLANDER BARITONE UKE

MASTRO CUTAWAY TENOR GUITAR

MACCAFERRI GUITARS
With High-Fidelity Tone and Pitch

Some outstanding features of the MACCAFERRI Plastic Guitar:

- **"Adjustable" Neck** — Practical device to regulate height of strings from frets to suit individual style of player. Precision engineered. Permanently lubricated.
- **"Feather-Touch" Machine Heads** — Six planetary gear heads in sealed assembly. Screw regulator for each gear. Precision engineered. Permanently lubricated.
- **"Slip-Free" Armored Neck** — Made of metal shell, plastic sheathed, with laminate bracket wood core to guarantee firm alignment.
- **"Pitch Compensating" Bridge** — New sharp "pitch compensator" bridge with decorated ends.
- **"Sound-Kinked" Body** — Professional cutaway made of moulding plastic material. Highly efficient inside wood construction.

No. G-40 PCC—½ doz. pack—31 lbs.

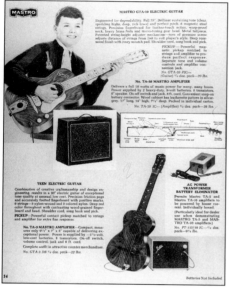

MASTRO GTA-10 ELECTRIC GUITAR

No. TA-10 MASTRO AMPLIFIER

TEEN ELECTRIC GUITAR

No. TA-3 MASTRO AMPLIFIER

AC POWER TRANSFORMER BATTERY ELIMINATOR

Batteries Not Included

MASTRO SELF-CONTAINED, BATTERY-OPERATED ELECTRIC GUITARS
PLAY THEM ANYWHERE!

TENOR CUTAWAY ELECTRIC GUITAR

No. TA-5 MASTRO AMPLIFIER

GTA-5 ELECTRIC GUITAR

No. TA-5 MASTRO AMPLIFIER

Batteries Not Included

"FEATHER-TOUCH" MACHINE HEADS

ISLANDER GUITAR

No. G-40 PCC—½ doz. pack—20 lbs.

MASTRO G-5 GUITAR

MASTRO G-10 GUITAR

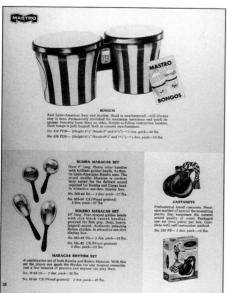

BONGOS

Real Latin-American beat and rhythm. Head is weatherproof—will always stay in tune. Permanently stretched for maximum resonance and quick response. Non-slip foam discs on sides. Simple-to-follow instruction booklet. Each bongo is poly-bagged. Both in counter merchandiser.

No. 350 PDB—[Height 5", Heads 5" and 5½"]—½ doz. pack—10 lbs.
No. 620 PDB—[Height 6½", Heads 6½" and 7¼"]—½ doz. pack—15 lbs.

RUMBA MARACAS SET

No. MS-80 DL—2 doz. pack—17 lbs.

BOLERO MARACAS SET

No. ML-82 DL—2 doz. pack—19 lbs.
No. ML-82 CS [Wood-grained] 2 doz. pack—19 lbs.

CASTANETS

No. 210 FB—3 doz. pack—12 lbs.

MARACAS RHYTHM SET

No. M-84 DL—2 doz. pack—23 lbs.
No. M-84 CS [Wood-grained] 2 doz. pack—25 lbs.

SNARE DRUM OUTFIT

Full size snare drum, 14" x 5½". Handsome appearance, crafted of sturdy plastic with weatherproof tunable mylar head. Gold finish trim on rich red, gold-sparkled body. Brilliant tone quality, deep resonance. Adjustable tripod stand of sturdy plated steel. Balanced wood drum sticks. Simple-to-follow instruction book in sturdy, attractive carrying case with handles.

No. 1500 PCC—½ doz. pack—21 lbs.

WORLD'S LARGEST SELLING POPULARLY PRICED SNARE DRUM OUTFIT

The Uke that Arthur Godfrey made famous!

ISLANDER UKE WITH AUTOMATIC CHORDMASTER

Professional size ukulele. Produces mellow tone and perfect pitch. Precision fingerboard and metal plastic frets. Separate nylon strings. Patented pegs. Handsome grained body with ivory finished face. Distinctive decorations on head. Inlaid position marks. Contrasting bridge and sound hole decorative ring. Chordmaster automatically selects any one of six chords to accompany the melody of all popular songs. Complete with pick, instructions and song book in attractive box.

No. C-400 PFB—1 doz. pack—18 lbs.
No. 400 PFB [Islander Uke without Chordmaster] Poly-bagged in folding box. With pick and song book. ½ doz. pack—14 lbs.

BANJO UKE

Full size instrument with perfect pitch and mellow, penetrating tone. Beautifully grained white and gold satin finish body. Four different colored nylon strings. Neck is armored with steel and String height adjuster. Accurately fretted fingerboard with position marks. Adjustable tension rods to tighten the all-weather mylar head. Patented tuning keys. Pick, instructions and song book.

No. 320 DL Shrink-wrapped in deluxe tray. ½ doz. pack—13 lbs.
No. 320 PIC Poly-bagged in individual carton. ½ doz. pack—17 lbs.

DESIGNED AND MADE FOR MUSICAL ENJOYMENT. TUNE THEM! PLAY THEM!

MASTRO MASTRO INDUSTRIES, INC., 3040 WEBSTER AVENUE, BRONX, N.Y. 10467.

Tony Smith, Mario Maccaferri and Maurice Summerfield in New York, 1975 (courtesy Maurice J. Summerfield).

Two cutaway baritone ukes, the Mastro TV Pal (No. 610) and the Islander (No. 410), were offered, as well as the woodgrained Mastro Cutaway Tenor Guitar (No. CTG-6) and the TV Pal Cutaway Tenor Guitar (No. 666). Ukes included the Mastro Uke (No. 750), the Islander Uke (No. C-400), the Mastro Jr. Guitar (No. 725, a uke with six-strings) and the TV Pal Uke (No. 120). Two Chordmaster units were available, the Automatic and the Visual Chordmaster, complete with little lights to let you play the uke without lessons! The Mastro Ukette (No. 100) was still around, as well as the Mastro Banjolele (No. 110) and the Banjo Uke (No. 520).

Two plastic violins were offered, the cream-colored Square Dance Fiddle (No. 700) and the woodgrained Stradivarius Violin (No. 1000), both with plastic bows.

Finally, six wind instruments were available, a trumpet in gold or cream, a saxophone in gold or red, and a clarinet in gold or black. There were also six percussion instruments, a set of bongos, three maracas (rumba, bolero and rhythm), castanets and a remarkable plastic snare drum.

Gitarina

In 1966 the Mastro plastic line continued unabated with several new curious additions. Most curious was the Gitarina (No. 222), 25" double-cutaway hollowbody

acoustic basically looking like a Strat with an asymmetrical three-and-three headstock. This had 20 frets, the end of the fingerboard cut in a groovy stairstep design. Soundholes were twin "split-ribbon" shapes.

Also new were two electrics, the GTA-10 Electric Guitar and the Teen Electric Guitar. The GTA-10 was basically a 35" woodgrained Romancer (with neck-tilt adjustment) and the Mastro pickup. The Teen was a woodgrained 30" guitar with a small transducer pickup. Both could be played through the TA-5 amp, or the new TA-10 10-watt amp, or the smaller TA-3 3-watt amp (powered by 1½ volt batteries). If you wanted to plug these amps in, a new AC Power Transformer was now available.

Summer of Love

In 1967 Mastro enhanced the line once again. Most of the old plastics were still available, but new things were added. The Gitarina was the main focus of expansion. On the downside was the Monkey (No. 102), a tiny uke version of the acoustic Strat, now with a four-in-line headstock. Upside was the Disco Cutaway Guitar (No. 352), basically the Gitarina with a small pickguard sort of surround on the lower

soundhole, triple rectangle fingerboard inlays, and a fancier bridge with tailpiece.

New, too, was the 30", nylon-stringed Riviera Guitar (No. 303), a slightly offset double-cutaway with ribbon soundholes with little circles in the middle, a six-in-line headstock and optional bridge or molded tail string attachment. An upscale version of this was available called the Jet Star, with more coloration, a pickguard surround on the lower soundhole, a metal tail, and with triangular inlays. The Riviera (No. 551) was an electric version with a transducer pickup attached to the lower bout connected to the Mastro 4.11 amplifier.

The Sonora acoustic got a lift with the addition of the nylon-stringed Deluxe Sonora (No. 325). This had trapezoidal inlays, a black pickguard and a metal tailpiece. The nylon Mastro G3 Guitar (No. 358) was basically the same guitar with traditional worm-gear tuners, rather than friction pegs. The woodgrained Mastro G5 Guitar (No. 452) was virtually the same, too, except for hollow rectangle position markers and the through-body metal beam reinforcement.

Also new was the 32" cream-and-colored Mastro Classic Guitar (No. 451), pretty much identical to the G3. This was avail-

Ca. 1975 sales flyer for the Ibanez-made Maccaferri guitar (courtesy Maurice J. Summerfield).

able as the Classic Electric Guitar (No. 552) had the same transducer and 4.11 amp as the Riviera electric.

Plastic denouement

All this new development ended up as the end of the road.

In around 1967, Mario Maccaferri had an episode with his heart which precipitated some new thinking about his priorities. Other events were conspiring to confirm his conclusions.

Not long after his recovery, in 1969, Maccaferri decided to get out of the plastic instrument business altogether. The designs, molds and other equipment for making his more toy-oriented plastic creations were sold to Carnival industries, another plastic novelty company. Carnival never figured out what to do with the Maccaferri legacy which it purchased, and no Maccaferri plastic instruments were ever made again.

8-Track tapes

Never ones to remain idle, the Maccaferris continued to work in plastic, however. In around 1970 or '71, RCA came to Mario with the idea for an 8-track

cassette, needing plastic housings. Mario designed and produced the first 8-track cassette housing. Unfortunately, RCA had his design and process copied, closing out a major business opportunity. Nevertheless, Maccaferri turned his invention to good turn, and he sold many of these 8-track housings to other manufacturers. Eventually, in the later '70s, Maccaferri expanded into making cassette tape housings, as well.

Maria and Mario Maccaferri, Pat and Maurice Summerfield in New York, 1991 (courtesy Maurice J. Summerfield).

Selmer Revisited

As the '70s dawned there was renewed interest in Django Reinhardt and the guitars he played. Most folks at the time were unaware that Reinhardt actually played an instrument from after the Maccaferri hegemony at Selmer, and it became common currency among guitar enthusiasts that Django and Maccaferri were directly connected. The result was the beginning of a series of '70s replicas of the Selmer Maccaferri.

One of the first was "an authentic replica of the Selmer Maccaferri, the guitar Django played" built by French luthier Jacques Favino and offered in an ad in the December 1971 *Guitar Player*. This was advertised as a handmade guitar — production was limited to five a month, signed and dated by the maker — and offered through Favino-America, Box 1078 Radio City Station in New York. No prices or specs were offered, but the illustration showed a classic Maccaferri right-angle cutaway and an oval soundhole parallel to the fingerboard, which ended above the soundhole with a concave edge. The bridge was a long straight Maccaferri mustache. No other information is known, so it's impossible to tell how "authentic" these really were. This was the only advertising for these

Favino replicas, so we can probably assume they did not especially succeed. Still, if you find a Favino, you at least now have some idea where it fits in the Maccaferri canon.

In the early '70s Mario Maccaferri became acquainted with Maurice Summerfield in England. Summerfield is perhaps best known as author of books on classical and jazz guitarists, but has also been active as an instrument importer and publisher. Summerfield was an important player in the early days of the Ibanez story, bringing that brand into the United Kingdom and helping develop such guitars as the Joe Pass. In 1974, Summerfield and Maccaferri hit upon the idea of reviving the guitar designs Mario did for Selmer back in 1931. Mario revisited his original designs, updating them for the new times. Summerfield arranged for them to be built by Hoshino in Japan.

The Ibanez Maccaferri guitars were basically the old Selmer Jazz model, with a single cutaway, "D" soundhole, slotted headstock, wide moveable bridge, and metal trapeze tailpiece. At least four models were produced, including the MAC10. These were consecutively numbered and featured a label signed by Mario Maccaferri himself.

The Hoshino Maccaferri guitars began coming in to the U.K. in 1976, where they were sold by Summerfield's CSL Guitars as

Sales flyer for an early '80s Maccaferri MAC 100S made by Saga in Japan (courtesy Maurice J. Summerfield).

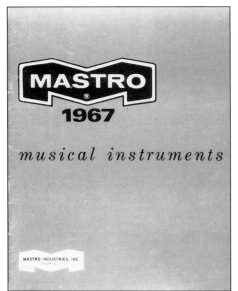

MASTRO
1967
musical instruments

MASTRO INDUSTRIES, INC.
Bronx, N. Y.

THE MONKEY

The perfect toy for the young Music-Makers that want to make the scene. A replica, over 15" long, of the popular double cutaway "Swedish Head" guitar used by leading musical groups. Comes in attractive two-tone contrasting bright colors. Nylon strings. Precision friction tuning peg.

No. 162
Shrink-wrapped on multi-colored display card perfectly suited for rack, counter or bin merchandising.
2 doz. pack—10 lbs.

A Musical Toy for Fun and Play

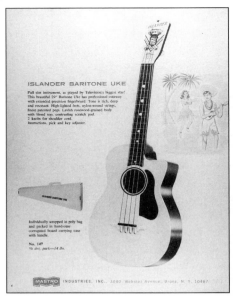

ISLANDER BARITONE UKE

Full size instrument, as played by Television's biggest star! This beautiful 29" Baritone Uke has professional cutaway with extended precision fingerboard. Tone is rich, deep and resonant. High-lighted frets, nylon-wound strings, finest patented pegs. Lavish rosewood-grained body with blond top, contrasting scratch pad. 2 knobs for shoulder cord. Instructions, pick and key adjuster.

No. 147
½ doz. pack—14 lbs.

MASTRO INDUSTRIES, INC., 3040 Webster Avenue, Bronx, N. Y. 10467

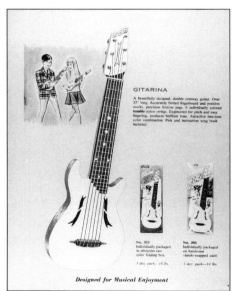

GITARINA

A beautifully designed, double cutaway guitar. Over 25" long. Accurately fretted fingerboard and position marks, precision friction pegs. 6 individually colored **tunable** nylon strings. Engineered for pitch and easy fingering, produces brilliant tone. Attractive two-tone color combination. Pick and instruction song book included.

No. 311
Individually packaged in attractive two color folding box.
1 doz. pack—16 lbs.

No. 301
Individually packaged on handsome shrink-wrapped card.
1 doz. pack—14 lbs.

Designed for Musical Enjoyment

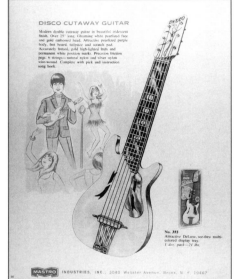

DISCO CUTAWAY GUITAR

Modern double cutaway guitar in beautiful iridescent finish. Over 25" long. Gleaming white pearlized face and gold embossed head. Attractive pearlized purple body, fret board, tailpiece and scratch pad. Accurately fretted, gold high-lighted frets and permanent white position marks. Precision friction pegs. 6 strings—natural nylon and silver nylon wire-wound. Complete with pick and instruction song book.

No. 352
Attractive DeLuxe, see-thru multi-colored display tray.
1 doz. pack—24 lbs.

MASTRO INDUSTRIES, INC., 3040 Webster Avenue, Bronx, N. Y. 10467

RIVIERA GUITAR

NEW SLIM LOOK

Modern double cutaway, slim body, 30" long instrument that produces clear, resonant tones. Beautiful contrasting colors—marbleized ebony body and fret board, white face and head. Extended accurately fretted fingerboard with position marks. 6 strings—nylon and nylon wire-wound. Precision friction tuning peg. Complete with pick and instruction song book.

RIVIERA
Sound of Music and Fun

No. 303
Shrink-wrapped on handsome self-merchandising display card.
½ doz. pack—15 lbs.

JET STAR

NEW SLIM LOOK

A handsomely crafted double cutaway, slim body guitar that produces clear, mellow tones. Near professional size, 30" long. Distinctive design featuring the modern "Swedish Head" with all metal worm gears for **micro-tuning.** Accurately fretted extended fingerboard with white embossed position marks and gold high-lighted frets. Rich red gold-sparkled body, fret board, scratch pad and new **string grip bridge.** White pearlized face with gold embossed head. 6 strings—3 natural nylon and 3 nylon wire-wound. Plastic tailpiece. Complete with shoulder cord, instruction song book and pick.

METAL WORM GEARS 12 to 1 RATIO FOR MICRO-TUNING

No. 356
Individually packed in attractive multi-colored, shrink-wrapped see-thru DeLuxe Tray.
½ doz. pack—20 lbs.

MASTRO INDUSTRIES, INC., 3040 Webster Avenue, Bronx, N. Y. 10467

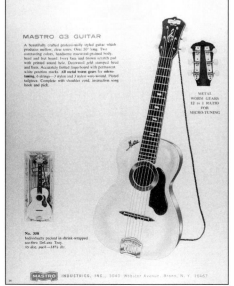

MASTRO G3 GUITAR

A beautifully crafted professionally styled guitar which produces mellow, clear tones. Over 30" long. Two contrasting colors, handsome rosewood-grained body, head and fret board. Ivory face and brown scratch pad with printed sound hole. Decorated gold stamped head and frets. Accurately fretted fingerboard with permanent white position marks. All metal worm gears for micro-tuning. 6 strings—3 nylon and 3 nylon wire-wound. Plated tailpiece. Complete with shoulder cord, instruction song book and pick.

METAL WORM GEARS 12 to 1 RATIO FOR MICRO-TUNING

No. 358
Individually packed in shrink-wrapped see-thru DeLuxe Tray.
½ doz. pack—18½ lbs.

MASTRO INDUSTRIES, INC., 3040 Webster Avenue, Bronx, N. Y. 10467

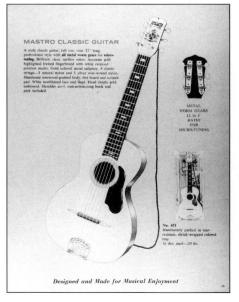

MASTRO CLASSIC GUITAR

A truly classic guitar, full size, over 32" long, professional style with all metal worm gears for micro-tuning. Brilliant, clear, mellow tones. Accurate gold high-lighted fretted fingerboard with white recessed position marks. Gold colored metal tailpiece. 6 classic strings—3 natural nylon and 3 silver nylon wire-wound. Handsome rosewood-grained body, fret board and scratch pad. White marbleized face and head. Head deeply gold embossed. Shoulder cord, instruction song book and pick included.

METAL WORM GEARS 12 to 1 RATIO FOR MICRO-TUNING

No. 451
Handsomely packed in tear-resistant, shrink-wrapped colored tray.
½ doz. pack—20 lbs.

Designed and Made for Musical Enjoyment

MASTRO G5 GUITAR

Steel String

Over 32" full size, professional style guitar with all metal worm gear for micro-tuning. Clear, mellow tone. Accurately inlaid fingerboard with white colored position marks and gold highlighted frets. New, rigid metal beam throughout the length of the guitar (patent pending). Metal reinforced. 6 strings—2 steel and 4 steel wire wound. Handsome rosewood-grained face and body with many color contrasting scratch pad and gold embossed head. Shoulder cord, instruction song book and pick.

New, rigid, metal beam throughout the length of the guitar (patent pending).

METAL WORM GEARS 12 to 1 RATIO FOR MICRO-TUNING

No. 452
Individually packed in shrink-wrapped, multicolored, DeLuxe Tray.
½ doz. pack—22 lbs.

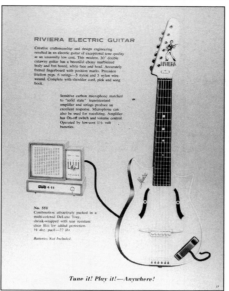

RIVIERA ELECTRIC GUITAR

Creative craftsmanship and design engineering resulted in an electric guitar of exceptional tone quality at an unusually low cost. This modern, 30" double cutaway guitar has a beautiful ebony marbleized body and fret board, white face and head. Accurately fretted fingerboard with position marks. Precision friction pegs. 6 strings—3 nylon and 3 nylon wirewound. Complete with shoulder cord, pick and song book.

Sensitive carbon microphone matched to "solid state" transistorized amplifier and strings produce an excellent response. Microphone can also be used for vocalizing. Amplifier has On-off switch and volume control. Operated by low-cost 1½ volt batteries.

No. 551
Combination attractively packed in a multi-colored DeLuxe Tray, shrink-wrapped with tear resistant clear film for added protection.
½ doz. pack—22 lbs.

Batteries Not Included.

Tune it! Play it!—Anywhere!

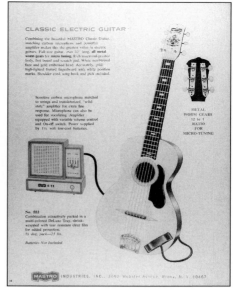

CLASSIC ELECTRIC GUITAR

Combining the beautiful MASTRO Classic Guitar, matching carbon microphone and powerful amplifier makes this the greatest value in electric guitars. Full size guitar, over 32" long, all metal worm gears for micro tuning. Rich rosewood-grained body, fret board and scratch pad. White marbleized face and gold embossed head. Accurately, gold high-lighted fretted fingerboard with white position marks. Shoulder cord, song book and pick included.

Sensitive carbon microphone matched to strings and transistorized, "solid state" amplifier for extra fine response. Microphone can also be used for vocalizing. Amplifier equipped with variable volume control and On-off switch. Power supplied by 1½ volt low-cost batteries.

METAL WORM GEARS 12 to 1 RATIO FOR MICRO-TUNING

No. 552
Combination attractively packed in a multi-colored DeLuxe Tray, shrink-wrapped with tear resistant clear film for added protection.
½ doz. pack—25 lbs.

Batteries Not Included.

MASTRO INDUSTRIES, INC., 3040 Webster Avenue, Bronx, N. Y. 10467

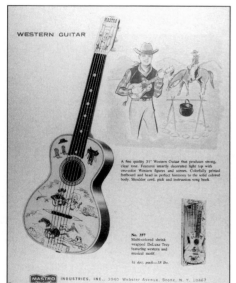

WESTERN GUITAR

A fine quality 31" Western Guitar that produces strong, clear tone. Features smartly decorated light top with two-color Western figures and scenes. Colorfully printed fretboard and head in perfect harmony to the solid colored body. Shoulder cord, pick and instruction song book.

No. 357
Multi-colored shrink wrapped DeLuxe Tray featuring western and musical motif.
½ doz. pack—18 lbs.

MACCAFERRI GUITAR

With High-Fidelity Tone and Pitch

Top-ranking musicians acclaim the MACCAFERRI GUITAR is easier to finger and play. The tone is rich, full and brilliant. This beautiful instrument is full standard size with professional cutaway and heavy brass frets. Made to the highest precision standards. The instrument has pressure type pitch compensator bridge, brass tailpiece with plastic insert, reinforced with wood sound-ribbing and metal-shell neck. Many new and exciting features. Designed to give years of satisfaction for exacting professional use, or for personal enjoyment.

Some outstanding features of the MACCAFERRI Plastic Guitar:

"Adjustable" Neck—Practical device to regulate height of strings from frets to suit musician's individual style of playing.

"Stay-True" Armored Neck—Made of metal shell, plastic covered, with specially treated wood core to guarantee true alignment.

"Pitch Compensating" Bridge—New style "pitch compensation" bridge with decorated ends.

"Sound-Ribbed" Body—Professional, cutaway style made of resounding plastic material. Highly efficient inside wood sound-ribbing.

'FEATHER-TOUCH' MACHINE HEADS
Six sets of all metal planetary gears in sealed assembly. Screw regulator for each unit. Precision engineered. Permanently lubricated.

No. 446
Each guitar is wrapped in a poly bag and packed in an attractive heavy-duty corrugated board carrying case with handle.
½ doz. pack—25½ lbs.

MASTRO INDUSTRIES, INC., 3040 Webster Avenue, Bronx, N. Y. 10467

New additions to the 1967 Mastro catalog (courtesy Maria Maccaferri).

1980s Saga DG500, a copy of the Selmer "Django Guitar" which appeared after Maccaferri departed Selmer.

the CSL Gypsy. They were accompanied by a booklet titled "The Rebirth of Django's Guitar." Outlets were reported to be available in the U.K., Europe, North America and Australia, but it's unknown how many units actually made it around the globe. Unfortunately, Mario was not pleased with the consistency of the products coming in from Japan and the model only lasted until around 1979. It's not clear how many of these Hoshino Maccaferri's were produced, but they are probably relatively rare. An unused 1979 signed label for an MAC10 with a serial number of 306 has been seen, so probably there were fewer produced of that particular model.

The Maccaferri Saga

Despite the lack of success of the Hoshino Maccaferris, Summerfield and Maccaferri did not give up on the idea of reviving the Selmer guitars, and in the early '80s they tried again, this time producing Maccaferri guitars by the Saga company in Japan.

This round of Saga Maccaferris yielded two models, the MAC 100S and the MAC

400S. These were essentially the same guitar except the MAC 100S had a small oval soundhole, similar to the post-Maccaferri "Django" guitars, while the MAC 400S had a large "D" soundhole.

Both Saga Maccaferri models had solid spruce tops, laminated mahogany sides and backs, single cutaway, rosewood fingerboard and bridge, 21 frets, dot inlays, spruce braces, celluloid rosette, slotted headstock, gold tuners and a gold plated Maccaferri trapeze tailpiece.

While no reference is available, Saga also marked a DG-500 guitar — presumably DG = Django Guitar which was identical to the Mac 100S.

The Saga Maccaferris were more satisfactory than the previous Hoshino models, but unfortunately demand proved less than sanguine, and the Saga Maccaferris lasted only until 1983 or so. These marked the end of the official Maccaferri Selmer guitar, although periodically smaller companies revive the idea, a tribute the power of Mario's creation.

Saving the reeds

In around 1981 several events occurred to wind down Mario Maccaferri's commercial ventures. One event was simply that Maccaferri was getting tired of making cassette housings, and wanted to get out of the plastic business. Another was that the city of New York wanted Maccaferri's building and purchased it from him. Rather than beginning over again at a new location — Mario was already 80 — Maccaferri decided it was time to stop and to liquidate the factory.

In 1981 *almost* all of the equipment was auctioned off for a relative pittance and Mario retired. However, Maria was *not* ready to stop working, and diverted the auctioneer from the reed-making equipment. She asked Mario to give her the reed making business. She had, after all, been involved with it since she was 16 years old. Mario agreed and signed the reed business over to Maria Maccaferri.

From that day on until his death, Mario would always tell Maria that "you're the boss" when it came to the reed business, although Maria adds that Mario was re-

ally always the boss.

As of this writing Maria Maccaferri continues as President of the French American Reeds Manufacturing Company, making reeds primarily for various private label retailers, rather than put the effort into advertising and marketing the Maccaferri brand. Among those labels which are really Maccaferri reeds, by the way, is the name Selmer...

Plastic violins

Although commercial production of instruments had ended at the end of the '60s, in his later years Maccaferri continued his interest in making instruments. For the remainder of his life he went to his workshop every day at 7:30 a.m. and continued working on various projects, including the development of a remarkable travel guitar, a classical guitar which folded up into its own body — without detuning — becoming the size of a shoebox, and a radical new plastic violin design. This violin project was completed in 1990 and a public debut was conducted at the Weill Recital Hall at Carnegie Hall. The critics were less than generous about the violin, but Mr. Maccaferri was feted by a number of chemical companies for his pioneering work in the field of plastics.

In the late 1980s Mario Maccaferri returned to experimenting with classical guitars, his first love, working in collaboration with luthier John Monteleone. These included guitars with and without internal sound chambers.

Although I never had the pleasure of his acquaintance, there has never been an account of meetings with the Mastro Maestro which didn't relate his warm nature and genuine enthusiasm and camaraderie with anyone who loved guitars.

Mario Maccaferri passed away on April 16, 1993, at the age of 92.

Many Maccaferri plastic guitars and other instruments remained unsold after 1969 and were stored at a Mastro warehouse in the Bronx for many years. Periodically lots of these would be liquidated to hopeful dealers, the first beginning in 1982, with a final purge being made shortly before Maccaferri's death in 1993, many instruments going both to A.S.I.A. and Elderly Instruments in Lansing, Michigan. These were all quickly sold. New-old-stock Maccaferri plastics should be relatively easy to find, and they are well worth seeking out, particularly the G30 and G40 models, with their funky tone and fascinating technology. Much harder would be finding Mario Maccaferri's older Selmer and Maccaferri guitars, which now command prices well into the five figure range.

In December of 1995 Mario Maccaferri's collection of Mozzani/Maccaferri lyre-guitars was sold to a private collector.

21st Century guitars?

In retrospect, there's no denying that Mario Maccaferri's vision of inexpensive but good guitars made out of plastic was quixotic, but the time has come to recognize them for the visionary instruments they were. It's highly unlikely that the idea of building acoustic guitars out of injection-molded plastic will prove to be the wave of the future, but increasingly luthiers are searching for alternative materials to the scarce tonewoods traditionally put into guitars. And, at this writing, at least one company, Kuau Technology, Ltd., of Maui, Hawaii, markets RainSong guitars, steel-string and classicals made entirely out of graphite, advertised as "stable and durable, impervious to climate," objectives laid out by Mario Maccaferri way back in 1953. So, who knows? Who would have thought how prophetic were the words of Mr. Robinson when he put his arm around Dustin Hoffman and said, "Plastics?"

However the next century turns out, we can certainly conclude that Mario Maccaferri contributed mightily to the guitar cause over the course of the 20th Century, as a trailblazing classical guitarist, award-winning luthier, and plastics innovator, the father of the plastic guitar. That Mario Maccaferri's best-known achievement should be his plentiful, accessible and totally delightful plastic instruments may not be totally adequate, but then again, how many of us are so fortunate to leave living epitaphs that serve as memorials to our creative vision?

MACCAFERRI GUITARS

Here's an approximate listing of Mario Maccaferri's many guitars and other instruments, including the plastics. As usual, take this as a rough guide only, and do not expect it to be all-inclusive or absolutely accurate. Maccaferri built a great many prototypes and one-offs during his lifetime.

Guitars/Lyre-Guitars

1923-27	No. 1 9-String Contraguitar
1923-27	No. 2 11-String Contraguitar
1923-27	No. 3 9-String Guitar
1923-27	No. 4 6-String Cutaway Guitar
1923-27	No. 5 6-String Guitar
1923-27	No. 6 6-String Spanish Guitar
1923-27	No. 7 short-scale Guitar
1923-27	No. 8 Terz Guitar
1928-c.31	Model No. 1 Chitarrone 9-String Cutaway Lyre-Guitar
1928-c.31	Model No. 2 Chitarra 9-String Cutaway Lyre-Guitar
1928-c.31	Model No. 3 Chitarra 11-String Cutaway Lyre-Guitar
1928-c.31	Model No. 4 Chitarra 9-String Lyre-Guitar (non-cut)
1928-c.31	Model No. 5 Cutaway Spanish Guitar
1928-c.31	Model No. 6 Spanish Guitar (non-cut)
1928-c.31	Model No. 7 Parlour Guitar
1928-c.31	Model No. 8 Terz Guitar
1932-34	Selmer Modèle Espagnol
1932-34	Selmer Modèle Concert
1932-34	Selmer Modèle Orchestre
1932-34	Selmer Modèle Jazz
1932-34	Selmer Modèle Hawaienne
1932-34	Selmer Guitare Eddie Freeman
1976-79	Ibanez Maccaferri MAC10 Guitar (plus 3 other models)
c.1981-83	Saga MAC 100S Guitar
c.1981-83	Saga MAC 400S Guitar
c.1981-83	Saga DG500 Guitar
1980s	Various handmade classicals

Mandolins/Mandolas

1928-c.31	No. 1 Mandolone
1928-c.31	No. 2 Mandoloncello
1928-c.31	No. 3 Mandola baritono
1928-c.31	No. 4 Mandola tenore
1928-c.31	No. 5 Mandola soprano
1928-c.31	No. 6 Mandolino
1928-c.31	No. 7 Quartino

Plastic Instruments

1949-c.69	U400 Islander Ukulele (by '65 C-400)
1951-c.69	U600 Islander Deluxe Ukulele
1951-?	Sparkle Plenty Islander Ukette
1951-c.65	Islander Visual Chordmaster
1952-c.58	G30 Flat-top Guitar
1952-c.58	G40 DeLuxe Arched Top
1953-?	Islander Baritone Ukulele
1954-?	U150 Islander Ukette
1954-?	MU25 Midget Uke
1954-c.69	No. 120 T.V. Pal Ukulele
1954-?	No. G16 Islander Guitar
1957-c.69	No. R20 Romancer Classic Style Guitar (No. 1010 by '65)
c.1959-c.69	ShowTime Classical Guitar (No. 1020, no decoration by '65)
c.1959	Roco Guitar

1964-c.67	No. 300 Mastro Beatles Jr. Guitar (tenor)	by 1965-c.69	No. 100 Mastro Ukette
1964-c.67	No. 320 Mastro Beatles Four Pop Guitar (tenor)	by 1965-c.69	No. 110 Mastro Banjolele
1964-c.67	No. 330 Mastro Beatles Yeah Yeah Guitar (6-string)	by 1965-c.69	No. 520 Banjo Uke
		by 1965-c.69	No. 700 Square Dance Fiddle
1964-c.67	No. 340 Mastro Beatles Beatle-ist Guitar (6-string)	by 1965-c.69	No. 1000 Stradivarius Violin
1964-c.67	No. 380 Mastro Beatles Ringo Snare Drum	by 1965-c.69	Mastro Trumpet (gold or cream)
1964-c.67	No. 360 Mastro Beatles Beat Bongo Drum	by 1965-c.69	Mastro Saxophone (gold or red)
1964-c.67	No. 370 Mastro Beatles Big Beat Bongo Drum	by 1965-c.69	Mastro Clarinet (gold or black)
1964-c.67	No. 350 Mastro Beatles Banjo	by 1965-c.69	Mastro Bongos
1964-c.67	Mastro Beatles Pin-Up Guitar (miniature)	by 1965-c.69	Mastro Rumba Maracas
by 1965-c.69	Mastro G-10 Guitar	by 1965-c.69	Mastro Bolero Maracas
by 1965-c.69	No. 452 Mastro G-5 Guitar	by 1965-c.69	Mastro Rhythm Maracas
by 1965-c.69	No. 727 Sonora Guitar A-SH (nylon strings, woodgrain)	by 1965-c.69	Mastro Castanet
		by 1965-c.69	Mastro Snare drum
by 1965-c.69	No. 727 Sonora Guitar IC (nylon strings, cream & black)	1966-c.69	No. 222 Mastro Gitarina
		1966-c.69	Mastro GTA-10 Electric Guitar
by 1965-c.69	No. 500 TV Pal Guitar A-SH (woodgrain)	1966-c.69	Mastro Teen Electric Guitar
by 1965-c.69	No. 500 TV Pal Guitar PIC (two colors)	1966-c.69	TA-10 Mastro Amp
by 1965-c.69	No. 775 Western Guitar	1966-c.69	TA-3 Mastro Amp
by 1965-c.69	GTA-5 Electric Guitar	1967-c.69	No. 102 Mastro Monkey (Strat-style uke)
by 1965-c.69	CT GTA-5 Tenor Cutaway Electric Guitar	1967-c.69	No. 352 Mastro Disco Cutaway Guitar
by 1965-c.69	TA-5 Mastro Amplifier	1967-c.69	No. 303 Mastro Riviera Guitar (nylon strings)
by 1965-c.69	No. 610 Mastro TV Pal Cutaway Baritone Ukulele	1967-c.69	Jet Star Guitar
by 1965-c.69	No. 410 Islander Cutaway Baritone Ukulele	1967-c.69	No. 551 Riviera Electric Guitar
by 1965-c.69	No. CTG-6 Mastro Cutaway Tenor Guitar	1967-c.69	Mastro 4.11 amplifier
by 1965-c.69	No. 666 TV Pal Cutaway Tenor Guitar	1967-c.69	No. 325 Mastro Deluxe Sonora Guitar (nylon strings)
by 1965-c.69	No. 750 Mastro Uke	1967-c.69	No. 358 Mastro G3 Guitar
by 1965-c.69	No. 725 Mastro Jr. Guitar (6-string uke)	1967-c.69	No. 451 Mastro Classic Guitar
by 1965-c.69	Automatic Chordmaster	1967-c.69	No. 552 Mastro Classic Electric Guitar
by 1965-c.69	Visual Chordmaster (with lights)	1990-93	Plastic violin

MARTIN
ELECTRIC GUITARS

Exotic Pilgrims From Nazareth

Mention the subject of American *acoustic* guitars and one of the first names that will undoubtedly pop into your head will be C.F. Martin. Not that there aren't many other estimable brands, but Martin, by virtue of its longevity — since 1833 — and incredible quality remains the standard by which almost all steel-stringed acoustics are judged. A pretty impressive achievement.

Bring up the topic of *electrics*, and Martin is hardly the first name of recall. By "electrics" is not meant the company's many fine acoustic-electric guitars, many sporting top-notch electronics (which ultimately remain acoustic beasts), but rather electric guitars meant for country chicken pickin' or raunchy rock and roll. How-

ever, beginning in the late '50s, Martin has periodically launched forays into the electric guitar marketplace with some very interesting, if commercially unsuccessful, results. Most coverage of the Martin brand is focused, quite rightly, on their substantial acoustic achievements. For this essay,

1962 Martin F-50 electric with one DeArmond pickup, Martin's first thinline (courtesy C.F. Martin Company).

however, let's take an alternative view and look at the company's various electric guitars, its thinline hollowbodies and later solidbodies.

The primary starting point for information about Martin guitars is, of course, *Martin Guitars: A History* by Mike Longworth, one-time pearl inlaying ace and former company historian (4 Maples Press, Minisink Hills, PA). Longworth's

book chronicles the company's history in very personal terms and provides wonderfully rich detail about Martin's many guitars through the ages. It should be an essential part of any Martin lover's library.

Fifties flattop electrics

Martin actually got into the electric guitar business in the late '50s when it started slapping DeArmond pickups onto some of its acoustic guitars, yielding the D-18E, D-28E and OO-18E. These pickups were the DeArmond humbuckers with chrome sides and a black center in a trapezoidal hole, large pole pieces along one side and smaller poles along the other. Prototypes of the D-18E began in 1958, and in 1959 production began on it plus the D-28E and OO-18E.

The D-18E was a mahogany dreadnought with the neck pickup and a second bridge pickup. The typical Martin pickguard had the front point cut off and a notch in back to make room for the pickups rings. A threeway toggle was mounted on the upper treble bout. Controls included one volume and two tones, with the big plastic knobs. D-18Es are the rarest of these early Martin electrics, lasting only from the '58 prototypes through 1959. These began with prototype #163746. Around 858 of these were produced.

The D-28E was essentially the same as the D-18E except for a rosewood body, gold-finished pickups and Grover Rotomatic tuners. D-28Es lasted from 1959 through 1964. These were the most common, with around 3083 produced.

The OO-18E was basically the small-

(Left) 1963 Martin F-65 in a cool sunburst with a pair of DeArmond's and a Martin Bigsby. (Right) 1966 Martin GT-70 with trapeze tail (courtesy C.F. Martin Company).

(Left) 1966 Martin GT-75 with Bigsby (courtesy C.F. Martin Company). (Right) A 19th Century Stauffer/Martin with the Austrian six-in-line headstock which may have inspired Leo Fender and certainly influenced the head on the 18 and 28 series electrics (courtesy C.F. Martin Company).

The F-50 was the bottom of the line, a single cutaway with a single DeArmond humbucker pickup, like those on the previous acoustic hybrids, in the neck position. Controls were one volume and one tone control mounted along the edge of the lower treble bout, with black, chrome-topped knobs. This had a trapeze tailpiece with a sort of cabinet of Dr. Caligari "M" cutout of the center. This was finished in a brown to yellow two-tone sunburst. The first prototype bore the serial number 179828. Only 519 F-50s were built from the middle of 1962 to the spring of 1965.

The F-55 was identical to the F-50 except for the addition of a bridge DeArmond humbucker, plus the attendant threeway toggle on the cutaway horn and a second set of volume and tone knobs flanking the treble f-hole. The F-55, too, had a Martin "M" trapeze tail. This series began with guitar #279831. Some 665 F-55s were made from mid-'62 to the summer of 1965.

The F-65 was the top of the line with two equal cutaways yielding a wide, tulip effect. Other than the bookmatched cutaways, this was the same as the two-pickup F-55, with the addition of a Bigsby-made Martin vibrato in which the stylized "M" had become a similar "V" shape. Probably the strangest feature of the F-65 was the fact that the heel of the neck did

bodied OO-18 acoustics with mahogany back and sides, spruce top, and the ring-mounted DeArmond tucked right at the end of the fingerboard. These featured one tone and one volume control, with large two-tone plastic knobs situated down on the lower treble bout. The first prototype was serial number 166839. OO-18Es were produced from 1959 to 1964. Around 1526 of these were produced.

These first Martins were fairly clumsy pilgrimages into electricity, but it's important to know about them because they could easily be construed as having been modified by owners when, in fact, they are quite original.

F Troop

Martin's first truly electric guitars were the Style F thinline cutaway archtops which began in prototype stage in 1961 and entered production in 1962. The F Series consisted of three models, the F-50, F-55 and F-65, all with bodies slightly less than 2" thick and made of maple plywood with bound tops. All three had shapes roughly reminiscent of the dreadnought that made Martin famous, though slightly exaggerated with a wider lower bout. The cutaways were fairly wide and radical, cutting out at almost a right angle from the neck. The glued in necks had unbound 20-fret rosewood fingerboards, dot inlays and the typical squarish Martin three-and-three headstock. Necks joined the body at the 14th fret. Each bore an elevated pickguard and had a distinctive moveable adjustable bridge made of clear plexiglass.

Ca. 1962-63 Martin #700 portable amplifier (courtesy C.F. Martin Company).

not change from the single-cutaway models, creating a sort of thick chunk of body extending up to the 14th fret. The first F-65 was #179834. 566 F-65s were made from 1962 to the summer of '65.

Mike Longworth's book shows at least

three guitar amplifiers carrying the Martin name from the early '60s. In 1961 Martin marketed a pair of combos, the Model 110T and Model 112T which were made by DeArmond, Martin's principle early pickup supplier. DeArmond's versions were almost identical except for lacking Martin's grillcloth and being covered in metallic lavender tolex! Both the 110T and 112T had top rear-mounted controls and very groovy geometrical grillcloths in a sort of M.C. Escher pattern. Presumably the 110 featured a 10" speaker, while the 112 had a 12". The "T" suggests a tremolo circuit. DeArmond amps offered the tremolo circuit as an option. In 1962 Martin offered a very cool #700 portable amplifier, a unit ensconced in a leather carrying case, presumably battery-powered. Who made this amp is unknown.

(Left) A ca. 1981 Martin EB-28 bass and a ca. 1966 Martin GT-75 in red with trapeze tail (courtesy C.F. Martin Company). (Right) Fall of 1974 ad for Martin Sigma "approved" copies with a quasi-Gibson SG SBG2-6 and a quasi-Fender bass SBB2-8 (C.F. Martin Company).

Sporty GTs

The Martin F Series bit the dust in mid-'65, to be supplanted by the somewhat updated, nattier GT Series of bound archtop cutaway hollowbody electrics. The first few prototypes were dubbed the XTE Series and produced in 1965. There were three each to the XTE-70 and XTE-75. The guitars were renamed the GT Series and swung into production in the beginning of 1966. The GT Series consisted basically of two models, the GT-70 and GT-75. These were thinlines with two f-holes, a 15th fret neck joint (actually more frets were clear of the body), bound 22-fret rosewood fingerboards, dot inlays, and new, bound, wide-flared three-and-three headstocks with a concave curve in the pointed crown. Both were offered with the V-notched Bigsby tailpiece, but examples can be found with trapeze tails as well.

The GT-70 was a re-styled two-pickup, single-cutaway recalling the F-55s. The cutaway retained the wide horizontal angle of before, however the upper bass bout received a more graceful treatment, with a slight inward curve as it met the neck at the 16th fret. The controls were the same as before; the elevated pickguard had become a large white affair. Pickups remained our familiar DeArmond humbuckers. Gone were the plastic bridges in favor of metal adjustable fine tune variety. Finishes were either burgundy or black. The first prototype serial number was 203803. Just 453 of these were made between January of 1966 and October of 1968.

The GT-75 was a re-tooled two-pickup, double-cutaway F-65 with the same appointments as the GT-70. The major changes were moving the heel forward to the body juncture, eliminating the awkward body extension of the F-65 and curving the upper shoulder back in a bit like a Tele.. The first prototype serial number was #204108. 451 GT-75s were built from January '66 to October '68.

Just one 12-string versions of the GT-75, a T-12-75 was produced. This had an extended headstock without the flared top, and a large M trapeze tailpiece. The pickguard covered most of the lower room.

As can be seen in the promotional photograph provided by Martin, there was also one XGT-85 Bass guitar made, shown on the right. This was a prototype.

The F Series Martin electrics were before my awareness of the diversity of the guitar universe, but I recall the appearance of the GTs, which got to stores in Wisconsin in the summer of '67. I recall admiring the cool shapes and burgundy finish, although I've never been a fan of DeArmond pickups and, rightly or wrongly, always considered them a weakness. As already indicated, the GT Series was hardly a winner and fell victim to the general guitar malaise that swept the world guitar markets in around 1968. The same guitar bust that did in Valco/Kay and a host of Japanese guitarmakers did in Martin's archtop electrics.

Martin's GTs never really made great inroads in the professional arena, however,

1979 catalog for Martin Electrics (C.F. Martin Company).

it's worth noting that Skip Spence played a GT-75 with the Bay Area psychedelic outfit Moby Grape. He can be seen with it on the back of their first album, *Moby Grape* (CBS, 1967).

Longworth also illustrates yet another Martin amplifier offered in 1966, the SS140, an OEM amp manufactured for Martin. This was one of those gigantic amps popular at the time. As the prefix indicates, this was a solid state amp with enough inputs to run a whole band, plus tremolo and reverb. This was a piggy-back amp, with a head separate from the speaker cabinet. The vinyl-covered cab featured two 15" J.B. Lansing speakers. Controls were on both the front and back of the

head. The front offered two channels with one input each. Controls for each channel were volume, bass, treble, presence, reverb and brilliance controls. The amp offered a separate pair of controls for tremolo. The back had an additional two inputs, one for another guitar (or bass), one for guitar or microphone, and jacks for reverb and tremolo footswitches. The 140 probably suggests the output wattage.

Japanese Martins

Martin' first era of flirtation with electrics ended with its GTs, and wouldn't resume until a decade later. However, in 1970 Martin joined the growing list of American manufacturers to begin import-

ing guitars made in Japan, introducing its Sigma series acoustics. In around 1973, Martin, like competitors Guild and Gibson, began importing a line of Sigma solidbody electrics made in Japan by Tokai.

Like virtually all Japanese-made guitars from that era, Martin Sigma solidbodies were basically copies of other American models. Martin Sigmas employed slightly different headstock designs, unlike many copies carrying Japanese brand names, but essentially these are similar to most other of these early copies.

In 1974 Martin Sigma electrics included two SGs, a Tele and a Fender bass. The SBG2-6 was pretty much a straightforward SG copy with a bolt-on neck, center-peaked three-and-three head, block inlays, large pickguard, twin humbuckers, finetune bridge, and stop tailpiece, in cherry. The SBG2-9 was pretty cool, with a natural-finished plywood body, white pickguard, rosewood fingerboard with white block inlays, gold hardware and Bigsby. The SBF2-6 was a Tele with rosewood fingerboard, three-and-three head, block inlays, neck humbucker and bridge single-coil. The SBB2-8 was the bass, with natural finished body, two-and-two head, rosewood 'board, block inlays, white 'guard, and two humbucking pickups.

Martin's Sigma electrics fared hardly better than its own electric guitar designs of the '60s. After little more than a year, the electrics were dropped from the Sigma line. Replicas marked by Japanese companies, of course, did swimmingly well.

Rock solids

Martin's re-entry into electric manufacturing is related to the association of Richard (Dick) Boak with the C.F. Martin company. Dick Boak, with dreams of being a luthier and constantly working on guitar projects on his own, joined Martin in 1976 as a draftsman. In 1977 Boak was assigned to the project of designing an electric guitar for Martin. This resulted in the development of the E-18, EM-18 and EB-18 guitars and bass. The first prototypes of this new electric guitar series were produced in 1978, ten years after the demise of the GT-70/75, and production commenced in 1979 with guitar serial number 1000.

The new Martin electrics were offset double cutaway guitars which, in terms of shape, fall very loosely into a Stratocaster category. The cutaways are a bit wider and shallower than a Strat, both pointing away from the body. The horns are much more rounded than a Strat. Like a Strat, the waist is slightly offset, and the lower bout has a slightly asymmetrical slant to it. The bodies were initially built of hard maple and rosewood laminates that imitate the look of neck-through guitars popular at the time, but actually have neck pockets with glued-in mahogany necks. These had unbound 22-fret rosewood fingerboards, dot inlays and a distinctive three-and-three variation on the old Stauffer/Viennese headstock, with script CFM logo decal, which may have originally inspired Leo Fender's Strat creation. [Prior to developing the Strat, Fender visited the Martin factory and was shown some of the old Stauffer/Martins with the round-hooked Eastern European headstock shape.] These all featured chrome Sperzel tuners, brass nuts, twin humbuckers, threeway selects, two volume and two tones with chrome dome knobs, and a Leo Quan Badass bridge.

The E-18 and EM-18 were basically the same guitar differing only in electronics. The E-18 featured two DiMarzio humbucking pickups, a DiMarzio PAF at the neck and a DiMarzio Super Distortion at the bridge. In addition to the regular controls, the E-18 had mini-toggle phase switch. Production of the E-18 began in April of '79 and only 341 were made until the guitar ended in early 1982.

The EM-18 came with either a pair of Mighty Mite humbuckers or a pair of DiMarzios. It was otherwise the same as the E-18 with the addition of a threeway mini-toggle coil selector switch which allowed a choice of both or either coil on the lead pickup. This arrangement allowed for a rather remarkable variety of tones, by the way. EM-18 production began in 1979 and only 1,375 before the guitar ended in February 1982.

The EB-18 was a bass version with a 33.825" scale. According to Longworth, early versions had a single DiMarzio "One" pickup and Grover Titan tuners, while later basses had a DiMarzio "G" pickup and Schaller pickups. Expect to find various combinations of those. Longworth also mentions the possibility that some might have Mighty Mite pickups, but this is uncertain. EB-18 production began in '79 and 874 were made until the guitar ended in early 1982.

According to Longworth, Martin began to use built-in Schaller Straploks beginning with guitar #2085. However, the example shown here is #1034, the thirty-fourth made if #1000 was indeed the first, and it has the Schaller Straploks, which are original. Pot dates are late 1978, confirming that it's probably one of the early examples. The serial number on #1034, by the way, was printed on a piece of tape in the cavity under the neck pickup. The control cavity had EM-18 stamped in it.

These guitars came with rectangular molded plastic cases.

The #1034 EM-18 illustrated has the impressed or branded Martin logo burned into the back of the headstock. According to Longworth, the Martin trademark began to be burned into the back at the neck joint beginning with #2377.

Again according to Longworth, early 18 Series instruments had brass-plated steel covers on the control panel, whereas later

(Left to Right) 1979 EM-18, E-18 and EB-18, Martin's first electric solidbodies (courtesy C.F. Martin Company). Martin EM-18 (#1034, April or May 1979) with Mighty Mite pickups. Martin EM-18 from late '79 or early '80 with vibrato, either a special order or addition.

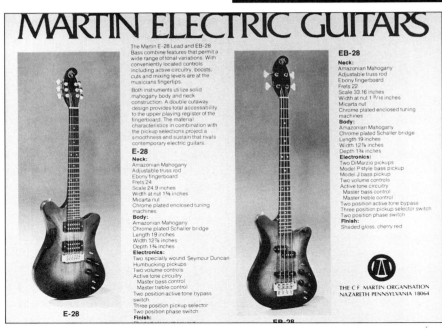

(Left) 1981 Martin E-28 and EB-28, neck-through guitars (C.F. Martin Company). (Right) Ca. 1981 flyer for the Martin E-28 guitar and EB-28 bass illustrating their "arched" tops (C.F. Martin Company).

versions had black plastic.

Finally, according to Longworth, the earliest examples of these instruments had laminated bodies made of maple, rosewood and mahogany. A second series was made with a combination of maple and rosewood. A third series was made with maple and walnut. The #1034 EM-18 shown here appears to be very early yet has maple and rosewood, so it's not clear if materials are indicators of chronology or simply the vicissitudes of fate (or the woodshop, as the case may be).

Despite what appears now to a somewhat dated design (all the quasi-organic shapes inspired by Alembic at the time can be tough to love with the passage of time), Martin's 18 Series electrics are actually quite comfortable and yield a versatile number of useful sounds. The neck profile is quite round, not unlike many acoustics, but very easy to play. The frets are small and squarish, which makes them a bit awkward for blues-style bending. Martin's 18 Series didn't turn the heads of the electric guitar world and these relatively rare models bit the dust in 1982.

Plus ten

In 1980, however, Martin had hired another guitarmaker, one John Marshall.

Marshall had studied lutherie with Eric Schulte whose base of operation was in the far western Main Line suburbs of Philadelphia around Frazer, Pennsylvania. Schulte himself had worked with the legendary Sam Koontz, who was responsible for Harptone and some Standel guitars, as well as his own. After learning the tricks of the trade from Schulte, Marshall became involved in the il-fated Renaissance guitar company of Malvern, Pennsylvania, just up the road from Frazer. Renaissance, you'll recall, made those exotic plexiglass guitars and basses in around 1979 (plus a later series in 1980 designed by John Dragonetti). These were designed by John Marshall. Marshall left Renaissance to join Martin, where he was hired to work on the electric guitars which would become Martin's 28 Series.

As suggested by the numerical designation, Martin's 28 Series was essentially an upgrade or refinement of the earlier 18 Series. Martin typically indicates fancier materials and appointments with a higher number (a D-28 is fancier dreadnought than a D-18, etc.). These consisted of one guitar, the E-28, and one bass, the EB-28. The first prototypes appeared in June of 1980; production began in January of 1981.

Essentially the 28s looked very similar to the E/EM/EB-18s. They had the same offset double cutaway body outline and the modified Viennese three-and-three headstock. Instead of maple laminate bodies with glued-in necks, the 28s had mahogany bodies and necks in a neck-through-body design. The basically slab bodies of the E-18 had gained a carved top, with a deep contour in the upper waist. The brass nut had become a Micarta nut. Fingerboards were now ebony. Finishes were sunburst.

The E-28 guitar now sported a two-octave fingerboard and a Schaller adjustable bridge/tailpiece assembly, in chrome. Pickups were twin active humbuckers specially designed for Martin by Seymour Duncan. The straplocking system was also by Schaller, as were the tuners. Controls included two volumes for each pickup plus a master volume and master tone (all with black knobs sort of like those found on Rickenbackers), a threeway select, a phase switch and an active circuit bypass switch. The headstock had an ebony veneer. The cover on the control cavity was made of black Boltaron.

The EB-28 bass was very similar to the guitar in appointments and controls. It had a 22-fret ebony fingerboard, 33.825" scale, a DiMarzio P-style neck pickup and a DiMarzio J-style pickup at the bridge. It, too, carried a Schaller bridge and Schaller M-4 tuners. Just 194 E-28 guitars and 217 EB-28 basses were built between January 1981 and February 1982, although another 98 unidentified solidbodies appaer on Martin production logs.

For better or worse, by 1982 the taste for natural-finished, neck-through guitars with lots of switches and active electronics had begun to move on. On the horizon were the brief affair with weird-shaped "heavy metal" guitars and the impending first Strat-mania and the rise of Superstrats which would pretty much define the remainder of the decade. 1982 and the 18 and 28 Series marked the end of Martin's direct manufacture of electric solidbody guitars.

Like a bumble bee

However, Martin did not completely abandon the marketing of solidbody electrics. In 1985, coincident with the dramatic increase in quality among Korean manufacturers, Martin unveiled its Stinger line of solidbody electrics made on the peninsula south of the DMZ.

As with most other imported Martin products, Stinger guitars were made in Korea and shipped to the Martin factory for a final inspection and set-up before being sent on to dealers. Essentially, Martin Stingers are well-made entry level guitars pretty much following conventional lines of the marketplace.

No Martin Stinger catalogs are available to me, so a detailed accounting is pretty difficult. However, there were four basic Stinger body styles, a fairly conventional Strat shape, a Strat-style with an arched top, a Tele and a Fender-style bass. These came in a variety of finish and pickup configuration options. Headstocks were a kind of modified Strat-style six-in-line, with a pointed throat and slightly hooked nose, with a painted triangular Stinger logo running under the strings. All had bolt-on maple necks. Guitars had a 25.4" scale, while the basses were 34"ers.

The core of this early Stinger line can

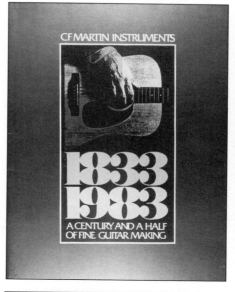

1983 Martin catalog with the Custom E-28, 19th century Stauffer reproduction, plus the E-28, EB-28 and EB-28 Fretless (C.F. Martin Company).

be seen in an undated flyer which could be anywhere from around 1986 to '88. Strat-style guitars included the SWG, SGV and SSX. The arched-top Strats were the SSL-1, SSL-10 and SSL-20. The Tele was the STX, and the basses were the SBX and SBL-10.

The principal difference among the Strats was in finish options. All had 21-fret maple necks, three single-coil pickups, volume and two tone controls, and fiveway select. The SWG came in yer basic red or black, with maple 'board and chrome hardware. These had traditional non-locking vibratos. The SGV was offered in red with white graphics. The SSX was the

dusey, with purple burst (white outside, purple in center), tiara turquoise, blue pearl, metallic white, black and candy apple red finish options with matching colored maple fingerboard *and* (that's and) matching chrome hardware.

Sources other than the flyer do not mention all the fingerboard and hardware color options. Since few of these show up on the market, I suspect these fancy Stingers are *quite* rare, indeed.

The STX "Tele" was pretty much a copy with a humbucker at the bridge and a single-coil at the neck. This had volume and tone, threeway select and a mini-toggle coil-tap on the 'bucker. Fingerboard

STINGER ELECTRICS
Quality you can afford.
Prices from $198*

Stinger electric guitars feature a stunning high gloss finish, low radius neck, and high output, precision electronics. Available in a wide range of colors and styles.

*SUGGESTED RETAIL

For further information write:

THE MARTIN GUITAR COMPANY
510 Sycamore Street, Nazareth, Pa. 18064

(Top) April of 1986 ad for Martin Stinger guitars (C.F. Martin Company). (below) January of 1987 ad for Martin Stinger guitars (C.F. Martin Company).

STINGER ELECTRICS
Quality that's affordable
Prices under $330*

Ask for our new SSL-1, SSL-10 and SSL-20 with the Whammy Bar™ Tremolo System.

*Suggested Retail

For further information write:

THE MARTIN GUITAR COMPANY
510 Sycamore Street, Nazareth, Pa. 18064

was rosewood, while hardware was black chrome. Finish options included cream, metallic red, purple burst and black.

The arched top Strats all had maple necks, rosewood 'boards, black hardware, Floyd Rose licensed locking vibrato systems, and slight finish variations. The SSL-1 had a single humbucker with a volume control that had a push-pull coil tap. This could be had in metallic black, purple burst, white pearl, red pearl, and pink fire. The neck on the early SSL-1 is described in different sources as having a stain finish or as having an oil finish; there's probably a clue to dating sequence here, but I don't know the answer.

The SSL-10 offered the humbucker/single/single arrangement, with one volume and two tones, fiveway select and mini-toggle coil tap. Substitute candy apple red and blue pearl for the red pearl and pink fire options.

The SSL-20 had two humbuckers, threeway select and push-pull coil taps on the two tone pots. This came in the same finishes as the SSL-1 minus the pink fire. Darn. Actually, the example shown here is finished off in tiara turquoise, a slightly pearloid, which was not listed, so you can expect to find a variety of guitar colors. Also of interest on this guitar is a Floyd Rose licensed locking vibrato system which is a pretty interesting hybrid. Instead of a knife-edge like most of these vibratos, these actually screw down in front with six screws like a Fender or traditional fulcrum vibrato. Yet they have the fine tuners of a Floyd Rose, albeit in a curious interpretation. This was probably not the most successful translation of the classic locking vibrato system, but it is sort of nifty.

The basses followed a similar pattern. The SBX sported one split-coil pickup, volume, tone and black, candy apple red, white pearl and gun metal finishes, with matching colored maple fingerboards and colored chrome hardware.

The SBL-10 offered a split neck pickup and single-coil bridge pickup, with two volumes, master tone,

threeway select, cream, black, white, and black pearl finish option, with matching maple 'board and hardware.

By the Fall of 1988 the Stinger line, as reflected in a November price list, had rearranged slightly. Still around were the SWG ($281), SGV ($294), SSX ($308), and STX ($330) guitars and the SBX ($337) and SBL-10 ($367) basses, the black SSX and SBX now available in lefty versions (add $15). Essentially these were unchanged in options.

New was the SSX-N ($347), basically the three single-coil SSX with an ash body and natural finish, set off with black hardware and a fixed bridge/tail assembly.

The arched top Strats were still available, but now with new names and details. Gone were the one-pickup SSL-1 and twin humbucker SSL-20.

The SSL-10 had become the SSX-10 ($387), with humbucker/single/single pickups, pretty much the same. This came with jumbo frets, a satin-finished neck and a 14 degree backward pitch on the head. The rosewood 'board now sported the "wave" or triangular wave inlays popular on Kramers, Charvels and Jacksons of the period. No mention is made of vibrato,

STINGER ELECTRIC STRINGS

Introducing the all NEW STINGER HI-TECH electric strings.

■ Designed from the beginning to offer every HI-TECH advantage—fast action feel and great sound.
■ **NEW** alloys to create the brilliant high-end response, increased sustain and longer life that today's player demands.
■ **NEW** ball end lock twist design for added strength when used with tremolo systems.
■ **HI-TECH**—precision—consistent gauge selection.
■ **STINGER ELECTRIC STRINGS**—the perfect match for your electric guitar—from the people who care about guitars—The Martin Guitar Company.

THE MARTIN GUITAR COMPANY
Stinger Electric Strings
Stinger Electric Guitars
Nazareth, PA 18064

1987 ad for Martin Stinger Strings (C.F. Martin Company).

but that doesn't mean it didn't have a tradition-style unit. Colors were now Carrera midnight blue, metallic black, purple burst, dark red, white pearl and blue pearl, all with chrome hardware.

New was the SSX-10L ($451), a deluxe SSX-10, adding a Whammy Bar II Floyd Rose licensed vibrato system and black hardware. Colors were Carrera midnight blue, dark red, white pearl and metallic black.

Two other totally new guitars debuted in November of '88, the ST-3 ($225) and ST-4 ($235). These were both Strats, with maple necks, rosewood fingerboards, volume and two tones, fiveway select, chrome hardware, SAT non-locking vibrato, in black, white or red with graphics. The ST-3 had three single-coils, whereas the ST-4 had a 'bucker and two singles.

Cases or gig bags were extra.

These guitars appear to have lasted through 1989 or so. In 1990 the Stinger line shrank dramatically. Three guitars and two basses were listed in the *Guitar World 1990-91 Guitar Buyer's Guide.* The three guitars in '90 were the SSX, SPX and SSL. These were basically Strats (gone were the arched tops). The SSX now had three

single-coils and fixed bridge/tailpiece. The SPX offered two humbuckers with a coil tap switch. The SSL had one humbucker and one single-coil, with a tap on the 'bucker, and a traditional vibrato.

Basses were the SBL and SBL-105. The SBL was a P-bass with split-coil and single-coil pickups, rosewood 'board, and black hardware. The SBL-105 was a five-string version of the SBL.

These last Stingers apparently hung around for a year or so. In the *Guitar World 1992-93 Guitar Buyer's Guide* only one Stinger guitar was listed, the ST-2, an inexpensive Strat with three single-coil pickups. No basses were listed.

In around 1988 Martin introduced a line of Stinger amps and effects pedals. Amps included the FX-1 (10 watts, 8" speaker, "Tube Synth" distortion circuit, $152), the FX-1R (15 watts, 8" speaker, Tube Synth, spring reverb, $220), FX-3B (15 watts, 10" speaker, compression, separate pre-amp and master volume controls, 3-band EQ, $189), FX-3C (30 watts, 12" speaker, Tube Synth, chorus, $299), and the FX-3RC (65 watts, 12" speaker, Tube Synth, chorus, reverb, effects loop, $379).

In the Spring of 1989 Martin added the

Ca. 1987 Martin Stinger SSL-20 in tiara turquoise (courtesy Society Hill Loan, Philadelphia, PA; photo: Mike Tamborrino).

FX-1R Mini-Stack (15 watts, 10" speaker, Tube Synth, reverb, $369) and the FX-6B bass amp (60 watts, 15" speaker, separate pre-amp and master volume controls, 3-band EQ, $469).

Effects pedals included the TS-5 Tube Stack (distortion, $77.50), DI-10 Distortion ($65.95), CO-20 Compressor ($73.50), OD-30 Overdrive ($65.95), FL-60 Flanger ($95.95), CH-70 Stereo Chorus ($90.50), DE-80 Analog Delay ($173.95), and DD-90 Digital Delay ($189.50).

The Stinger amps and effects lasted only a little over a year or so.

And that's about that. After '93 Martin Stingers, like their previous Martin-brand cousins, started drifting off into solidbody byways of guitar history.

(Left) Ca. 1987 flyer for Martin Stinger guitars (C.F. Martin Company). (Right) 1988 ad for the Martin Stinger guitar, bass and amplifier (C.F. Martin Company).

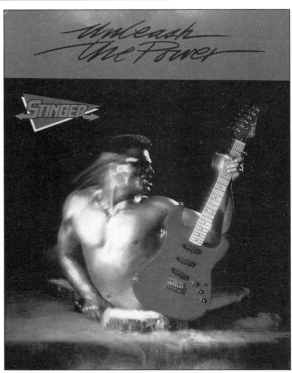

(Left) 1988 ad for Martin Stinger Strings (C.F. Martin Company). (Right) Ca. 1988 Martin Stinger flyer cover showing the Stinger SSL-1 (C.F. Martin Company).

The Stinger ST-2, basic fulcrum-vibrato Strats with pickguards, three single-coils, black, red and white finishes, and the now ubiquitous droopy pointy headstock (not the Stinger Strat variation), was still listed in the 1996 Martin catalog, but these were pale reflections of the peak years.

It must be said, by the way, that Martin Stingers, were not bad guitars, setting up and playing well, with a decent, hefty feel. But they never really caught on, bringing to an end — for the time being, at least —

the sporadic story of Martin electric guitars.

Why Martin electric guitars have never been more popular isn't too hard to figure out. Martin, whose expertise has always been in top-notch acoustics, never really put a lot of effort into marketing its electrics. They were always well made, and, especially in the necks, clearly "Martins." In the final analysis, however, it probably comes down to being victims of the success of their acoustic brothers, and players have just never seemed to warm up to the idea of Martin "electric" guitars. For the savvy collector with a taste for quality and relative rarity, Martin electrics remain excellent and attainable prizes.

Martin Electric Guitars, Amps and Effects

Here's an approximate outline of Martin electric guitars. Fortunately, most of these are fairly well documented, but, as usual, understand that no list such as this should be taken as gospel.

Dates Available	Models
1958-59	Martin D-18E
1959-64	Martin D-28E
1959-64	Martin OO-18E
1961-65	Martin F-50
1961-65	Martin F-55
1961-65	Martin F-65
1965	Martin XTE 70
1967	Martin XTE-75
1965	Martin XGT-85 Bass
1966-68	Martin GT-70
1966-68	Martin GT-75
1966-68	Martin GT-75 12-String
1978-82	Martin E-18
1978-82	Martin EM-18
1978-82	Martin EB-18 bass
1980-82	Martin E-28
1980-82	Martin EB-28 bass
1973-74	Sigma SBG2-6
1973-74	Sigma SBG2-9
1973-74	Sigma SBF2-6
1973-74	Sigma SBB2-8 bass
c.1985-88	Stinger SSL-1
c.1985-88	Stinger SSL-10
c.1985-88	Stinger SSL-20
c.1985-89	Stinger SWG
c.1985-89	Stinger SGV
c.1985-89	Stinger SSX
c.1985-89	Stinger STX
c.1985-89	Stinger SBX
c.1985-89	Stinger SBL-10
1988-89	Stinger SSX Lefty

Dates Available	Models	Dates Available	Models
1988-89	Stinger SBX Lefty	c.1988-90	Stinger FX-1
1988-89	Stinger SSX-N	c.1988-90	Stinger FX-1R
1988-89	Stinger SSX-10	c.1988-90	Stinger FX-3B
1988-89	Stinger SSX-10L	c.1988-90	Stinger FX-3C
1988-89	Stinger ST-3	c.1988-90	Stinger FX-3RC
1988-89	Stinger ST-4	1989-90	Stinger FX-1R Mini-Stack
1990-91	Stinger SSX (new version)	1989-90	Stinger FX-6B bass amp
1990-91	Stinger SPX	**Martin Effects Pedals**	
1990-91	Stinger SSL	1989-90	Stinger TS-5 Tube Stack
1990-91	Stinger SBL bass	1989-90	Stinger DI-10 Distortion
1990-91	Stinger SBL-105 bass	1989-90	Stinger CO-20 Compressor
1992-96	Stinger ST-2	1989-90	Stinger OD-30 Overdrive
Martin Amplifiers		1989-90	Stinger FL-60 Flanger
1961-?	Martin Model 110T	1989-90	Stinger CH-70 Stereo Chorus
1961-?	Martin Model 112T	1989-90	Stinger DE-80 Analog Delay
1962-?	Martin #700 portable amplifier	1989-90	Stinger DD-90 Digital Delay
1966	Martin SS140		

VELENO
GUITARS

Shiny Metal (Rare) Birds

Throughout the years luthiers have built guitars out of a lot of exotic materials, from Torres' paper mache acoustics to Danelectro's masonite to Dan Armstrong's lucite guitars to Steinberger's all-graphite headless wonders. While all of these instruments are absolutely cool, few have the magic of those shiny metal guitars with bird-like headstocks and gleaming ruby eye crafted of aluminum named Veleno. Veleno guitars are the essence of glam, perfect icons of the decadence of the Me Decade.

And, as it turns out, quite rare. To learn their story we have to travel back in time to those innocent days of 1966, or, indeed even back further, to the formative years of a young machinist by the name of John Veleno.

The Rhythm Masters

John Veleno was born in 1934 and began studying guitar in Massachusetts in around 1958, eventually playing part-time in a rock and country band called the Rhythm Masters. Veleno progressed in his studies, well enough to teach, and from 1961 to '62 he worked as a guitar teacher at the studio where he had been taking lessons. As most of us know, music teaching hardly proved to be a reliable source of income, so during the day Veleno pursued a trade as a machinist. John had completed his apprenticeship in 1956 and had held down his day job until 1963, when his wife's health condition caused him to relocate to Florida. Two days after his arrival in the Sunshine State, he was offered a job in a machine shop in St. Petersburg.

Aluminum

Once in St. Petersburg, Veleno' job at the Universal Machine Company was to make aluminum boxes which were designed to contain the electronic components used on the rockets launched from Cape Canaveral. These boxes were of various shapes and had to be both strong and lightweight. The most common way to make them was by taking a 35 pound billet of solid aluminum and cutting it down to a rib-reinforced box of around $1^1/_2$ to 3 pounds in weight. It was this background in working with aluminum which would eventually give birth to Veleno's unique guitar designs.

While working by day at the machine shop, Mr. Veleno continued to give guitar lessons in his off-hours. To do this he obtained an occupational license allowing him to teach guitar in his home. To advertise his guitar lessons, he wanted to put up a sign, however, to his dismay he discovered that local ordinances only allowed him to put a one foot by one foot sign attached to the outside of his house, hardly something that would catch the attention of people passing by.

The guitar mailbox

Veleno thought about it and decided to make a guitar-shaped mailbox out of aluminum to sit at the street curb shaped like a guitar. This was not technically speaking a "sign" and therefore he could draw attention to the sign on his house with the mailbox. Since he was an aluminum worker, Veleno naturally decided to machine the mailbox stand out of aluminum.

As it turned out, the fellow who was Veleno's aluminum supplier was also a guitar player, and while they were talking, the supplier asked: "Why make a just a guitar-shaped mailbox out of aluminum? Why not make a guitar out of aluminum?" A little light went off in Veleno's head, and it

John Veleno in a later photograph. One of the earliest Veleno aluminum guitars with the V headstock, the only one still in possession of John Veleno (photos courtesy John Veleno).

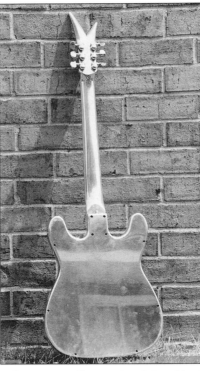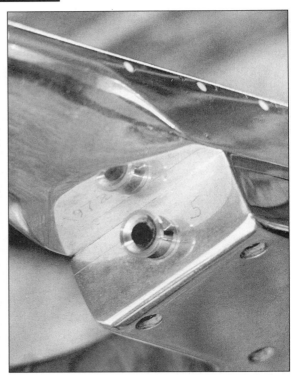

Veleno Original #5, 1972 with Gibson pickups, originally owned and signed by Ace Frehley of Kiss. Back of the Veleno Original #5. Closeup of neck joint engraved #5, 1972 (photos: Bill Baker).

was only a matter of time until Veleno aluminum guitars came into being.

Prototype

Veleno began to hand-make his first guitar in 1966, working at home, constantly changing the design to overcome problems as he progressed. Finally, in 1967, it was complete.

Since he was not particularly well connected with the local music scene, the only way Veleno could think of to market his new guitar was to take it around to area niteclubs. Like many a visionary before him, all Veleno received from the local musicians was laughs and insults. Dispirited, the aluminum guitar went into the closet to collect dust, and John Veleno thought his guitar-making career was over.

However, as fate would have it, in around 1970, Veleno ran into his old friend the aluminum supplier, who asked if he had ever built that aluminum guitar. Veleno reluctantly admitted that he had. The aluminum supplier asked to look at it and got very excited when he saw the design. He took John Veleno and his aluminum guitar to a local niteclub called the Cheshire Cat

where the guitarist in the band playing that evening loved Veleno's guitar. They stayed at the club until 1 or 2 AM in the morning, after which Veleno's friend took him to the south side of St. Petersburg, not the nicest neighborhood in town at the time.

Clothes for the stars

Veleno recalls that night with amusement. "My friend took me to this house that looked like a haunted house. The grass hadn't been cut for ages. It was about 18" high! The house had paint peeling off it. A real horror house. We went into an apartment in the house where I was introduced to a couple named Michael and Tony, I forget their last names. Michael and Tony made costumes for rock stars and they were completely surrounded by racks and racks of wild clothes and shoes with 5" soles on them. They supplied some of the clothes Sonny and Cher were wearing for their act at the time. I remember that Michael and Tony had just completed a wardrobe for Jimi Hendrix. I remember the Hendrix connection because this was just about the time that Hendrix died."

Veleno's aluminum guitar was shown to

Michael, who was also excited by it and offered to show Veleno how to sell his idea. He insisted the only way was to get guitar players to see it, and that he could show Veleno how to get into the big rock shows which were frequently visiting the area coliseum at the time.

James Gang

"Remember this was around 1970, before there was so much security," muses Veleno. "Michael took me to the first show, which was the James Gang, I believe. I didn't know anyone's names in the band at the time. Michael's suggested technique was to show up carrying a guitar case in the afternoon, between 1 and 3 PM. No one ever stopped someone entering backstage with a guitar case at that time of day. The idea was then to get near the stage during the soundcheck, take out the aluminum guitar and begin to polish it. Michael assured me that there was no way that the guitar player wouldn't come over to look at it. He was right. It worked like a charm for years."

"By the way," adds Veleno, "later on I would always go to the record store before a band was coming to town so I could find

Closeup of hand-engraved back of headstock of 1972 #5 (photo: Bill Baker).

out the names of the band members and see their pictures before I showed up!"

The other Santana

The first group to really take a look at Veleno's guitar was led by Jorge Santana in either 1970 or 1971. "I was really excited that I was going to see Santana, but then I found out it was actually Carlos' brother," recalls Veleno with a self-deprecating chuckle. Veleno followed the pattern, going in for the soundcheck, pulling out the guitar and polishing it. Jorge Santana couldn't resist his curiosity and came over to try the guitar. He liked it so much, he took it out and used it on his first three songs that night. His manager was furious, Veleno remembers, telling Jorge that he should stick to the guitar he was familiar with for the show, but Santana was adamant and used the Veleno.

After the show Jorge Santana met with Veleno and offered about a dozen ideas that would improve the design, all of which were incorporated in subsequent guitars.

V headstock

Veleno's first few prototype guitars had a bird-shaped headstock with six-in-line tun-

ers. One of Jorge Santana's suggestions had been to change it to a three-and-three arrangement, since it was easier to find the string you wanted to tune while performing onstage. Veleno went home and got his five children around the kitchen table and had a brainstorming session. One of his children suggested using the family's last name and came up with a "V" design, and that was it. The trademark red corundum ruby set in the middle of the headstock was inspired by Veleno's first wife's birthstone. Some of the heads are all chrome, but some (on black necks, especially) were black with a silver V highlight. At least one example is seen in all black with no highlight.

The Veleno Original

The main Veleno guitar design is called the Veleno Original, although several other models appeared over the course of his brief luthier's career. The Original is sort of an equal double cutaway cross between a Strat and a slab Tele with an aluminum body and a bolt-on aluminum neck. Some differences can be seen in guitar shapes; some are a bit slimmer like a Gibson Les Paul Junior and some are a bit chunkier like a Tele.

Veleno's necks were cast from Almag 35 aluminum, the most corrosive-resistant alloy available at the time. Veleno came up with his ideal profile and took it to a pattern maker who made a board which allowed casting three necks at a time. Casting was then done at a local foundry.

To come up with the neck profile Veleno studied many popular guitars. He liked the flatter fingerboard radius of Gibson guitars, but he preferred the shallower back of Fenders. He was fortunate to have access to quite a number of people in the neighborhood who had retired from the guitar business, so he was able to consult with them and learn why companies did things. Veleno chose a compromise that combined the Gibson radius with the Fender back. Their designs, of course, had been dictated in part by the necessities of truss rod installation, whereas Veleno, with his warp-proof aluminum neck, was free of such concerns, and could make any shape he liked. Many of Veleno's necks were coated in a black finish, making them feel more like a conven-

tional neck finish.

Originally the Veleno fingerboard had 21 frets, but this was quickly changed to 22. Frets were seated with a special quick-drying glue. In theory, this design was supposed to allow easy refretting as often as required or desired. Veleno admits that the necks were a little heavy, causing the guitars to be a bit unbalanced, although he tried to compensate by putting three different places to connect the guitar strap so the player could adjust somewhat. Still, this was a design flaw that was never corrected.

Fingerboards could be finished in black with white dots or in chome with white or black dotes. The typical dot pattern on Velenos was an alternating one/two pattern, with three dots at the octave.

The Veleno Original is actually a hollowbody guitar which is carved from two solid blocks of aluminum, 17 pounds of raw material reduced to a pound and a half! The first five or so guitar bodies were actually cast like an automobile engine, but Veleno quickly switched to the method familiar from his job. Veleno bodies are not stamped and have no bends or welds. Backs were removable to allow access to the electron-

Another view of a black Veleno (photo: O.J.Henley).

Chrome-plated 1974 Veleno Original #90 with Guild humbuckers.

ics. The final guitar was $8\frac{1}{2}$ pounds, lighter than a Gibson Les Paul. The first cast Originals did not have a pickguard, but when John switched to carving he addied a clear plexiglass pickguard to protect the finish.

Colors

The first Veleno bodies were made of 7075 aluminum, but these quickly tarnished and changed color. Veleno switched to 6061 aluminum which was then chrome plated. Eventually, in addition to the most common chrome finish, Velenos were offered in real gold plating, polished aluminum (similar look to chrome plated), plus anodized finishes of blue, red, green, gold and two blacks, ebony and "super finish." The super finish was a special process which yielded a harder finish that regular anodizing. This availability does not mean that Veleno guitars were necessarily produced in these colors. Chrome was the most common, with a few in gold and at least one in a black finish.

Occasionally Veleno would make his own bridges, although he sometimes used Gibson Tune-o-matics or Guild bridges. He actually preferred the way the Guild bridges adjusted.

Electronics on Veleno guitars were pretty straightforward. Typical controls consisted of two volume and two tone controls, two threeway mini-toggles (off in the middle, coil taps in the up position), and a mini-toggle phase switch. Since the guitars were made of aluminum, they were automatically shielded to reduce feedback.

Pickups

Pickups on the first few guitars were DeArmond humbuckers, but Veleno quickly switched to chrome-covered Gibson humbuckers, when he could get them. When he couldn't, he sometimes used Guild humbuckers, although he didn't care that much for their more trebly output. Somewhere between guitar #25 and guitar #50 Veleno was approached by Larry DiMarzio and asked to use his early pickups, which he did, when they were available.

Veleno guitars sold for $600.

At least one gold-plated Veleno Original was built with three DiMarzio pickups. This can be seen on page 95 of Tony Bacon and Paul Day's *The Ultimate Guitar Book* (Alfred A. Knopf, New York, 1991). This featured three volumes and three tones, three on/off mini-toggles under the knobs, three mini-toggles on the upper bout bass horn and a single mini-toggle on the lower horn.

Black anodized V headstock of the '74 Veleno Original #90.

The first sale

While the Jorge Santana connection was productive in terms of input, it didn't result in a sale. That would come shortly thereafter when John — using the same surreptitous entrance technique — went to a T-Rex gig, and made his first sale. Or actually first *two* sales.

Veleno recounts his meeting with the eccentric Mark Bolan with amusement. "I got into the soundcheck that afternoon," recalls John, "and started to polish my guitar. Mark Bolen came over to look at the guitar and asked me to go to his motel with him after the show. We went back to his room and he got down on his knees to inspect the guitar. He loved the guitar and said, 'I want two, one for me and one for my good friend Eric Clapton.'"

"Okay," said Veleno in a deadpan voice, who had no idea who Eric Clapton was.

"Don't you know who Eric Clapton is?," exclaimed Bolen in amazement. "My best friend is the greatest guitarist in the world."

"No," replied Veleno, thinking to himself that everyone says his friend is the best guitarist in the world. He'd heard that claim before.

Bolen began rolling around on the floor laughing hysterically. "I can't believe someone who makes guitars doesn't know who Eric Clapton is!"

Bolen gave Veleno the shipping address for the guitars, which was in care of Warner Brothers studios in California. "Gee," thought Veleno, "these guys really are in show business!"

"My daughter Michelle was in college at the time," adds Veleno, "and when I went home and told her I'd just sold two guitars to T-Rex and Eric Clapton, her awed response was 'Wow, Eric Clapton is the greatest rock and roll guitarist in the world!' I realized Bolin had been right. That's when I figured out that I'd better begin to read up on this stuff."

Glory days

In those heady days of the early '70s, between venues in St. Petersburg, Tampa and Lakeland, there were as many as 57 concerts a year, which kept Veleno busy polishing his guitars.

John remembers showing one of his guitars to Gregg Allman. He was backstage and Allman's manager came over and opened the case. "Gregg has to see this. Close it up and we'll show it to him after he cleans up."

After the show Allman, tired and sweaty, showered and dressed, poured a drink and came to look into the guitar case. As he looked inside he exclaimed, "Oh my God, a motorcycle in a guitar case!" He bought the guitar.

Later Veleno recalls selling another one to Sonny Bono of Sonny and Cher. They were playing in Florida. John recalls that they were using the Playboy jet and took their guitarist, Dan Fergusson, and a couple other members of the band along to lead things, filling in the rest of performers with local union pick-up musicians. Veleno showed one of his guitars to Fergusson, who wanted it, but didn't have the money right then. Fergusson gave John a backstage pass and asked him to return that night. John was so excited about making a sale, he forgot to take the pass with him.

Well, that night he arrived at about quarter to eight, just before the show. He didn't have his pass, but he'd dressed up like an important person. Two big burly security cops stood in front of the backstage door. Veleno just tucked his guitar case up under his arm, barged right through the crowd, went right through the guards, and grabbed the door knob muttering worriedly, "Oh, man, I'm late for the show." He got in and got paid for the guitar!

A few weeks later he got a call from Sonny Bono's manager, ordering another one for Bono. Later he recalls hearing that, after Cher had married Gregg Allman, Bono sold his Veleno guitar, but John doesn't know if it was because Allman also had one...

Standardization

Word began to get around the rock world and before long Veleno began getting more and more calls from famous rock guitarists. The problem was that most of them wanted custom jobs, and would always say, "Now, here's what I want you to do with it," John recalls. Unfortunately, Veleno Guitars was just a two-man operation by this time and the design depended on mak-

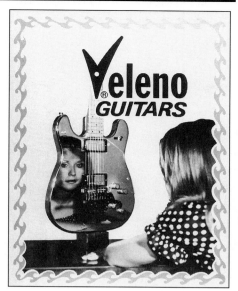
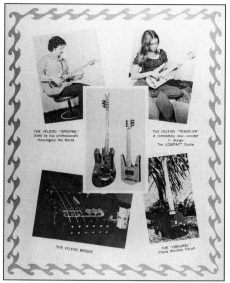

The Veleno catalog showing both the Original and the Traveler.

ing "cut and dry," standardized guitars, so Veleno could not accommodate all the custom requests. The callers would become insistent, and would invariably use the line to Veleno, "Do you know who I am?" Of course, the joke was that John mostly *didn't* know who they were!

Sometimes players had reservations about Veleno for curious reasons. Johnny Winter, interviewed in the July 1974 *Guitar Player* talked about his current gear: "I've also got a really strange, all-metal guitar made by John Veleno. It's got the thinnest neck in the world. Since it's solid metal, you don't have to worry about it warping. But I'm not quite used to it. The neck's a little too thin. The worst part about it is

that the neck is silver, and it's got little black dots on it, and when the spotlight is shining on the neck I really can't see the dots, so I haven't been using it on stage. But he makes pretty nice guitars. If I played it, and got used to it, I think it'd be a real nice guitar to play."

The players

Who else played Velenos? During the '70s some significant artists were seen playing Veleno aluminum guitars. We know that Mark Bolan, Eric Clapton and others owned Velenos. Jorge Santana eventually bought one. Other well-known guitarists who played Velenos included Pete Haycock of the Climax Blues Band (a gold Veleno

(Left) Gold anodized Veleno Original with Guild humbuckers. (Right) Polished aluminum Veleno Original with Gibson humbuckers and no clear pickguard.

B.B. and the Traveler

In addition to the Original, Veleno also offered a down-sized Traveler guitar, which was only $27^1/_4$" long, $8^1/_2$" wide, with 24 frets, tuned to a "G" tuning, a third above a normal tuning. In essence, this was a one-pickup terz guitar.

Actually, the idea for this guitar came from none other than B.B. King! One night B.B. was performing in the area and John went backstage to meet him after the show. The line was a mile long, but B.B. told his people to let them all in. He'd just say "Hi" to each one. John was in the middle of the line, and when he finally got up to King and identified himself, King asked him if he could do a favor. King asked him to go to the back of the line again so they could talk more. "It won't take long, I'm just going to say 'Hi' to these folks and sign some autographs."

Well, at around 3:30 in the morning — Veleno wryly remarks that musician's don't go to jobs like everyone else, they work all night and sleep all day — Veleno came up again. King was sitting in a chair. He stuck out his hands and said he wanted a guitar about this long. Veleno pulled out something he had with him and measured it. King explained. He did a lot of travelling,

can be seen on the cover of their *Gold Plated* lp), Alvin Lee of Ten Years After, Ronnie Montrose, then of the Edgar Winter Group, Martin Barre of Jethro Tull, Ace Frehley of Kiss, Dave Peverett of Foghat, and Mark Farner of Grand Funk Railroad. One of the last appearances of a Veleno was on the album cover of *Panorama* by the Cars. Not all of these folks purchased their guitars directly from John.

Who did purchase new guitars from Veleno? Veleno did not keep detailed records of everyone who bought his guitars from him, but a partial list in his scrapbook reveals some interesting names. The list includes Eric Clapton (#2), Mark Bolan (#3), Mark Farner (#4), Lou Reed (#5), Gregg Allman (#6), Ray Manet of Rare Earth (#7), Dave Peverett (#8), Dan Fergusson (#9), Sonny Bono (#10), Pete Haycock (#11), Ronnie Montrose (#12), Jeff Lynne of ELO (#13), Miami-area guitarist Johnny Olafson (#14), Terry Blankenship of Damon (#18), John Stone of Chocolate and Vanilla (#19), Robert Bond of the Texas band Rise (#21) and Mark Klyce of Love Date (#58). Clearly the celebrity exposure early-on had its ef-

fect down the guitar pecking order later.

Reportedly, several guitars were made for Ronnie Montrose with thicker necks reminiscent of late '50s Gibsons. The normal Veleno neck is quite thin, reflecting necks like Kapa and Hagstrom in the '60s and anticipating tastes of the late '80s.

Veleno recalls that shortly after Jeff Lynne bought his Veleno guitar Electric Light Orchestra appeared on a New Years Day celebration television program during which ELO performed on the Thames river in London. There, shining brightly, was the Veleno Original for the world to admire.

The sleeve of the album "Panorama" by the Cars with the drummer holding a Veleno.

including on planes. When he travelled, he was always getting his best ideas for songs or for guitar licks, but he couldn't do anything about it. He couldn't whip out a guitar while sitting on a plane. But, if he had a small one, he could just take it out and work out his ideas. "I'd call it my Travelling Companion," King concluded.

Veleno went home and developed the Traveler, named in honor of B.B. King. The first one was supposed to be for King, but Veleno had forgotten to get an address or telephone number, and he didn't know how to get in touch with King. So, B.B. never got his Travelling Companion. Nevertheless, B.B. did come up with the idea for that guitar. Mark Farner of Grand Funk Railroad helped John develop the final Traveler guitar design, which was an unusual shape that looked something like a mask out of a Buck Rogers episode. The edges were horizontal with deep extended cutaway horns, a three-segment rounded lower bout. The Traveler had a small squared-off three-and-three head, a 24-fret fingerboard (no markers), a single middle pickup, combined compensated bridge/tailpiece like on early Gibsons, a volume on the lower wing, tone back near the bridge, and a tone toggle on the upper horn.

Very, very few of these were ever produced. John recalls setting up around 10 to 12 Travelers for production, however, he made only one or two himself. One was sold to Mark Farner. The remainder of the leftover parts were given to John's son Chris, who assembled some more. The total tally should be no more than a dozen at most.

The bass

Rarest of the rare of Veleno's creations was one electric bass guitar which he built. He can't recall who ordered it, but it was part of a guitar and bass set. The fellow who bought them said in his will he was going to leave the guitar to the Smithsonian Institute museum because the Veleno guitar was an "All-American original." He got that right.

Ankh

The final two Veleno guitars were made for Todd Rundgren in 1977, the last Velenos

Flyer for Larry DiMarzio's Super Distortion humbucker, with Veleno's added notice in the upper right (courtesy John Veleno).

made by John himself. These were duplicate, atypical "custom-made" guitars shaped like an "ankh," the ancient Egyptian mystical symbol, or as Veleno put it, an "ox."

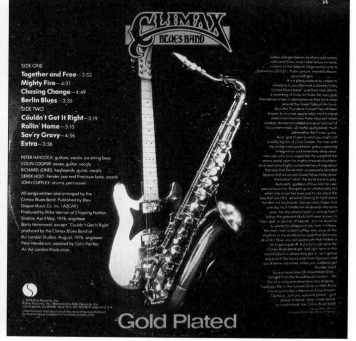

(Left) The sleeve of the album "Gold Plated" by the Climax Blues Band with Peter Haycock playing a Veleno guitar (courtesy Sire Records). (Right) Reverse side of the Climax Blues Band Gold Plated *album.*

An April 1978 running of the Veleno ad (same as earlier versions), probably run by one of John's friends long after he had closed up shop.

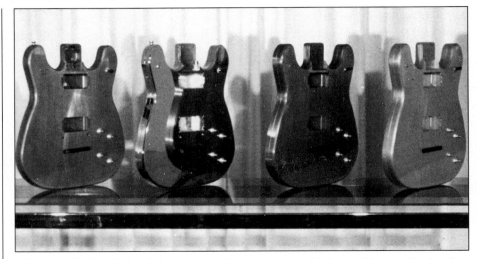

A line-up of Veleno bodies, left to right in chrome plating, gold plating, blue anodized and gold anodized (courtesy John Veleno).

These had hollow round-rimmed bodies with a straight cross or bar perpendicular to the neck. These had a bridge humbucker and a single-coil pickup mounted on the cross bar, with three controls for volume and tone. Rundgren kept two while performing just in case one had a problem.

These guitars, one of which Rundgren can be seen playing on the cover of the October 1977 *Guitar Player*, were actually designed by Rundgren himself. Veleno recalls getting a call from Rundgren, who had come up with this exotic guitar shape and had contacted several major guitar companies about making it for him, but they declined. The days of Custom Shops had not yet arrived. So he called John. John said to send him the drawings, which Todd did. John said he could make the guitars and he did.

Veleno recalls Rundgren's reaction upon receiving the axes: "They look just like my drawings!" Rundgren explained he was surprised because most makers changed things around rather than following exactly what he had in mind. The Veleno ankhs were just as Todd had conceived them.

Veleno's "cut and dry" aluminum guitars were built from approximately 1970 to 1976 or possibly 1977, except for the Rundgren special-orders. It was at about this time that John experienced some health problems and decided he didn't want to hear anything more about guitars. "In fact," says Veleno with a chuckle, "I didn't even want to talk about guitars for about five years after I quit making them."

Rare birds

If you have a Veleno guitar, you have something especially rare. Accounts vary, but the outside estimate is that only about 185 total were ever produced by John. It's possible that the number of John Veleno originals is some 40 guitars less at around 145. There were around one or two Travelers, one bass and the two ankhs for Rundgren. All were numbered consecutively, so you know where you fall more or less in that chronology. If yours says #5, it's the fifth one built. When John decided to leave the guitar biz, he turned over enough parts to make maybe 10 or 12 Originals and another 10 or so Travelers to

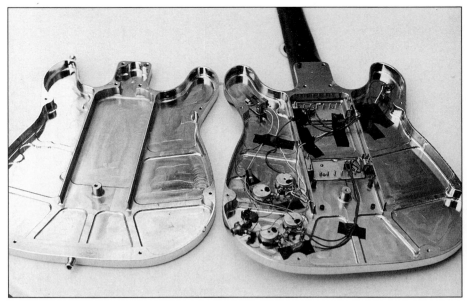

Inside of Veleno Original #90 showing "modular" electronics.

his son Chris, who had helped him build the guitars. Chris did in fact assemble and sell some of these guitars after his father stopped, so there are another 20 or so Velenos which were finished by Chris. An exact tally is not possible, but whatever the total, these are extremely rare birds.

Many people tried copying Veleno guitars, but none were successful. John recalls with amusement getting a call from a guitarmaker in Japan (he doesn't remember who it was), who said he had a Veleno guitar disassembled in front of him and his

(Left) 1980 Guitar Player article on Todd Rundgren who's still playing his Veleno "Ankh" guitar (©1980 GPI Publications). (Right) October 1977 cover of Guitar Player with Todd Rundgren clutching his Veleno "Ankh" guitar (©1977 GPI Publications).

engineers gathered around. He wanted to know how Veleno could make this guitar for under $1,000. The caller requested a visit Veleno's factory to see how production went. Veleno relates with glee his answer: "Well, I rent a garage with a drill press by the day and I assemble the guitars in my living room while watching TV. I have no employees, no overhead, no engineers. That's my production method and that's why I can make them for under $1,000."

Denouement

One final mystery remains, though. In early 1978 a couple of small space ads for Veleno guitars were placed in *Guitar Player* magazine, almost a year after John ceased making guitars. John is at a loss to explain

these, except he does recall that a good friend asked for permission to try his hand at building Veleno aluminum guitars, and John said it was ok with him, believing that his friend could never pull it off. His friend did not, in fact, ever build any Velenos, but it's possible he did have high hopes and placed the ads. In any case, if you encounter one of these late ads, don't let that confuse the chronology presented here.

And that's the Veleno story. John had thought about developing a new guitar. He wanted to develop a carbon graphite neck, which would be lighter and solve the problem of the heavy aluminum neck, which threw the guitars slightly off balance. "That would have been my guitar forever," muses Veleno. However, it was not to be.

John had no regrets about leaving the guitar business and had no plans to return to it. When I spoke with Mr. Veleno, he really hadn't played guitar for about 20 years. "I either go all the way or I don't," he said.

Well, Veleno certainly did go all the way on his exotic carved aluminum guitars. Even though fewer than 200 were ever made, they were played by some of the biggest names in '70s guitardom, and stand among the most interesting guitars of their often maligned decade. In fact, in 1996 Lonesome Dave Peverett's #8 was ensconced in the Hard Rock Cafe in Orlando, Florida, so Veleno figured his guitars had finally arrived. Indeed. If you're lucky enough to have a Veleno, be sure to keep it well polished.

INDEX

References page numbers for photographs are printed in *italics*.

SUBSCRIBE NOW and save 58% off the cover price. That's like getting 6 issues FREE!

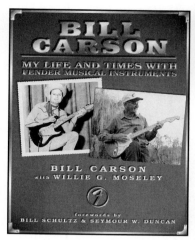